SLOW TRAVEL

Scotland's North Highlands

plus Inverness

Local, characterful guides to Britain's special places

T0355922

Emma Gibb

EDITION 1

Bradt Travel Guides Ltd, UK
The Globe Pequot Press Inc, USA

First edition published February 2025
Bradt Travel Guides Ltd
31a High Street, Chesham, Buckinghamshire, HP5 1BW, England
www.bradtguides.com
Print edition published in the USA by The Globe Pequot Press Inc,
PO Box 480, Guilford, Connecticut 06437-0480

Text copyright © Bradt Travel Guides Ltd, 2025
Maps copyright © Bradt Travel Guides Ltd, 2025; includes map data ©
OpenStreetMap contributors
Photographs copyright © Individual photographers, 2025 (see below)
Project Manager: Anna Moores
Editor: Samantha Cook
Cover research: Pepi Bluck, Perfect Picture
Picture research: Faeze Shad and Daniel Austin

ISBN: 9781804691380

British Library Cataloguing in Publication Data
A catalogue record for this book is available from the British Library

Photographs © individual photographers credited beside images & also those from
picture libraries credited as follows: Alamy.com (A); AWL Images; Dreamstime.com (DT);
Shutterstock.com (S); Superstock.com (SS)

Front cover Loch Assynt with Ardvreck Castle (Alan Copson/AWL Images)
Back cover Plockton village (AnnetteWillacy/S)
Title page Sandy Beach, Coldbackie Bay (SS)

Maps David McCutcheon FBCart.S. FRGS, assisted by Daniella Levin

Typeset by Ian Spick, Bradt Travel Guides
Production managed by Gutenberg Press Ltd; printed in Malta
Digital conversion by www.dataworks.co.in

Paper used for this product comes from sustainably managed forests, and recycled and
controlled sources.

AUTHOR

Emma Gibbs is a freelance travel writer and editor, specialising in Scotland's North Highlands and with a particular interest in slow and sustainable travel. She is the author of *North Coast 500: Britain's Ultimate Road Trip* (a best-selling, illustrated guide to the touring route) and *i-SPY Scotland*. She has written for *The Guardian*, *The I*, *The Independent*, BBC Travel and *Scotland Magazine*, among others, with articles that have seen her snorkelling in the North Sea, stargazing from the back of a campervan, and (perhaps hardest of all) sampling local whisky and beer. You can follow her updates on  emmgibbs_words.

AUTHOR'S STORY

I'm ashamed to admit I was a latecomer to the North Highlands: it had long been on my list of places to go, but it took having children – and, I suppose you might say, slowing down my own travelling – to get me there. That first trip will forever be one of my very favourite holidays: playing on vast, golden beaches that were ours alone; hiding behind massive dunes during a sandstorm; stone-skimming on a rain-splattered loch; and every corner seeming to reveal a panorama better than the last.

I had expected the mountains, the lochs, the empty beaches and – of course – the rain. What I hadn't expected were the colours – the way that the view from any one place never stayed the same but constantly shifted across a spectrum of shades, even under the heaviest of skies. Nor had I expected the people: whether born-and-bred Highlanders or incomers, all fiercely proud of their home and, above all, willing to share its secrets. Then there was how it *felt* to be there; the way the landscape crept into my bones and refused to let go.

Countless trips later and these things are all still true. There is not one particular place or area that I could claim to be better or more of a favourite than the others. How could I choose between the endless skies of Caithness and the brooding mountains of Assynt? Between the coves and caves of the north coast, the pretty fishing villages of the east and the turquoise waters of the west?

In researching this book, I've spent the last few years comprehensively exploring the region – largely on foot and by car, taking every path or road that I could – and learning its landscape. I could spend a lifetime seeking out the secrets of the North Highlands and still have more to discover. I'm more than happy to give it a shot.

ACKNOWLEDGEMENTS

A book is so much more than just the name on the cover, and there are so many people without whom this guide wouldn't exist. First and foremost, thanks to the amazing team at Bradt, particularly Claire Strange for the commission, Faeze Shad and Daniel Austin for picture research, Alex Whittleton for proofreading, and David McCutcheon and Ian Spick for their map and typesetting skills respectively. Massive thanks are also due to Anna Moores for her editorial guidance, support and numerous glasses of wine, and with whom it's always a joy to work.

I couldn't have chosen a better editor than Sam Cook – thank you for your thoughtful suggestions, improvements and encouragement.

So many people have helped me along the way, from welcoming me into their homes and businesses to telling me about their favourite places and answering my many, many questions. Thank you – I hope I have done justice to the things and places you have shared with me. Particular thanks must go to: Kendra Ballantyne, Alexandra Black and Rob Dawkins, Jane Cumming and Garry Coutts, Sue and Andy Groocock, Dee and Nigel Hart, Davy Holt, Joanne Howdle, Katie and Owain Jones, Ellen and Nick Lindsay, Rhionna Mackay, Fiona Mackenzie, Joanna Macpherson, Ken McElroy, Billy Mckechnie, Jon Perkins, Monica Shaw and Mark Washer, Cat Thomson, Mike Unwin, Yvonne and Alan West, Connor Williams and Jay Wilson.

Huge thanks to Helen Ochyra, without whose knowledge and amazing writing I might never have made it to the North Highlands, and to fellow Bradt author Katie Featherstone for all the insight and reassurance she's provided over the last few years. I owe a lot of my love of this region to my dear friends Juliet and Jon Stubbington – thank you both so much. I also couldn't have done this without the encouragement (and voice notes) of Frankie Gilman and Esme Wilks. On the home front, thanks to Mum and Dad for their unwavering love and support.

Finally, my biggest thanks to my little family. Lydia and Alex, I know it hasn't always been easy having a mum who disappears for weeks at a time, but I've loved sharing so many Highland adventures with you, too. (Oona, forever!) And last, but not least, the biggest of thank yous to Matthew, without whom I really could not have done this. All the whisky in the world could not tell you how grateful I am for everything you have done. (But it's a start…)

DEDICATION
To Matthew, Lydia and Alex

SUGGESTED PLACES TO BASE YOURSELF

These bases make ideal starting points for exploring localities the Slow way.

ORKNEY ISLANDS

Pentland Firth

John O' Groats

Wick

A99

A882

A9

Lybster

DUNNET BAY page 156
A huge, surf-friendly beach close to cliffs full of breeding seabirds.

Dunnet Bay

Thurso

A9

Loch Thurso

CHAPTER 3
page 116

Caithness

A9

A836

A897

Flow Country

Bettyhill

BETTYHILL page 179
A remnant of the Highland Clearances, wedged between two superlative swathes of golden sand.

Tongue

A838

N

0   5 miles
0   10kms

Ben Hope
▲ 3,041ft

CHAPTER 4
page 168

Durness

Loch Eriboll

S u t h e r l a n d

A838

A836

Cape Wrath

Loch Shi...

SCOURIE page 213
The perfect springboard for exploring Handa Island and the rugged northwest coast.

Scourie

A838

Conival
▲ 3,238ft

Handa Island

COIGACH page 249
A tucked-away peninsula that epitomises the joy of Slow travel, with mountains and water never far away.

Lochinver

CHAPTER 5

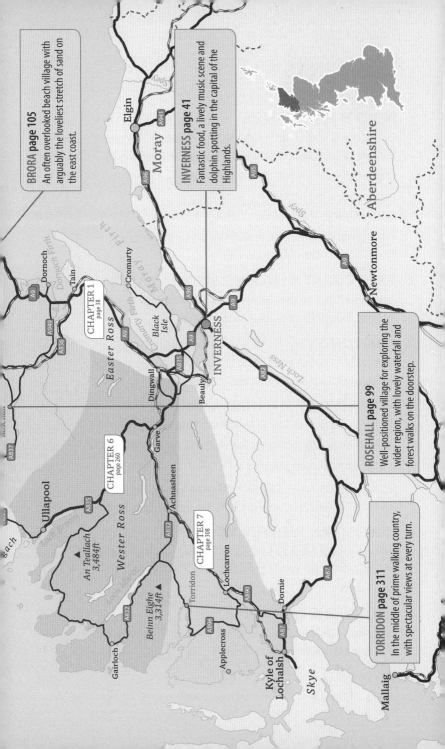

BRORA page 105
An often overlooked beach village with arguably the loveliest stretch of sand on the east coast.

INVERNESS page 41
Fantastic food, a lively music scene and dolphin spotting in the capital of the Highlands.

ROSEHALL page 99
Well-positioned village for exploring the wider region, with lovely waterfall and forest walks on the doorstep.

TORRIDON page 311
In the middle of prime walking country, with spectacular views at every turn.

CHAPTER 1
page 38

CHAPTER 6
page 260

CHAPTER 7
page 308

An Teallach
3,484ft

Beinn Eighe
3,314ft

Elgin
Moray

Inverness

Aberdeenshire

Newtonmore

Dornoch
Tain
Cromarty
Dingwall
Beauly

Easter Ross

Black Isle

Dornoch Firth
Cromarty Firth
Moray Firth

INVERNESS

Loch Ness

Ullapool

Garve

Achnasheen

Wester Ross

Lochcarron

Torridon

Gairloch

Applecross

Kyle of Lochalsh

Dornie

Mallaig

Skye

Loch Maree

Loch Broom

CONTENTS

GOING SLOW IN

SCOTLAND'S NORTH HIGHLANDS

The word 'Highlands' suggests an area of craggy mountains, moody skies and glittering lochs – which is certainly true in this region, particularly on the west coast, but far from the whole story. Here, too, are coves of white sand and vertical cliffs, small crofting townships and old fishing villages, rolling moorland and heather-clad hills, windswept blanket bog and flat, fertile farmland.

For the purposes of this book, the North Highlands covers the mainland area north of Inverness in the east and north of the village of Dornie in the west – a huge, vast swathe of Scotland that is home to some of the UK's most dramatic and evocative landscapes. In the west, among the stereotypical Highland scenery of mountains and lochs, are quiet peninsulas, tucked-away bays of pale sand and craggy rocks that tell stories of how the world looked billions of years ago. In the north, miles of golden beaches punctuated by dark cliffs are turned into seabird cities every summer. In the east, under the huge, constantly shifting skies of Caithness, are wind-battered fishing villages and countless ancient sites. And in between these wild and varied coasts, neat farmland gives way to brooding moorland, scarred by the ghosts of the people who were cleared from them.

This geography – and a lack of motorways, dual carriageways and widespread public transport – makes Slow travel the order of the day here. Ironically, the existence of the North Coast 500 (page 26) touring route means that many people experience the region by whizzing around the coast in a rush to tick off as many sights as possible: the antithesis of going Slow. But doing so misses so much: the opportunity to connect with the landscape, to watch the way the weather and light changes almost constantly, to meet the people who live and work here,

and to be able to follow your instinct and head down that intriguing track off the main road. This, really, is what Slow travel is about; taking your time to get to know a place and, in doing so, forming a deeper appreciation of, and connection with, it.

The North Highlands is not somewhere to try and see everything in one trip, not least because to do so is something of a Sisyphean task – there will always be a footpath you didn't have time to explore, or a loch that only appeared as a glimmer in your rearview mirror. I'd even go so far as to say that this book should be used largely as a starting point – consider it a friend who'll point you in the right direction, and then don't be afraid to let your eyes and your feet guide you. There is, in my opinion, no better way to experience this landscape than by simply being out in it: tramping across a lonely hill, standing at a shoreline or putting your hands on ancient, sun-warmed rocks.

THE LANDSCAPE OF SCOTLAND'S NORTH HIGHLANDS

One thing you'll often hear from visitors to the region is that 'west is best' – if nothing else, I hope this book will prove otherwise to you. The west is, undeniably, a land of high drama; for large stretches of it, every curve of the road will have your mouth dropping a little further open in awe, unable to quite believe what you are seeing. Here you'll find some of the region's most distinctive peaks, including An Teallach, Ben Mor Coigach and Suilven and, at a lower level, craggy hills that are often the sole domain of sheep. Climb to the top of any of these and the landscape below will likely glitter with lochs and lochans.

The coast here, too, is rugged and undulating, punctuated by large headlands, studded with islands and full of little nooks and crannies that often reveal glorious stretches of sand, lapped by water so blue it would put the Mediterranean to shame, were it not for the temperature. Trees are often few and far between (page 14), meaning that when they do appear, such as around the villages of Plockton, Applecross and Gairloch, they often create the feeling of lush little oases.

◀ 1 The village of Plockton on the southern shore of Loch Carron (page 335).
2 Looking towards Quinag across Loch a' Chàirn Bhàin (page 220).

THE SLOW MINDSET

Hilary Bradt, Founder, Bradt Guides

> We shall not cease from exploration
> And the end of all our exploring
> Will be to arrive where we started
> And know the place for the first time.
> T S Eliot, 'Little Gidding', *Four Quartets*

This series evolved, slowly, from a Bradt editorial meeting when we started to explore ideas for guides to our favourite part of the world – Great Britain. We wanted to get away from the usual 'top sights' formula and encourage our authors to bring out the nuances and local differences that make up a sense of place – such things as food, building styles, nature, geology, or local people and what makes them tick. Our aim was to create a series that celebrates the present, focusing on sustainable tourism, rather than taking a nostalgic wallow in the past.

So without our realising it at the time, we had defined 'Slow Travel', or at least our concept of it. For the beauty of the Slow movement is that there is no fixed definition; we adapt the philosophy to fit our individual needs and aspirations. Thus Carl Honoré, author of *In Praise of Slow*, writes: 'The Slow Movement is a cultural revolution against the notion that faster is always better. It's not about doing everything at a snail's pace, it's about seeking to do everything at the right speed. Savouring the hours and minutes rather than just counting them. Doing everything as well as possible, instead of as fast as possible. It's about quality over quantity in everything from work to food to parenting.' And travel.

So take time to explore. Don't rush it, get to know an area – and the people who live there – and you'll be as delighted as the authors by what you find.

The further north you go on the west coast, the more ancient the landscape feels; unsurprising, perhaps, given that here you will find **Lewisian gneiss** rocks which, at three billion years old, are among the oldest in Europe. Even total amateurs will be able to spot these striking geological marvels, commonly striped with pink.

On the far north coast, the western side – **Sutherland** – is particularly notable for its lochs, which for centuries made travelling in the region difficult, and now mean that it often feels as though there's more water here than land. If you've heard people wax lyrical about Scotland's west-coast beaches then it might surprise you to learn that the north coast's are also phenomenal, in the main part boasting a deep golden colour and often backed by huge, rolling sand dunes. As you cross into **Caithness**, there's an almost immediate change in the coastal landscape, with the moorland flattening and soon shifting to neat farm fields. In the far northeast, sheer cliffs tower over the tumultuous **Pentland Firth**, their ledges filling with breeding seabirds every spring and summer.

The east coast might not hit you in the face with its drama in the same way as the west, but that's good reason to take your time here: the coast is dotted with historical sites, both ancient and modern, and away from the crowds you'll be able to appreciate the quiet charms of its gentler, but equally beautiful, coastline. The A9 here hugs the coast for much of its journey, providing superlative coastal views, but exploring on foot (particularly along the handy John O'Groats Trail; page 145) will enable you to experience just how varied and dramatic it can be.

As you near **Inverness**, the coast is interrupted by four notable water features: Loch Fleet and the firths of Dornoch, Cromarty and Moray. This is prime farming territory, with much of **Easter Ross** feeling more akin to the lowlands further south than the Highlands, though the hint of mountains on the horizon will tell you otherwise.

Perhaps even more ignored than the east coast is the interior of the North Highlands, which is often little more to visitors than something to pass through from east to west. The farmland and forestry of the south gives way to moorland and mountains further north, and, for a large swathe, the mesmerising expanse of **Flow Country**, one of the world's largest areas of blanket bog.

Of course, to see this region as little more than scenery would be wrong: this is very much a place where people live and work. While there are few big settlements north of Inverness (which itself often feels more like a town than a city), there are hamlets and villages throughout and while you might drive for an hour or more without meeting another car, it's unlikely that you'll travel for so long without seeing at least one house. What might seem 'remote' to those of us who live in more populated areas may not be considered remote to the people who live there, who are more than used to travelling an hour and a half (or more) to get to a big supermarket, but have a well-stocked local shop close by and can still get all the deliveries that the rest of us are acquainted with.

WHERE ARE ALL THE TREES?

If you've never been to the North Highlands, you might be taken aback by just how bare parts of the landscape are: craggy, rocky, barren and sparse are all words that easily come to mind as you gaze across it. That's not to say that it's not beautiful, but it's important to understand that what appears to be a wild and unmanaged landscape is in fact very much the result of human interference.

Native woodland covers just 1% of the Scottish Highlands: an astonishingly low number for an area that was once predominantly tree covered. Many of the trees that you will see as you travel around the region are **Forestry Commission** plantations: non-native conifers, like Sitka spruce, planted because they grow quickly and can be easily replenished once chopped down. (You'll also come across areas of decimation, where trees have been cut down for timber – they're rather unsightly on the landscape but are more managed than they look.) Do look out for patches of so-called granny pines, particularly on heather moorland; majestic, wide-crowned trees that are remnants of Scotland's original forest.

Cutting down trees for timber is just one part of the story; for thousands of years, forests have also been destroyed for livestock grazing. By the time the **Highland Clearances** (page 90) took place in the late 18th and early 19th centuries, much of Scotland's native tree cover had already

BIRDS & BEASTS

Bears, lynx and wolves once roamed the North Highlands, but today this human-managed landscape can feel rather wildlife-light. Many of the animals that make their home here are rather elusive, particularly **red squirrels** and **pine martens**, and seeing them involves equal amounts of luck, patience and time. Translocations of the former mean they can often be seen around Ullapool (page 264), Ledmore & Migdale (page 93) and Alladale Wilderness Reserve (page 94), the last being the only place I've been fortunate enough to see them myself. Saving Scotland's Red Squirrels (⊘ scottishsquirrels.org.uk) has a handy map of recent red-squirrel sightings. Pine martens are even harder to spot, being well camouflaged in their woodland habitat; they're rather fond of an evening snack from the visitor centre bins at Beinn Eighe (page 300) and are frequent visitors to the bird table at Ceol Mor Highland Lodges (page 99).

You're much more likely to encounter **deer** on your travels around the North Highlands, which is home to three species – roe, red and sika – though only the first two are native; the last was introduced into deer parks (such as at Rosehall; page 99) from Japan in the 18th century.

been felled but the move towards large-scale sheep farming meant that it was all but impossible for natural regeneration to take place. This was further compounded during the Victorian period when deer stalking and other game shooting became increasingly fashionable – grouse moors were burnt and deer numbers rose rapidly, both of which were ecologically devastating.

'Rewilding' has become something of a buzzword, and in Highland Scotland often refers to planting native trees to restore the landscape to something closer to its natural state. With **deer** numbers still high, this generally has to be managed by fencing off young trees (you'll see deer fences around areas of tree replanting) and the human management of deer as the animals are rather fond of eating young trees. If apex predators like lynx and wolves are eventually reintroduced, as some rewilding charities and estates like **Alladale** (page 94) would like to see happen, this will help control deer in a more natural way.

One of the best places to see reforestation in action is **Beinn Eighe** (page 300), where planting trees grown in the on-site nursery and careful deer management has seen a rich woodland forming around the ancient granny pines. More information about rewilding in the wider Scottish Highlands can be found at Trees for Life (⊘ treesforlife. org) and Scotland: the Big Picture (⊘ scotlandbigpicture.com).

You'll have most luck seeing deer in autumn and winter, when they come down from the hills. Listen out for red deer in the autumn months, when the stags start their rut – they can be heard bellowing, particularly in valleys where the sound ricochets around the strath walls, which is the precursor to fighting over the females. Particularly good deer-spotting areas include around Kinbrace (northwest of Helmsdale; page 113), Lochinver (page 235) and Inchnadamph (page 244).

Though of course they're not wild, ridiculously photogenic **Highland cows** can often be seen on the region's farmland. While russet-red is the colour most associated with these cattle, they were originally black; selective breeding took place after Queen Victoria declared that she preferred them in a ginger coat.

The shoreline is often a great place for wildlife watching. **Seals** are particularly prolific, with harbour seals found along the west coast and larger grey seals more common on the east coast. A large colony of the latter can be seen south of Brora (page 106), but I've spotted seals from beaches all the way up and down both coasts, including at Loch Fleet (page 83), Duncansby Head (page 153), Handa Island (page 211),

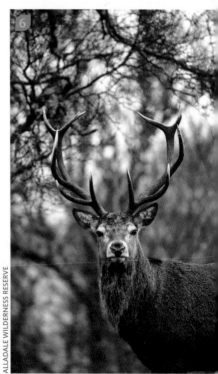

Ullapool (page 264) and Balmacara (page 342). You'll need a lot of patience to spot **otters** – look out for them at dusk on rocky, sheltered shores on the west coast, particularly where there's a lot of seaweed.

Also along the shoreline, keep an eye out for oystercatchers, always distinctive with their orange beaks and legs, little ringed plovers and curlews. **Puffins** can be seen between May and July at a few sites in the far north, including Duncansby Head (page 153), Dunnet Head (page 155), Handa Island (page 211) and, my personal favourite, Wester Clett (page 171). Other nesting birds you'll likely see on stacks and cliffs include skuas, shags, guillemots and razorbills.

Clifftops are a great place from which to spot **cetaceans**: porpoises and dolphins are usually the easiest to see, but orcas can be quite prolific along the Caithness coastline, and minke whales and basking sharks are also sometimes present. Chanonry Point (page 55) is the most famous land-watching spot in the region, thanks in part to the Moray Firth's large resident population of dolphins; several companies offer dolphin-spotting trips near here (page 45). If you're spending time on the east coast, I'd recommend joining the Caithness & Moray Firth Cetacean Sightings Facebook group; members post live updates when they catch sight of any cetaceans and you can join the small clifftop crowds when something is spotted.

Golden and **white-tailed eagles** breed on and near the west coast: your best bets are often inland for the former, with the mountain and moorland area between Gruinard and Gairloch particularly good, while along the coast tends to be best for the larger white-tailed eagles. Other birds of prey you might spot are ospreys (Loch Fleet is a good place for these; page 83), red kites and buzzards.

WEE BEASTIES

Not all creatures in the North Highlands are a joy to encounter, unfortunately. Top of the list has to be the dreaded **Highland midge**,

◀ 1 Saving Scotland's Red Squirrels has information on recent sightings. 2 Look for Highland cows on farmland on your travels. 3 White-tailed eagles breed on or near the west coast. 4 You will need a bit of luck to spot pine martens. 5 Dolphin-spotting trips in the Moray Firth are a great way to see these playful cetaceans. 6 Red deer are one of three deer species found in the region. 7 Otters can be elusive, but dusk is a good time to look for them along the rocky shores of lochs.

notorious for its summertime swarms. Though they can be active as early as May and still going into early October, the most bothersome months tend to be July and August and they are most often experienced at dawn and dusk.

The good news is that travelling to the North Highlands in the summer doesn't guarantee you'll be attacked by these tiny biting flies: for a start, they love damp, humid places – so inland areas are often worst affected – and hate wind, which there's often an abundance of, particularly along the coast. Secondly, they tend to almost exclusively stick to the west coast – head east in the summer months and you'll have no issue with them. Thankfully, midges don't carry disease, so the worst you're likely to experience is itchiness and annoyance.

You can get numerous repelling sprays – most people swear by either Avon's Skin So Soft body spray or Smidge repellent (⊘ smidgeup.com) – and Smidge has a handy 'Scottish Midge Forecast' on its website if you want to get an idea of what midge levels are like. If you're planning on spending some significant time outside during peak midge times, perhaps camping, then investing in a very glamorous head net is worth considering.

Another nuisance, and one that can potentially be more dangerous, is the **tick**, a blood-sucking parasite that starts out barely visible and becomes bigger as it swells with blood. Ticks live in the countryside, particularly in overgrown areas of grass – sticking to paths and wearing long trousers and boots is a good way to avoid them, but not necessarily foolproof (I once found a tick on my ankle despite doing all of these things). In most instances, a tick bite will cause little more than itching, but they can occasionally pass on Lyme disease, so it is important to check yourself and your companions after a walk in order to remove any that may have found their way on to you.

If you're spending any time walking even short distances in the Highlands, I'd recommend investing in a tick-removal tool. I have a Lifesystems tick remover card (⊘ lifesystems.co.uk/products/tick-removal-tool), which I've found invaluable – I keep it in my wallet so I don't have to worry about remembering where I've put it and it's always on me. You can also remove them using tweezers, but you need to be careful not to squeeze or crush the tick. Clean the bite area with antiseptic after removal; if a large rash appears on the site within a few months of being bitten, or if you feel unwell, see a doctor and tell them you've been bitten by a tick.

A TASTE OF SCOTLAND'S NORTH HIGHLANDS

The region's coast and countryside provide an abundant larder for restaurants and shops across the North Highlands – and means that eating locally sourced food often doesn't even have to be a conscious decision. Fish and seafood are at the forefront of this, and in coastal villages you'll often be served dishes made with ingredients that are fresh off the boats that day. Look out for Cape Wrath **oysters**, **salmon** from Loch Duart, **mussels** from Loch Dubh and **langoustines** and **crab** from Applecross and Handa Island. You might also see mention of local fish and shellfish brought in from Kinlochbervie and Scrabster – these are two big fishing ports, in the far northwest and near Thurso respectively; Scrabster haddock and chips is a particular favourite on menus.

BATHTUBS OF CHEESE

I'll admit that I'm rather snobby about cheese: give me something so strong it could walk out the door of a fromagerie and I'm happy. French cheese, yes, but Scottish cheese – I wasn't convinced it was really a thing. But then, staying in Easter Ross, every welcome basket we received had at least one cheese from **Highland Fine Cheeses** (hf-cheeses.com) and I found my preconceptions about Scottish cheese blown out of the water.

'My father complained that no-one made crowdie [a traditional soft cheese] any more – so my mother stuck a ten-gallon churn of milk in the bathtub to sour it,' company director Rory told me when I visited the Tain headquarters of Highland Fine Cheeses. They still make crowdie today (albeit not in a bath), but it's now just one of nine cheeses, ranging from two types of brie and blues to my personal favourite, Minger. With a washed rind, gooey middle and pungent aroma, it gives some of my favourite French cheeses a run for their money.

On the day I visited, they were making blue cheese in huge vats which didn't look all that dissimilar to bathtubs. 'When we started making blues in the late 1990s,' Rory said, 'we filled some skips.' Even today, quality is paramount – before I leave, Rory is handed a slither from a new batch of Fat Cow that he tastes and immediately declares not good enough.

It's not possible to visit the cheese headquarters, but you'll find Highland Fine Cheeses stocked in shops and restaurants across the North Highlands (and beyond), including Black Isle Dairy (page 54), The Storehouse (page 63) and The Walrus and the Corkscrew (page 48).

Don't miss the chance to try some locally **smoked fish**. There's a number of smokehouses in the region, including in Shieldaig (page 320). As well as hot and cold smoked salmon, Applecross Smokehouse (⌀ applecrossmokehouse.co.uk) sells smoked sea trout, smoked scallops and mussels, and smoked cheeses; Ullapool Smokehouse (⌀ ullapoolsmokehouse.com) also sells its own pork and venison chorizo and salami.

One of the most sustainable things you can eat in the Highlands is **venison**. Deer culling is an important part of land management, not least in terms of biodiversity and allowing trees and other plants to thrive, and eating the meat of these deer closes the circle and adds another positive to this necessary work. If you see Beinn Eighe (page 300) venison on offer, don't miss the opportunity to try it; the deer are shot on the Beinn Eighe estate, brought off the hills and inspected for disease before being stored in the nature reserve's on-site larder and being sold on, often to The Torridon (page 316) and other local people and places. 'Many of our volunteers start out vegan,' reserve manager Doug Bartholomew told me, 'but they end up making an exception for our venison, when they realise how sustainable it is to eat it.'

Locally reared **beef**, **lamb** and **pork** are also easy to come across; many village shops will sell local sausages and other meat products. If you're passing through Drumbeg, on the west coast north of Lochinver, stop by Lochview Croft (⌀ lochviewcroft.co.uk) for some of its excellent free-range meat, including sausages, burgers and lamb, and eggs. You'll see honesty boxes selling **free-range eggs** throughout the region – there are even egg-box vending machines (yes, really!) on the Black Isle (on the A832, two miles southwest of Cromarty) and the Easter Ross Peninsula (1½ miles northwest of Hilton of Cadboll).

The Black Isle and Easter Ross are also excellent for **dairy produce**, with a highlight being a visit to the self-serve farm shop of Black Isle Dairy (page 54), though you'll find its produce, including its **ice creams**, sold all over the region. Speaking of ice creams, a visit to the east coast isn't complete without a stop at Capaldis of Brora (page 109), either in Brora itself or in nearby Golspie. Look out for the excellent Highland

---

1 Catch of the day in Ullapool. **2** A traditional crofting cottage in Shieldaig (page 319).
3 Whisky tasting at Clynelish Distillery (page 107). **4** The Black Isle Brewing Co brews organic beer and has strong sustainable credentials (page 51). ▶

BOBBROOKY/DT

BOBBROOKY/DT

EMMA GIBBS

BLACK ISLE BREWING CO

Fine Cheeses (page 19) – especially their evocatively named Minger – in grocery shops and on many menus throughout the North Highlands.

BOOZE

There are some excellent local **beers** made in the North Highlands, many of which are well stocked in local shops. (Pubs, unfortunately, can be rather few and far between.) Based near Inverness, **Black Isle Brewing Co** (page 51) makes brilliant organic beer and has a fantastic sustainable ethos. A similar eco-focus can be found at **Uile-bheist** (page 50) in Inverness, where the beer is pumped direct from the brewery to the bar – it is also in the process of making its own whisky, though it'll be a little while before it's ready to drink. A pint of beer at the Applecross Inn (page 328) is the perfect pay-off for driving the infamous Bealach na Bà (page 330); **Applecross Craft Brewery** (⊘ applecrossbrewingcompany. co.uk) makes three fantastic beers – a pale, a red and a dark ale – which are served on draught in the pub but can also be bought by the bottle.

Strathcarron Brewery (⊘ strathcarronbrewery.com), just south of here, produces four beers – you can find these, and Applecross beers, at the well-stocked Lochcarron Food Centre (⊘ lochcarronfoodcentre. co.uk). Also on the west coast is **Ewebrew** (⊘ ewebrew.beer), run by husband and wife James and Jo Struthers – they currently have nine beers, including a barley wine, with evocative packaging and named after local places.

The well-placed **John O'Groats Brewery** (page 150) sells its beer from 'The Last House' in Groats itself, and can be found in a number of shops and restaurants in the northeast of the region, particularly in Thurso and Wick. On the east coast, **Cromarty Brewing Company** (⊘ cromartybrewing.com) has a wide range of beers, both in cans and bottles, and often turns up on draught too.

Whisky making is not quite as widespread as it is elsewhere in the Highlands, but the distilleries that are here generally fit very well with the Slow ethos, being deeply rooted in their location. Most can be visited on tours (book in advance) or you can pop in to buy direct from the shop.

The big hitter of the region is **Glenmorangie** (⊘ glenmorangie.com), on the outskirts of Tain, which has been making whisky since 1843 and famously has giraffe-height stills. Five miles northwest is the much smaller operation at **Balblair** (⊘ balblair.com), which was established in 1790, albeit with a hiatus in production between 1911 and 1948. On the outskirts of Brora, further up the east coast, is **Clynelish** (page 107); don't let the fact that it's part of the Johnnie Walker empire put you off – the whisky, which has famously waxy notes, has a real connection to its surrounding landscape. Its sister, **Brora Distillery** (⊘ malts.com), in the original Clynelish buildings, reopened in 2021 after being closed in 1983; visits are by appointment only.

Despite being a familiar name on supermarket shelves, **Old Pulteney** (page 142) in Wick remains a small-scale operation that still uses traditional techniques and water from a nearby loch. On the outskirts of Thurso is **Wolfburn** (⊘ wolfburn.com); the original distillery was founded here in 1821 but closed in 1858 – its latest incarnation dates to 2013 and its whisky, which is still made by hand, includes the lightly peated Morven and a number of small-batch bottles.

Even smaller in scale is **Badachro Distillery** (page 294), which produces Bad na h-Achlaise whisky, finished in Madeira, Tuscan oak and rum casks. Badachro also produces its own gin and vodka (the latter in a very cute puffin-branded bottle). **Dornoch Distillery** (page 78) has been bottling its own whisky since 2017 and also does a fantastic line in independent bottling of whiskies from other producers. Like Badachro, it also produces its own gin.

A number of other fantastic **gins** in the region include **Seven Crofts**, the signature gin of Highland Liquor Company (⊘ highlandliquorcompany. com), which has a well-stocked bottle shop (featuring other local whisky and beer brands, too) in Ullapool itself. Try too the gin produced by the even smaller **Rhidorroch Distillery** (⊘ rhidorrochdistillery. co.uk), based just up the road and with a handily located pop-up bar next to the Seafood Shack (page 268) in Ullapool. On the east coast is **The Geologist** (⊘ cromartydistillers.com), its name an homage to local boy Hugh Miller (page 58), and Caithness-based **Ice and Fire** (⊘ iceandfiredistillery.com).

Although Badachro can be visited on a tour, the other gin distilleries listed above are not open to the public. There are, however, two you can visit on the Caithness north coast. **North Point** (⊘ northpointdistillery. com) produces Crosskirk Bay Gin, which has a sublime citrusy taste, as well as its own rum and – though it's not due to be ready until 2028 at the earliest – single-malt whisky. My personal favourite is Rock Rose gin by **Dunnet Bay Distillers** (page 157), which makes incredibly smooth spirit infused by local botanicals, with a sustainable ethos that includes refills in recyclable pouches. Like North Point, Dunnet Bay is in the process of establishing its own whisky, at Stannergill Mill in Castletown (⬚ stannergillwhisky.co.uk; page 161).

GETTING THERE & AROUND

Unless you already live in the Highlands, there's no denying that the North Highlands is rather a long way from most other places in the UK. Inverness, sitting at the confluence of major road and rail routes, is the natural starting point for most people; if you're coming from London or other places in the south, I'd argue that there's no better way to arrive here than by sleeper train. The **Caledonian Sleeper** (⬚ sleeper. scot) has nightly departures to Inverness from London Euston from Sunday to Friday, all year round, arriving into Inverness after breakfast the following morning. I love the romance and lack of hassle of the trip – eating dinner in the dining car, waking to mountains and lochs outside, and arriving in the middle of the city – but I know others find it harder to deal with the noise and lack of sleep. It's also possible to take a daytime LNER (⬚ lner.com) service from London, which takes about eight hours but is particularly scenic once you get past Newcastle. Inverness is also served by regular trains from Edinburgh, Glasgow and Aberdeen, making connections from southern Scotland easy. Car hire is available from Inverness station (page 26).

Another option is to take the train to Edinburgh or Glasgow and drive north from there; train fares and car hire are often cheaper to/from these cities, and the time it takes to travel north is roughly equivalent to the time it takes by train – particularly convenient if you want to head first to the southern reaches of Wester Ross, avoiding Inverness.

It is possible to travel around the North Highlands without a car, but the ease of doing so depends on where and when you want to travel. From Inverness, two Scotrail (⬚ scotrail.co.uk) **train** lines serve the region: the **Kyle Line**, which runs west to Kyle of Lochalsh (gateway to the Isle of Skye) via Strathcarron, Attadale and Plockton; and the **Far North Line**, which runs north to Wick via Tain, Golspie, Brora, Helmsdale, Forsinard and Thurso. Both of these, but particularly the Kyle Line, are regarded as among the UK's most scenic rail routes; from the Kyle Line, you'll be treated to classic Highland mountainscapes.

There are roughly four services a day on each route, so you'll need to check times in advance if you're using either to get around.

Bus services are most frequent along the east coast, with Stagecoach (⊘ stagecoachbus.com) running the X99 route from Inverness to Thurso via a number of helpful stops along the east coast. Citylink (⊘ citylink. co.uk) buses run from Inverness to Ullapool and Skye; the latter stop at Dornie Bridge and Kyle of Lochalsh. More localised bus services are covered at the start of each chapter of this book, with those that exist often limited to school term time and/or a few days a week. If you do intend to travel around entirely by public transport, plan your route in advance and allow plenty of time.

DRIVING IN THE NORTH HIGHLANDS

As much as I'm loath to say it in a guide dedicated to Slow travel, exploring by car is the easiest way to visit the North Highlands, allowing you to get out to more places than you would be able to reach on public transport – and without quite the same effort as cycling or walking everywhere. That's not to say that it isn't without its challenges, however – single-track roads are the norm in vast swathes of the region, particularly the west, and if you're not used to them can initially be quite daunting.

Fortunately, the presence of **passing places** (in large part marked by white diamond-shaped signs) makes driving single-track roads easier, and a lack of hedges and walls along them means that visibility is often much better than on winding country roads in other parts of the UK. A few basic rules (page 26) do apply, though, which may not be obvious if you've never driven on roads like this before.

If you are a nervous or inexperienced driver, you might find some of the single-track Highland roads a little overwhelming. Generally speaking, a good indication that one of these is going to be particularly tricky is if it has a sign recommending against use by motorhomes. I've mentioned roads that are particularly difficult in the guide text. If you do find the driving hard work, my best advice is to take it slowly – that way you have plenty of time to think when you see an approaching vehicle – but do make sure you pull over for any faster vehicles behind you to overtake.

Be aware that Scotland's **drink-driving limits** are significantly lower than elsewhere in the UK: 22mcg of alcohol in 100ml of breath; 50mg of alcohol in 100ml of blood; and 67mg of alcohol in 100ml of urine. These levels mean that just one drink could put you over the limit.

RULES OF THE (SINGLE-TRACK) ROAD

Even if you've driven on single-track roads elsewhere, I'd advise making yourself aware of the rules of driving on single-track roads in the North Highlands. Not only will it make your own experience of driving here more enjoyable, it'll also help make things easier for locals who are trying to go about their lives without tourists getting in their way.

• Only pull in to a passing place on the left-hand side of the road; if the passing place is on the right, wait in the middle of the road by it and allow the other car driver to pull in to the passing place when they reach it.

• Use passing places to allow faster traffic to overtake you, regardless of what speed you're travelling at.

• Don't park in passing places.

• Be prepared to reverse into a passing place if you're closer to one than the oncoming vehicle is.

• Don't travel in a convoy – this makes driving much harder for other road users.

• Don't stop in the middle of the road, regardless of whether it's single- or dual-lane, except to let vehicles pull in to a passing place.

• Vehicles travelling uphill have priority; if you meet a car when travelling downhill you should pull over or reverse uphill to the nearest passing place.

Petrol stations can be few and far between and are generally limited to the larger towns and villages. Many of them are unmanned in the evenings and on Sundays, in which case there's always a card machine on hand to take advance payment.

 CAR HIRE

Enterprise 4 Seafield Rd, Inverness IV1 1SG ℰ 01463 235525 ◌ enterprise.co.uk. Station pick-up available.
Jack's Self Drive 17 Henderson Dr, Inverness IV1 1TR ℰ 01463 236572 ◌ jacksselfdrive. co.uk. Excellent local company that will deliver the car to Inverness station and meet you off the sleeper train. Highly recommended.

The North Coast 500

A huge number of visitors to the North Highlands are there to drive the **North Coast 500** (NC500; ◌ northcoast500.com), a 516-mile touring route circling the coast, beginning and ending in Inverness. The drive is really just a nifty bit of marketing – the roads all existed long before the route was established in 2015 – but there's no denying it's a fabulous road trip, taking in the huge variety of coastal scenery in the region.

It is, however, a hugely divisive and tricky subject locally. There are many people who have benefited from the route, particularly those offering accommodation along or just off it. But there have also been many negative side effects. One of the biggest complaints is often that there just wasn't (and still isn't) the infrastructure in place for such a popular touring route: not enough toilets, accommodation, places to eat, bins, parking spaces and so on.

On top of this are the complaints about visitors' behaviour. Travel along the route, but particularly on the western side, for any length of time in the late spring and summer months and you'll no doubt see some of it for yourself: convoys of fast cars and slow motorhomes; viewpoints full of touring vehicles parked up for the night; rubbish left by the side of the road; cars parking in passing places just to take a photo; 'wild camping' (page 31) by the side of the road; slow vehicles that refuse to move over for faster ones. There's also plenty that you hopefully won't see, like the toilet canisters being emptied into burns (streams), or the piles of human waste locals have stumbled across in beauty spots.

As always, this kind of behaviour is displayed by (hopefully) a minority of visitors to the region, but it's bad enough that many locals feel a strong antipathy towards the route. One local woman, who lives near Durness and didn't want to be named, told me that 'in summer I just want to stay inside my house and not come out until everyone has gone home.' Just the day before, she'd refused to budge for a driver who wouldn't reverse into the nearest passing place and had suffered a litany of abuse as a result. 'It makes me want to go and live in the most boring place ever, where no one will want to go,' she said.

Part of the problem with the NC500 is that many drivers treat it like a tick-list of places that they have to see. They drive from one beauty spot to another, nip out, take a photo, then get back in their vehicles and head on to the other. Speaking to people driving the NC500 often reminds me of backpacking in my youth, when you would talk to other travellers and try to outdo them with the places you had seen and been to. Many people see that it's *just* 516 miles and figure it can be done in just a handful of days, but of course 516 miles in the North Highlands is very different to 516 miles in most other parts of the UK.

SUSTAINABLE CAMPERVANNING
– A CONTRADICTION IN TERMS?

I've spent long enough in the North Highlands to have formed a strong antipathy towards touring vehicles. On too many occasions I've been stuck behind a slow-moving motorhome, opposite ones whose drivers refuse to manoeuvre them into a passing place, or unable to stop to look at a view, visit a beach or go on a walk because motorhome drivers have already claimed all the parking spaces and set up camp for the night. My children, however, felt none of this, and after one summer holiday where every car park seemed to have at least one brightly bedecked campervan with a party-like atmosphere, were desperate to try it out for themselves. Which led me to wonder, is it possible to camp sustainably and conscientiously?

With this in mind, we hired a van from **Big Sky Campers** (07768 973804

 bigskycampers.co.uk), based just across the Forth from Edinburgh and easily reached by train. I'd chosen them largely because their small VW vans ('not much bigger than a regular VW car,' owner Rob told me) would be easy to manoeuvre on the single-track Highland roads and were completely unbranded, so we could travel around without looking too much like tourists. In addition, Big Sky's ethos very much aligns with my own, encouraging their guests to camp and drive responsibly, shop locally rather than in the supermarkets, and to get away from the main tourist hotspots.

'The only way to sustainably camp is to stay in campsites,' a business owner on the Applecross Peninsula had told me on a previous trip, and so that's what we did, making use of a suggested itinerary drawn up by owner Alex to find places that were

This isn't to put you off driving the NC500 – not least because by travelling in the North Highlands you will, inadvertently or otherwise, have to do so at some point. But if you do want to drive it, my advice is to take as much time as possible: spend more than one night in each place, get out and explore on foot, and remember that you don't have to do everything in one trip.

WALKING & CYCLING

In my opinion, there is no better way to see the North Highlands than **on foot** – by walking the landscape you can gain a better understanding of it, and have the time and space to really appreciate it. You don't have to be an experienced hiker to enjoy walking here – there are plenty of options for even brief leg-stretchers that will offer up invigorating views. One thing I would say is to come prepared: walking shoes or boots are still open when we travelled in October. In actuality, camping sustainably was not hard: the campsites we chose were all in amazing places, such as at Clachtoll (page 233), and Port a Bhaigh (page 259) where the shore was just steps away, and there was always either a shop on site or within an easy stroll where we could stock up on dinner supplies – or, even better, a nearby pub or restaurant for a meal.

One thing we noticed was the mass exoduses from campsites every morning, as touring owners trundled on to the next place. Instead, we maximised our time, staying right up until check out so that we could finish exploring the local area, climbing hills and finding nooks and crannies on the beaches. I was pleasantly surprised by how magical it was, playing cards with the kids at the small table every evening and then climbing into bed together (because, of course, despite there being a roof tent, they both wanted to share the bed with me), falling asleep most nights to the sound of the surf outside.

I had worried that I would feel conspicuous, driving a large lumbering vehicle on these small roads, but the truth was that Rob was right and the van was small enough to get in and out of passing places as easily as if I had been driving my regular car. We made a particular effort to be courteous throughout our travels, pulling over when we were going too slowly for the vehicle behind, leaving enough room for other drivers every time we stopped, only using campsites, and having toilet stops in proper loos.

So yes, it is possible to sustainably camp, but you have to make the effort. But it's worth it – the kids still brand it 'the best ever holiday', and it won't be long before we're hiring a Big Sky van again.

invaluable up here, as is a waterproof coat and enough layers to keep you warm or cool depending on the weather.

Scottish access rights mean that you are free to walk (or cycle, or horseride, among other things) on most land in Scotland; this is great news if you want to just get out and explore, though you should be mindful of dwellings and other private property. The Scottish Outdoor Access Code website (⊘ outdooraccess-scotland.scot) is a good place for clarity on what is and isn't allowed. Do also be aware that some areas, particularly but not limited to the Flow Country (page 113), can be rather boggy, especially from autumn to spring, and so you should always walk with care.

There are excellent **footpaths** in many areas, ranging from long-distance routes to short ambles; I've included some of my favourite walks within the guide but there are countless more. It's worth investing

WILD CAMPING

Scotland is often lauded for its **access rights** (page 29), which include the ability to 'wild camp'. This is often spoken about as though it applies to any kind of camping, but in actuality it is just camping in tents that is permitted, and not vehicles. The idea behind wild camping is that it is 'lightweight camping' – basically as much as you can carry on your back – that takes place in tents with small numbers of people, staying for a maximum of two or three nights in one place. You should keep a good distance from both roads and buildings – if you have no choice but to pitch your tent near someone's house, you should seek permission before doing so. In addition, you should make sure to **leave no trace**, taking away your rubbish at the end of your stay to dispose of in bins and burying your own toilet waste (but not paper, which should be binned) – you should carry a trowel to do so. More information can be found at ⊘ outdooraccess-scotland.scot.

If you are travelling in a **touring vehicle** – a motorhome or campervan, or with a caravan – note that these are not included in the rules about wild camping. You will see many people parking up at night, often in very scenic spots by the side of the road, but I'd urge you to stick to campsites instead – it lessens your impact on the local environment and helps put money into the local community. There are some excellent campsites in the region, many of which have wonderful views and access to amazing places.

in the **Ordnance Survey** app (⊘ osmaps.com), which provides close-up detail on terrain and footpaths. **Walkhighlands** (⊘ walkhighlands. co.uk) is a comprehensive and celebrated website of (you've guessed it) Highland walks; you can download the app and save walks to it, which is handy, though I'd recommend always using the walks in conjunction with a decent map as they lack in-route distance information and can at times become confusing.

With the exception of Stac Pollaidh (page 250), I've stayed away from describing mountain walks in the region, though there are, naturally, a number of them on offer, including a number of Munros (mountains over 3,000ft) to climb. Again, Walkhighlands is the place to go for information. If you do want to climb a mountain, make sure you head out adequately prepared, with enough food, water and battery power, and that you choose a mountain suitable for your ability and experience.

◀ **1** Mountain biking the Balblair Mountain Bike Trails (page 77). **2** Wild camping near Plockton (page 335). **3** An amusing road sign near Grummore, Strathnaver (page 185). **4** Hill walking on Beinn Eighe, Beinn Eighe National Nature Reserve (page 300).

There are a couple of long-distance footpaths in the North Highlands. The main one is the **John O'Groats Trail** (page 145), a signposted route that runs largely along the coast from Inverness to John O'Groats – some sections are harder than others but the website does a good job of breaking it all down. Around two-thirds of the intensely challenging **Cape Wrath Trail**, which runs from Fort William to the Cape Wrath, falls within this region, too. More information about this unmarked route can be found on ⊘ capewrathtrail.org.uk.

CYCLING IN THE NORTH HIGHLANDS

Stevie Christie, managing director of Wilderness Scotland (⊘ wildernessscotland.com)

Cycling in the North Highlands is wonderful – the scenery is amazing and the volume of traffic is lower than in many other parts of the world, especially once you get off the main roads. There are some lovely climbs to take on, as well as lots of beautifully winding roads to explore.

The far north is not, however, a great destination for less experienced cyclists: there can be long distances between towns and the nearest bike shop could be a day's ride away. So you need to be self-sufficient and to consider in advance where you're going to stay, where you will source food and how you will cope with mechanical issues. You might find it better to base yourself in one town (which has a bike shop) and do loop rides, rather than attempt a long point-to-point journey.

As a general guide, you want the wind on your back – as the prevailing wind in Scotland is (usually) from the southwest, you ideally want to ride northeast as much as possible. Or plan a loop that goes into the wind in the morning (when you have more energy) and then has the wind on your back in the afternoon (when you feel tired). But whatever you plan, be prepared for the wind to do the opposite!

If you're carrying all your gear, you'll need a touring bike, but otherwise a road or gravel bike is fine – ideally with a wider tire width for more comfort and grip. While the volume of traffic is low, be prepared to negotiate narrow roads with lots of fast-moving traffic. Also be aware of vehicles behind you and let them pass to avoid queues forming on roads where it is not easy to overtake.

Cycle touring requires a lot of planning if you're doing it independently – and even with a route mapped out you can often pass very close to some of Scotland's greatest sights without knowing it. A good tour, such as the ones we offer at Wilderness Scotland, should let you just focus on riding your bike, enjoying the scenery and having some cool experiences as you travel – your guide and support team will look after everything else, plus you can pop into the van for a few miles if you're feeling tired or finding the route hillier than you expected.

The region's terrain makes **cycling** (see opposite) a challenge at times – but that doesn't stop the many hardy folk you'll pass on the roads and struggling up vicious hills. **National Cycle Route 1** heads north from Inverness to Tain and Dingwall, with an eastern option that loops to include Cromarty, Balintore and Nigg. More information can be found on the Sustrans website (⊘ sustrans.org.uk), along with a plotted, largely inland route from Inverness to John O'Groats. There are a number of dedicated **mountain-bike trails**, including Learnie Red Rocks and Balblair, both of which are on Forestry and Land Scotland (⊘ forestryandland.gov.scot) sites, and the Highland Wildcat Trails (⊘ highlandwildcat.com) on the slopes of Ben Bhraggie near Golspie (page 85). Bike hire, where available, is listed in the guide chapters.

ACCESSIBILITY

As you might expect, the terrain in this region doesn't always lend itself to accessibility, particularly when it comes to getting out and about. Euan's Guide (⊘ euansguide.com) is a good starting point for information about accessible attractions, places to stay and other facilities; you can search for specific destinations and locate them on the map.

There are a few **all-abilities paths** in the region that are suitable for wheelchairs: my favourite is the Leitir Easaidh path (page 242) near Lochinver, but other options include around Ferrycroft Visitors' Centre (page 96) in Lairg, around the Beinn Eighe visitors' centre (page 300), and at Aldie Burn near Tain (⊘ forestryandland.gov.scot). Corrieshalloch Gorge (page 274) is also wheelchair accessible, though be aware that there are some steep gradients to negotiate.

In Dornoch, wheelchairs can be hired for use on the beach (page 82). A lot of the region's museums are in old buildings that aren't particularly accessible, but notable exceptions include those at Gairloch (page 289), Strathnaver (page 178) and Ullapool (page 265).

TOURIST INFORMATION

There are, unfortunately, no longer any official Visit Scotland tourist offices in the North Highlands. Many towns and villages run their own, often seasonal information centres, usually out of small shops, and you'll find stacks of flyers at restaurants and accommodation throughout the region. The following websites are handy for planning your travels:

Black Isle Info ⟡ black-isle.info
Discover Assynt ⟡ discoverassynt.co.uk
Easter Ross Peninsula ⟡ easterrosspeninsula.com
North Coast 500 ⟡ northcoast500.com
Venture North (Caithness and Sutherland) ⟡ venture-north.co.uk
Visit Inverness Loch Ness ⟡ visitinvernesslochness.com
Visit Scotland ⟡ visitscotland.com
Visit Wester Ross ⟡ visitwester-ross.com

HOW THIS BOOK IS ARRANGED

The area that this book covers includes the historic counties of Ross and Cromarty, Sutherland and Caithness – you'll still see signs welcoming you to these areas as you travel around. For the purposes of this book, I've broken the region down into geographical chapters, taking a little

WHAT'S IN A NAME?

Throughout the Highlands you'll see that place names, both on village signs and road signs, are presented in both English and Gaelic. A Celtic language, **Gaelic** was brought over from Ireland some 1,500 years ago; today around 65,000 people in Scotland speak the language, with the majority of Gaelic speakers living in the Western Isles, and a significant proportion in the Highlands.

Sometimes English place names don't seem remarkably different to their Gaelic counterparts: Inverness is *Inbhir Nis*, Ullapool is *Ulapul* and Dornoch is *Dòrnach*, for example. At other times they seem hugely different: Rosehall is *Innis nan Lìon* and Cape Wrath is *Am Parbh*. In addition, many place names in the region, particularly on the east coast and in Caithness, have Pictish or Norse origins, reflecting the history of settlement in those areas.

In this book, I've generally used the English-language names for places, reflecting what you will usually hear and encounter on the ground. There are a few exceptions where I use the Gaelic, notably Stac Pollaidh (anglicised – and pronounced as – Stac Polly) and a few other mountainous areas, which again reflects their common use in the region. Gaelic pronunciation is notoriously difficult and not easy to gauge from spelling alone – for example, Beinn Eighe is pronounced *bayn ay* – but Gaelic speakers are usually understanding of this and will help you.

liberty here and there to include places where they more comfortably fit as part of a journey through the region.

Away from towns and villages, the vast majority of places I've included in this guide are natural sights: beaches, hills, cliffs and peninsulas. As such, giving addresses, or even just postcodes, doesn't tend to work. In most instances, putting the place name into your map app or satnav should suffice, but I have also included OS grid references (prefaced with ♀) so they can be easily located in the OS app. Hard-copy maps are, as always, useful, but if you're doing a fair amount of travelling you could end up needing dozens of maps – the app is infinitely easier both to carry and on your wallet.

MAPS

The double-page map at the front of this book shows which area falls within each chapter, with suggestions for places to base yourself. Each of the chapters also begins with a map, on which the numbers correspond with the numbered headings in the text – most often sights or settlements of particular interest. The ♀ symbol on these chapter maps indicates that there is a walk (featured in the text) in the area; these walks also have simple maps accompanying them, but I'd recommend you always have an **OS map** to hand for complete clarity and peace of mind. For each walk, I've included the relevant OS map title, marked with ❄, as well as a grid reference (marked ♀) for the starting point.

ACCOMMODATION

Throughout this book I've listed a handful of carefully selected places to stay under the **Special Stays** heading, encompassing bed and breakfasts, campsites, self-catering cottages and a handful of very special hotels – places that struck me for their location, friendliness, character, or a mixture of all three.

Hotels, bed and breakfasts and hostels are indicated by the symbol 🏠 under the heading for the nearest town or village in which they're located; self-catering options by 🏡 and campsites by ⛺. Be aware that prices vary widely between low and high seasons, and many places close during winter.

There are of course countless other accommodation possibilities in the region. Sawday's (⊘ sawdays.co.uk) is always a reliable site for wonderful places to stay, while a decent range of self-catering options can be found on Unique Cottages (⊘ unique-cottages.co.uk) and Wilderness Cottages (⊘ wildernesscottages.co.uk).

OPENING HOURS & ADMISSION FEES

Opening hours are notoriously fickle and tend to be the bane of a guidebook-writers' life. In the North Highlands, this is further compounded by the fact that many places, whether museums, hotels or restaurants, are only open during the spring and summer months, or only open sporadically during the winter. With this in mind, I've included opening hours for those sights that are not open daily and year round, but I've not included them for places to eat or stay, as these chop and change so regularly. Please do check in advance whether places will be open, to save yourself a potentially wasted journey (and a growling belly).

I've not included **admission prices** in the guide, largely because they are also subject to regular changes. Instead, I've mentioned where sights are free to enter – with the exception, of course, of nature reserves and other natural sights, which as a rule are always open access. Note that National Trust for Scotland (NTS) sites can be visited for free by National Trust England members, on production of a valid membership card.

FEEDBACK REQUEST

At Bradt Guides we're aware that guidebooks start to go out of date on the day they're published – and that you, our readers, are out there in the field doing research of your own. You'll find out before us when a fine new family-run hotel opens or a favourite restaurant changes hands and goes downhill. So why not tell us about your experiences? Contact us on ⊘ 01753 893444 or ✉ info@bradtguides.com. We will forward emails to the author who may post updates on the Bradt website at ⊘ bradtguides.com/updates. Alternatively, you can add a review of the book to Amazon, or share your adventures with us on social:

⨐ BradtGuides
✕ BradtGuides
⊙ BradtGuides & emmgibbs_words

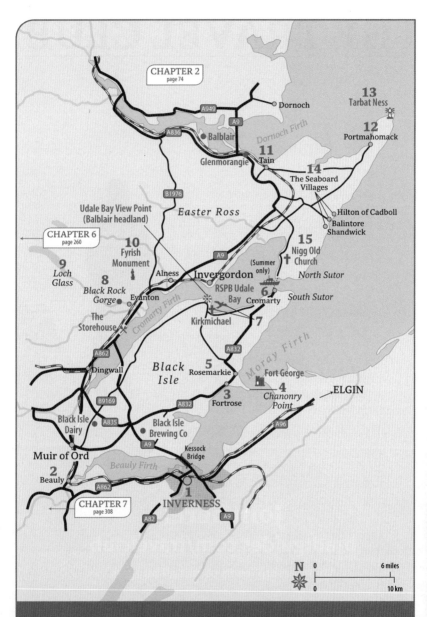

CHAPTER 6
page 260

CHAPTER 7
page 308

13 Tarbat Ness

Dornoch

12 Portmahomack

Dornoch Firth

A949

A9

A836

Balblair

11 Tain

Glenmorangie

14 The Seaboard Villages

Hilton of Cadboll

Balintore

Shandwick

B1976

Easter Ross

Udale Bay View Point
(Balblair headland)

15 Nigg Old Church

10 Fyrish Monument

9 Loch Glass

8 Black Rock Gorge

Alness

Evanton

A9

Invergordon

(Summer only)

North Sutor

RSPB Udale Bay

6 Cromarty

South Sutor

The Storehouse

Kirkmichael

7

Cromarty Firth

A862

Dingwall

Black Isle

5 Rosemarkie

A832

Moray Firth

Fort George

4 Chanonry Point

ELGIN

B9169

3 Fortrose

A832

Black Isle Dairy

A835

Black Isle Brewing Co

A9

A96

Muir of Ord

Kessock Bridge

Beauly Firth

2 Beauly

A862

1 INVERNESS

A82

A9

N   0   6 miles
    0   10 km

INVERNESS, THE BLACK ISLE & EASTER ROSS

1

INVERNESS, THE BLACK ISLE & EASTER ROSS

Sitting at the confluence of major roads from the south and east, and with direct trains running from as far south as London, the Highland capital of **Inverness** is the natural starting point for explorations of the North Highlands. Its petite size, combined with its river- and firthside setting, and thriving food, drink and music scene, makes it an ideal Slow city. Immediately north, where the narrow neck of the Beauly Firth becomes the much wider (and wilder) Moray Firth, is the **Black Isle** – not actually an island but a peninsula of lush farmland and small coastal communities. Agriculture lies at the heart of **Easter Ross**, too; a predominantly low-lying region that's considered one of Scotland's best farming areas. This association stretches as far back as the Picts (page 67), who left behind evidence of their existence in the striking cross-slabs that still pepper the countryside today.

Two more firths – **Cromarty** in the middle and **Dornoch** at the northern end – further characterise this gentle part of the North Highlands, meaning that water, or at least the glittering promise of it, is almost always in view. As are distant mountains, which you'll often catch in your rear-view mirror or as you stand at the tideline. Sure, this region may lack the in-your-face showiness of further west, but don't be tempted to skimp on it because of that – it has its own, quiet drama that rewards a little time and effort.

GETTING AROUND

This is the easiest of the regions in this book to get around by public transport, due largely to its proximity to Inverness. In summer, the small **car ferry** (⊘ highlandferries.co.uk ☉ Jun–Sep 08.00–18.15 daily) between Cromarty on the northern tip of the Black Isle and Nigg at the southern point of the Easter Ross Peninsula is hugely convenient for getting to the northern reaches of the area covered in this chapter, replacing a 38-mile road journey with a short water crossing.

TRAINS

Inverness's train station is conveniently located on Academy Street in the city centre, with Scotrail (⚲ scotrail.co.uk) services running to Beauly (3–6 daily; 15min) and Tain (2–5 daily; 1hr 10min). Be aware, however, that services can be a little irregular so if you're planning a return journey you should check times with ScotRail in advance.

BUSES

Several Stagecoach (⚲ stagecoachbus.com) services run from Inverness bus station on Margaret Street (and other city-centre bus stops) to places in this chapter. Of particular use are the 28 to Beauly (usually hourly; 30min), the 26A to Cromarty (every 30min–1hr; 50min) via Fortrose and Rosemarkie, and the hourly X25 to Tain (1hr 20min–1hr 45min).

WALKING & CYCLING

There are a number of easy-to-follow but rewarding **walking paths** in the region, of which my favourite is the Fairy Glen walk at Rosemarkie (page 56) on the Black Isle. For wide-ranging views that stretch – on a clear day, at least – as far as the Cairngorms, you can't beat the lung-busting walk up to the Fyrish Monument (page 64), just north of Evanton; the village is also the starting point for a lovely woodland walk to dramatic Black Rock Gorge (page 62).

The long-distance John O'Groats Trail (page 145) cuts inland for most of its journey through Easter Ross, though it thankfully gives the A9 a wide berth much of the way.

The relatively low-lying nature of this region makes it ideal for **cyclists** of all abilities. Learnie Red Rocks (IV10 8SN ⚲ forestryandland.gov. scot/visit/learnie-red-rocks), on the Black Isle, three miles north of Rosemarkie, has a number of mountain-bike trails suitable for a range of abilities.

 BIKE HIRE

Inverness Bike Hire Caledonian Gifts, Church St, Inverness ⚲ 01463 710664
⚲ invernessbikehire.co.uk

Ticket to Ride The Pavilion, Bellfield Park, Inverness ☏ 01463 419160
⊘ tickettoridehighlands.co.uk

1 INVERNESS

⌂ The Glen Mhor, Ness Walk

Despite being the 'capital of the Highlands', Inverness has more the laid-back feel of a medium-sized town than the frenetic energy of a city. While it may lack traditionally 'big' sights, this is just part of the charm; spend a few days wandering by the river, eating fabulous local food and

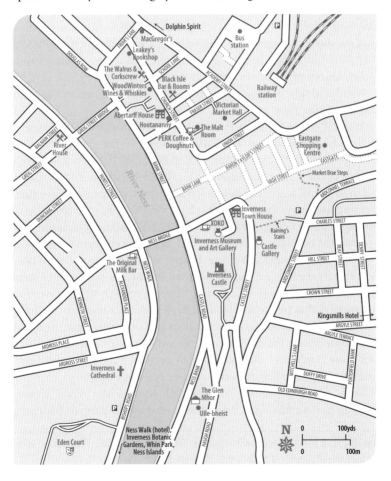

ducking into bars for live music, and the appeal of this small but vibrant city will slowly work its magic on you.

My first stop – until they closed it off for renovation, at least – in Inverness has always been the grounds of the impressive red sandstone **Inverness Castle** ($\mathring{\partial}$ invernesscastle.scot), which overlooks the wide River Ness from its vantage point at the southern edge of the city centre. If the site is back open, this is a great spot from which to get your bearings, looking upriver towards the hills of the Black Isle and – on a clear day at least – Ben Wyvis. At the time of writing, the castle was undergoing a huge redevelopment project, which will see it reopen in 2025 (keep an eye on the website for the latest details). Though there has been a fortification on this site since the 11th century, the building you see today dates from the 19th century, and is actually two different castellated buildings, built as a courthouse and a prison respectively. Mary, Queen of Scots was famously denied entry to the castle in 1562 – unsurprisingly, her supporters then laid siege to it and managed to capture it after three days.

Halfway down the steps that lead to High Street from the castle is **Inverness Museum and Art Gallery** (Castle Wynd $\mathscr{D}$ 01349 781730 $\mathring{\partial}$ highlifehighland.com $\odot$ Apr–Oct 10.00–17.00 Tue–Sat; free entry), which crams a decent amount of local and Highland history into a relatively small space. The gallery space on the first floor is my favourite, hosting temporary exhibitions that have ranged from an exploration of the work of the Glasgow Boys and Girls to contemporary sculpture.

From the museum, turning right up High Street will bring you almost immediately to **Inverness Town House**, with four narrow, fairy-tale-like turrets on its main façade. Opened in 1882 as the home of local government, it is now occupied by (largely empty) office space. The two wolves that sit either side of its steps are in fact modern creations, carved to replace two missing stone dogs that originally sat at the top of the Town House; the originals were found in unmarked crates in 2017 and have since been reinstated to their original positions at the top of the building – you'll need to crane your neck to see them.

High Street becomes pedestrianised beyond the Town House, leading past a rather bland assortment of shops to Eastgate Shopping

INVERNESS: **1** The castle and the River Ness. **2** The imposing cathedral. **3** Town House with its fairy-tale-like turrets. **4** Exhibits in the Museum and Art Gallery. ▶

42

JACQI/DT

CHRIS DORNEY/DT

AYOME WATMOUGH/DT

INVERNESS MUSEUM & ART GALLERY

Centre, full of the usual chain stores (including an excellent branch of Waterstones). A right turn just before the shopping centre will take you up **Market Brae Steps** to Ardconnel Terrace in the upper part of town. I love wandering the streets up here, with the city centre quickly giving way to attractive pale-stone Victorian houses. You can head back down to Castle Street, coming out almost opposite the castle, by heading down **Raining's Stairs** at the western end of Charles Street. Head immediately left at the bottom of Raining's Stairs to reach **Castle Gallery** (43 Castle St ✆ 01463 729512 ⌂ castlegallery.co.uk ⌚ 10.00–17.00 Mon–Sat), which has excellent exhibitions by artists from Scotland and the rest of the UK; all art on display is available to buy. I was particularly taken by the work of Shazia Mahmood when I visited last, who beautifully captures the way light plays on water in the northwest.

Many of the city's most imposing buildings are a testament to the Victorians, including the **Victorian Market Hall** (⌂ thevictorianmarket. co.uk), which has a rather austere front on Academy Street (and can also be accessed from Union Street, Queensgate and Church Street). Inside, be sure to look up at the domed roof with its elegant red cast-iron beams; I'm often reminded, walking through here, of Parisian *passages*. The market hall is home to an assortment of shops, including a long-established butcher, a sweet shop and some gift shops, and has a food hall at its Church Street end.

Church Street, although less busy than High Street, always feels like the focus to me – though I can neither confirm nor deny how much of that it down to its abundance of bars. Blink and you'll miss **Abertarff House** (⌚ mid-Jul–Oct 10.00–16.00 Tue–Sat; NTS; free entry), tucked back from the road. The city's oldest house, it was built in 1593 and now has displays on Inverness in the 17th century.

A little further north are two of the city's finest independent shops. At number 99, **WoodWinters Wines & Whiskies** (⌂ woodwinters. com ⌚ 10.00–19.00 Mon–Sat) doesn't just stock an impressive range of whiskies (among which they'll be more than happy to find the right one for you) and wines, but also Scottish gins and beers. The grand old 18th-century church at the northern end of the street is now **Leakey's Bookshop** (⌂ leakeysbookshop.com ⌚ 10.00–17.30 Mon–Sat), Scotland's largest second-hand bookshop and (unsurprising given that title) crammed with books on every possible subject; this is less a bookshop than a temple to the art form. Many original features abound,

THE MORAY FIRTH DOLPHINS

It's no coincidence that the world's most northerly resident population of bottlenose dolphins is also its largest – they've evolved to have a particularly thick layer of blubber that helps them cope with the colder waters here. (Having spent some time in these waters, I can confirm that an extra-thick layer of blubber would be highly beneficial.) Theoretically, you can see them all year round, particularly from Chanonry Point (page 55) – your best bet is on a rising tide (one hour after low tide) when the dolphins chase their salmon supper inland – but your chances hugely increase in late spring and summer when conditions are (in theory, at least) calmer and sunnier.

If you're in the area during these months and keen on **dolphin spotting**, I'd really recommend taking a RIB (rigid inflatable boat) trip. Though they can't of course guarantee sightings, in my experience the boat trips alone are hugely fun, led by knowledgeable, friendly skippers who provide great insight on the landscape and marine life; on all three trips I've taken, I've seen dolphins, plus on one occasion, a rather unexpected minke whale. Both companies listed below follow strict marine standards, which means giving the animals space and treating them with respect. That's not to say that you won't be able to get close to them, but encounters will be on the animals' terms: on one memorable trip, we had a pod of common dolphins escort us all the way back to the Kessock Bridge.

Dolphin Spirit Stadium Rd, Inverness IV1 1FF ✆ 07844 800620 ⬥ dolphinspirit.co.uk
EcoVentures Victoria Pl, Cromarty IV11 8YE ✆ 01381 600323 ⬥ ecoventures.co.uk

including the pulpit (now perfect for peering at oversized tomes), and there's a well-stoked wood fire for colder days. Good luck getting out in under half an hour.

ALONG THE RIVER

One of the best things to do in the city is to walk along the river to the botanic gardens and Ness Islands. The nicest route, in my opinion, is to cross to the west side of the river at graceful Greig Street Bridge and follow the road south, past a string of lovely Victorian buildings and **Inverness Cathedral** (⬥ invernesscathedral.org). Built in 1866 and imposing from the outside, the cathedral has a surprisingly compact interior that is, if I'm honest, rather underwhelming. Just beyond is the excellent **Eden Court** (⬥ eden-court.co.uk), home to two theatres, two cinemas, three art galleries (free entry) and the summertime **Under Canvas** music festival.

About half a mile after the cathedral, the footpath becomes lined with trees on both sides, and you'll get a sense of the city dropping away. At low tide, you can pick your way along the pebbly shore here, the view widening around the lush green islands.

Inverness Botanic Gardens (Bught Ln, IV3 5SS ⌀ highlifehighland. com/inverness-botanic-gardens; free entry) is another half a mile to the southwest. Though small, this is one of my favourite spots in the city, and one that always feels busy with locals rather than tourists. In the Tropical House, you'll be ducking under palm leaves as you wander around; adjoining is a display of carnivorous plants, where on one visit we watched an unfortunate bee submit to a North American Pitcher Plant. Outside are neatly cultivated herbaceous borders that pop with colour in spring and summer, and the slightly wilder confines of the Grow Project's area, where horticultural therapy is offered.

Whin Park, to the south of the gardens, is home to the **Ness Islands Railway** (⌀ nessislandsrailway.co.uk ⊙ Easter–late Oct 11.00–16.00 Sat & Sun, school holidays daily), a 7¼-inch gauge miniature railway that winds through trees for just over half a mile. Despite the railway's name, you'll have to backtrack slightly downriver to reach the actual **Ness Islands** (cross over the white bridge opposite Bught Road), where paths wind gently through the trees and across bridges. There's a wild feel to these lovely islands, with the rushing of water always around you and a sense of the city being far away. Children will love climbing on the carved wooden Nessie, and there are lots of places to sit and contemplate. From here, you can follow the paths north to eventually cross the river on yet another slender white bridge; a left turn at the end (before you meet the road) will take you back to the city, following the river along its eastern bank.

 SPECIAL STAYS

The Glen Mhor Ness Bank ⌀ 01463 234308 ⌀ glen-mhor.com. Set across a number of attractive 19th-century buildings, The Glen Mhor has a prime riverside position just a short and very pleasant walk from the city centre. Rooms combine subtle Highland touches like tartan cushions with contemporary colours and smart bathrooms, and there's also a number

◀ INVERNESS: **1** The Botanical Gardens. **2** Eden Court is home to theatres, cinemas and art galleries. **3** Boats for hire at Whin Park. **4** Story-telling, music and whisky tasting with The Highland Malt Whisky Experience.

of apartments with kitchens and living spaces. The excellent Uile-bheist (page 50) is on site, as well as the Waterside Restaurant, which serves local meat and fish, and the hotel has admirable sustainability credentials, including its own energy centre.

Ness Walk 12 Ness Walk ✆ 01463 215215 ⌂ nesswalk.com. Tucked away on the west side of the river, south of the cathedral, five-star Ness Walk feels every inch a sophisticated city retreat. As well as an excellent fine-dining restaurant, Torrish, and a cocktail and whisky bar, guests have access to the leisure facilities (including a pool) at Ness Walk's sister property, **Kingsmills Hotel** (Culcabock Rd, IV2 3LP ⌂ kingsmillshotel.com), 15 minutes' walk east of the city centre and well suited to families.

¶¶ FOOD & DRINK

The **Food and Drink Hall** at the Victorian Market Hall (page 44) has a number of casual food options, including delectable cakes from the Bad Girl Bakery and authentic Indian street food from Namaste Inbhir Nis.

Restaurants & cafés

Black Isle Bar & Rooms 68 Church St ✆ 01463 229920 ⌂ blackislebrewery.com. This large, relaxed bar is always popular – and deservedly so. The beer, from its own brewery (page 51), is excellent, with no fewer than 26 on tap, and the pizzas are too (my kids, after extensive testing, have declared them the best in the region), with most toppings coming from the brewery farm and garden.

The Original Milk Bar 3 Ness Walk ▪. Tiny coffee shop serving up great cakes and cookies alongside strong coffees, plus sandwiches, paninis and Black Isle Dairy ice cream. On a sunny day, grab a table outside and watch the river (and the city) go by.

PERK Coffee & Doughnuts 33 Church St ⌂ perkcafe.co.uk. One of my favourite places in the city, not just for the amazing, creative doughnuts but for its brilliant coffee. Also pastries and granola for breakfast, and toasties and soup for lunch. Reopens most evenings for fantastic coffee cocktails.

River House 1 Greig St ✆ 012463 222033 ⌂ riverhouseinverness.co.uk. Intimate and unpretentious restaurant with an emphasis on seafood and shellfish, sourced from within Scotland – oysters (the freshest I've tasted) from Cape Wrath, hot smoked salmon from the Hebrides, haddock from Peterhead. Meat and veggie options, too.

The Walrus & Corkscrew 105 Church St ✆ 01463 221237 ⌂ thewalrusandcorkscrew. co.uk. Candlelit tables and sheepskin throws on the benches make this small wine bar extra cosy. The menu is simple – single or sharing platters of local meat and/or cheese, with a vegan option also available, complemented by excellent wine by the glass or bottle.

XOKO 13 Bridge St ⌂ xoko.co.uk. You're greeted by piles of pastries as you enter XOKO, the work of pastry chef Fernando, which set the scene for great breakfasts. Lunch options include

HISTORY THROUGH STORIES

Highland history is such that it's written across the land: in the bare hillsides, ruined villages and old fishing ports. Two experiences in and around Inverness offer up the ideal opportunity to learn a bit more about this history, while enjoying a great night out.

Held in a fairy-light-festooned cellar room below MacGregor's bar (see below), **The Highland Malt Whisky Experience** (◌ highlandmaltwhiskyexperience.co.uk ◌ Apr–Oct Mon–Fri) takes you on a journey through Highland history – from the days of clan control and the Battle of Culloden to the resurgence of Gaelic – with storytelling interwoven with music (which could be fiddle-, guitar- or accordion-based, depending on your host) and local whisky tasting. It may sound like a lot to cram into 90 minutes but it doesn't feel like it when you're there; Davy Holt, who hosted the evening I attended, combined all these elements

with such a lightness of touch (and excellent comedic timing) that it flowed seamlessly. As a group, we veered from convivial laughter to wiping away tears.

'Dinner with stories about Scottish history,' is how owner Garry Coutts describes **Downright Gabbler** (◌ downrightgabbler. co.uk) in Beauly (page 50). Meals here come in the form of 'events', each with a theme, such as the Super Scots Supper (famous Scots) and A Write Good Night (Scotland's literary heritage). I joined them for the six-course Highland Banquet, where the food – which included haggis bonbons and a deconstructed tea cake that I still regularly think about – was accompanied by stories from the region's past. With his background in politics, Garry is a natural raconteur, and the experience feels like an intimate dinner party at a friend's house.

---

tacos and soups, the coffee is fantastic and there's a wide range of hot chocolates on offer, including orange and chilli.

Bars & live music
Hootananny 67 Church St ◌ 01463 233651 ◌ hootananninyinverness.co.uk. Affectionately known as 'Hoots', this is an Inverness institution and you're likely to be crammed in, shoulder to shoulder, with locals as well as tourists. Live music every night, including a Saturday afternoon 'super ceilidh' and famous Sunday sessions where anyone can get up and jam.
MacGregor's 109–113 Academy St ◌ macgregorsbars.com. Home of the Malt Whisky Experience (see above), this cosy bar at the northern end of Academy Street was established by eponymous Bruce MacGregor of the band Blazin' Fiddles – unsurprisingly, it's a great place to hear live music throughout the week.
The Malt Room 34 Church St ◌ 01463 221888 ◌ themaltroom.co.uk. Tucked up a narrow alleyway, this smart little whisky bar manages to ooze cool without pretension. Staff will

help you negotiate the extensive menu of malt whiskies, and there are cocktails (with or without whisky) and other drinks on the list, too.

Uile-bheist Ness Bank ⊘ uilebheist.com. Inverness's only distillery serves up fantastically fresh (they're literally piped in from the adjoining brewery) beers and a huge range of whiskies (and other drinks) in its large bar room. Tables outside in sunny weather, and often live music on weekend afternoons. Book in for a whisky tour while you're here.

BEAULY & THE BLACK ISLE

Whether you head northwest on the A9 from Inverness to cross the Beauly Firth on the Kessock Bridge or west on the A862 to run alongside it, it doesn't take long before you've shaken off the city confines. Taking the latter will lead you to the appealing village of **Beauly**, approached through an avenue of neatly spaced oak trees that create something of a French feel – appropriate, given the village's connections to Mary, Queen of Scots. The former takes you straight on to the **Black Isle**, the name of which is a misnomer, being neither black nor an island but rather a peninsula wedged between the Moray and Cromarty firths.

2 BEAULY

🏠 **Big Sky Lodges, Downright Gabbler**

Popular belief has it that Beauly's name comes from Mary, Queen of Scots, who on a visit here in 1564 apparently remarked 'C'est un beau lieu' ('It's a beautiful place'). Though the village sprawls along the main road for almost a mile, its centre is neat and compact, with the large central square (now given over to car parking) as its focus.

The atmospheric red-sandstone ruin of **Beauly Priory** (⊘ historicenvironment.scot; free entry) is set back from the road at the northern end of the square. Founded around 1230, it is notable for being one of only three priories founded by French Valliscaulian monks in Scotland (the other two are in Argyll and Moray). Central to life in the Valliscaulian order were obedience, chastity and poverty – despite this, the original size of the complex betrays the fact that the monks were in fact rather well off. Today only the now-roofless abbey church remains; Oliver Cromwell had stone from the other buildings repurposed for

"I'm not a religious person, but I've spent many hours here, standing in the quiet of the abbey church ruins."

his fort in Inverness (built in the 1650s and then demolished upon the restoration of Charles II to the throne).

I'm not a religious person, but I've spent many hours here, standing in the quiet of the abbey church ruins, enjoying the juxtaposition of the solitude offered between the old walls and the sounds of modern life beyond. The interior of the church houses some gravestones, reflecting its change of purpose after the Reformation, when it became a local burial ground. Take time to wander around the outside, too, where the

NATURE FIRST, BEER SECOND

Black Isle Brewing Co Old Allangrange, Munlochy IV8 8NZ ⬧ blackislebrewery.com
🕙 10.00–18.00 Mon–Sat

I'm a naturally cynical person, so when I first encountered Black Isle Brewing Co's slogan 'Save the Planet, Drink Organic', I thought it was a nifty bit of marketing – with the bonus that they made beer that tasted really good. However, visiting their brewery, seven miles northwest of their Inverness bar (page 48) and set among 130 acres of farmland, it soon becomes clear that it's anything other than a gimmick.

This farmland sits at the heart of what the brewery does: 40% of the barley is grown on site (with the rest coming from sources as local as possible), though only one field is used for the crop at a time, so that the land can have time to recover and allow nature to thrive.

'We operate on a "nature first, beer second" basis,' shop manager Catrin Anderson-Hayman tells me when she shows me around. It's a bold move for a company but it's just one of the things that led to Black Isle Brewing Co becoming a certified B Corp in 2023 (meaning it meets high standards of social and environmental performance).

'Production is only as important as biodiversity,' Catrin says, telling me that they compost their spent grain which then helps to grow crops and increase biodiversity. The five-acre on-site market garden provides ingredients for the brewery's two bars (the second is in Fort William) and benefits from an organic and appropriately regenerative focus. But the knowledge and benefits that the brewery brings aren't just limited to its beer and its beer drinkers – there's a committed community focus here, too, with a local school coming in once a week to work in the garden, a weekly volunteer day, and regular workshops and events.

Anyone can pop in during opening hours to either buy beer or enjoy a free tour (or both!), and you can even stay on site in a cosy little shepherd's hut. And as for the beers themselves – they're good enough that I always bring a handful home from any trip up here. My personal favourite is the amber Red Kite, while my husband loves the Scotch Ale – at 6.8%, the biggest you can buy at the bar is two-thirds of a pint.

CAMPBELL & C°

crumbling walls, protrusions and high-up imprints of doorways tell just as much of a tale of the site's history and its one-time size.

South of the square is a shop that surely rivals the priory for tourist numbers: **Campbell's of Beauly** (⟨ campbellsofbeauly.com), also known as 'The Highland Tweed House'. It was established in 1858, and stepping inside feels a bit like stepping back in time, with rolls of tweed stacked neatly on the wooden shelves behind the counter. The warren of rooms holds ready-made items of Highland and sporting clothing, and you can also book a tailoring appointment.

To appreciate the beauty that Mary, Queen of Scots saw here, venture away from the main road: the roads to the east will take you down towards the wide, meandering river, while the grid of roads to the west is lined with neat cottages and heads out towards the hills. Downright Gabbler (see below) has an excellent free walking tour available to download from its website.

 ## SPECIAL STAYS

Big Sky Lodges Muir of Ord ✆ 01463 870919 ⟨ bigskylodges.co.uk. Among my very favourite places to stay, the Scandinavian-style lodges here make perfect, cosy bases for exploring the region. Each has been beautifully decorated, with lots of Highland-inspired touches, and with its own fire pit (the welcome pack includes marshmallows for toasting). There's also a romantic two-person loft and a cosy caravan. Ailsa and Jonny are excellent hosts, and the little on-site shop stocks local produce.

Downright Gabbler High St, Beauly ✆ 01463 782800 ⟨ downrightgabbler.co.uk. Four one-bed apartments in this old coaching inn – which also houses one of the region's best and most inventive restaurants (page 49) – each with a mini kitchen and comfortable living area. An extensive information pack is provided and, despite the frequent events held downstairs, rooms feel private and tucked away.

 ## FOOD & DRINK

In addition to the below, book ahead for the excellent Downright Gabbler (page 49).

Café Biagiotti 11 High St ✆ 01463 782036 ⟨ cafebiagiotti.com. Friendly Italian café where everything is made in-house. The focaccia is perfectly salty, crispy and chewy – try it with butternut squash and goat's cheese. Pasta meals to take away, too.

◀ **1** Fortrose Cathedral. **2** The atmospheric remains of Beauly Priory. **3** A Highlands institution: Campbell's of Beauly. **4** Volunteers gardening at the Black Isle Brewing Co.

Corner on the Square 1 High St ℐ 01463 211410 ♟ corneronthesquare.co. Bright, big-windowed deli café where the shelves groan with local produce. The menu (eat in or take-away) includes sandwiches and salads, as well as more decadent platters – 'From the sea' features homemade mackerel pâté and sautéed king prawns.

3 FORTROSE

The approach to Fortrose on the A832 is a rather genteel one thanks to the gabled Victorian houses that sit just back from the main road (some of which must boast rather impressive firth views from their gardens), just before the road narrows to become High Street and buildings press in on either side.

Tucked just off High Street, on Cathedral Square, are the striking red sandstone ruins of **Fortrose Cathedral** (♟ historicenvironment. scot; free entry). As at nearby Beauly (page 50), what remains today is significantly smaller than the original – here, helpfully, markings on the floor show the area (and shape) the cathedral would have covered, giving a sense of just how big it once was.

The earliest remaining buildings here date back to when the Bishop of Ross's seat was relocated to Fortrose in the early 13th century, and the cathedral remained in use even after the Reformation. Like Beauly, it's said that many of the bricks were taken away by Oliver Cromwell to build his citadel in Inverness. Unlike at Beauly, however, you can't go inside, but you can still gain quite a sense of its interior, particularly the impressive ribbed vaulted ceiling and some beautiful marble memorials, by peering through the railings.

DIY DAIRY

Black Isle Dairy Rootfield Farm, Mulbuie IV6 7RF ♟ blackisledairy.co.uk

Tucked off the B9169 north of Muir of Ord, with the peaks of Ben Wyvis in the distance, the **Black Isle Dairy** is a farm shop with a difference: it's all self-service. The highlight is the milk vending machine: buy a reusable glass bottle (attractive enough to keep as a souvenir) and fill it up with milk from the machine. The milk is produced by the mixed herd at the farm just a little further up the track, making it about as fresh as you can get. You can even – much to my kids' delight – turn it into flavoured milk. Other produce on sale includes fantastic ice cream, plus cakes, bread, fish, pork and even skincare – some products are only available on certain days, so check the website in advance.

¶¶ FOOD & DRINK

Fortrose is a great place to pick up a picnic lunch if you're spending the day exploring the Black Isle, with two bakeries to choose from: **Cromarty Bakery** (49 High St) and **Bakhoos Bakery** (85 High St).

IV10 18 High St ⟡ iv10.net. In a low modern building on the corner of Academy and High streets, this smart, contemporary 'café bar deli' is reason enough to come to Fortrose. The menu focuses on seasonal food, with the wood fire leading to the likes of smoky piri piri prawns and charred sweetheart cabbage. Everything can be ordered to take away, as well.

4 CHANONRY POINT

The near-straight line of the Black Isle's eastern coast is broken by a sharp finger of land that points into the Moray Firth between Fortrose and Rosemarkie. Once the houses drop away, the road cuts directly down to Chanonry Point, through Fortrose and Rosemarkie Golf Course, the water a silvery streak in a distance. Just three-quarters of a mile separate Chanonry from Fort George (though it's 25 miles by road), diagonally across the firth, creating a deep, narrow channel that's the perfect feeding ground for the point's most famous residents: bottlenose dolphins (page 45).

As with any kind of wildlife watching, spotting the cetaceans is down to a mixture of timing and luck – though they live here all year round, a rising tide (as the tide changes from low to high) and the summer months are your best bet. The peninsula's shape means that the winds are often high here, and it's easy to mistake the curve of a breaking wave for a cresting dolphin.

The best place to spot dolphins is from the beach on the northern side of the peninsula – you can cut across on the narrow footpath that runs along the back of the rather squat lighthouse or, when the tide is low enough, follow the pebble beach around the front of it. Regardless of whether you have luck with the dolphins or not, this is a lovely spot. The pebble beach is ideal for stone skimming while you wait, becoming sandy as it stretches around to Rosemarkie – a very pleasant walk of just under two miles.

5 ROSEMARKIE

At low tide, Rosemarkie's lovely biscuit-coloured beach feels as though it stretches on endlessly past the village. At the far, northern end are some fantastic rocks for clambering on and rock pooling; press on past here (use the footpath behind the beach if the tide is up) to reach some fascinating sea caves about a mile further on. The closest, Caird's Cave, was inhabited as recently as the beginning of the 20th century.

Red sandstone and painted buildings crowd Rosemarkie's narrow High Street, including the attractive white 18th-century building that houses the **Groam House Museum** ($\mathcal{O}$ groamhouse.org.uk $\odot$ Apr–Oct 13.00–16.00 daily). This is the perfect example of what a local-history museum should be like – bright, engaging and not overcrowded. It's the kind of place where you think 'I'll just pop in for five minutes' and then emerge over an hour later.

The museum is crammed full of an astonishing array of Pictish stones (and replicas), all of which were found within just 220yds of it. In pride of place is the 7ft Rosemarkie cross-slab, where the detail and variation of the carving is staggering. Dating from the late 8th century, it is thought to have originally been 9ft tall. Rosemarkie was the site of a Pictish church that stretched from the beach to the present-day church (next to the museum) – a huge site that was, from the mid 600s, the centre of Christianity for the Inner Moray Firth.

While you're here, don't miss a walk up **Fairy Glen**, an RSPB site (signposted) to the northwest of the village. An easy walk of just shy of a mile along clear footpaths will take you to a couple of twin waterfalls (the second involves a bit of a steep climb up some steps) via bridges and an old millpond that was once used as a source of ice for the fishing industry. The glen is so named because local children used to decorate a pool here with flowers for the fairies, in the hope they would keep the water clean. I've always found it a magical walk, even in the depths of winter, with the path winding through a delightful mixed woodland of oak, ash and beech that is alive with birdsong.

6 CROMARTY

⌂ The Factor's House

Sitting on a triangle of land that juts into the Cromarty Firth just as it swerves out to meet the North Sea, the Black Isle's best-known village is

---

1 The lighthouse at Chanonry Point. 2 Take a boat trip to look for bottlenose dolphins or try your luck from the beach at Chanonry Point. 3 RSPB Fairy Glen at Rosemarkie. 4 The postcard-perfect beach at Rosemarkie. ▶

made up of huddles of neat, whitewashed old fishing cottages and grand merchant's houses. While gentrification has felt like it's started creeping in over the last few years – not least along Church Street with its Scandi-style homeware shop and smartened-up pub – this is still a place where the past feels deeply tangible.

Bounded on two sides by water, Cromarty can feel like a place of two halves. To the northwest is the harbour, built in 1784 and used as the firth's principal port until a larger one was built across the water at Invergordon. The Cromarty Firth's deep waters have made it ideal for trade, fishing and naval fleets – and, from the 1970s, the oil industry. You'll likely see one or two offshore oil rigs on your visit; these are not drilling here but rather moored while they await repair or deployment. The harbour is a great spot to watch the sun set over the Easter Ross hills, with the silhouetted oil rigs providing a striking contrast against the natural landscape behind and the much smaller fishing boats in the foreground. To get a real sense of the village and its location, I'd recommend getting out on a boat with EcoVentures (page 45) or taking the Cromarty-Nigg ferry (page 39).

The eastern side of the village, hemmed into a rough rectangular shape by Shore and Church streets, is what was known as 'Fishertown'; many of the old, low fishing houses still stand, with narrow pedestrian streets called vennels running between them. As you'd expect from such a picturesque seaside community, there's a thriving arts scene here today: on Shore Street, **Gallery48** (⊘ gallery48.scot ☉ Feb–Dec) showcases and sells a varied array of local artwork, jewellery and other trinkets; tucked just behind is **Cromarty Pottery** (⊘ cromarty-pottery.com ☉ Feb–Dec), selling beautiful (and often quite quirky) handmade pottery. On the corner of Church and Shore streets is the **Old Brewery**, owned by Cromarty Arts Trust (⊘ cromartyartstrust.org.uk), which hosts theatre, music, arts workshops and exhibitions throughout the year.

> *"Many of the old, low fishing houses still stand, with narrow pedestrian streets called vennels running between them."*

As you continue up and along Church Street, many of the houses become rather grand, telling of the wealth gained by local merchants in the 18th and 19th centuries. About halfway up, on the left-hand side, is **Hugh Miller's Birthplace Cottage & Museum** (☉ mid-Mar–May, Sep & Oct 11.00–16.00 Wed–Sun; Jun–Aug 11.00–16.00 daily; NTS) – two

ELECTRIC TOOTHBRUSHES ACROSS THE FIRTH

Stand on Cromarty foreshore and you'll notice the tall, skinny white cylinders across the water at Nigg, which look – as my kids said – like the handles of electric toothbrushes. These are in fact the bases of wind turbines, which are being built for offshore and onshore wind farms. The largest open port in the Moray Firth, the Port of Nigg is also the largest offshore wind staging port in the UK, making it critical to the development of this green energy.

adjacent buildings that provide an overview of the life of the celebrated Scottish geologist and folklorist. Start in the large, street-facing Georgian villa, which was built by Miller's father, for an overview of his life – I particularly liked seeing his desk, worn and battered by use, and found his final letter to his wife, Lydia, before his death by suicide at the age of 54, particularly poignant.

The real treat, however, lies next door in the thatched cottage in which Miller was born in 1802. Here, you duck under doorways into plain but hugely evocative rooms where everyday items – like a tiny child's rocking chair and a bed that's so enclosed it almost seems like a cot – bring to life a sense of what it would have been like to live here.

Next to Hugh Miller's House is the rather austere-looking **Cromarty Courthouse Museum** (⊘ cromarty-courthouse.org.uk ⊙ Apr–Oct noon–16.00 daily; free entry), which uses soundscapes to illustrate the history of the building.

A little further up, just past the Hugh Miller Institute (now the library), look for a signpost pointing the way to the **Gaelic Chapel**, a rather overgrown ruin on the hill. From the outside, the chapel, built in 1783 to meet the needs of Gaelic speakers who moved to Cromarty following the Highland Clearances (page 90), seems rather more intact than it actually is. Step inside and it has a rather enchanted (or spooky, depending on your disposition) feel, with trees and plants growing in the middle of it.

The eastern end of the Cromarty Firth is guarded by two headlands – **North and South sutors**, said to be named for two shoemaking giants who would throw tools at each other across the water. A lovely walking route takes you up on to South Sutor – look for the pathway down the side of Clunes House as Miller Road (an extension of Shore Street) turns right to become Causeway, and then follow it along the shore. You can

also walk up Causeway to St Regulus Burial Ground, signposted on the left, which has a quiet, elevated position with views through the trees to the water. It's also known as the pirates' graveyard, owing to a number of gravestones bearing skulls and crossbones, though in reality this just reflects the funerary art of the 17th and 18th centuries.

SPECIAL STAYS

The Factor's House Denny Rd ✆ 01381 600384 ☍ thefactorshouse.com. Elegant but unstuffy rooms in this former estate manager's house at the southern end of the town, with firth views from the grounds and one of the rooms (Forsyth). Rooms are large, bright and extremely comfortable, and Fiona is a perfect host – three-course dinners can be booked (Mon–Thu), or she can set out a cheese plate for you. There's a lounge with a well-stocked honesty bar (the gin selection alone is impressive), and an excellent selection at breakfast.

FOOD & DRINK

The Fishertown Inn Church St ✆ 01381 600988 ☍ fishertowninn.com. This pub has been considerably smartened up since my first visit years ago, but it remains unpretentious and friendly, with an excellent range of Scottish beers on tap (including from local Cromarty Brewery) and the menu features local meat and fish, with decent options for veggies and vegans too.
Slaughterhouse Coffee Marine Tce North ⬛. Next to the ferry slipway, this small coffee house is particularly cosy on winter days when the fire is roaring. As well as excellent coffee, there's a small selection of equally delicious cakes, and outdoor seating for warmer weather.
Sutor Creek 21 Bank St ✆ 01381 600855 ☍ sutorcreek.co.uk. This small, dark-walled restaurant near the harbour serves celebrated pizzas as well as seafood, including Shetland mussels and scallops. You can also pop in to peruse its impressive whisky, gin and beer selection.

7 RSPB UDALE BAY & KIRKMICHAEL

The intertidal nature of Udale Bay makes it a great spot for watching waders like snipe and lapwing. The first of the RSPB Udale Bay hides (◔ NH 71233 65071) is just five miles west of Cromarty, looking across the water to the low headland of Balblair. My favourite spot

◄ **1** Cromarty Pottery is jam-packed with beautiful handmade items. **2** The pretty waterfront at Cromarty. **3** Hugh Miller's Birthplace Cottage & Museum, Cromarty. **4** Inside Kirkmichael you will find striking medieval tombstones. **5** Pink-footed geese flocking near RSPB Udale Bay.

for birdwatching, however, is on the headland itself, reached via a right turning off the B9163 (signposted 'Newhall Point') by the large graveyard for **Kirkmichael** (♀ NH 70590 65852 ♂ kirkmichael.info), which overlooks the bay's mudflats. It's worth pausing here: from outside, you'd be forgiven for thinking it was nothing more than a small, rather plain church – its two rooms, however, have been repurposed to house some striking medieval tombstones. The sandstone ornamental crosses are particularly remarkable in their level of detail and clarity.

It's just under a mile further up this road to **Udale Bay View Point** (♀ NH 70952 67147), where the view takes in a wide sweep of the bay, from Invergordon's port to the sutors in the east. On one visit, in late April, the water was silver and flat like a mirror, with the squawks of the birds a contrast with the drone of industry across the firth. I sat and watched two herons, one picking on spindly legs through the shallows, the other stooped old-man-like on the exposed rocks, while a hulking cruise ship lumbered into port.

INLAND EASTER ROSS

It's far too easy to whizz along the A9 once you cross the Cromarty Firth and not stop along the way – and most visitors do exactly that. Venture inland, however, and you'll find a few spots of hidden drama that the gentle vistas from the main road do little to give away.

8 BLACK ROCK GORGE
♀ NH 59337 66820; Wood entrance on Camden St, Evanton ♀ NH 60331 66416
♂ evantonwood.com

Often a community woodland suggests a young and/or very managed forest – but **Evanton Wood** is delightfully neither. Despite being obviously looked after, and with clear paths that wind through the trees, it has a sense of wildness that I love, and is the kind of place that I can spend hours happily wandering through, with little care for where I am going.

The star attraction here is undoubtedly Black Rock Gorge, on the woods' northern edge (and famously used as a location in the film *Harry Potter and the Goblet of Fire*). Narrow and deep, the gorge cuts like a scar through the ground. Moss-covered, undulating walls tower over the caramel-coloured ribbon of the river, while water drips from the ferny sides above. The gorge is in the woods' furthest northeastern corner; take a photo of the map at the entrance to the woods and meander your way up from there.

FOOD & DRINK

The Storehouse Foulis Ferry, Evanton IV16 9UX ✆ 01349 830038 🖥 thestorehouse.scot. The Storehouse's location on the A9 makes it the ideal stop for picnic food – either from the well-stocked farm shop or a take-away from the restaurant. As well as substantial meals like fish and chips, there are soups, sandwiches and salads – plus meringues as big as your head.

9 LOCH GLASS
📍 NH 53354 70297

On a still day, this loch five miles north of Evanton more than lives up to its name, providing such a perfect reflection of the hills that surround it that they seem to be rising directly from the water. Just under four miles in length, Loch Glass tapers to its narrow, most southerly point where it meets the River Glass (which runs all the way to Black Rock Gorge; see opposite).

It's a staggering setting, with Ben Wyvis rising above the western shore, but what brings many people out here these days is the **Pink House** (📍 NH 52696 70708) on its southwestern side. Strikingly coloured against the surrounding hills, this two-storey building is little more than a shell – there are no interior walls, at all – and has, apparently, always been like this. It's near impossible to find out any concrete facts about the building, but it's likely – particularly as it doesn't appear on Canmore (🖥 canmore.org.uk), the online catalogue of Scotland's historical and archaeological buildings – that it is a relatively recent construction. This mystery adds to the appeal of the house for many visitors, and it has been the subject of countless Instagram posts – and even appeared in an episode of TV reality show *The Traitors*. Note that you'll often see it referred to as Culzie Lodge; this was actually the name of a cottage a mile further up the loch, which was demolished a few years ago.

Social media appeal aside, the loch itself is more than worthy of a visit – particularly if you're not pressing on further west. You can't drive into the Wyvis Estate, on which the loch sits; there's a parking area (unmarked; 📍 NH 54807 69006) about 350yds from the estate gate – on foot, turn right out of the car park to follow the road over a bridge and through the estate's pedestrian gate. After just over 100yds, you'll meet a crossroads; turn right and follow the road through pines that tower over mossy ground, with the sound of water to your right. It's just over a mile along a clear, flat track to the start of the loch, and another half a mile further to the Pink House. It's not possible to do a full loop of the loch, but you can walk as far as its northern end, by Wyvis Lodge (now a very luxurious holiday house), and from here head into the hills on either side. Alternatively, to avoid entirely retracing your steps, you can cross the river at the reservoir (about a quarter of a mile south of the start of the loch) and return on the opposite side of the river; the woodland here is forestry land and feels markedly different to that on the estate.

10 FYRISH MONUMENT
Fyrish car park, Boath Rd, V17 0XL ♀ NH 62748 71500

As you drive north along the A9, you might catch a glimpse of an unusual structure in the hills above Evanton. This is the Fyrish Monument, built in 1782 on the orders of General Sir Hector Munro. If you've heard of it, it may well be in terms of a benevolent landowner who created work for the cleared and starving local people. In reality, it is likely that this construction had as much to do with vanity – after all, Munro himself had been responsible for clearing people off his land in order to install large-scale sheep farming. Nonetheless, the creation of the monument would have provided employment – albeit an exhausting, unrelenting one that involved heaving stones up to the top of an almost 1,500ft-high hill. (Another common story holds that Munro would roll some of the stones back downhill at night so that the labourers could then engage in extra work…)

Vanity project or not, the monument – which apparently was modelled on the Gate of Negapatam in Madras (now Chennai), India – commands fine views from its position. Designed to look like a ruin, with three central, linked arches and two truncated columns on either side, it is a little too stumpy to be considered elegant – I like it best as a frame from which to appreciate the view beyond. The two-mile walk to reach it is well worth the effort, on a clear, straightforward path that undulates so you're not constantly slogging uphill. As you gain in elevation, you'll catch tantalising glimpses of the Cromarty Firth

1 The Fyrish Monument. 2 Looking towards the Tolbooth from the grounds of Tain's museum. 3 You can take a tour of Balblair Distillery near Tain. 4 Evanton Wood. ▶

FIONA THOMPSON/DT

IVAN VDOVIN/A

13THREEPHOTOGRAPHY/DT

BECKY DUNCAN

through the trees; you know you're on the home straight when the trees start to give way to heather. At the top, you can see (weather providing), the Cromarty Firth's sutors (page 59), oil rigs and cruise ships, and, beyond the patchwork fields of the Black Isle, the Moray Coast.

TAIN & THE EASTER ROSS PENINSULA

Wedged between the Dornoch Firth and the A9, **Tain** marks the northern boundary of Easter Ross – cross the bridge over the firth and you're in Sutherland (page 75). To its east lies the hammer-headed **Easter Ross Peninsula**, edged by three firths and home to Pictish stones that'll make you feel rather small and young.

11 TAIN

The birth- and burial place of St Duthus, Tain was an important medieval pilgrimage site and later a well-regarded market town and royal burgh (a town that had been granted a royal charter). Despite this, today it's the kind of place that you need to scratch the surface of. The High Street is a little run down in places, with a couple of notable exceptions. The grandest building here is undoubtedly the **Tolbooth**, which was once used to collect taxes; it's actually younger than its medieval appearance suggests, having been completed in 1733 to replace the original one built a century earlier. The adjoining courthouse, whose roof has spiky little turrets, was built over a century later.

Tucked away just to the north is the **Tain & District Museum and Class Ross Centre** (⊘ tainmuseum.org.uk ⊙ Apr–Oct 10.00–16.00 Tue–Fri), set across three buildings. The museum itself is small but jam-packed. 'Sorry about the smell,' the lady on the desk said to me when I visited, 'but a snake escaped from some whisky.' Once I'd established that there wasn't a drunk snake slithering about, I discovered that the museum usually keeps its (dead) reptiles in whisky donated by the local Glenmorangie distillery. Among details about the Clearances (page 90), town history and illicit whisky distilling, there is also a thought-provoking display about the role Easter Ross played in the slave trade.

Across the graveyard is the **Collegiate Church of St Duthus**, built as a shrine to the eponymous saint in the 14th century. It felt smaller – and barer – inside than I had expected, but there's some beautiful stained glass, particularly at the eastern end, resplendent with flowers and fruit. The third building on site is the **Clan Ross Centre**, particularly of interest to those who wish to research their Ross heritage.

For a lovely **walk** – and this might be my favourite thing about Tain – head down to the firth and cross the wobbly white suspension bridge over the river. Signposted as 'Plaids Circular', it heads first along the shore before looping back along the river via the golf course. It's a gentle but thoroughly pleasant walk – and if you're with kids, there's the bonus of being able to promise a playground at the end.

Tain these days is perhaps most famous for its connection with whisky, in particular **Glenmorangie** (⊘ glenmorangie.com) on its western edge. For more of a Slow (and a much smaller) experience, however, head a further five miles up the coast to **Balblair** (⊘ balblair.com), where the 90-minute tour provides insight into its processes and two drams.

FOOD & DRINK

Platform 1864 Station Rd ⊘ 01862 894181 ⊘ platform1864.com. Tain's train station building has been converted into a bright, modern restaurant with a few nods to its past,

THE PICTS IN EASTER ROSS

The gentle agricultural landscape of Easter Ross – in particular, the Easter Ross Peninsula – is home to some of the most artistically accomplished Pictish sculptures in the country. Even if that claim makes you feel rather ambivalent, I'd still urge you to seek out some of the area's cross-slabs; I too felt the same, until I saw them in person.

Little is known about the Picts, who are thought to have lived in northern Scotland from AD300 to 900 and to have descended from the indigenous people of the region. Though they have a reputation as somewhat savage warriors – no doubt stemming in part from the fact that they were able to defend their lands from the conquering Romans – the vast majority of the tribe were livestock farmers, proving that this land has been fertile agricultural land for centuries.

The remains of Pictish life in the region stem – much as they do elsewhere – from their religion, in cross-slabs and, perhaps most remarkably, the remains of a major Pictish monastery in Portmahomack (page 68). It's accepted that the Picts were converted to Christianity in the 6th century by St Columba; as well as depicting hunting scenes, the cross-slabs feature hugely ornate crosses and some religious scenes, including the first ever depiction of the Eucharist (page 72).

For an introduction to this rich heritage, head to the excellent museums at Rosemarkie (page 56) and Portmahomack (page 68).

such as framed timetables, giving it character rather than a themed feel. It's a relaxed place throughout the day, with a good range of local meat and seafood on the menu.

12 PORTMAHOMACK

This lovely old fishing village sits in a bowl-shaped crescent on the peninsula's west coast, some ten miles from Tain. Its position gives it the honour of being the only west-facing settlement on Scotland's east coast, and as a result sunsets here can be something special, with the sky behind the Sutherland hills changing from deep blue to orange to pink to red – and all the shades in between.

The golden stretch of beach is backed by Main Street and its predominantly pale-coloured, sea-facing houses, which turns into Harbour Street just before – you guessed it – the harbour, where you'll still see clusters of stacked-up lobster pots lining the walls. Built in 1816, it could initially only accommodate 20 herring boats, but it's said that during the height of the herring boom (from around 1850 to 1890), as many as 120 vessels were docking here. Today the harbour is only used by a small number of commercial fishing boats; you can get out on the water yourself during the summer months by hiring a kayak or paddleboard from the village shop (Main St ✐ 01862 871623).

"This lovely old fishing village sits in a bowl-shaped crescent on the peninsula's west coast, ten miles from Tain."

What you might not guess from the seafront alone is that Portmahomack's heritage doesn't lie entirely in its fishing industry: the village was home to a large Pictish monastery from the 6th to 8th centuries AD, discovered during excavations between 1991 and 2007. Tucked away behind Main Street is **Tarbat Discovery Centre** (Tarbatness Rd ✐ tarbat-discovery.co.uk ☉ Mar 13.00–16.00 Mon–Sat; Apr–Oct 10.00–16.00 daily; Nov–Feb by appointment only), based in the old parish church – what you see today is in fact the fifth iteration of a place of worship on this site, with the original having been established by the Picts (page 67) in the 8th century.

This is one of my favourite museums in the region – and that of my kids, who spent a happy half hour uncovering 'treasures' in the archaeological pit, allowing us grown-ups to actually engage with the displays. The highlight is undoubtedly the small Treasury, home to a number of Pictish carvings discovered on site, including the striking

Calf Stone, decorated with clearly recognisable cattle and another, larger animal that resembles a lion.

🍴 FOOD & DRINK

Inver Inn 1 Shop St, Inver ✆ 01862 871399 ⌂ theinverinn.com. In the firth-facing village of Inver, five miles west of Portmahomack, this is a great pub. The menu features pub classics, pizzas and seafood including creel-caught langoustines – but the real standout is the incredibly light and fresh scampi.

13 TARBAT NESS

Heading north from the discovery centre, a single-track road cuts through largely flat farmland towards the tip of the peninsula at Tarbat Ness. The headland here is topped by the strikingly striped red-and-white **lighthouse**. Engineered by Robert Stevenson and first operated in 1830, it's the third-tallest lighthouse in Scotland. You can't enter the compound, but it's possible to walk around it by heading north through the gate by the car park (you can also walk out here from Portmahomack, three miles away; see ⌂ walkhighlands.com for details). Keep your eyes peeled for seals, gannets and dolphins while you're here (the first two are easiest to spot). The path around the headland varies from grassy (and a bit muddy) to stony, curving low on its western side (with great views towards Dornoch) and then looping back up towards the lighthouse through the heather. If you head east of the car park, you'll find a path that leads down to the cliffs, where there's a little pebble cove and a particularly photogenic angle back towards the lighthouse.

14 THE SEABOARD VILLAGES

🏠 The Mill at Fearn Farm

From Tarbat Ness, the east coast of the peninsula stretches all the way down to the cliffs opposite Cromarty. There are few settlements along this gentle 14-mile stretch, with the main exception being the so-called Seaboard Villages of **Hilton of Cadboll**, **Balintore** and **Shandwick**. Though each is signed, there's no other delineation between the villages from the main road that follows the shore through them, with each being composed of low buildings (predominantly houses) facing the Moray Firth.

Arguably the villages' most noteworthy aspect is their connection to Pictish history (page 67). Just north of Hilton, the most northerly of

the villages, standing proud (if a little lonely) in a field, is the **Hilton of Cadboll stone** (♀ NH 87284 76855; park in the lay-by on the west side of the road). This is in fact a reconstruction by stonemason Barry Grove, erected here in 2000 – the original, which was carved in the 9th century AD is in the Museum of Scotland in Edinburgh. Don't let this put you off: it's a remarkable carving that shows off the intricacy and skill of the Picts' decorative arts. What's particularly striking about this stone is that the hunting scene features a woman in a central position – unusual in Pictish art and believed to represent an important woman of the time. The back of the stone is in fact Grove's imagining of what it might have looked like – that of the original was replaced in 1676 by an inscription commemorating a local man and his three wives. The lumpen, enclosed ground adjoining the field the stone stands in is thought to be the site of an early chapel dedicated to the Virgin Mary.

The base of the stone, which was excavated in 2001, can now be seen just inside the entrance of the **John Ross Visitor Centre** (King St, Hilton ☉ summer daily; winter Mon–Fri).

Two doors down is the **Seaboard Centre** (East St, Balintore ⊘ seaboardcentre.com), a community hall that's home to a café, small gift shop and facilities for campers. Among the rocks on the shore, 350yds south, is the bronze-cast *Mermaid of the North* sculpture.

"What's particularly striking about this stone is that the hunting scene features a woman in a central position."

Commissioned in 2007, the sculpture was originally made of wood but was replaced in 2012 after it was damaged by a storm; at high tide, the rock on which she sits appears cast out to sea.

Press on south, past Balintore's harbour, to reach the jewel in the crown of these villages: **Shandwick Bay**. North of here, the sea is backed by dark rocks, but at Shandwick there's soft, golden sand flanked by low dunes that leave the villages feeling miles away. You can follow the shore, or the faint path through the grasses on the dunes, a short distance south, until the sand tapers out and a dark cliff rises to your right.

Less than half a mile southeast of the last village is the 9ft-tall **Shandwick Stone**, enclosed in glass and overlooking the villages from

◀ **1** The lighthouse at Tarbat Ness. **2** The Hilton of Cadboll stone is a recent reconstruction of the original. **3** Walking through the dunes at Shandwick Bay. **4** The village of Portmahomack. **5** The Treasury is a highlight of a visit to the Tarbat Discovery Centre.

its hilltop position. Seeing it through glass does little to diminish the beauty of this stone, which was thought to have been erected here in AD780; its sea-facing side is carved with an intricate cross, flanked by angels, beasts and serpents. While its landward side is rather more smoothed by time, the real power from this angle comes from studying the stone while the firth glitters in the distance, in the same way it would have done hundreds of years ago.

SPECIAL STAYS

The Mill at Fearn Farm Near Fearn IV20 1TL ⌂ fearnfarm.com/holidays. Two stylish and comfortable holiday cottages – The Mill and The Wee End – sleeping ten and four respectively, and which can be combined into one large holiday property for big groups. Just two miles inland from Balintore, this is an excellent position from which to explore the peninsula and further afield.

SHOPPING

ANTA Fearn IV20 1XW ✆ 01862 832477 ⌂ anta.co.uk. This is one of my very favourite shops in the whole of the North Highlands, selling Scottish-inspired textiles and homeware. Nothing feels twee or tourist-oriented but instead classically stylish and elegantly simple. Prices are on the steep side, but there are often specials such as 'Tartan Tuesdays', plus seconds on offer, and the quality – all items are made in the on-site, environmentally conscious factory – is superlative. There's also a **café** selling soups, coffees and indulgent cakes.

15 NIGG OLD CHURCH

IV19 1QR ⌂ spanglefish.com/niggoldchurch ⊙ Apr–Oct 10.00–17.00 daily

The roads from Shandwick to Nigg Old Church, 4½ miles to the southwest, are among my favourite to drive on the peninsula – through rolling farmland that's a paint chart of shades of green in spring, contrasted against bright splodges of gorse. Set back from the road, alongside a narrow burn (stream), Nigg Old Church was built in 1723–25, though the earliest recording of a church on this site dates to the mid 13th century. The church itself is infrequently used these days; the main reason to come here is to see the last of the peninsula's Pictish sights: the **Nigg Stone**. Carved in the late 700s, the intricate carvings on this sandstone cross-slab include what

"Nigg Old Church was built in 1723–25, though the earliest recording of a church dates to the mid 13th century."

is thought to be the earliest-known representation of the Eucharist in Britain. Unpretentious and unadorned, the church's pleasing simplicity makes the stone's artistry even more powerful.

Running alongside the burn next to the church is **The Bishop's Walk**, which follows the waterway all the way to the Nigg Bay end of the Cromarty Firth. At just over half a mile (one way), it's a short stroll, but it takes you through lush, mixed woodland and feels secluded and magical. I saw no-one except a couple of pheasants, as surprised by my presence as I was by theirs. At the end of the route, across the road, is a wide panorama of the bay – at low tide you might have luck spotting waders here.

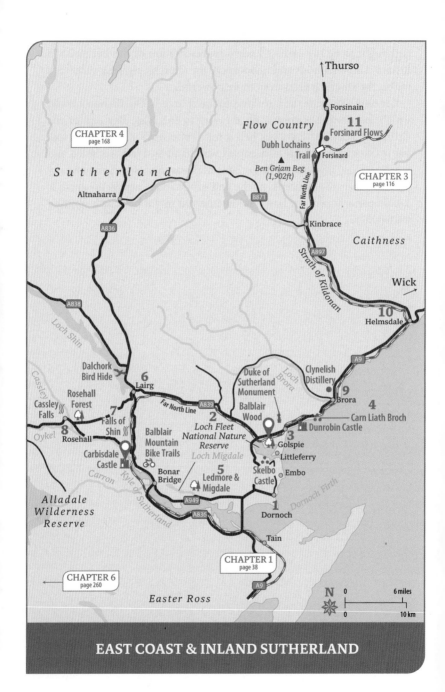

↑ **Thurso**

Flow Country

Forsinain

11
Forsinard Flows

Dubh Lochains
Trail Forsinard

Ben Griam Beg
(1,902ft) ▲

CHAPTER 4
page 168

S u t h e r l a n d

Altnaharra

B871

Far North Line

CHAPTER 3
page 116

A836

Kinbrace

A897

Caithness

Strath of Kildonan

A838

Loch Shin

Wick

10
Helmsdale

A9

Dalchork
Bird Hide

6
Lairg

Cassley

Rosehall
Forest

Cassley
Falls

7
Falls of
Shin

Far North Line

A839

Duke of
Sutherland
Monument

Balblair
Wood

Loch Brora

Clynelish
Distillery

9
Brora

4

Carn Liath Broch

Oykel

8
Rosehall

2
Loch Fleet
National Nature
Reserve

Loch Migdale

3

Dunrobin Castle

Golspie

Carbisdale
Castle

Balblair
Mountain
Bike Trails

Littleferry

Carron

Kyle of Sutherland

Bonar
Bridge

5
Ledmore &
Migdale

Skelbo
Castle

Embo

Dornoch Firth

Alladale
Wilderness
Reserve

A949

1

A836

Dornoch

Tain

CHAPTER 1
page 38

CHAPTER 6
page 260

Easter Ross

A9

N

0   6 miles

0   10 km

EAST COAST & INLAND SUTHERLAND

2
EAST COAST & INLAND SUTHERLAND

The Dornoch Firth marks the boundary of southern Sutherland – as you cross its wide waters on the A9, there's immediately a sense of the landscape shifting, with layers of hills rising up to the west and north. Compared to the northwest, this part of Sutherland is much gentler, with – in the south and east, at least – pretty villages, patchwork fields and swathes of golden sand punctuating an undulating landscape, though without the dizzy heights of further north.

A couple of the North Highlands' best beaches can be found along this stretch of the east coast, at **Dornoch** and **Brora**. Both long, wild-feeling strands with distant views of hills, they are – particularly less well-known Brora – often overlooked by other tourists on their journey north, leaving them largely the preserve of locals and making you feel as though you've stumbled on a well-kept secret.

"Pretty villages, patchwork fields and swathes of golden sand punctuate an undulating landscape here."

The scars of the Highland Clearances (page 90) are never far away in this region, from the brooding figure of the Duke of Sutherland looming over **Golspie** from Ben Bhraggie and his French-inspired castle just up the road to the neat old fishing village of **Helmsdale**, built to house people removed from further up the strath (valley). From here, the drive inland is one of the loveliest in the region, winding through the valley to reach the sparse, haunting beauty of **Flow Country**, one of the largest expanses of blanket bog in the world. Keeping inland, the area around the **Kyle of Sutherland**, further south, is fabulous walking country, with abundant woodland, gushing waterfalls and gentle hills to tempt you away from the coast for a while.

I haven't included all parts of inland Sutherland in this chapter: the Strathnaver Trail (page 184) and Dun Dornaigil Broch (page 193) can be most easily accessed from the north coast and so are included in the chapter on Northwest Sutherland.

GETTING AROUND

If you're travelling along the coast, the A9 is unavoidable: it swerves inland after crossing the Dornoch Firth until Golspie, from where it runs more or less in parallel with the coast, providing big sea views over neat fields and gorse-covered hills. The major roads inland, specifically the A897 to Forsinard (and beyond to Melvich) and the A836 and A839 to Lairg, are among some of my favourites in the whole region, trundling through beautiful and varied countryside and following the River Helmsdale and the Kyle of Sutherland respectively for much of the way. If you're driving the A897, keep your eyes peeled for red deer, particularly around Kinbrace.

This area is also home to the only major roads that allow you to cut directly from the east to the west – the A836 from just north of the Dornoch Firth Bridge and the A839, which connects to the A837 (another fabulous road) to Ledmore Junction in Assynt.

TRAINS

The **Far North Line** ($\mathcal{O}$ scotrail.co.uk) between Inverness and Wick is often celebrated as one of Scotland's finest train lines, cutting inland along the Dornoch Firth and then up the east coast before heading inland again through Flow Country. The most convenient stations in this chapter are Lairg, Golspie, Brora, Helmsdale and Forsinard (for Flow Country). In the summer months, a request service is also offered at Dunrobin Castle station.

BUSES

Coastal towns are served by the Stagecoach ($\mathcal{O}$ stagecoachbus.com) X99 service between Inverness and Scrabster (1–3 daily), which stops at Dornoch, Brora, Golspie and Helmsdale. Buses between inland villages are pretty much non-existent, though Lairg is a good place to travel on from, being served by the Far North Bus ($\mathcal{O}$ thedurnessbus.com ☉ May–Oct Mon, Tue, Thu & Sat; Nov–Apr Tue, Thu & Sat) between Durness (1hr 45min) and Inverness (1hr 15min), and Transport 4 Tongue ($\mathcal{O}$ transportfortongue.co.uk), which runs a Wednesday service between Lairg and Talmine (1hr 20min), via Tongue (1hr 5min).

WALKING & CYCLING

Walking opportunities are numerous and great in this region, particularly if you strike inland, such as at Ledmore & Migdale Woods (page 93) and around Carbisdale Castle (page 102); the latter is hands-down the prettiest woodland route I've ever walked. Flow Country also has some fantastic walks, including an easy boardwalk trail at Forsinard (page 114). The long-distance John O'Groats Trail (page 145) provides some great day-walk options even if you're not doing the whole route, including the very pleasant and straightforward path from Golspie to Brora (which can be walked along the shore at lower tides); a nice option is to walk one direction and catch the train for the return journey.

Off-road bike trails can be found a mile north of Bonar Bridge (which you'll pass through if you're travelling east to west at any point), at Balblair Mountain Bike Trails (♀ NH 60410 92865 ⊘ forestryandland. gov.scot/visit/balblair), and in Rosehall Forest (♀ NC 48349 02900). More challenging are the trails on Ben Bhraggie (page 85), managed by Highland Wildcat Trails (⊘ highlandwildcat.com), which range from moderate to severe.

BIKE HIRE

Dornoch Bike Hire Bridge St, Dornoch ⊘ 07939 139139 ⊘ dornochbikehire.co.uk
Sutherland Adventure Company Brora ⊘ sutherlandadventurecompany.com
☺ summer only. Pick up from the Visitor Information Point in Brora (Otter's Couch, 1 Rosslyn St); walk-ins available, or book online.

DORNOCH TO GOLSPIE

With a staggering beach on its doorstep, in season genteel Dornoch has something of a laid-back holiday feel. To its north is the tidal beauty of Loch Fleet National Nature Reserve and the small beachside village of Golspie, from where a handful of historical sites – including Dunrobin Castle and ancient Carn Liath – are in easy reach.

1 DORNOCH

⋔ **Heartseed House, Links House**
There's no doubt about it, Dornoch is extremely pretty – catch it in the right light (just before sunset is always a good bet) and its honey-coloured sandstone buildings seem to glow. The town is focused

around Castle and High streets, which, together with Bridge Street, form a kind of square around **Dornoch Cathedral** (⊘ dornoch-cathedral.com; free entry). Technically speaking, this isn't actually a cathedral as it's part of the Church of Scotland, which has no bishops; its name certainly suggests a larger, more dominating building than this one, which is rather small and squat, albeit still appealing in its warm sandstone. Dornoch was flung into the spotlight in December 2020 when Madonna and Guy Ritchie christened their son here – the pair married the following day at nearby Skibo Castle (now a private members' club); the wedding of actor Talulah Riley and businessman Elon Musk was also held here, in 2010.

The original 13th-century cathedral on this site was almost totally destroyed by a fire in 1570; what can be seen today is largely the result of a 17th-century reconstruction, though significant internal changes were made during renovations financed by Elizabeth, Duchess of Sutherland (she of Highland Clearances fame; page 90) in 1835–37. Inside, it feels rather enclosed and compact – definitely more like a parish church than a cathedral. My favourite part is its stained glass, much of which dates from the 20th century. Look out for 'Praise' on the north wall, which features the outline of a figure with arms raised, surrounded by the heads of musicians and singers in blue, pink and red. The work of visual artist Alison Kinnaird, it was commissioned in memory of Stuart Anderson, a former choirmaster and organist at the cathedral, and has a simplicity about it that makes it all the more striking. I'm also particularly fond of the two windows in the South Porch, which are full of flowers, birds and animals, created in 1985 to commemorate a young farmer who had been killed at work.

Directly opposite the southern entrance to the cathedral is **Dornoch Castle**, thought to date back to the 15th century and now a hotel. It's home to a celebrated whisky bar, which is a particularly good place to sample Thompson Bros' excellent whisky and gin, currently produced at the **Dornoch Distillery** (⊘ thompsonbrosdistillers.com). One of the smallest distilleries in Scotland, it produces around 12,000 litres of alcohol annually, as well as bottling that of other brands. Plans are afoot to build a second, larger distillery to the south of the town, but

1 Dornoch Beach. 2 Dornoch Distillery is one of the smallest in Scotland. 3 Stained-glass windows in Dornoch Cathedral. 4 Loch Fleet National Nature Reserve. ▶

VISITSCOTLAND/PAUL TOMKINS

DORNOCH DISTILLERY

KLODIEN/DT

©LORNE GILL/NATURESCOT

you can currently see much of its range at the Thompson Bros' bottle shop (see below).

Immediately east of the castle is the 19th-century courthouse, now home to a spa, restaurant, gift shop (appropriately called Jail Dornoch – pop in to see the original jail cells) and **Carnegie Whisky Cellars** (⊘ carnegiewhiskycellars.co.uk). As well as stocking an impressive range of whisky (don't be afraid to ask for recommendations based on your budget, however limited), it also has a great selection of wine and gin, and offers insightful and relaxed tastings (book in advance) in the courthouse's old records room.

On the other side of the cathedral is one of my other favourite shops in town, **Dornoch Bookshop** (High St ◻ ⊙ Mon–Sat), which always has an excellent array of books and gifts in store, including a particularly good selection of Scottish children's titles. Just round the corner from here, on the town's small industrial estate, is the **Thompson Bros Bottle Shop** (Station Sq ⊘ thompsonbrosdistillers.com ⊙ 10.00–17.00 Mon–Thu, 10.00–16.00 Fri); if you can find it (rumours are that it's coming to the end of its run), grab a bottle of the TB/BSW – though it's a blend, it's predominantly made using a celebrated Speyside single malt and is astounding value.

"From up here, you can enjoy far-reaching views over the green and the dunes beyond to the firth."

It's easy to forget Dornoch's coastal location when you're in the town centre, but great views can be had by walking up Argyll Street, about 350yds south of the bottle shop; the road soon becomes Grange Road, running along the back of the celebrated **Royal Dornoch** golf club (⊘ royaldornoch.com). From up here, you can enjoy far-reaching views over the green and the dunes beyond to the firth and, on the other side, Tain and the Easter Ross Peninsula.

Immediately south of the castle is **Historylinks** (The Meadows ⊘ historylinks.org.uk ⊙ Apr–Oct 10.30–16.00 daily), another one of those local museums that manages to pack a huge amount into a small area, covering everything from Viking history to crofting and the Clearances. Look out for the pair of Sutherland chairs, common in the region during the 18th and 19th centuries and designed so the sitter could sit low to the ground and avoid getting a faceful of smoke from the constantly burning peat fire. At the time of writing, a new 'Heritage

THE LAST WITCH OF SCOTLAND

The small stone memorial to **Janet Horne**, the last woman to be executed for witchcraft in Britain, feels rather inadequate today — but I suppose, given that so many women suffered this fate and so few are remembered, maybe we should be pleased that there is anything here at all.

Janet and her daughter were tried and found guilty of witchcraft in 1727: Janet's daughter apparently had a deformity in her hands that other people said were in fact 'hooves' and the result of her mother using her as transport for her witchy endeavours.

While her daughter was able to escape, Janet was not so lucky. She was first tarred and then covered in feathers before being paraded through the town in a barrel. Finally, she was burned in Littletown, on the southeastern edge of Dornoch, where her memorial stone now stands.

Though Janet was the last person in Britain to be tried and killed for witchcraft, it wasn't until nine years later that the Witchcraft Acts of England and Scotland were repealed, making execution for supposed witchcraft unlawful.

Hub' extension was being built, which will allow for more exhibition space; check the museum's website for the latest updates.

It's roughly half a mile from the centre of town to Dornoch's glorious beach. The most direct route is down Golf Road (turn right at the eastern end of Castle Street and then take the first left) which, unsurprisingly, cuts straight through the golf course (watch out for flying golf balls as you walk). An alternate, more suburban route is to follow Church Street south and then east as it becomes River Street and then Beach Road. At the corner with Well Street, look into the garden on your left-hand side for a glimpse of the **Witch Stone**. This small and otherwise unremarkable stone marks the spot on which, in 1727 (rather than 1722, as the stone confusingly says), the last person was executed for witchcraft in Britain (see above). It is some distance from the road, and seems somewhat incongruous among an otherwise normal garden, but a signboard gives some information about it.

From here, you can reach the sea either by cutting through the sprawling caravan site and taking one of the sandy paths over the dunes, or by continuing along Beach Road, eventually curving up to meet Golf Road. At the end, just beyond the car park, the dunes that shelter the beach give way to the wide expanse of pale golden sand.

Dornoch's long **beach** is one of the finest on the east coast, with its position a little apart from the town centre – and its long spine of grassy

BEACH ACCESSIBILITY

Free, specially adapted wheelchairs for the beach can be hired all year round, from **Dornoch Beach Wheelchairs** (✆ 0300 770 4624 ◌ dornochbeachwheelchairs.co.uk); prospective wheelchair users (anyone who would have difficulty walking on the beach) need to have someone with them who can push the rather heavy chairs.

dunes – giving it an away-from-it-all feel. The sands stretch for over 1½ miles down to Dornoch Point, which, from above, resembles a stumpy elephant's trunk; the further you walk, the more you're likely to have only oystercatchers and ringed plovers for company. At low tide, you can walk all the way down to the point and then head back north on the other side of the dunes, following a path alongside them and the salt marsh towards the caravan site.

To the north, the beach is a little rockier, with the low Sutherland hills as a backdrop (look for the towering spike of the Sutherland Monument directly ahead of you). It's possible to walk 2½ miles north along the sands to **Embo**, a tightly packed little village of narrow lanes. On approach, the sand is interrupted by black, seaweed-clad rocks and overlooked by green mobile homes – making it feel a little less hidden than Dornoch's beach. As at Dornoch, however, the sands appear to stretch on forever; at its northern end, a walkable 1½ miles away, is Loch Fleet (see opposite).

⬛ SPECIAL STAYS

Heartseed House 2 The Pillars ✆ 07904 946708 ◌ heartseedhousebedandbreakfast. co.uk. Hands down one of the best B&Bs I've had the pleasure of staying in, with just three very comfortable and serenely decorated bedrooms, two of which (Firth and Loch) have distant sea views. Each room has a mini fridge with fresh milk for tea and coffee, and the breakfasts are delicious (don't miss the mushrooms!). Dee and Nigel are the loveliest hosts, full of passion for their local area and tips for how to get the most out of it. Just over a mile from the centre, but walkable in about half an hour.

Links House Golf Rd ✆ 01862 810279 ◌ linkshousedornoch.com. The best kind of luxury hotel – sophisticated but unpretentious and unstuffy. Rooms are spread across the original manse house, built in 1843, and two other buildings which are modern but just as elegant. Some have views over the golf course, with the sea shimmering in the distance. The restaurant, MARA, focuses on local produce including venison and Highland Fine Cheeses (page 19), and the guest lounges are the perfect spots for curling up with a post-dinner dram.

¶¶ FOOD & DRINK

In warm weather, head to **Dornoch Stores** (12 Castle St *✐* 01862 811288 **f**) for a Mr Whippy ice cream.

Milk & Honey High St *✐* 01862 811235 **f**. This bright café does a roaring trade throughout the day so there's often a wait for a table. Lunch options include filled bagels, soup served with a cheese scone, and ridiculously delicious cakes.

Surf & Turf 8 Castle St *✐* 01862 811181 **f**. The bricks-and-mortar outpost of the Surf & Turf trailer at Kylesku Bridge (page 224), serving up outstanding seafood and game dishes. You can't go wrong with whatever you choose, though my personal favourite are the haddock tacos. Look out for specials like hot seafood platters, too.

2 LOCH FLEET NATIONAL NATURE RESERVE

✐ nature.scot

Three miles north of Embo is the tidal basin of Loch Fleet, which is, in my opinion, one of the most captivating spots in the North Highlands. While the easiest point from which to explore is on the northern side of the loch, I'd recommend driving up here from Dornoch (follow Station Road north out of town and turn left at the T-junction after about three miles) to skirt around it, rather than rejoining the A9 when you leave.

THE FORGOTTEN BATTLE

On the northern side of Ferry Road, about a mile off the A9, is a small but easy-to-miss stone memorial (♀ NH 81875 98343) dedicated to the people who died during the **Battle of Littleferry**. This little-known battle on 15 April 1746 was rather overshadowed by the events of the following day: the devastating Battle of Culloden. The Littleferry battle, which, like Culloden, was between government militia and the Jacobites, began with an ambush of the Jacobites near St Andrew's Church in Golspie, with the action soon moving down Ferry Road in a 'running firefight'. Unknown to the Jacobites, two government companies

were hiding in the hills to the northwest; when they attacked on Ferry Road, it caused confusion and succeeded in breaking up the Jacobite regiment. While some Jacobites managed to escape on boats across the loch, it is thought that up to 100 were killed and another 200 were captured; as at Culloden, the government side saw only a fraction of their regiments injured and wounded.

The memorial to the battle was established in 2022 as part of a trail that begins and ends at Dunrobin Castle (page 87). You can pick up a trail guide from shops in Golspie and the Dornoch Bookshop (page 80).

The single-track road swerves around the ruins of Skelbo Castle to run along the southern shore of the loch for 2½ miles before it joins the A9, with plenty of places to pull in and enjoy the view across the water. In autumn, look out for wigeons and dunlins; in summer you may have luck spotting a swooping osprey. At any time of year, but particularly at low tide, you'll see large numbers of harbour seals, lounging on the exposed sand banks or bobbing in the shallows.

To really appreciate Loch Fleet's wild beauty, however, you need to explore its northern shore; this is reached by heading across The Mound

A loop through Balblair Wood

✳ OS Explorer 438; start: Balblair Wood car park ♀ NH 81483 976620; 4½ miles; easy

This is a straightforward walk that takes in the best of Loch Fleet, with fabulous views opening up when you get down to the shore. Do be aware of the tide as you head down, however – if it's coming in then you'll want to retreat inland as it can entirely cover the shoreline.

From the entry gate, follow the path through the towering pines; after just over three-quarters of a mile you'll see a short path on your left that leads down to a bird hide. From here, continue another 350yds until the path splits – veer left and follow it past a house and garden, with the loch visible through the trees on your left-hand side. Some of the trees in this area are so ancient and wizened they look as though someone has bewitched them. About a quarter of a mile beyond the house, look for a faint path down to the shore and follow it; turn right to walk along the pebbly beach, keeping the woods on your right. When the tide is completely out, it feels as though you could stroll across to the loch's southern side.

As you walk, look out for birds like eider ducks, wigeons and curlews, and ospreys swooping above the treetops, as well as seals. Follow the shoreline as it curves around mini triangular headlands; after just over half a mile, you'll turn right to head northeast, with the Mound and the A9 to your left. Keep following the coast northwest for another half a mile, with a grassy path at the top of the shoreline faintly discernible for much of the time. When you reach an old waymarker (♀ NH 78500 97651), follow the rough route to your right through the heather. It can be a little overgrown at times but you'll soon emerge on to the main path. When you do, turn right, even though it may look a bit overgrown, and pick your way through the gorse; the forest here feels decidedly different from earlier, but these are just younger trees.

You'll emerge from the gorse at a crossroads; continue straight and you'll soon meet the path you entered on, which will lead you back to the car park.

(the causeway over the loch) to Golspie, and then taking the right-turn down Ferry Road just after the train station. After 1½ miles, you'll reach **Balblair Wood** on your right-hand side, with parking directly opposite the entrance (♀ NH 81483 97620). The wood is a great place from which to explore Loch Fleet's many different landscapes and habitats. You can follow a number of flat and easy paths through the trees; the walk on the opposite page is a particularly lovely option.

The eastern end of Loch Fleet feels markedly different to this woodland, with vast, rolling dunes, crisscrossed with paths, that seem to stretch on for ever, with the roar of the sea ahead of you for a while before you see it. To get here, continue down Ferry Road to just north of the small settlement of **Littleferry** (as the name suggests, there was once a ferry here, which ran over to Skelbo), about 1½ miles from Balblair Wood, where there is a large parking area (♀ NH 80669 95769) on the eastern side of the road. The sand on the other side of the dunes is vast and softly golden at low tide and feels much wilder than Embo and Dornoch beaches to the south. There are usually seals in the shallows here, and to the north you should be able to make out both the Sutherland Monument and Dunrobin Castle.

3 GOLSPIE

Separated from Loch Fleet by a golf course, the neat village of Golspie sits at the foot of Ben Bhraggie (a hill rather than a mountain), ten miles north of Dornoch. Like so many other villages along the east coast, Golspie started life as a fishing settlement; it grew during the 19th century in order to house people cleared off the inland area, and then again when the establishment of a train station (still in operation, at the southwestern point of town) started bringing in holidaymakers. Today, it's an unassuming place, with an appealing, sheltered sandy beach that's perfect for paddling (though note it can all but disappear at high tide), and Ben Bhraggie looming to its northwest, and is the starting point for some the region's best walks.

The most famous of these is arguably the 1½-mile walk up Ben Bhraggie to the **Duke of Sutherland Monument**, known locally as 'The Mannie'; it's a pleasant hike for the most part, if a bit of a heart-thumper towards the end. To climb the hill, start from Fountain Road (there's a handy car park just behind High Street) and walk north up the road, past gabled grey-stone houses – built using the distinctive local

Clynelish stone. A little further up, on the left-hand side, is the Gothic-style Fountain Road Hall, originally – and unsurprisingly, given how it looks – built as a church in the early 20th century and now repurposed for community use. Directly opposite, in the middle of the road, is the eponymous fountain – dedicated to the memory of Elizabeth, Duchess of Sutherland (page 90), it is rather functional and ugly which, given her role in the Clearances, always pleases me somewhat.

Continue straight on, under the railway bridge; it doesn't take long before you've left behind the confines of the village. Once you've passed the farm buildings behind fine Rhives House, on your left, the road splits; take the right branch, which soon narrows to become a path, with the sea in the distance. The path to the top is fairly well signposted, but be aware that the hillside is criss-crossed with wider mountain-bike tracks (page 77) – take care as you cross them and stick to the narrower footpath.

"When I walked this in June, the top of the hill was patterned with fluffy white cotton-grass bouncing in the breeze."

The final push up the 1,302ft hill is rather steep but, thankfully, there are steps. When I walked this in June, the top of the hill was patterned with fluffy white cotton-grass bouncing in the breeze, skylarks flitting low above the grass. The monument at the top is surprisingly huge when you get to it, unscuppered by distance – at 100ft, it looms over its surroundings. Topped by a statue of the first Duke of Sutherland, and built after his death, it remains a subject of much discussion due to the duke's role in the Highland Clearances (page 90): some say it should be removed, while others argue it serves as a reminder of what he did. Either way, the reason to come up here is for the views that stretch along the coast – if it's a clear day, south past Loch Fleet and Dornoch to even as far as the Black Isle, and north to Brora with its neat old harbour. Don't miss the views behind the monument, either, across the lumpen, moorland landscape, and a striking contrast to the coast. You can return the way you came or make a wider loop back along the clear paths.

While there's undoubtedly a huge satisfaction to be gained from hiking up a hill and back (particularly on a day when the Golspie outpost of ice-cream shop Capaldis of Brora, 34 Main St, is open), my favourite walk in Golspie is the there-and-back to **Big Burn waterfall**. The starting point is from a car park ($\mathcal{Q}$ NC 84015 00549) around 85yds beyond the Golspie Inn (look for the narrow track that runs alongside the old warehouses, just as the A9 begins to climb and curve uphill, with a blue footpath sign), though it's an easy walk from the village. From the car park, follow the signposted path; at first it seems like little more than a pleasant walk, but when you reach the second bridge over Golspie Burn, the river tumbling and frothing over the rocks and water dripping down the moss-covered walls, the magic of the route is fully revealed.

After crossing the sixth bridge, taking the path to your right leads you alongside the water and on to a wooden platform from where, at the end, the falls are fully revealed: rampaging down the rocks, with birds often flitting in and out of the water. It's so lush here that it feels almost tropical, with ferns and plants clinging to the dark, rugged rock faces. From here, retrace your steps and take the uphill path (now on your right) to climb and wind around to another bridge, this time at the top of the falls, from where you can appreciate the full force of the water. You can then either retrace your steps or take a right at the end of the bridge to walk a different path, through the trees; after about three-quarters of a mile, look to your left to see the old skating pond, which makes a peaceful spot for a picnic. It is possible to combine this walk with Ben Bhraggie; see WalkHighlands ($\oslash$ walkhighlands.co.uk) for the full route.

Dunrobin Castle

KW10 6SF $\oslash$ dunrobincastle.co.uk $\odot$ Apr–Oct 11.00–16.00 daily

Graceful Dunrobin Castle, around 1½ miles northeast of Golspie, looks more like a French château than a stately home, particularly when seen from the coast, with its skinny turrets rising above neat, ornamental gardens. Lush woodland encloses the castle to the east and west, and the wide Moray Firth borders it to the south. This picturesque setting is best appreciated by visiting on foot from Golspie; to get there, walk down pretty Duke Street in the north of the village, or approach from the south via the seafront, and cross Golspie Burn on a small wooden bridge in front of a turreted house. When the path splits, take the left-hand branch that soon leads uphill through the woods, with the sea below you. The path winds through the woodland, carpeted with bluebells in spring, and you'll more often than not have it more or less to yourself. On bright days, the sea glitters below you like a sequinned party dress.

A castle has stood here since the mid 13th century, when the Earldom of Sutherland was created – the original, square keep was quite a

different beast, and you can still make out some of it as you walk around, though it was much added to from the 16th century onwards. The castle as it appears today, however, is largely due to the work of Sir Charles Barry who, in 1845, was engaged to remodel the building into the Scots Baronial style, which had gained in popularity thanks to Queen Victoria's new pile at Balmoral.

I'll be honest: I always love spotting dream-like Dunrobin from afar, but as an experience it leaves me a little cold. This is no doubt because it was the home of the 1st Duke of Sutherland, George Granville Leveson-Gower, and his wife Elizabeth, who in the 19th century were instrumental in clearing people off their lands (page 90). Knowing this, I found it hard wandering around the house and looking at portraits of the couple and various items that had been presented to them by their tenants, none of which were (as far as I could see), accompanied by any information about their role in the Clearances. In this day and age, this feels like a considerable oversight, but perhaps is to be expected when the castle remains in the Sutherland family.

"Among the perfectly coiffed quince trees and neat croquet lawn, there's also The Grove."

Nonetheless, a visit isn't without its merits. I particularly enjoyed the phenomenal views from the drawing room, and the old photos here of glamorous if rather bored looking women from the 1920s. The room guides are also worth chatting to – one man I spoke to had worked at Dunrobin as a 15-year-old, returning to be a guide after his retirement, and had been to school with the current Earl.

The small museum in the gardens is more a Victorian leftover than a modern beast, and is stuffed with countless hunting trophies – animal heads, in the main, with details of when they were shot and by whom. It feels a little tasteless, to be honest – the life of the very rich, eh? – but if you're able to get past them, there are some interesting Pictish stones on the lower floor, though with minimal background detail.

For me, the highlight of a visit is undoubtedly the elegant gardens, which are surprisingly compact but split into different areas. Among the perfectly coiffed quince trees and neat croquet lawn, there's also The Grove, which has been allowed to grow wild, with paths cut through

◀ **1** The gardens at Dunrobin Castle are a highlight. **2** The Duke of Sutherland Monument on Ben Bhraggie. **3** Golspie village. **4** The Iron Age Carn Liath Broch.

THE HIGHLAND CLEARANCES

The landscape of Highland Scotland has been shaped by numerous things, but many of its lasting scars are from the Highland Clearances, which took place here (and on the islands) from the late 18th to mid 19th centuries. In the most simplistic terms, the Clearances saw the forced evictions of local people to make way for large-scale sheep farming, destroying the traditional way of life for countless Highlanders.

The events were set into motion following the Jacobite defeat at the Battle of Culloden in April 1746, which led to the forfeiture of lands belonging to Jacobite-supporting Highland lairds and the dismantling of the traditional clan system. The new landowners introduced sheep (instead of more traditional cattle) and crop rotation, with a new focus on commerciality, and rents were increased. This soon led to the reorganisation of the tenants on these lands.

Perhaps the most notorious – not to mention cruel – of all the Highland Clearances was that under the **1st Duke of Sutherland**, George Granville Leveson-Gower, and his wife, Elizabeth, **Duchess of Sutherland**. Between 1809 and 1821, the pair cleared almost 15,000 people from their land in order to convert it to highly profitable sheep farming.

Instrumental in the Sutherland Clearances was **Patrick Sellar**, a sheep farmer who managed the estate and oversaw the removal of tenants. Initially, it seems that he treated them with some consideration, but he soon became more violent in his actions. One report of 1814 tells of how he set fire to the home of William Chisholm while Chisholm's mother-in-law was still inside – she died a

it. Regular falconry displays are held in the gardens, which are worth making time for – Andy, the castle falconer, is an informative and humorous guide, and the birds fly low over the audience's heads, making kids and adults alike squeal with surprise and delight.

The castle woodlands can be explored without paying the entrance fee, and the coast path runs along the front of the castle, offering up some great views.

4 CARN LIATH BROCH

♀ NC 87041 01380 ⟁ historicenvironment.scot

On a gentle hillside overlooking fields and the rocky shore beyond, halfway between Golspie and Brora, are the remarkably intact remains of this Iron Age broch (page 92). Well, I say intact – what has survived is thought, at 10ft tall, to be only around a third of its original size – but it's nonetheless an impressive site, with enough of its shape preserved to conjure up a sense of it.

few days later. Sellar was tried for culpable homicide in 1816 but acquitted.

The Sutherlands, like many other estate owners, created new coastal villages (including Bettyhill, page 179) for many of their displaced tenants, in order that they could find new employment (to the estate owners' benefit, of course) in fishing. Some of these new settlements, like Helmsdale (page 111), were more successful than others; Badbea (page 122), for example, now sits in ruins on the southern Caithness coastline. As benevolent as this may seem, it was a huge upheaval for many families, and didn't work for everyone. In addition, many other tenants moved south into the cities, where they often sought out dangerous factory work and lived in cramped, unsanitary tenements. Others emigrated to Australasia and North America – many of these people ended up being arguably more prosperous than they ever could have been back home, with some owning plantations and slaves in the Americas.

As well as the remains at Badbea, the landscape of Sutherland (and the Highlands as a whole) is littered with the ruins of old crofting houses that tell of the people who once lived out their lives in this region. **Canmore**, the National Record of the Historic Environment (⬧ canmore.org. uk), is an invaluable resource for finding out more about the buildings and ruins you may encounter on your travels; you can easily locate places by searching on the map. Understandably, the Clearances are covered by almost every local museum in the region; particularly noteworthy is the Strathnaver Museum (page 178) near Bettyhill.

You can enter the broch through a low doorway; standing inside, and despite the rush of the adjacent A9, there's a sense of the past not being far away. As well as walking around the interior, you can also circle the broch on top of the walls, from where you can make out the clearly discernible shapes of outbuildings beneath the grass beyond. Carn Liath is quite unusual among Scotland's brochs in having surviving outbuildings (Ousdale Broch in Caithness is another; page 120). It's thought that this broch may have belonged to a wealthy family.

Carn Liath was excavated in the late 19th century by the 3rd Duke of Sutherland; some of the finds, which included quern stones (used for grain grinding) and soapstone cups, are on display in Dunrobin's museum (page 87).

To reach the broch by car, park in the large parking area directly opposite, on the northern side of the A9. From here, walk to the far, southern end of the car park, where a clear crossing point has been made – do take care, however, as this is a very busy road! You can also

WHAT THE BROCH?

Brochs – huge, circular drystone towers – are uniquely Scottish buildings, dating back to between 400BC and AD100 and largely found in the north and west of the country. Their purpose has been heavily debated; for years, they were believed to have been defensive structures, but now it is thought they were more likely used as living places. These are no regular houses, though – rather, they are thought to have been also used for storing and processing food, making crafts and clothes, keeping animals and even storing the remains of dead family members.

It is the size of brochs that make them particularly notable – it's thought that, including their conical, thatched roofs, they may have stood up to 50ft tall. They would have had multiple floors, and the walls of the broch itself were often as thick as 16ft at its base, becoming thinner as it gained height. No mean feat, especially when you consider that this was thousands of years ago.

There are hundreds of brochs in Caithness and Sutherland, most of which have never been excavated. I asked Ken McElroy, co-founder of the **Caithness Broch Project** (page 121), why there are so many. 'It's likely to be something to do with the geology – the stone here is good for building with, and there was a distinct lack of trees in the area even by the Bronze Age,' he said. 'Atlantic Scotland – that is to say, Caithness, Shetland, Orkney and Sutherland, the Hebrides, even Skye – is quite wind-scoured in places, so this is probably why so many brochs were built here.'

Some of the best-preserved brochs in the North Highlands include Carn Liath (page 90), Ousdale (page 120) and Clachtoll (page 231). More information and background can be found on the Caithness Broch Project's website (⊘ thebrochproject.co.uk).

reach the broch on foot along the coast path from both Golspie and Brora (roughly 2½ and 3½ miles away, respectively).

INLAND FROM DORNOCH & GOLSPIE

From Dornoch, the Dornoch Firth winds its way northwest, getting gradually narrower until it becomes the **Kyle of Sutherland**, an estuary that weaves into the heart of the North Highlands, where it starts out as the rivers Oykel and Cassley. If the east coast feels like a well-kept secret, then that's even more true of this inland area – many visitors who come this way are doing little more than passing through en route to the west coast, which means that often you'll drive or walk for ages before meeting another person. This is a great area to base yourself, with both coasts within easy driving distance, and plenty to explore on the doorstep, including some magical patches of woodland.

5 LEDMORE & MIGDALE

Parking at ♀ NH 66839 90728 ♂ woodlandtrust.org.uk

Just north of the pretty hamlet of **Spinningdale** (which I always think sounds more Yorkshire than Highlands) is this glorious 1,730-acre native woodland, home to the most extensive of the UK's northerly oakwoods. The wide variety of habitats here, from scrubby moorland and marshes to ancient and newly planted trees, makes it fantastic for biodiversity; keep your eyes peeled for red squirrels, which were relocated here from Moray and Inverness in 2019 with great success.

The main car park (follow the road north, signposted 'Migdale' from Spinningdale) is the best starting point for walks; from here, it's just a short walk to reach the waymarked trails that wind through the woodland. The easiest path (marked by yellow posts) is a two-mile there-and-back route to the northern shore of **Loch Migdale**; a relatively flat option that should be possible with both push- and wheelchairs, it takes you through the pine forest before skirting the edge of the loch, with a few opportunities to go down to the pebbly shore. As you walk through the woods, look out for willow sculptures, such as a red squirrel peeking out from between the trees.

If you have the time and energy, though, my personal favourite is the 4½-mile **A' Chraisg route** (marked with purple posts), which initially takes you through the forest and up the eastern edge of the loch. Look for little paths down to the shore here; I sat for a while just listening to birdsong and watching the mirror-still water, the steep, wooded cliffs rising on my right-hand side. Soon after the loch, the path begins to ascend quite steeply (and can be a little boggy underfoot), but it doesn't take long before the views to Migdale Rock, on the other side of the water, open up, and the path is lined with heather, young Scots pines and gorse, egg-yolk yellow in spring. From the very top, you can see Loch Migdale, the Kyle of Sutherland, Dornoch Firth and, if it's a particularly clear day, beyond to the Black Isle and Moray Coast.

As you walk in Ledmore & Migdale, you'll come across three beautifully carved benches, which have been placed in strategic positions so you can catch your breath while taking in the views. These were carved by a local woodworker, Bill Ross, using wood from damaged and fallen

INTO THE WILDERNESS

Alladale Wilderness Reserve Alladale IV24 3BS ⬦ alladale.com

It's early December, and the landscape is painted in muted shades of green and brown, against which the mauve branches of the downy birch lining the river seem to shimmer in the pale sunlight. The mountains in the distance have just received their first dusting of snow, and the wide river below is gushing so fast that at first I mistake the sound for traffic – until I remember that the closest main road is some 13 miles away.

I'm in **Alladale Wilderness Reserve**, in the very south of inland Sutherland, where – appropriately, given the 'wilderness' in its name – I am the only guest on the 24,700-acre estate. In a country where so much of the land seems to be made up of private estates, Alladale is a literal breath of fresh air – its owner, Paul Lister, sees himself as a 'custodian of the land' and has moved the estate away from the traditional pursuit of deer stalking to one of rewilding and regeneration.

If you've heard of Lister and/or Alladale before, chances are it's because of wolves: Lister has been rather vocal in his desire to reintroduce these predators to his reserve. A large part of this is to do with deer control: rewilding is only really possible when deer numbers are managed (deer like to munch away at saplings and young trees), and a wolf can work '24/7, while we're just nine to five,' as ranger Ryan Munro tells me.

In reality, the reintroduction of wolves is likely to be some time off (probably for the best, given how controversial an idea this is), but in the meantime there are plenty of other things going on here, including a wildcat-breeding programme. Ryan takes me to see these gorgeous felines, who look like a fiercer version of our domestic pets, and which will be later transferred to the Royal Zoological Society of Scotland's 'breed and release centre' in Kincraig in the Cairngorms. This is important work: only around 150 wildcats are thought to exist in the wild in Scotland, pushing them dangerously close to extinction.

trees. Ross died before his third, which sits overlooking Loch Migdale, could be completed – a plaque on the bench reads 'He was never good at finishing projects but this was taking it a bit far'.

6 LAIRG

Roads from all compass points converge at **Lairg**, inland Sutherland's biggest settlement, making it likely that you'll pass through – or certainly nearby – at least once if you're travelling from east to west or down through the middle. As a result, it often feels like quite a functional village – signs tell you that it's the last place to stock up on petrol for 40-odd miles, and there's a choice of two shops for supplies, both of which

The benefits of the work being done at Alladale can easily be seen on a trip around it: more than 900,000 native trees have been planted over the last decade, changing the face of the reserve; peatland is being restored to help prevent erosion and improve water quality; and you're very likely to catch a glimpse of some of the red squirrels that were reintroduced here in 2013 and have now ventured into the neighbouring communities. It's brilliant that the work that they do here isn't just something that happens at a distance, but can be seen by visitors for themselves. It's also not something that's happening at a distance from the local community: Lister is keen to encourage interaction between locals and the estate, to move away from the mentality of 'us' and 'them'. One of the best examples of this is the work Alladale does with schools within a 50-mile catchment area, getting the children into the reserve with an ecologist to connect them with nature and the landscape.

Walkers are welcome at Alladale (though you'll have to park off-site and enter on foot), but the best way to experience it is as a guest in one of the three **accommodation** options: Alladale Lodge (sleeps up to 14), Eagle's Crag (sleeps up to eight) and Ghillie's Rest (up to four). They're all beautifully but comfortably furnished and fully catered: in the case of the latter two, this means that the supplies for your meals will be delivered to your cottage with a menu and (simple) instructions on how to heat up and serve. The food is really excellent (I still think about the venison cottage pie I had there), and there's something really luxurious about being able to eat food prepared by someone else in your own space and at your own pace.

Often luxury experiences leave you feeling a little cut off from the place in which you're staying, but here at Alladale I feel totally ensconced in the landscape. Being able to see positive change in action is both enlightening and reinvigorating.

are open daily (often unheard of in the North Highlands). It's also home to the huge **Lairg Lamb Sale**, held each August, which sees some 15,000 sheep from around northern Scotland being auctioned off.

The village sprawls at the southern tip of **Loch Shin**, Sutherland's largest loch – known here as Little Loch Shin, thanks to being separated by a dam from the main part of the loch. Travelling north on the A836 alongside the water, approaching the main part of the village, you'll likely notice the appropriately named **Wee Hoose**, on an equally tiny island in the loch. The story commonly told is that it was built in 1824 by a local poacher after being gifted the land by a local laird, but that he died shortly afterwards having (accidentally) shot himself in the foot. It was actually built as a float for the Lairg Gala in the 1990s and afterwards placed on a little island in the loch rather than be thrown away. (The information board near the 'hoose', which seems to confirm the first story, was put up 'as a bit of a joke', according to an article in *The Scotsman* in 2017.)

On the western side of town is **Ferrycroft Visitor Centre** (IV27 4AZ ⬧ highlifehighland.com/ferrycroft-visitor-centre ⬧ Easter–Oct), which has displays about local life and history, and a small shop. The centre is also the starting point for a couple of pleasant **walks** (⬧ forestryandland. gov.scot/visit/ferrycroft), which can easily be combined into one longer walk. The easiest are the one-mile Lochside Trail, which takes you through the pine woods and then along the shore of Little Loch Shin, and the Broch Trail, which continues on for a quarter of a mile to reach the remains of a broch, though there's little more than a grassy mound to be seen. More strenuous is the 1¾-mile Ord Hill Trail, which involves some steep climbing up to the eponymous hill where there are chambered cairns, hut circles and extensive views over the village and loch.

Two miles north of the village is **Dalchork Bird Hide** (⬧ NC 56728 09346), perched on the marshy eastern shore of Loch Shin. Parking is available by the side of the A836 (⬧ NC 57139 09023), just before the left-hand turn to the hide. Follow the track for about 400yds until you see another left turn on to a path. It can be quite easy to miss this turning, but you'll otherwise find yourself right at the shoreline, where the path runs straight into the water – the left-hand path will lead you all the way to the little wooden hide from where there are expansive views across the loch. We spotted black-throated divers ducking in and out of the water; other birds to look out for include merlins, ospreys, lapwings and greenshanks, the last of which breed in large numbers in Flow Country (page 113), to the north of Lairg.

¶ FOOD & DRINK

The Pier Lochside ⬧ 01549 402971 ⬧ pier-cafe.co.uk. Bright, modern café, beloved by both locals and tourists, in a prime position beside the loch. On a sunny day, sit out in

1 Alladale Wilderness Reserve. 2 Look out for red squirrels in the woodland at Ledmore & Migdale. 3 You might spot black-throated divers on Loch Shin from the Dalchork Bird Hide. 4 Loch Migdale. ▶

the garden and watch the water glitter while you eat. The lunch menu ranges from open bloomer sandwiches with toppings like hot smoked salmon and avocado to venison burgers and a battered haddock wrap, or just pop in for coffee and a cake from the abundant display of sweet treats.

7 FALLS OF SHIN

🏠 **Ceol Mor Highland Lodges**

📍 NH 57668 99346 ⌖ forestryandland.gov.scot

South of Lairg, Little Loch Shin soon becomes the River Shin, a relatively short river that's famous for its large fish: salmon. Between May and November you can watch the improbable spectacle of the fish trying to jump up waterfalls at the Falls of Shin, five miles south of Lairg. The Shin is just one of four rivers (the others are the Cassley, Oykel and Carron) that branch off the Kyle of Sutherland; wild Atlantic salmon come in from the sea in shoals and travel up the firth and then the kyle before heading upriver to return to where they were born in order to spawn. As at Rogie (page 302), there is something quite astounding (and

THE CASTLE OF SPITE

One of my favourite historical stories in the North Highlands is that of **Carbisdale Castle**, which overlooks the Kyle of Sutherland from its hillside perch just five miles northwest of the village of Bonar Bridge. It was built in the Scots Baronial style between 1906 and 1917 for the Duchess of Sutherland, the second wife of George Sutherland-Leveson-Gower, 3rd Duke of Sutherland; when the duke died in 1892, the duchess initially inherited most of his estate, but his son and family contested the will and she was imprisoned for six weeks in Holloway Prison, London, for burning related documents. Eventually, a financial settlement was reached and the Sutherland family agreed to build the duchess a castle, at their own expense but to her specifications – providing it sat outside their lands.

The position of the castle – just inside the Ross-shire boundary but overlooking Sutherland from an elevated position – was allegedly chosen by the duchess out of spite, not least because the Sutherland family would be unable to avoid seeing it on any of their travels in the region. In addition, the square tower was given just three clock faces; the story goes that the side of the tower facing Sutherland was left blank to reflect the fact that the duchess would not give the family the time of day.

At the time of writing, the castle had just been put on the market for £5 million. You can explore the beautiful (public) woodland on a walk (page 102), which provides a great view of Carbisdale's exterior.

a little amusing) about watching the fish make what is essentially a leap of faith – and often failing.

The falls themselves are a little less spectacular than those at Rogie, but are nonetheless worth a visit even out of season, with the coffee-coloured water crashing down with force over the rocks. The falls are directly across the road from the car park, reached by a short but steep path that leads to a couple of viewing points. Back at the road, you can follow the blue waymarked Riverside Trail north along the Shin before looping back to cross the road and then head through the forest; a pleasant walk of about half a mile in total. Two other trails here, the Pond and Play, and the Woodland, head deeper into the forest to the west of the car park. They're both pleasant walks (three-quarters of a mile and 1¼ mile respectively), but a little too managed for my liking – kids will find plenty to explore, sit on and climb over along the way, though. There's also a decent playground here, by the car park, as well as a sit-in and take-away café, The Salt & Salmon Company (🖪), making it a good choice for a leg-stretcher on a longer journey.

🧳 SPECIAL STAYS

Ceol Mor Highland Lodges IV27 4EU ✆ 07887 563238 ⬙ ceolmor.co.uk. Two modern wooden lodges overlooking the Kyle of Sutherland, with the hills rising up all around. Each lodge has its own terrace, perfect for soaking up the views (not to mention the phenomenal sunsets) and listening to the birds in the grasses on the floodplain – which include snipes, siskins and, at night, tawny owls. The interiors are smart but homely, with hugely comfortable double beds and an additional sofa bed in the living area. No TV, but excellent internet so you can easily stream on your devices, and the kitchen has everything you need for self-catering. Alan and Yvonne are the perfect hosts and can provide ample suggestions for how to make the most of your time here, including several on-site experiences such as cooking classes and afternoon tea in their lovely sun room. Pine martens and red squirrels are regular visitors, too.

8 ROSEHALL

West of the Falls of Shin, the A837 follows the sinewy passage of the Kyle of Sutherland. This is a wonderful road to drive: in winter, the bare, skinny trees and moss-covered ground lend a ghostliness to the surroundings, while in summer the route is abundant in colour. In terms of amenities, there's little to the village of Rosehall, nine miles from the falls, except a café and a hotel/pub, but its setting, at the confluence of

the Oykel and Cassley rivers, is really lovely and provides some great opportunities for walking.

Tucked away in the hills that climb up to the east of the hamlet, just north of the village hall, is the gorge of **Raven's Rock** (♀ NC 49799 00848 ♂ woodlandtrust.org.uk). Landslips mean that you can no longer get too close to the gorge itself, but the two pleasant paths from the parking area take you through towering trees down to the gushing burn and out to a viewpoint over the dark streak of the water. You will see evidence of landslips on both routes but particularly on the lower one, where countless trees look as though they've been ripped up from their roots; a testament to the devastation wrought by nature. Both paths are easy with kids (though little legs might find the uphill return from the burn a little tiring), and there's an attractive bear carving to look out for at the beginning.

Continuing west along the A837 you come to **Rosehall Forest** (♀ NC 47986 01906 ♂ woodlandtrust.org.uk), which is crisscrossed by a handful of walking (and biking) trails. At the car park a community-constructed log cabin provides information on the wood, which is also known as Deer Park, due to the fact that sika, red and fallow deer were once kept here. The sika in particular flourished, despite coming from Japan; so much so that they escaped from the park and spread out across the region –

"Four trails wind through the woodland, including one that features artwork and poems by local schoolchildren."

the information board claims that the thousands of sika deer that now live in Sutherland are descended from the original imported deer here. Four trails wind through the woodland, including one that features artwork and poems by local schoolchildren.

One path, the Cassley Trail, takes you all the way to my favourite spot at Rosehall: **Cassley Falls** (♀ NC 46805 02839). I'd argue that, though significantly less well known, they're far superior to those at Shin (page 98). These can also be reached from Rosehall itself; for the nicest route, take a right turn (signposted 'Glencassley') just east of the bridge over the River Cassley and follow the road up past the Achness Hotel for about half a mile until you see a parking area by a gate on the right

◀ **1** Carbisdale Castle overlooks the Kyle of Sutherland. **2** Between May and November you might see wild Atlantic salmon leaping up the waterfalls at the Falls of Shin. **3** Cassley Falls.

A walk around Carbisdale Castle

❋ OS Explorer 441; start: parking area north of the railway bridge in Invershin ♀ NH 57908 95345; 4 miles; moderate.

This is a long but hugely enjoyable walk that explores the mixed woodland around Carbisdale Castle (page 98), which sits in a striking position above the Kyle of Sutherland. I've started the walk from the other side of the kyle, which allows for great views of the castle and the water as you cross the bridge; you could, however, make it a shorter walk by starting at Culrain station (if you come in by train) or from the car park within the castle grounds (♀ NH 57490 95104). The first half of the walk involves a fair bit of winding your way up and then downhill, while the second half weaves through woodland that becomes increasingly magical; pack a picnic and make a day of it.

While this route does follow paths, they can be overgrown and blocked at times (as I found on my last visit). As a result, I've kept this as simple as I can, but I'd advise you to arm yourself with an OS map before you walk it, so you can easily detour if necessary. Thanks to Alan West of Ceol Mor Highland Lodges (page 99) for pointing me in the direction of this walk.

1 From the parking area, walk south towards the railway bridge, climbing over the low metal barrier just after the information boards to reach the path to the pedestrian bridge. Cross the kyle, enjoying the wide view of the river and the castle, and once on the other side go up the steps and then follow the path down the side of the railway track. At the end, turn right along the road; you'll see the castle gates on your left after about 100yds.

2 Follow the road through the castle gates; you'll pass a car park on your left and then the road will start climbing uphill, passing the rather grand converted stables before meeting a wooden gate across the road, marked 'Private'. Go through the pedestrian access gate on the right-hand side, and shortly after you'll see the castle on your right. When the road curves round towards the castle, keep left, on to the rougher track that runs north. Shortly after, the track will curve left – take the sharp left turn just before this, between two stone markers, to go uphill on a clear footpath. The path curves around in almost a semi-circle to your left: keep straight on, ignoring any other paths. After 300yds, you will come out of the denser forest to walk among heather and younger trees; about 100yds further on you will see a prominent rock to your left. Keep straight on the path, which continues to wind gently to your right and then left before descending towards View Rock, where there are fabulous views over the Kyle of Sutherland.

3 Take the path to the right, just before the viewpoint, descending down to a clear track. Turn left here. After about 260yds, you'll reach a T-junction; turn right to walk gently uphill through the forest, ignoring the path to your left that heads over a bridge. When the path splits by a red

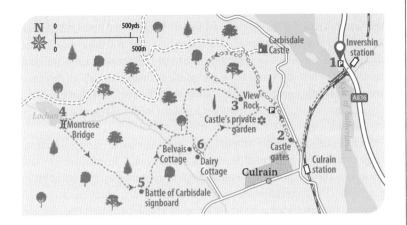

and white routemarker, keep left to stay close to the burn. You'll see waterfalls as you climb and can veer to the left to get closer to the biggest. As the burn widens, the path moves away from it, and at the top of the hill is joined by another path coming in from your right. Continue straight on and you'll soon see a path down to the lochan in front of you – a lovely spot for a picnic.

4 From the lochan, head back to the path and turn right; the sound of water should be on your left. The path curves in a horseshoe and you'll soon see a sign for Montrose Bridge. Cross the bridge over the burn as it gushes downhill and then take the path immediately to your right after the bridge to briefly climb up the side of the burn again. The narrow path winds through heather towards pines and you'll soon be heading gently downhill, weaving in and out of the trees with a view of the kyle in the distance.

5 Turn left when you reach a signboard about the Battle of Carbisdale and head into the trees again; the path curves through the woodland and descends towards the burn. Here, cross the little wooden bridge and then follow the path up to meet the one you followed alongside the burn earlier. Turn right and continue till you reach the T-junction again.

6 Turn right, and after a very short distance go through the metal gate by the bright blue Belvais Cottage, and shortly after turn left at the crossroads by the yellow and white Dairy Cottage. Follow the footpath along the base of the hill and then go through another gate. After about 70yds, look for a narrow path on your right and follow that into the car park you passed earlier. Turn right on to the road to exit the castle grounds, and retrace your steps back the starting point.

($\mathbb{Q}$ NC 46997 02829). Diagonally opposite here, a signpost points the way through a metal gate to the falls (which are, confusingly, marked as 'Achness Waterfall' on the OS map); it's just under 200yds from here to the water. There's a handily placed bench right by the river where you can sit and watch these lovely falls tumbling over the dark rocks; note though that the first falls you see aren't the only ones – keep walking south and you'll soon find the next, more dramatic set, where multiple small waterfalls combine in one great roar. To see the full force of it, cross over the small wooden bridge and turn back to look; the rocks are cut in such a way that they look like giant steps.

The Cassley is a good salmon river, so you may see people fishing, their lines looping through the air like whips, or – from spring to late autumn – the fish jumping in an attempt to continue upriver (as at Shin; page 98). The riverside walk south is really lovely, breaking out from between the trees after a short while on to grazing ground. Pass the old graveyard and you'll see a mound on your left – the remains of an old broch, which you can climb up on to see its outline and walk its walls, now almost entirely grassed over. The larger mound to the south also has remnants of a broch, and you can see some of its stones on the river-facing side. It's not hard to see why this position, surrounded by hills and close to the river, was chosen; today it's largely populated by sheep.

You can climb up and over the bridge (taking care with the road) to continue along the river, or loop back to the start via the road. I'd also recommend heading north from the falls, following the path over the rocks. The river becomes rockier as you head in this direction and it feels wilder and more magical among the downy birch; you'll pass another set of small waterfalls and the path will eventually wind its way back to the road.

BRORA TO HELMSDALE

The wildness of Sutherland begins to kick in as you head north from Golspie, with hills rearing up to the west and north, and the coast almost always in sight, often with glimmers of empty stretches of golden sand. Arguably the most glorious beach can be found at Brora, an often overlooked but lovely seaside village. Further north, just before the Caithness boundary, is the appealing fishing village of Helmsdale, hemmed in by gorse-covered hills.

9 BRORA

🏠 **Royal Marine Hotel**

Brora is the kind of place that makes me go a little misty-eyed, though I'll admit that I drove through the village on countless occasions before I actually took the time to stop. And boy, did I wish I'd stopped here sooner. Driving through the centre, there is little to give away the fact that this is a seaside village – with the exception perhaps of Capaldis 'Big Pink Shop' (page 109) – but in truth it is home to one of the most gorgeous stretches of sand in northern Scotland. I'd go so far as to say that there's nowhere finer to be on the east coast on a sunny day than Brora.

What you also can't tell from a first glance is that, for a period, Brora was something of an industrial powerhouse. Coal – the most northerly deposits in Britain – was first discovered and quarried here in the early 16th century, and the first pits were sunk in 1598 and the mined coal was used to fuel the production of salt (which was used locally and further afield for the curing of meat and fish). Rather terrifyingly, the local coal's high sulphur content meant it had a reputation for spontaneous combustion. Coal mining took place on and off here until the mines were permanently closed in 1974. Mining and salt production weren't the only industries in this busy little village, either – there were also brickworks, whisky distilleries and a woollen mill: the last brought electricity to Brora as early as 1913, earning it the nickname the 'Electric City' for being the first and only place with electricity north of Inverness.

You can learn more about the history of the village at **Brora Heritage Centre** (🗗 Brora Heritage), run enthusiastically by the Clyne Heritage Society and crammed full of village detail and artefacts. At the time of writing, the museum was located in the west of the village, on Coal Pit Road (signposted from the village centre), but it is due to open in new premises in the Old Clyne School on the A9 in summer 2025; for up-to-date information, visit the centre's Facebook page. Having seen the plans and spoken with Nick Lindsay, the society's president, I'm confident the new museum will be well worth a visit. Guided walks of the village and the surrounding area (including out to old Clearance villages) are often on offer; check the society's website for more details (🖊 clyneheritage.com).

The river from which the village takes its name somewhat cuts the settlement in half. To the south is a cluster of shops near Fountain

Square (including Capaldis' unmissable Big Pink Shop; page 109), with its commemorative Queen Victoria Jubilee Fountain and 19th-century buildings predominantly built of local Clynelish stone. Just to the northeast is Cunningham's – the place to head to if you need a bucket and spade for the beach. About 100yds further northeast, just before the bridge, is the rather fanciful war memorial – a clock tower that looks like it's been shaved off the side of a castle (it hasn't), and which is only just over a century old.

Harbour Road, directly opposite, runs southeast alongside the river; after about 170yds, as the water drops out of sight, look for the curved roof of the old ice house, thought to have been built around 1820 for storing fish. A further 130yds on and you'll reach the harbour; you're unlikely to see more than a handful of boats and a scattering of lobster pots lined at the side, but when it was first built in 1813 (by the 1st Duke of Sutherland, page 90), it would have been incredibly busy, not just for salmon fishing but for transporting coal, salt and bricks. From here you'll get your first glimpse, across the water, of Brora's northern beach (more on that later), but if you follow the road round you'll reach its **southern beach**.

"The southern beach has a much wilder feel, punctuated by seaweed-wigged rocks when the tide is out."

This has a much wilder feel, punctuated by seaweed-wigged rocks when the tide is out and little more than a pebbly strand when the water is in, which makes it great exploring territory – particularly at low tide when you can peer into rock pools – and also perfect for snorkelling (page 108).

This stretch of the coast seems to change constantly as you walk it – if the tide is high, look for the narrow coast path (part of the John O'Groats Trail; page 145) through the grasses. After about a mile or so, you are likely to see seals, either bobbing like little dark-eyed balls in the water or lounging rather precariously on rocks depending on the tide. I've spent hours watching them here as they swim in the shallows and ride the swell of the waves. On one occasion when the tide was out, I took an evening stroll to the rockiest part of the beach, and as my eyes adjusted to the gloaming, I realised that not all of the rocks were rocks but some were in fact seals. As I stood alone on the beach, the distant hills shrouded in mist, the seals' singing was both mesmerising and haunting.

You can walk along the coast all the way to Golspie (six miles), via Carn Liath (page 90) and Dunrobin (4½ miles; page 87); it's a straightforward and relatively easy walk (the sand makes for a bit of a workout but you can also follow a path behind the shore), with fabulous views, a waterfall and plenty of empty spots for a picnic.

To reach Brora's **northern beach**, return to the village centre, cross the bridge over the river and take the first right down Golf Road. This winds along the watercourse with some lovely views towards the harbour once you're about halfway down. At the far end of the road is the **golf course**; a wooden gate on the right of the car park leads down to the southern side of the beach, initially running along the mouth of the river. At this point you might be thinking, 'hang on Emma, you promised me an amazing beach' – stick with me (and it). This first part of the beach is punctuated by a considerable swathe of rocks at low tide but round the corner, leaving the river behind, and then curve around the next corner, and the whole, wide sweep of golden sand will be revealed to you.

'There's two miles of beautiful beach and nobody on it,' Billy Mckechnie, manager of the Royal Marine Hotel (page 109) said to me, and it's true – I've been here in all weathers, including on a Saturday during a summer heatwave (yes, they do sometimes have them in the North Highlands) and the sands have always been all but empty – plus, they're big enough that even if there was a sudden deluge of visitors, they'd still feel far from busy. I particularly love the beach at sunset on a clear day, when the sands and the sky shimmer in so many different colours it feels like stepping inside a Georgia O'Keeffe painting.

Clynelish Distillery
KW9 6LR 🥃 malts.com

To be totally honest, I wasn't going to visit Clynelish. I'd seen a photo of the Johnnie Walker statue outside and had written it off as too mass market (despite, admittedly, never having heard of the brand before). But a conversation with a local, who told me that touring Clynelish had moved her to tears because 'I'd never seen my local area represented like that before', changed my mind.

And ultimately, this is a place deeply connected to its location: the 1st Duke of Sutherland (yes, *that* one; page 90) established a distillery here in 1819 in order to deal with his tenants' illegal activity – he was personally fined every time one of his tenants were found to be distilling illegally, and so built a distillery here to curb the problem and thus make himself a huge profit in the meantime. (Never a self-seeking man, this one.) The present-day Clynelish is in fact the sister distillery of the original, which is now called **Brora Distillery** (⊘ malts.com ☺ appointment only), famous for peated whisky and only reopened in 2020, having closed in 1983. (With tour prices in the hundreds, a visit to Brora Distillery is very much the preserve of the truly dedicated – and moneyed – whisky connoisseur.)

This is not a staid tour – it's interactive and informative without being gimmicky, starting in a beautiful room where the surrounding hills

ON & UNDER THE WATER IN BRORA

Sutherland Adventure Company ✆ 07854 991601 ⊘ sutherlandadventurecompany.com

I am not a natural sportsperson – balance, speed and general coordination are all words I would never use when describing myself – and yet, somehow, I found myself on the placid waters of Loch Brora, calmly standing up on a paddleboard and staring at the beautiful, gorse-clad hills around me.

'That's it,' my guide, Rhionna, said from her own board, a few yards away, 'you're doing it!' Barely daring to breathe, I followed her instructions to start paddling, and within minutes had done a circle of the little island in the middle of the loch. Not bad for the woman who has consistently fallen off every other kind of board she's ever stood on.

Stand-up paddleboarding with Rhionna was so much fun that my hour's lesson passed in a blur – I even, despite my immense dislike of cold water, willingly went into the loch just so I could learn how to get back on to my board. It's a testament to Rhionna's skills as a teacher that I was able to paddle so calmly and confidently, despite being a complete novice, and – for

once – not actually worry what anyone else thought of me.

Stand-up paddleboarding is the main focus for Brora-based Sutherland Adventure Company, which you can experience on a 90-minute lesson, or by hiring the gear and setting off by yourself on the loch (only really advisable if you've already paddled). Rhionna and her small team also offer bike hire and tours, guided walks, and – much to my delight – **snorkelling** from Brora beach. For the last, you do have to be somewhat prepared to waddle to and from the beach in your wetsuit and flippers (both provided), during which time you'll likely be watched with varying levels of amusement by anyone in the car park, but once you're in the water, swimming among seaweed that billows like mermaids' hair, you'll have forgotten all about that. On my own snorkel, just at the tail end of high tide, I saw little in the way of marine life, but it was still utterly thrilling and left me buzzing for hours afterwards.

have been recreated on the walls out of slats of wood, with audience involvement bringing the history of the whisky, and the landscape and people of the region, to life. What I appreciated was that, in stark contrast to Dunrobin (page 87), the less savoury history of the company wasn't shied away from but discussed openly. Afterwards, you're taken to see the production process, with the opportunity to see how the grain changes and a handy cafetière-based explanation of mashing. It's great fun.

The tour finishes in the big-windowed bar that looks out towards the coast, where three whiskies and a highball are provided, paired with chocolate. You're talked through each whisky and encouraged to talk about what flavours and smells you find. 'Whatever you get is correct,' said my guide, Alfie. 'It just might not be the correct way to describe it.' Which might be the kindest way of saying that you're wrong I've come across. What marks out Clynelish's whisky is its waxy character – it's much more pleasant than that sounds, and you'll see what I mean when you swill it around the glass and take a swig. There are a number of different tours available, and you can also just pop up to the bar for drinks or food.

SPECIAL STAYS

Royal Marine Hotel Golf Rd ✆ 0333 2576977 ⏂ royalmarinebrora.com. Set in an attractive building that dates back to 1913, this is an elegant but relaxed hotel, with a snug bar and a sophisticated restaurant, the Curing Yard, which serves up lots of local seafood and meat. It's all topped off by the friendly and informative manager, Billy, who takes the time to get to know guests – everyone from locals to hikers, golfers, fishers and families. Breakfast is often accompanied by Billy playing the bagpipes.

FOOD & DRINK

Capaldis of Brora Fountain Sq ✆ 01408 622713 ⬛. A visit to Brora isn't complete without an ice cream from the 'Big Pink Shop' (the 'Wee Pink Shop' is in Golspie). The ice cream, which is still made to the top-secret recipe used back in 1929 when the business started, comes in a mind-boggling array of regularly changing flavours, from Belgian chocolate orange to Turkish delight.

Cocoa Skye London House, Station Rd ✆ 01408 621954 ⬛. Lovely café by the station, famous for its home-made chocolates and waffles, and decorated with local art. The short menu also features hot chocolates, milkshakes, soups, sandwiches and toasties – the BLT, made with chipotle mayonnaise, is amazing.

10 HELMSDALE

It's not hard to see why there's been a settlement here, at the mouth of the Helmsdale River, since at least Viking times: approaching over the bridge from the south, with the sea crashing on one side, the wide river on the other, and hills to the north and west, there's no doubt that it's both a very scenic and strategic position. Little remains of Helmsdale's earlier incarnations, however – even its 17th-century castle is long gone – and what you'll see of the village today much reflects its role as a planned settlement at the start of the 19th century, when it was laid out to house crofters who had been evicted from the straths during the Highland Clearances (page 90). Much like other towns and villages dating from this time, the streets to the northwest of the A9 follow a neat grid plan, of which Dunrobin Street is the main focus, being home to a handful of shops and restaurants.

A left turn at Dunrobin Street's northwestern end leads to the striking yellow and black building of **Timespan** (KW8 6JA ✆ 01431 821327 ⌾ timespan.org.uk ⊘ mid-Mar–Oct 10.00–17.00 daily; Nov–mid-Mar 10.00–15.00 Sat & Sun), the town's heritage museum. There's a huge amount of information on display here about the village's history – I'd even say maybe too much information, as it feels like a lot to take in in one visit. There are, however, a good number of interesting artefacts to look at: my kids were particularly taken by the huge fishermens' socks. My favourite part was at the very back of the museum, where there is a recreation of a smiddy (a blacksmith's) as well as a shop, crammed with old bottles, and a croft house and byre. The upstairs gallery hosts interesting art exhibitions throughout the year and has a great view of the old Telford Bridge and the hills behind.

From the museum, you can follow Shore Street along the river and under the A9 to the large harbour, which remains fairly busy compared to other east-coast villages, even if pleasure boats seem to dominate these days. Just east of here is the pebbly beach, which is worth a visit if, like me, you enjoy searching for and collecting sea glass – I'm not exaggerating when I say that I've never come across such an abundant spot for it. A footpath runs behind the rocky shore, with increasingly

---

◀ **1** The sandy beach at Brora. **2** *The Emigrants* statue, Helmsdale. **3** Helmsdale.
4 & 6 Flow Country is a great place to look for flowers like bog asphodel and to try your hand at activities like pond-dipping. **5** Paddleboarding in the lochs and rivers around Brora.

THERE'S GOLD IN THEM THAR HILLS

Today, the rivers around Helmsdale are particularly prized for their fishing, but in the mid 18th century the **Strath of Kildonan**, to the northwest of the village, was the site of a frenzied gold rush. A local man, Robert Gilchris, found significant amounts of gold in the burns here in 1868 and by the spring of the following year around 600 prospectors had descended on the valley, setting up settlements of tents and wooden huts.

Unsurprisingly, the Duke of Sutherland wasn't best pleased that people were making money from his land, and soon introduced gold-mining licences and a royalty charge on any gold found. The final blow to the gold rush, however, came at the start of 1870, when the duke, finding it conflicted with the work of those people grazing sheep and fishing in the strath, decided to stop all gold panning.

It's still possible to gold pan on the Kildonan and Suisgill burns today; the former requires a permit and the latter is only open to guests at a couple of nearby self-catering properties. Full information can be found at ⊘ suisgill. co.uk/things-to-do/gold-panning.

good views of the cliffs north along the coast, though it does get a little rougher under foot after a while; WalkHighlands outlines a nice route that loops round the back of the village.

Looking out over the sea on the western side of the A9 bridge is *The Emigrants*, a statue erected in commemoration of the people from the Highlands and islands of Scotland who emigrated to other countries. It's a moving work of art, composed of four people: a man in a kilt facing out to sea, as if he is walking towards it; a young boy, also in a kilt, looking beseechingly at his father; and a mother with a baby, turning back to look at the hills she is leaving behind. I particularly love the sense of movement created by the sculptor, Gerald Laing, in the group's clothes.

From here, you can walk north to the war memorial, which looms over the western side of the village (just behind which is the train station, all but hidden from view). Immediately east of the memorial is the old bridge, still in use today but much less busy than the A9 – engineered by Thomas Telford, it was built in 1811 and its two arches look particularly pretty against the backdrop of the dusky hills.

¶ FOOD & DRINK

River Café Timespan, Dunrobin St ✆ 01431 821327 ⊘ timespan.org.uk/visit/river-cafe.
Right by the wide, dark river, with a view of the double arches of the old Telford bridge and

tables outside for fine weather. The menu is focused on savoury and sweet crêpes, including one with smoked salmon and local crowdie cheese, plus sausage rolls, soups and a small selection of cakes.

FLOW COUNTRY

theflowcountry.org.uk

The A897 heads north out of Helmsdale to wind its way alongside the Helmsdale River for 17 miles until the village of **Kinbrace**, which, despite its diminutive size, has a train station on the Far North Line. This stretch of the road is particularly beautiful: look out for the wide loop of fly fishers as you travel, and for large groups of grazing red deer by the side of the road. Beyond this, it doesn't take long before the lush green fields give way to moorland, marking the start of Flow Country.

Stretching across northern inland Caithness and Sutherland, Flow Country is home to the most extensive and intact blanket bog system in the world. While that claim alone might not excite you – I appreciate the word 'bog' likely only has a thrill for a very small percentage of people – this mottled land of peat and pools is nonetheless captivating in its own way, particularly when you explore it on foot. A word of warning, though: this is an incredibly fragile and – surprise! – boggy landscape, so it's best to explore on established paths. The Flow Country website has a map of the numerous sites that are possible to explore – the two included below are the main options when it comes to experiencing this fascinating landscape, but it's also worth considering Camster Windfarm (page 133) for an alternate view. Do also bear in mind that even the paths can become saturated and impassable at certain times of year.

The landscape of Flow Country is such that for much of the year it can appear to be little more than scrubby shades of the same colours (brown in winter, green in summer); take time to get down to ground level and you'll soon notice the diversity of plants that thrive here. A huge amount of this peatland is covered in sphagnum mosses (also known as bog mosses) – 29 species in total grow here, some red and flowerlike, others narrow, long and almost furry in appearance – it is these that form layers of peat when they die. In summer, the landscape is spotted with colour: look out for the purple shades of heath-spotted and northern marsh orchids, and the star-shaped sun-yellow petals of bog asphodel.

In July 2024, Flow Country was inscribed as the first peatland UNESCO World Heritage Site; it's hoped that this accreditation, which is the result of years of work by the Flow Country Partnership, will further aid conservation, education and tourism here. Above all, it helps to acknowledge the positive role that the bogs can play in the climate crisis – able to soak up carbon from the atmosphere and store it, Flow Country contains more than double the amount of carbon found in the entirety of UK woodlands and forests.

11 RSPB FORSINARD FLOWS

Forsinard KW13 6YT ⚘ rspb.org.uk; **visitor centre** ☺ Apr–Oct 09.00–17.00 daily; Nov–Mar 10.00–15.00 Mon–Fri

Arguably the easiest and most accessible way to visit the heart of Flow Country is at the RSPB Forsinard Flows nature reserve, which extends for more than 50,000 acres; its position right by Forsinard train station even makes it accessible by public transport, which feels like a rarity in these parts. Regardless of how you arrive, the station is a great place to start your visit; here you'll find the helpful visitors' centre, which provides easy-to-digest insight into the area.

From the station, head 200yds south along the A897 to reach the start of the one-mile **Dubh Lochains Trail**, signposted on your right. You'll see the wooden lookout tower in the distance, which is what you're aiming for – the curved, modern structure looks striking yet harmonious against the bogland backdrop. The trail is over a mix of boardwalks and flagstones – you do need to stick to them both to avoid damaging the bog's fragile ecosystem, and to avoid doing damage to yourself. As someone who likes her walks to feel a bit less 'managed', I didn't have huge hopes for this one, but I was pleasantly surprised at how enjoyable I found it; the boardwalk ahead of you often disappears from view, so you don't feel too conscious of where you're going.

As you walk out towards the lookout tower, with the hills rising up in the distance against the flatness of bog country, you begin to appreciate the patchwork nature of this landscape, with little pools dotted around that glitter even in the half-light of a rainy, overcast day. Small explanation boards at foot-level explain the make-up of the landscape as you walk – helping to identify common bog plants like the carnivorous sundews with their bright red tentacles, and sphagnum moss, which – apparently – some people think looks like a kitten that's fallen into the water. (I was quite glad not to have made this association myself, no matter how hard I tried.)

From the lookout tower, you get a great, uninterrupted view of **Ben Griam Beg** in the distance, with the vast, pool-spotted bog stretching towards it. The pools become mirror-like in still weather, blurring the delineation between land and sky. While you're here, look out for birds including golden eagles, hen harriers and ospreys, though you'll have more luck catching the song of skylarks in the spring. Spring can also be a good time to spot frogs and frogspawn in the water.

For a longer, more immersive experience in this vast landscape, head four miles north to the hamlet of **Forsinain**. A parking area (NC90380 48577) on the western side of the road sits directly opposite the start of the four-mile trail (there's a handy RSPB information board at the parking area), which initially leads up a track through farmland before heading across the peat bog. The route is marked by posts throughout, making it easy to find your way along the paths, and boggier areas have flagstones to make walking easier – though if it's very wet it could be impassable, as I found out one damp March.

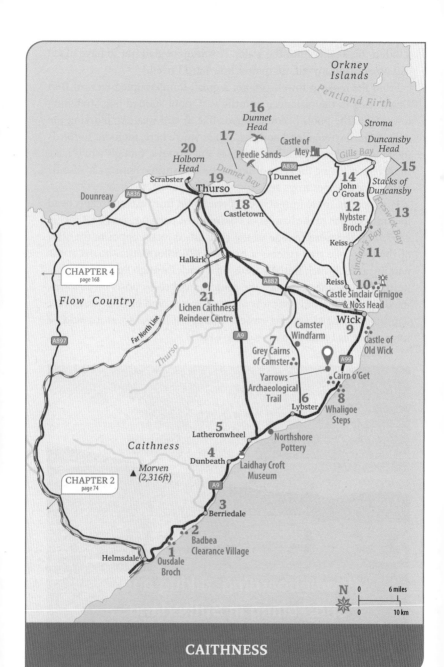

Orkney
Islands

Pentland Firth

16
Dunnet
Head

17
Peedie Sands

Castle of
Mey

Stroma

Duncansby
Head

Gills Bay

A836

Dunnet Bay

Dunnet

15

14
John
O'Groats

Stacks of
Duncansby

20
Holborn
Head

Scrabster

19
Thurso

Dounreay

A836

18
Castletown

12
Nybster
Broch

13

Keiss

Halkirk

11

CHAPTER 4
page 168

Flow Country

A882

Reiss

10

Castle Sinclair Girnigoe
& Noss Head

A897

Far North Line

Thurso

21
Lichen Caithness
Reindeer Centre

A9

Camster
Windfarm

Wick

9

Castle of
Old Wick

7
Grey Cairns
of Camster

Cairn o'Get

A99

Yarrows
Archaeological
Trail

6
Lybster

8
Whaligoe
Steps

5
Latheronwheel

Northshore
Pottery

Caithness

4
Dunbeath

Laidhay Croft
Museum

▲ Morven
(2,316ft)

CHAPTER 2
page 74

A9

3
Berriedale

2
Badbea
Clearance Village

Helmsdale

1
Ousdale
Broch

N
0   6 miles
0   10 km

CAITHNESS

3
CAITHNESS

This is the northland, the land of exquisite light.
Neil M Gunn, *Highland River*

Gunn's words, from his celebrated 1937 novel, perfectly encapsulate Caithness, a place where the word 'vast' can be applied to both sky and land, with the two often seeming to melt into one another, and where the light shifts constantly, changing the surrounding landscape as it does so. On a coast that is often overlooked, this northeastern corner is often the most bypassed, too often unfairly branded as 'dull' and 'flat' – neither of which are true. It is, however, noticeably different to the rest of the North Highlands, often referred to as 'the lowlands beyond the Highlands', and with a history that is more Norse than Gaelic.

The name 'Caithness' comes from both the Picts and the Norse: a Pictish tribe, known as the Catt people, were known to live here, while 'ness' comes from the Old Norse for headland – the Norse themselves referred to the area as *Katanes*, or 'headland of the Catt people'. The translation of its Gaelic name, *Gallaibh*, is perhaps even more telling: 'the place of the non-Gaels'.

The A897 more or less marks the western boundary of Caithness, with the northern and eastern sides of the region enclosed by water: the Atlantic, the Pentland Firth and the North Sea. The east coast is characterised by old fishing villages, indicative of the herring boom experienced in the 19th and early 20th centuries, and a number of archaeological sites, which tell stories of the Iron Age people that lived here. To the north are steep, dark cliffs and sea stacks, the summertime home of thousands of seabirds, including puffins, and golden stretches of sand. Here, too, is Thurso, the biggest town north of Inverness, though far from a metropolis. Inland Caithness is a mix of farmland, scrubby moorland and the rolling expanse of Flow Country's (page 113) blanket bog; in the far south, you'll find its highest peak, Morven, the triangular shape of which, thanks to the low-lying nature of the rest of the region, you can often make out for miles and miles around.

'Caithness is a playground for those who prefer to take the time to truly immerse themselves in the places they visit,' artist Lisa Poulsen (see opposite) told me, and I don't think there's a better way of encapsulating what this region is like. Whizz through en route to other places and you'll be in danger of falling into the trap of agreeing that 'west is best'; take the time to explore, however, to wander its cliffs and its inland paths, to marvel at its ancient sites, and to just stand and watch the colours constantly changing across the sky, and you'll uncover its quiet, captivating drama.

GETTING AROUND

The A9 remains the major artery in Caithness, running parallel to the coast as far as Latheron before swinging inland, at first across the barren expanse of the eastern Flow Country and then through neat farmland before it reaches the town of Thurso, where it continues on another two miles to the busy port of Scrabster. The A99 continues along the coast north of Latheron all the way to John O'Groats, becoming the A836 to run west along the north coast.

TRAINS

The **Far North Line** ($\oslash$ scotrail.co.uk) runs from Inverness as far as Thurso (4hrs) and Wick (4½hrs); the latter involves the train backtracking somewhat in order to reach this east-coast town. Two other stations, Georgemas Junction and Scotscalder, 2½ miles and five miles from Halkirk respectively, are only really useful if you're planning to walk or cycle (with your own bike).

BUSES

Stagecoach ($\oslash$ stagecoachbus.com) runs a handful of useful buses in Caithness. The 80 runs from John O'Groats to Thurso (5–7 daily Mon–Sat; 1hr), via Dunnet (35min) and Castletown (40min); on weekdays, one bus runs on to Scrabster (1hr 5min), and two services run to/from Wick, half an hour before/after John O'Groats, stopping at Keiss and Freswick en route (15 & 20min from Wick respectively). The X99, which starts in Inverness, runs between Dunbeath and Thurso (1–3 daily; 1hr 20min), calling at Lybster (15min), Wick (40min) and Castletown (1hr 5min). The 276 runs from Staxigoe (near Wick) to Dounreay

INSPIRED BY CAITHNESS

Caithness to me is a land of sky, light and sea, and no matter how much I try to capture that in the photographs I take, I never seem to manage to accurately do so. Discovering the work of local artist Lisa Poulsen, then, felt almost revelatory – creating digital landscapes using photographs of stone, she manages to capture the sense of ever-shifting light and colour that feels so intrinsic to my own experience of the region.

'My process usually involves exploring Caithness with my bashed second-hand camera, stumbling over ditches, staring at cliff faces and flagstone fences,' Lisa told me. 'My artworks tend to start as a piece of stone I stumble across on the beach when I'm out with my dog. I see waves or skies in the surfaces of stones and cliff faces, so I photograph and then digitally enhance them on the computer to bring more of what I see out of them.'

The use of stone in Lisa's work – stonescapes, as she calls them – creates a fluidity in her images of landscape that is so fitting in this place of huge skies. It seems appropriate that stones, cliffs and boulders, which have been as she says 'chiselled by wild weather' should be repurposed to convey the sense of a landscape influenced by ever-changing skies and weather. In the print that I own – of Dunnet Bay – the texture of a large boulder (found on the same beach) streaks the sky in pale pinks and blues, reminding me of my own sunset walks there, when the colours of dunes, sea and sky all glow duskily. It's a rare quality, I think, to be able to capture something that so mirrors how somewhere had *felt* to be.

You can buy Lisa's work direct from her website (inspiredbycaithness.com) and from several shops in the region, including Coo's Tail Gallery (page 163) in Thurso.

(3 daily; 1hr 15min) via Wick (5min), Halkirk (15min), Reiss (20min), Castletown (40min) and Thurso (55min).

WALKING & CYCLING

Don't assume that Caithness's comparatively low-lying landscape means less interesting **walking** opportunities: here you will find some of the most enjoyable – and quietest – walks in the North Highlands. The John O'Groats Trail (page 145) runs along the coast here for its final seven stages; even if you're not walking the entire trail, the path makes a great way to take in some of the area's staggering coastal scenery and its fishing heritage. Particular coastal highlights include the walks south from Duncansby Head to the Stacks of Duncansby (page 153), the area south of Wick (page 142), and from John O'Groats to Sannick Bay (page 151). There's also a fantastic, tucked-away north-coast beach that can only be reached by a walk of just over half a mile (page 158) and, inland, a walk around a wind farm (page 133) and a fascinating archaeological trail (page 136).

If you fancy more of a challenge, you could tackle the conical-shaped **Morven** – its height makes it a Graham (rather than a taller Munro) – and its neighbour, Maiden Pap; see WalkHighlands (⌂ walkhighlands. co.uk) for details.

Caithness isn't so flat that it makes for easy **cycling**, and there are still a few hill climbs to challenge road cyclists, particularly along the southeast coast. John O'Groats of course marks the northern end of LEJOG (⌂ cyclelejog.com) – the Land's End to John O'Groats cycle route. For more of a relaxed ride, there are bike trails at Dunnet Forest (⌂ dunnetcommunityforest.org) immediately to the south of Dunnet Bay (page 156).

THE SOUTHEAST COAST

From Helmsdale, the A9 weaves alongside the coast through scrubby moor- and farmland, the sea dipping in and out of view – when it is visible, it seems to stretch on infinitely. (The nearest landmass to the east is Norway, some 300-odd miles away, which gives you an indication of how far north you are here.) Tucked among this landscape are scenic old fishing villages and some fascinating historical sites.

1 OUSDALE BROCH
♀ ND 07051 18846 ⌂ thebrochproject.co.uk

Look at a map of broch sites in Caithness and the land seems almost pock-marked by these ancient buildings (page 92); of them all, Ousdale Broch is, thanks to the dedicated team behind the Caithness Broch Project (see opposite), the best preserved. Access is from a small car park immediately east off the A9, halfway between Helmsdale and Berriedale, from where it's just over half a mile to the broch on a well-maintained path through an exposed, heather-clad landscape, with the sea always in view ahead of you.

En route, you'll cross the **Ord Road**; one of Caithness's oldest roads, this was – until the A9 was built – the main route into and out of the region from the south. The first site you'll reach after this is the remains of **Borg village**, which was home to tenant farmers until they were forced to leave during the Highland Clearances (page 90) at the beginning of the 19th century. You can climb over the stile in the fence to wander around the remains; some houses are clearly discernible, though a huge amount has been taken over by bracken and grass. No doubt it would have been a hard life here, but the village's distance from the sea makes it feel at least a little sheltered – it's hard not to contrast it with nearby

THE CAITHNESS BROCH PROJECT

The ambitious Caithness Broch Project (�‍ thebrochproject.co.uk) was founded in 2013 with the aim of constructing the first broch (page 92) in Scotland for more than 2,000 years. 'But we realised early on that we had to "start small" by building a portfolio of successful projects first, in order to build up our own credentials,' co-founder Ken McElroy told me. The first of these was to install interpretation panels at broch sites in the region and to produce a 'broch map' leaflet (⌍ thebrochproject.co.uk/caithness-adventure-map).

In 2020, the team finished a £140,000 conservation project at what Ken says is 'arguably the most exceptional broch in Caithness', **Ousdale Broch** (page 120). 'In effect, we added a new heritage site to the region,' he says. 'As it's situated only a few miles north of the Caithness border, Ousdale Broch is the first thing many people see when they enter the county – a fitting introduction to what we think is the "Home of the Broch".'

The **Big Broch Build** itself is of course no small task. For a start, finding the right place for it was a lengthy process – and now that that has been done, the land needs to be purchased and de-crofted, and planning recommendations have to be met.

It's an ambitious project – and not just because brochs are huge structures. The team plans to use Iron Age techniques during construction, and to train people in historical conservation skills as well as traditional crafts such as weaving and leather work. Once the broch is completed there will be opportunities for visitors and locals to learn these skills themselves, and further construction, of a broch village and other structures, is planned. Perhaps most importantly of all, the broch will serve a local, economic purpose, providing employment opportunities and bringing tourists to the region.

With luck – and funding – it shouldn't be too much longer before the project can be further developed; keep an eye on the website for the latest information. There are also several ways you can get involved in this work, including by become a member for just £10 a year. 'We're always looking for volunteers and members,' Ken says. 'A lot of work can be done remotely, but we do appreciate it if people can lend a hand locally.' If you're interested in doing so, contact the team via their social media accounts (𝕏 TheBrochProject ⬛CaithnessBroch Project ⬛ caithnessbrochproject).

Badbea (see below), which you can walk to along the John O'Groats Trail, where people were forced to live following the Clearances. Many of those cleared from this village were moved to nearby Berriedale (see opposite) to make a living from fishing, while others were given financial assistance by the landowner to help them emigrate.

The broch itself is quite remarkable, thanks to the work done by the Broch Project. The remaining structure was comprehensively surveyed in 2019, and gaps in the walls were filled with stone from a collapsed buttress (which itself was built in 1891 by amateur archaeologist Captain James Mackay, who originally excavated the broch), rather than bringing new stone on site. Though it looks to an outsider as though this was done to restore the broch, it was actually in order to stabilise it and prevent future collapse. As with most brochs elsewhere, the original walls would have been much higher than what you see today – it's thought at least 19ft – but what remains is nonetheless still impressive.

"You can also go inside, where the circular interior has been laid with gravel; a handful of other rooms lead off it."

I'd recommend circling the broch first to get a sense of its size and position, which provides views over the hills beyond to the seemingly infinite sea. You can also go inside, where the circular interior has been laid with gravel; a handful of other rooms lead off it. My only companion on one visit was a chattering wheateater perched on top of the walls, seemingly unbothered by my presence.

2 BADBEA CLEARANCE VILLAGE
ND 08898 20075

Undoubtedly one of the most haunting and evocative sites on the east coast is the remains of this Clearance village, perched on the cliffs less than a mile (or two miles by road) northeast of Ousdale Broch. The setting is beautiful, particularly when the heather is in bloom, with the sea shimmering and crashing in the distance, but there's no denying that it's also a rather desolate and isolated site.

From the car park, the path winds its way for about 500yds through gorse and heather; look out for a long, low stone wall as you walk – this is the boundary dyke, which many of Badbea's men were employed to build. The village was created to house people who had been cleared off the land as part of the Highland Clearances (page 90); while some people lived here as early as 1793, most of those who settled here did so in 1802 after being cleared off nearby fertile glens at Ousdale, Kildonan and Auchnacraig in order to make space for sheep farming. The contrast between those lush, fertile glens and this harsh, wind-whipped sea-facing land must have been huge. As well as being on bare, inhospitable moorland, the village was perched rather precariously at the edge of the cliffs: the information boards tell how both cattle and children were tied up to stop them being blown over the edge.

The last family left Badbea in 1903; some had moved to nearby villages, while others emigrated to New Zealand. The large brick monument on the northern side of the site was erected by the son of one family who emigrated, and it makes a sombre memorial to their harsh lives. Today, just enough remains of the cottages to give a sense of there once having been a community here (it's known that at least 12 families lived in the village), though plants have taken over much of it.

3 BERRIEDALE

Blink and you'll miss little Berriedale, which is scattered on either side of the A9. Until 2020, driving through it involved travelling along what was regarded as one of the most treacherous parts of the A9: Berriedale Braes ('brae' is Scots for a steep hillside), and its tight hairpin bend – thankfully, the new, wider meander of the road makes for a more enjoyable drive these days.

From the A9 you'll get little sense of the village, the name of which is thought to come from the Norse *birka-dair* ('valley of the birches'), aside from its compact church up the hill. To explore its lovely setting, park by the River Bothy café (page 126), tucked off the northwestern side of the A9 (and which gives you a good excuse to stop for a slice of cake). A clutch of graceful 19th-century buildings are set along this side road, including the office of the Welbeck Estate which, despite being based in Nottinghamshire, owns the Braemore and Langwell Estate, which includes Berriedale. (It was the 19th-century owner of Langwell, Sir John Sinclair, who was responsible for moving people to Badbea; see opposite.)

Despite the A9 running in parallel, this side of the village still has a tucked-away feeling. Head south from the estate office and the road soon becomes grassed over to cross two old bridges, built by Thomas Telford in the 19th century: the first crosses Berriedale Water and

the second Langwell Water, with the confluence of the two just to the east, beyond the A9. After the second bridge, the track heads up to the left to meet the A9: cross very carefully to head down Mill Road, directly opposite. Follow the road, with the river running behind some handsome old cottages and, a little further on, the old saw and grain mills; rocky, tree-clad cliffs rise up on the opposite side of the water. When you reach a gate, walk through it, passing a strip of immaculate, cream-coloured cottages.

At the end, the river makes a sharp left, leaving an exposed, jagged cliff jutting out. When I visited in early summer, the hillsides were a bright green and the cliffs crammed full of noisy, nesting kittiwakes. Look up on your right here to see a 19th-century tower that was used as a navigation building; if you look back up at it from the other side of the river, you'll see it's actually one of a pair, known as the Duke's Candlesticks. (It's possible to reach the hilltop and navigation towers by heading back to the A9, turning left and then taking another left turn on to a tarmac road, directly opposite the road to Langwell House; from here, a track and then a path leads up the hill – a walk of about quarter of a mile). On the lower cliffs directly ahead is the remains of medieval Berriedale Castle; there's not much to see now but it clearly would have commanded quite an imposing position.

The view of the opposite shore from here is exceedingly pretty, with a neat white line of shore cottages set against the green hills. You can cross to this side via a narrow wooden bridge, which should only be used by a maximum of two people at a time and is very bouncy. In front of the cottages is a pebble beach, steeply sloping and sandy in places, with dramatic rocky outcrops at both its northern end and to the south across the river. It's a peaceful spot, broken only by the kittiwakes, who sound at times like amateur trumpeters. Considering how wide the peaty river is further up, it's surprising how narrow it is by the time it channels through the pebbly shore. It's possible, particularly at low tide, to pick your way across the river mouth to explore the rocks and crevasses on the other side. On both sides of the shore, the cliffs look like they've been assembled from neat, sloping slices of rock.

◀ **1** The old fishing village of Dunbeath. **2** Pretty pink sea thrift can be found all along the coast in spring and early summer. **3** The remnants of Badbea Clearance Village. **4** Berriedale.

¶¶ FOOD & DRINK

River Bothy KW7 6HE ☎ 01593 751569 ⊘ theriverbothy.co.uk. Tucked just off the A9, this lovely deli café is stuffed full of delicious food, as well as tasteful gifts and homewares. It's a popular place, with tables outside in nice weather and cosy tables inside when it's less clement. Staff are friendly, and the menu ranges from hearty breakfasts to freshly made sandwiches and bagels, burgers and afternoon tea. Amazing cakes, too.

4 DUNBEATH

The old fishing village of Dunbeath feels like a place of two halves, split as it is over both sides of Dunbeath Water. My favourite place to start a visit here is on its northern side, by the harbour, where a large breakwater now dominates. Compared to other harbours on this stretch of coast, this is a particularly large one, thanks in part to Dunbeath's wide bay, though still far from crowded with boats – I counted just four on my last visit. On the far eastern side of the harbour are a few interesting relics of its fishing heritage: the large, three-storey building was the warehouse for the industry, while the white, curved-roof building a little further on that juts out from a wall in the hillside was the ice house; beyond this is a white bothy, once used for storing equipment and with bunks for fishermen to stay in. Just beyond is a grassy, flat area with picnic tables and a fine view towards the white, clifftop **Dunbeath Castle** (⊘ dunbeath.co.uk) on the other side of the harbour. The castle, which was built in the 15th century but remodelled in the mid 19th century, is a private residence and was put on the market for a cool £25 million in 2023. At the time of writing, it was still possible to visit the gardens by appointment but this may change once the new owners are in place, so check online for the latest information. Beyond the picnic area, the path leads to a little cove at the base of the cliffs where, at low tide, the rocks give way to golden sand.

Retrace your steps back up towards the harbour from here; on the left, facing the water, between the warehouse and the ice house, is a statue of a small boy and a giant fish: this is Kenn and his salmon, from Neil M Gunn's novel *Highland River* – Dunbeath Strath, the valley in which the village sits, was the main inspiration for this book by the esteemed local author (see opposite), who wrote extensively (and beautifully) about Caithness.

Just north of the warehouse, on the northern edge of the car park, is the **boat shed**, now part of the museum (see opposite) and home to a restored yacht that was built here in 1880 for the Berriedale Estate. Here you can also see old photos of Dunbeath and information about how the fishing industry grew in the village.

For more insight into Dunbeath, head up to the main museum on the southern side of the river; on a map it looks some distance away but it's a very pleasant walk of just under half a mile. Cross the river on the footbridge just north of the harbour. On the other side, turn left and then almost immediately right when the path splits soon after; about 35yds further on, veer right again to follow the footpath as it curves uphill to eventually meet the road. At the top, there are great views over the harbour; from here, continue straight up to follow the road towards a cluster of buildings straight ahead; the museum is the first building on your left.

The most striking aspect of the **Dunbeath Heritage Museum** (The Old School, KW6 6ED ✆ 01593 731233 ⌂ dunbeath-heritage.org.uk

NEIL M GUNN

Strength was the keynote of this coast, a passionless remorseless strength, unyielding as the rock, tireless as the water...
Neil M Gunn, *Highland River*

Born in Dunbeath in 1891, Neil Miller Gunn is widely regarded as one of Scotland's most important early 20th-century writers. His work captured life in the Highlands, particularly Caithness, during this period, and beautifully evokes a sense of the landscape that remains true today – I've frequently been stopped in my tracks by how much his lyrical descriptions match my own experience of the light and scenery of Caithness.

Gunn's father, James, was the skipper of a herring fishing boat, and his mother was a domestic servant – Gunn's books often have a strong matriarchal figure in them, said to have been inspired by her. He published his first novel, *The Grey Coast*, in 1926, while living and working in Inverness as a Customs and Excise Officer, but it was his second, *Morning Tide* (1931), that brought him critical acclaim.

Highland River, one of his most celebrated novels, was published in 1937 and dedicated to his brother John. In a later-written introduction to the novel, John's son Diarmid provides insight into how much the book – and its protagonist, Kenn himself – reflects John's life. 'If the river is central to young Kenn's life,' Diarmid writes, 'the sea occupies another dimension; it is about him in the same way the sky is above him.'

After the publication of *Highland River*, Gunn left his career to concentrate on writing – publishing 20 books in total before his death in 1973, though he gave up writing after the death of his wife, ten years earlier.

⊙ Apr–Sep 10.00–17.00 Mon–Fri, 10.00–16.00 Sun; Oct–Mar 10.00–16.00 Tue, Wed & Fri) is arguably the beautiful decoration on the floor of the first room, in which a river – the 'Highland River' of Neil M Gunn's eponymous book, meanders and flows, while salmon leap and birds swoop, accompanied by quotes from Gunn's work. As well as providing more information about Gunn's life and work (page 127), the museum covers both ancient and modern local history – not just limited to Dunbeath but to Caithness as a whole.

If Gunn's words inspire you to explore his Highland river, take a walk upstream along the river on its eastern side; WalkHighlands details a very pleasant 6½-mile option, but you can easily just walk the beginning part of it, to just beyond Dunbeath's nicely intact broch, which avoids a steep climb.

These days, very few thatched croft houses can be found in the region, but there is one preserved example a mile north of Dunbeath, at **Laidhay Croft Museum** (KW6 6EH ⊘ laidhay.co.uk ⊙ Easter–Sep 10.00–16.00 daily). Set inside a 250-year-old Caithness longhouse, this little museum, which has been in operation since 1974, reflects what life would have been like for its occupants – the Bethune family, who lived here from 1842 to 1968. There's also a small tea room on site.

¶¶ FOOD & DRINK

Tasty Toes The Harbour ⊘ 07584 568565 ⬛. It doesn't get much fresher than this: the seafood served up from this little trailer opposite the harbour has come straight off the previous night's boat. The brioche rolls crammed with either lobster or crab are absolutely delicious, especially when enjoyed with a sea breeze by the water.

5 LATHERONWHEEL & SURROUNDS

Pretty cottages, a butcher's and a lovely old church line the main street at Latheronwheel, three miles northeast of Dunbeath. The grand three-storey building with griffins above the porch on the northern side of the main road as you enter is known as 'The Blends' – built as the Latheronwheel Hotel in 1835 (the first building in this planned village), it got its nickname in the 1890s as its proprietor blended his own whisky. It's a B&B today.

At its far, southern end, the main road twists down to the harbour, built around 1840 when the herring boom (page 130) was in full swing. The cliffs enclosing it have a wild feel, with a small rock stack sitting just offshore; come when the weather is inclement and the tide is high and it feels especially so, with the spearmint-coloured water crashing against the harbour walls. You can get a fabulous view over the harbour by walking up over the headland at its southern end, reached by crossing the river on the old bridge and following the John O'Groats Trail signpost. Continuing south along here reveals the nooks and crannies of the coast, which is really quite spectacular.

A particularly delightful walk up **Latheronwheel Strath** begins from the harbour; it's just a mile and a half and, though it involves a bit of an uphill climb,

"Continuing south along here reveals the nooks and crannies of the coast, which is really quite spectacular."

is easy enough to do with children. From the harbour, head northwest up the road, past the old bridge; as the road curves right, look for a small footpath sign on your left. Follow the path through the trees, alongside the Burn of Latheronwheel, which widens as the path crosses a bridge to gush over dark rocks. It is an easy path through trees full of birdsong in what is clearly a loved area of woodland, with bird feeders, birdhouses and a small patch of tasteful fairy houses carved out of old tree stumps.

After the fairy glen, steps climb uphill through the mixed woodland, with the sound of water constantly accompanying you. When the path reaches the A9, cross over (carefully) to go up the road (signed for Smerral) diagonally opposite; follow the road as it curves right past a beautiful old house. When the road turns left, continue straight, following the footpath sign to Latheronwheel bridge, 200yds further on. After the bridge, the road curves right to run alongside the north side of the burn. Continue to follow the road, keeping left when it splits just before the A9: at the end a short flight of steps leads down to the pavement alongside the main road. Cross carefully again and turn left to walk up the road; after about 100yds you'll see another short set of steps on your right – take these and then walk diagonally opposite to reach the main road through the village. You can then follow the road back down to the harbour. For a particularly great view en route, follow the John O'Groats Trail sign (♀ ND 19060 32270) up on to the northern headland, located on the left just before a scenically placed bench. You can continue north along the coast here, too, for more excellent views and beautiful scenery.

SILVER DARLINGS

The harbours of the east coast tell the story of the once-mighty **herring industry**, which began to expand at the end of the 1700s but reached its peak in the following century. Today, the harbours at villages like Dunbeath, Latheronwheel and Lybster – and even at Wick – seem too big for the size of their villages, but in the 19th century these would all have been crammed full with boats and the people who came here to work on them.

Known as 'silver darlings' (a term later memorialised in Neil M Gunn's 1941 novel of the same name), herring has been fished in Scotland since Neolithic times, but it was in the 19th century that cured herring from the region dominated the European markets. This was aided by the development and expansion of the railways, which meant that the fish could reach the markets more quickly.

The success of the herring industry depended not only on the fishermen but also the women on land, gutting and preserving the catch. It was common for women to follow the boats down the coast, working as 'herring lassies'; evocative pictures in the museum in Wick (page 139) show just how busy the harbourside was with women gutting and packing herring.

The industry was interrupted by the two world wars but its ultimate collapse in the 1960s was due to overfishing. Herring fishing does still take place today but is limited by strict quotas and management.

Two miles northeast of Latheronwheel is **Northshore Pottery** (Mill of Forse, Latheron KW5 6DG ✆ 01593 741777 ⌂ northshorepottery. co.uk ⊙ Apr–mid-Dec 10.00–17.00 Tue–Sat), based in an old mill. Ceramic artist Jenny Mackenzie Ross' beautiful and slightly quirky work ranges from geologically inspired sculpture to more traditional pots and mugs, with shapes and glazing that feel full of movement and rooted to the earth. Don't miss the wood-fired kiln outside, which she built herself.

6 LYBSTER
🏠 North Star Glamping

During the 19th-century herring boom (see above), Lybster was the third-biggest herring port in Scotland – which goes some way to explain the wide, rather grand main road that you're greeted by in the heart of this now quiet village, which was laid out in 1802. As at Latheronwheel, the road curves down to the harbour through fertile hills; though you'll likely see only a few boats bobbing in the water today, its size is a giveaway as to how busy it would have been at the height of the herring industry, when 101 boats worked from here. At the head of the harbour is the old cream and red lighthouse, built in 1884.

In one of the old harbour buildings is the village's heritage museum, **Waterlines Heritage Centre** (✆ 01593 721520 Waterlines Lybster ⊙ May–Sep 10.00–15.00 Wed–Sat), where you can learn more about Lybster and its fishing history. In the exhibition room upstairs, a great diagram of the cliffs describes the animals that live in and above them – from kestrels in the air to voles on the ground and seals and orcas in the water. Interactive elements, such as being able to make rubbings of fossil casts and lift lids on barrels to find out interesting facts, provide plenty to interest younger visitors. I loved the photo of the gutter girl with her fingers bandaged in cloots (cloths) to avoid them being cut while she did her work. Downstairs is a café (cash only) – snap up a crab roll if they're available. For a particularly exciting approach to the museum, you can get here by boat with Caithness Seacoast (page 143) from Wick.

SPECIAL STAYS

North Star Glamping Norland Rd ✆ 07747 588253 ⊘ northstarglamping.co.uk. These two lovely pods are like little Tardises – considerably bigger inside than they look from the outside. Though they may be compact, everything you need for a self-catering stay is here, with the bonus of delicious homemade shortbread to welcome you. They're beautifully designed, but also supremely comfortable and cosy, with a lovely view over fields and a private barbecue area outside. Within walking distance of Lybster, it's in the perfect position from which to explore this stretch of coast, and the handy welcome pack has loads of information to get you started.

7 GREY CAIRNS OF CAMSTER

♀ ND 26124 44141

Six miles north of Lybster, these two cairns appear almost like huge, elongated molehills on the moorland landscape that surrounds them. Originally built over 5,000 years ago, they were restored in the 1980s and now provide an insight into what these structures might have looked like in their day – particularly interesting if you've seen or are going to see the cairns on the Yarrows Archaeological Trail (page 136).

From the parking area, a boardwalk leads over boggy ground to the cairns – if you look down as you walk you'll understand that there's a very good reason for the boardwalk here, so do stay on it. The cairn on the left is the Round Cairn; it's possible to go inside by a combination of

ROB ATHERTON/DT

ADRIAN SZATEWICZ/DT

STEVE ALLEN/DT

LINDAMORE/DT

crawling and squatting (depending on how tall you are), but it is rather tight and claustrophobic for a short while before you reach the end, where there's room to stand. This tunnel originally allowed access to the dead for a chosen few – burnt human bones and parts of skeletons, plus pottery, were found here, though my children were relieved to find they were empty now. If you can make it inside, it is quite amazing to do so and be able to stand and look at how these structures were made, with their stacks of stones – and to contemplate just how old they are.

To the north along the boardwalk is the Long Cairn, almost 200ft in length, with doorways leading into two separate and unconnected chambers. Of the two, the left-hand door provides the easiest access, with the tunnel opening up into a tall chamber with a concrete roof with a skylight in it (modern additions, of course). It's quite interesting to speak in here – you'll hear your voice come back to you a fraction of a second after you've spoken, causing an odd kind of vibration. I'll admit that I couldn't bring myself to crawl into the tight, puddle-strewn right-hand tunnel – not even in the name of research – but my adventurous seven-year-old did and said it was 'fun'. Make of that what you will.

A mile and a half north of here is **Camster Windfarm** (♀ ND 25721 46193), which sits on the very eastern edge of Flow Country (page 113). I know windfarms are quite divisive – and here in Caithness it's no different, particularly as many people feel that they get more than their fair share of them – but personally I love the striking juxtaposition between the modern turbines and the surrounding, rather flat countryside. From the car park on the site's southwestern side, you can do a straightforward four-mile walk around the turbines – it's a level walk through a landscape that doesn't vary hugely, but there's a fascination in being able to walk in the shadows cast by these huge structures.

Interestingly, this area shows two different approaches to blanket bog: parts that were drained in the 1970s and '80s to allow for the planting of non-native conifers for forestry, and – in the **Flows of Leanas**, which borders the windfarm to the northeast – an area of peatland that was never planted. Many of the trees have now been cleared from the site

◀ 1 In Latheronwheel the road twists down to the harbour which was built around 1840 during the herring boom. 2 Some 365 steps make up the Whaligoe Steps, well trodden by fisherwomen who brought the herring from the harbour to Wick. 3 During the boom, Lybster was the third-biggest herring port in Scotland. 4 The Grey Cairns of Camster.

to restore it to its previous state – one of the conditions given in order to establish a windfarm here. The route follows a gravel track the whole way, but I'd recommend taking a photo of the map on the signboard at the start to help keep track of where you are, as numerous other paths lead off towards the turbines themselves. In spring, listen out for skylarks in the grasses and bees zipping low across the path.

8 WHALIGOE STEPS

Parking at ♀ ND 3197 4034; take the unsigned road on the east side of the A99, opposite the signed turning for the Cairn of Get

Of the many remnants of the North Highlands' herring industry along the northeast coast, this is arguably the most evocative: 365 steps cut up the steep cliffside from a narrow natural harbour. Built in the 18th century, they were used by fisherwomen who would carry the fish (once they'd gutted them) that were brought in here up the steps and then on to Wick, eight miles north; no small feat in itself, and you'll struggle not to feel sympathy for them as you climb back up from the bottom.

"In spring, the wildflowers and sea thrift on the cliffs are beautiful, adding colour to the dark stone."

The steps are rather tucked away, to the east of a little row of houses; parking is round the back of here but limited so I'd advise coming early or late in the day for the best chance of a space. From the car park, you take the right turn to follow the track around a house. Look to the right just before the start of the steps to find a path (signposted) to a viewpoint on the other side of the cliffs; it involves a bit of a climb but affords a view of the whole of the stairway. In spring, the wildflowers and sea thrift on the cliffs are beautiful, adding colour to the dark stone.

At the start of the descent there's a rock memorial to Etta B Juhle – in 1975 a landslide covered the steps with a huge amount of rubble, and Etta was responsible for clearing it all, apparently using little more than a bucket and a small shovel. Today, the steps are maintained by a team of volunteers; you might meet one of them, Davy Nicholson, who lives in one of the cottages at the top. Davy, whose father was a fisherman here, is a mine of information, and may even invite you into his home to look at a photo of Whaligoe from the 1940s. The last boat stopped using the harbour in the 1960s.

The first time I walked down the steps, I was pleasantly surprised – I'd expected them to feel much more perilous but they feel surprisingly contained as they zigzag down the cliffside. Just before the final flight of stairs, a wide, flat, grassy area – the Bink – leads to the remains of the old salt store; look too for the round barking kettle, set in the grass. This would have been filled with a solution made from tree bark that was used to help preserve fishing nets. You can walk along here a short way for a view of the cliffs on the northern side, where noisy birds swoop in and out. At times, the force of the water against the rock is such that it sounds like someone is banging a door. Standing among these ancient cliffs makes you feel rather small, and you can't help but wonder how it would have felt to have been here centuries ago, knowing you had to walk up with a basket full of herring on your back, before another long walk to Wick.

At the very bottom is the Neist, where boats would have been pulled out of the water before the Bink was constructed. You can see a rusting old winch here, which would have aided this – it's not hard to see why it was needed, given the distance still from the water. It's humbling to stand at the bottom, enclosed by the dark cliffs and accompanied by the squawk of the seabirds, the steady drip of water down the rocky walls and the relentless passage of the waves, and think how this view hasn't changed much in hundreds of years – except for the lack of boats, and the wind farm on the distant horizon.

On your way back up, look for a sign in the obviously newer stretch of wall that says 'Etta 1975', just above the second corner. At the third corner, a plaque states that flights two and three were repaired by Charles Juhlenski – Etta's son.

Just before you reach the top, it's possible to follow a narrow path to the right, which takes you out to the top of the northern cliff above the steps. The view from here is somewhat vertigo-inducing but allows you to see a waterfall plunging down a sheer cliff face; as you return to the main path you'll see another, smaller waterfall on your right, which tumbles so prettily down the rock it almost looks artificial.

If the parking area is full when you arrive, one option is to park instead in the parking area ($\mathcal{Q}$ ND 31879 40822) for the **Cairn o'Get**, 600yds northwest, on the other side of the A99. The cairn itself can be reached via a 500yd waymarked walk through fields and up a hill that starts (signposted) just southwest of the parking area. This burial site

Yarrows Archaeological Trail

✳ OS Explorer 450; start: parking area at South Yarrows ♀ ND 30599 43588;
2½ miles; moderate

This walk is a great way to see a few of Caithness's many archaeological sites, including a broch (page 92), as well as offering an opportunity to appreciate the variety of the region's landscapes. Though this is an established trail, the waymarkers disappear at times, so I'd advise not relying on them – the instructions below and the map here should help avoid confusion. Be warned that it can get quite boggy underfoot.

1 Begin by going through the gate in the southeastern corner of the car park and following the path east towards Loch of Yarrows (actually a reservoir); it can be a bit muddy so you may have to pick your way, keeping to the left of a farm fence. Cross the stile on your right just before the loch and walk alongside the water – you'll be able to see the broch ahead of you as the path curves through rushes. Go through a gate and the broch is directly ahead; the path is faint now and heads up to an information board. From here, you can wander up to and around the broch, which is most impressive from its northern side, where its shape is most obvious. Afterwards, go through the gate immediately behind the information board, then turn slightly left to follow the farm fence, keeping it on your left.

2 After just over 100yds, the fence on your left is broken by a gate – go through it and cross the burn to go through another gate. Turn immediately right and follow the fence until you reach another gate. If you look ahead, slightly to the left, you'll see a stile; walk up to this (there is no path at this point, so you'll be walking across the field) and climb over it. Almost immediately after, across a narrow path between the fences, is another stile – climb over this one as well and walk straight towards the fence ahead. When you reach it, go through the gate on your right and follow the faint path up to the hilltop ahead, the path undulating through the heather. Once you start to descend from here, you'll see a white-topped post ahead, which is what you're heading for, though the path is fairly indistinct en route.

3 At the post, follow the path southwest over moorland; it winds down through rushes to another white-topped post by a stile: climb the stile and wind through heather towards the next post ahead. After this one, the path soon turns left and heads back uphill through tightly packed heather to an information board by some hut circles that are quite hard to discern. Continue straight on from here, veering right to cross a burn on a flagstone bridge before climbing again through heather. It does get increasingly boggy as you climb steadily towards another post visible on a hill; en route you meet and cross a stile and then follow the path uphill to your right (the post will disappear from sight for a little while but keep climbing up). ▶

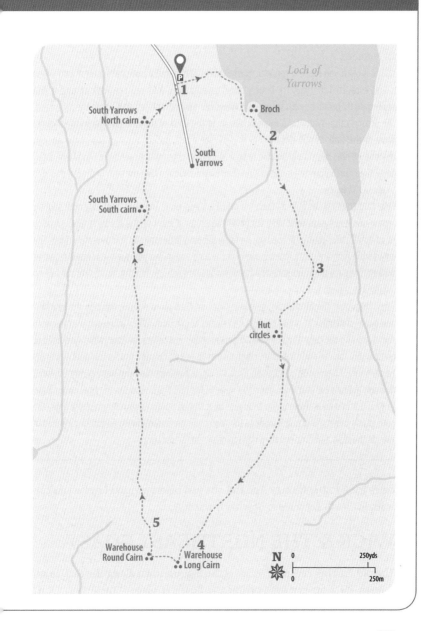

South Yarrows
North cairn

Loch of
Yarrows

Broch

South
Yarrows

South Yarrows
South cairn

6

3

Hut
circles

5

Warehouse
Round Cairn

4

Warehouse
Long Cairn

N

0 — 250yds

0 — 250m

Yarrows Archaeological Trail (continued)

◄ When you reach the post, you'll see the first cairn ahead and realise that you haven't finished climbing. At this point, however, the views to your left are increasingly good, looking out over the North Sea.

4 The first cairn you meet is the Warehouse Long Cairn; pottery and skulls were found when it was excavated in 1853. It's largely grass covered now, and you can walk around it and appreciate its position, with staggering views out towards the sea and across the moorland. The second cairn, Warehouse Round Cairn, is to the west of this one and marks the highest point of the trail; as you climb up to it you'll see a tall modern cairn on top of the ancient chambered one. You should be able to spot Morven to the south, beyond the wind farm. From here, head north downhill to the information board and then take the path to the left down to a stile in the fence.

5 Take care crossing the stile as there's a bit of a steep drop. The path goes downhill slightly afterwards and heads west first; it's boggy again for a short while, before it turns right to head uphill. After you've climbed up, it's fairly flat for a little while as you traverse a ridge. The views from here are great, looking out over the loch and giving you a sense of how far you've walked. The path then undulates its way downhill, through heather that was full of bees when I walked in spring.

6 You'll then start climbing again, gently at first and then more steeply, through the heather- and gorse-clad hillside, as you near South Yarrows South cairn. When you reach the top, you'll see a gate and the cairn ahead. The path gets muddier just before the gate, which you need to go through. You can circle the cairn, climb up on top and go through the narrow doorway on its eastern side. Afterwards, go through the gate on its northern side and head gently downhill through the heather and then along the ridge of the hill. You'll soon see the final cairn ahead of you, reached by walking down to a gate by it. This is South Yarrows North; from here, the path winds down the grassy hillside to the road, with green farm fields and the loch ahead of you. At the road, turn left and then right to return to the car park.

dates back to the Bronze Age and sits just below ground level – you can walk inside to get a sense of what it was like.

WICK & THE NORTHEAST COAST

The old herring centre of Wick is the biggest town along the east coast, though it's a far cry today from the bustling place it once was. Don't write it off, though: it's worth at least an hour or two of your time to appreciate its heritage, and from here you can strike out on some fabulous coastal walks. Most visitors pass through the town to reach the ruins of nearby **Castle Sinclair Girnigoe**, which overlooks the wide sweep of **Sinclair's Bay** and its lovely beaches. From here, many press straight on to the literal end of the road – **John O'Groats** – but the coast en route is littered with interesting historical sites, both ancient and modern, as well as lovely, often deserted, beaches. This stretch of the coast is often prime **orca**-spotting territory, particularly in the summer months – you'll need patience, luck and a decent pair of binoculars.

9 WICK

There's no denying that Wick has seen better days: arrive here on an overcast day and its grey-stone buildings can feel rather forlorn. This is particularly true on the northern side of the wide River Wick – on Bridge Street, where the grand old Victorian buildings look like they could do with a bit of love, and on High Street, which has more than its fair share of closed-up shops. However, plans are afoot for a much-needed regeneration of this area, so this will hopefully change over the next decade. Immediately south of the bridge is tiny Ebenezer Place – just two yards long, it holds the world record for being the shortest street in the world.

At the height of the herring-fishing boom (page 130) in the 1860s, Wick harbour was used by over 1,100 fishing boats – a staggering number that's easier to imagine when you see just how big the port is. Today, it is comparatively empty and home to rather more pleasure boats then it would have been in the 19th century. If you're here in the summer months, look out for the graceful red sails of the *Isabella Fortuna*: it dates back to 1890 and is now looked after by the Wick Society (⌂ wickheritage.org).

The harbour, which sits in Pulteneytown (page 143) on the south side of Wick Bay, makes a good place to start exploring. From here, streets spread south in a neat grid: this was just one of a number of Caithness settlements that were planned out in a grid system in the early 19th century. Immediately west of the harbour is the jam-packed **Wick Heritage Museum** (18–27 Bank Row ✆ 01955 605205 ⌂ wickheritage. org ⊙ Easter–Oct 10.00–17.00 Mon–Fri, 11.00–15.00 Sat). The exhibits range from old shop items (all of which have been donated rather than bought) and examples of Caithness Glass (including the *Mastermind* trophy), which was established in the town in 1961 but is now based in Perth and Kinross, to a photographers' studio and a school room. In the last, look on the back wall to see the photographic recreation of an L S Lowry painting, *Steps at Wick* (1937), with local schoolchildren in high-vis jackets.

In the courtyard, you can climb up the stairs to see a huge anchor that was dredged from Sinclair's Bay (page 146) – no one knows which boat it was from – and for sweeping views over Pulteneytown roofs and the harbour. In the cooperage you can see how the barrels – for fish rather than whisky – were made, while nearby is a kippering kiln, which still retains its smoky smell.

For me, it is the 19th-century photos dotted around that really bring the museum and the town to life, from the evocative portraits of divers and a girl lounging with a book and looking older than her years to the images of the harbour crammed with boats. Don't miss the picture of seated families in a cave; it has 'Tinklers At Home' written on it and shows some of the people who lived in nearby Tinker's Cave, which is thought to have been inhabited into the early 20th century.

Bank Row, where the museum is, was badly hit by bombs during World War II, which is evident in the architectural makeup of the street now. Two 100lb bombs were dropped here on 1 July 1940, in what was mainland Britain's first daylight bombing raid; 15 people were killed, seven of whom were under ten years old. Just under 100yds east of the museum is a peaceful **memorial garden** dedicated to them, and to the three people who lost their lives during another bombing raid in the October of the same year, on the site where the July bombs were dropped. The garden incorporates parts of the destroyed buildings, which have been decorated with murals. It's a nice spot to sit for a while – look out for the lovely herring mosaics on the back wall, and the wooden boat full of flowers.

Immediately east of the garden are the **Black Stairs**, immortalised by L S Lowry's painting (see above) and built around 1820 to link the higher residential area to the harbour. If you walk up the stairs and straight on for about 150yds, you'll reach large Argyle Square, which feels

1 Sinclair's Bay – an almost three-mile, white-sand beach. 2 Castle of Old Wick – only the remains of the tower survive today. 3 Displays at the Wick Heritage Museum. 4 Old Pulteney Distillery, Wick. 5 The atmospheric remains of Castle Sinclair Girnigoe. ▶

almost too grand for the houses that surround it. From here, it's a short walk east along Grant Street and then south on Huddart Street to **Old Pulteney Distillery** (⊘ oldpulteney.com ⊙ Apr–Sep 10.00–17.00 Mon–Sat; Oct–Mar 10.00–16.30 Mon–Fri). With it being a familiar brand, I was surprised at its small size – and even more surprised to discover that only eight people work here. This is a perfect Slow distillery: established in 1826, it remains firmly rooted in its community and surroundings, using water from Loch Hempriggs, which, if you take a tour, you can see being channelled into the distillery. New technology is eschewed in favour of long-established methods of production – though the whisky now travels by road rather than water, which was used when it was first established and the region lacked road links. Amusingly, the stumpy appearance of the wash still is due to it having been too tall to fit into the still house – and the top of it (the classic swan's neck) being chopped off to fit. Four tours are offered, ranging from 90 minutes to 2½ hours and finishing with tastings in the small shop.

From the distillery, heading north up Huddart Street will bring you to Bexley Terrace where, on the grassy area in front, is the **Seafarers Memorial**, unveiled in 2023 in honour of 'those who were lost in the wild seas around our coast'. Sculpted by Alan Beattie Herriot, it shows a man with one arm outstretched, holding a fish, his body partly made up of scales and waves. The view from here over the harbour is worth the climb up alone.

From the memorial, you can head down to follow a path east and then south along the coast. Shortly after the path joins the road, look for a painted white rock with the word 'cave' on it to your left, from where a path leads down to **Tinker's Cave**. Though it was once occupied by cave dwellers (a photograph of whom you can see in the museum, page 139), it's now very much the domain of gulls and terns, whose cries echo around the salt- and seaweed-emblazoned rocks.

Back on the road, after another 200yds you'll see the **Trinkie** below you – this well-loved swimming pool, built in 1931, is set into the rocks and filled by the tide, with its flat-rocked sides providing the perfect spot for picnicking and sunbathing after a dip. The coastline south of Wick is fabulously craggy, and you could easily spend hours walking, spotting caves, sea stacks and natural arches (it's part of the John O'Groats Trail; page 145). If you want something to aim for, you could head out to the **Castle of Old Wick**, just over half a mile south of the Trinkie, which is

A TALE OF TWO TOWNS

It's thought that Wick's name comes from the Norse word *vík*, meaning bay, and it was mentioned in documents as early as 1140, during Norse rule. The wide bay on which the town sits would have been used as a harbour for Viking vessels like longboats, and the Castle of Old Wick (see opposite) was also built during this period. It became a Royal Burgh in 1589, which gave it special privileges, including trading rights, by way of a royal charter and meant it was represented in the Parliament of Scotland. Wick's heyday came as the herring industry expanded: within just five years at the end of the 18th century, the number of fishing boats in the town had expanded from 32 to 200.

Following a visit in 1790, a young Thomas Telford recommended that a new harbour and town should be built on the southern side of the river; the British Fisheries Society subsequently bought 390 acres of land there to build a new town. Designed by Telford, this new town was split into two distinct areas: a lower industrial area around the harbour, and a higher residential area – linked by the Black Stairs (page 140). The foundations for the new town – called **Pulteneytown** after the Chairman of the British Fisheries Society, Sir William Pulteney – were laid in 1806.

By the time the harbour was completed in 1811, it was already too small for the boats using it so a new extension was designed and built, opening in 1830. At the height of the herring boom, 1,100 boats fished from here, supplemented by around 3,000 gutters and packers on the shore. It was said that it was possible to walk from one side of the harbour to the other just by going from boat to boat.

The two sides of the harbour – Wick and Pulteneytown – remained effectively separate until the start of the 20th century. Today, you'll likely experience them as one entity, separated by the river, but they still feel very much like separate areas in many ways. This is particularly true to many residents – one volunteer at the heritage museum told me how she had moved to Wick after living in Pulteneytown for her whole life, but how she had to move back because 'it didn't feel right'.

thought to have been built in the 1160s by the Earl of Caithness, during Viking rule of the region. Only the remains of the tower still exist today, though it's believed that this would have formed the main part of the small castle. It's not possible to access the castle, but its position is fantastic, perched on a grass-covered rocky outcrop. From here the coast path weaves and winds along the cliffs with staggering views and blissful solitude; at times the dramatic headlands and stacks almost resemble castle ruins themselves.

For an alternate view of the coast here, you can take a boat trip with **Caithness Seacoast** (Harbour Rd ✆ 01955 609200 ◈ caithness-seacoast.co.uk ☺ Apr–Oct), which offers a number of trips, including a leisurely harbour cruise aimed at children, a rather thrilling three-hour tour out to the uninhabited Pentland Skerries islands, and a trip down to the Waterlines Centre at Lybster (page 131).

10 CASTLE SINCLAIR GIRNIGOE & NOSS HEAD

🏠 **Lighthouse Keeper's Cottage**

📍 ND 37879 54971

In my opinion, the ruined Castle Sinclair Girnigoe, four miles north of Wick, is the most atmospheric and worth visiting of all castles in the North Highlands. Though what remains today is just a fraction of the original buildings, there is more than enough to conjure up a sense of the castle's size and grandeur, and its position, perched on rocky crags, is hugely evocative.

"In my opinion, the ruined Castle Sinclair Girnigoe is the most atmospheric of all castles in the North Highlands."

Access is via a car park (📍 ND 38423 54670) at the end of the public road to Noss Head, though you can also walk out here on the John O'Groats Trail (see opposite). From the car park, it's only about 700yds along the signposted path to the castle; a wooden bridge provides access into the ruins, though at my last visit this was closed off, with no indication of when it would reopen. Assuming you will be able to re-enter at some point, there's plenty to explore inside the crumbling walls, with paths winding up to nooks and crannies, and windows you can peer through.

Castle Sinclair Girnigoe is actually two castles: the more easterly and better-preserved ruin, Castle Girnigoe, dates from the late 15th century, while the westerly side of the ruins is Castle Sinclair, built in the early 17th century. Both belonged to the Sinclair Earls of Caithness – the newer building was an addition to the original. The English Parliamentary army used the castle from 1651, during which time its condition suffered; a family dispute over succession led to doors, roofs, floors and furniture being removed in 1680, and it was never repaired or lived in after this.

Even if you can't go inside, it's still a fantastic place to be close to, with fabulous views over the wide curve of Sinclair's Bay (page 146), and the craggy coastline peppered with sea stacks and arches. The castle is so much a part of the cliffs on which it was built that it's hard at times to tell where one stops and the other begins. If you can, time your visit to coincide with sunset – you'll often have the site much to yourself, and the setting sun casts the ruins in blushing shades of pink, purple and orange.

On the castle's southern side is a small, pebbly cove; it's a peaceful spot and the water here is beautifully clear and blue, if surprisingly deep. You'll often find countless rock piles stacked up here – at the risk of sounding like a spoilsport, I'd urge you not to add your own as doing so can damage the shoreline's natural defences and disturb the natural habitat of shore and sea creatures.

From the castle, you can follow a faint path northeast along the coast, which reveals little coves and stacks that look almost like Jenga puzzles.

THE JOHN O'GROATS TRAIL

⌀ jogt.org.uk

One of the best ways to explore the coastal landscape of the east coast, but particularly Caithness, is on the John O'Groats Trail, a 147-mile **walking route** between Inverness and John O'Groats. If you do any coastal walking in the region you'll likely walk part of it, whether by accident or design. Work on the trail started in 2016 and it was fully marked by 2019, but it very much remains a work in progress.

'It's wild and often remote, while having some of the most dramatic coastal scenery in the UK,' Jay Wilson, one of the trail founders, told me. 'And, as it's still in development, it's less crowded than most coastal trails in the UK.' This is certainly something I've found to be true, even when I've walked more popular parts of the trail on warm and sunny days.

If you do fancy taking on the entire route, Jay recommends that you should have already done an easier multi-day walk like the West Highland Way so that you have an idea of what's required. 'This walk is more

demanding, with more obstacles, less secure footing and – most probably – harsher weather,' Jay said.

For more casual walkers, Jay recommends the walk south from Wick (page 142), which within two hours will take you to one of the UK's highest sea arches, or heading south from Duncansby Head (page 153). Trail markers are in place along the whole route, with the exception of a couple of short sections where there's not yet agreement with the landowner.

The route requires constant maintenance, from the strimming of bracken and cutting of gorse in the summer to repairing stiles and bridges. Visitors are welcome to volunteer to check a section and can be lent tools to help with the removal of bracken and gorse. The trail's website has extensive, useful information about the route (including details on a bag-transfer service if you're doing the whole thing), with helpful colour coding to identify the difficulty of each section.

After about half a mile, you'll meet the low wall surrounding **Noss Head Lighthouse**, sitting at the far northeastern point of the headland. Built in 1849 and engineered by Alan Stevenson, this attractive lighthouse has appealing stripes of yellow and a couple of cottages (one of which you can stay in; see below). You can walk into the lighthouse compound – turn right at the wall to reach the road and then turn left to enter – but do be aware that it is also someone's home. From here, you can head out of its southeastern side to walk south along the coast – the views, south towards Wick and east across the seemingly endless water, are stunning, and orcas are often spotted.

SPECIAL STAYS

Lighthouse Keeper's Cottage Noss Head, KW1 4QT ☎ 07733 443037
⌂ lighthousekeeperscottage.co.uk. Gorgeous accommodation in the old lighthouse keeper's cottage at Noss Head, with sea views from every window. Sleeping six in three bedrooms, it's incredibly comfortable and has been beautifully furnished with lots of coastal and Caithness-inspired art, as well as stocked with all the books, maps and information you could need, and plenty of games for rainy days as well. Quite honestly one of the best cottages we've stayed in as a family, and a perfect base from which to explore Caithness and beyond.

11 SINCLAIR'S BAY

West of Castle Sinclair Girnigoe, the coast forms a wide curve around Sinclair's Bay, with an almost three-mile white-sand beach forming the middle part of it and a beach break that's considered good for surfing. Access is possible at **Reiss**, at its southern end, with parking just beyond Wick Golf Course (♀ ND 34396 55490), or at **Keiss** at its northern end (parking ♀ ND 34366 60141). A word of warning: come at high tide and the beach is reduced to a long, skinny line of pebbles – not without its charms, as my kids will attest, but it might make you wonder where the beach you've been promised is.

For a lot of the way, the sands (and pebbles) are backed by bulbous, grass-covered dunes. From the Reiss end, you can look south and east as far as Noss Head and Castle Sinclair Girnigoe; the castle you can see in the foreground is 15th-century Ackergill Tower, which was a luxury hotel until 2019 when it was bought by an American millionaire and turned back into a private residence. From the Keiss end, you should just about be able to make out the ruins of Old Keiss Castle to the north, perched rather precariously on the cliff edge, which is part of an estate that includes the larger – and lived in – Keiss Castle, built in the Scots Baronial style in the 18th century. The ruins are in a poor state and cannot be accessed, though the John O'Groats Trail (page 145) offers good and relatively close views.

The bay was the site of a large minefield during World War II – in total, 3,000 mines were laid here during the war, making it the largest minefield in Britain at the time; it took three years for it to be entirely cleared after 1945. At the Keiss end of the bay, you can still see some square anti-tank blocks and pyramidal 'dragon's teeth' that were used to stop armoured vehicles.

12 NYBSTER BROCH

KW1 4XP ♀ ND 37010 63141; parking at ♀ ND 37031 63520 – take the turning directly opposite the village sign for Auckengill if coming from the south

The remains of this broch (page 92), two miles northeast of Keiss, have been largely taken over by grass and wildflowers. The setting, above steep-edged cliffs and the pancake-flat rocks beyond, is a dramatic one, with views to the south taking in the sweep of Sinclair's Bay to Noss Head.

From the car park, it's a 500yd walk along a clear path to the broch remains. (You can also walk here along the John O'Groats Trail from Keiss.) The first thing you come to is **Marvyn's Tower**. A memorial to the nephew of the man who excavated the broch in the 19th century, Sir Francis Barry, it is thought to have been built out of stone from the broch itself. Astonishingly, it was originally erected in the middle of the roundhouse but (thankfully) relocated and rebuilt in its current position in the 1980s.

Rough paths weave in and around the broch (do watch your footing as there are sudden drops in places). The stones here at first look like haphazardly scattered rocks, but soon show themselves to be the shapes of buildings; climb up to the highest mound and you'll see the outline of a few of them. It's thought that a huge roundhouse was first built here around 500BC, though people had already built enclosures on this site around 1000BC, and once the broch had been abandoned it was still used for a while to house the dead. It is possible to wander inside the broch, though it is quite overgrown.

When you head back to the car park, look for a path to your right after about 300yds that cuts down to a small beach. At low tide, you can walk across the amazingly flat-cut rocks – so flat they look as though someone has sliced the top off them – and peer down into the clear waters of the rock pools; I watched countless tiny fish swimming in and out of the seaweed. The layers of rock jutting out into the sea here look almost fortress like. You can then walk north to the next cove, where there's an old landing stage for fishing boats and a couple of old fishing huts, one in better shape than the other.

13 FRESWICK BAY
Parking at ♀ ND 37701 67939

There are no signs on the A99 to this long stretch of beach, so it's very much a place that you need to know about to get to – and all the better for it. It's a beautiful curve of pale sand, enclosed by two headlands: the steep, rather imposing cliffs of Ness Head to the south, and lower, gentler Skirza Head to the north. At the lowest tide, the sand gives way to rocks (perfect for rock pooling) in the shallows at its southeastern end, which is overlooked by imposing **Freswick Castle**. More a house than a castle, it's thought to have been built in the early 17th century, with additions in the following century – and below it is the foundations of a 12th-century Viking settlement. Today, the house, which has been extensively restored, is largely used as a holiday home.

From the car-parking space at the beach's northern end, it's just a 250yd walk south down the signposted footpath to the sand. Before you get on to the beach, you'll notice the huge, square blocks lining the back of it at this end: these are anti-tank blocks, used in World War II to stop armoured vehicles.

14 JOHN O'GROATS
🏠 John O'Groats Luxury Holiday Lodges & Apartments by Together Travel

In many ways John O'Groats feels like it should be the anathema to Slow travel: after all, it's a place that people come to just to take their photo against the famous sign before jumping back in their vehicle to head on to the next place. In the middle of a summer's day, it can seem like a steady chain of coaches arrives to spit out tourists. But it is, despite this, exactly the kind of place that rewards a little Slow exploration: come early in the morning or late in the day and you can avoid the worst of the crowds and use the time to explore the beautiful coastline that surrounds it.

Many people equate John O'Groats with the northernmost point on mainland Britain – after all, it's the northerly finish line for the LEJOG bike route from Land's End – but that accolade actually goes to Dunnet Head (page 155), 14 miles to the west. Still, it is the literal end of the road north, so it's not hard to understand the appeal of making it out here.

What always strikes me about John O'Groats is how low-key it is – there is relatively little in the way of traditional tourist attractions and I can't help but think that in most other places in the country, if not the world, it would be overrun with cheap gimmicks and tat. There are a couple of souvenir shops, a handful of cafés and take-aways, a campsite, a distillery and a brewery – and that's about it.

The opening of **8 Doors Distillery** (KW1 4YR 🖉 01955 482000 🖉 8doorsdistillery.com) in 2022, in a big-windowed modern building at the southeastern corner of the main car park, has helped smarten John O'Groats up a little. The village's first distillery since 1837, it was founded by local couple Kerry and Derek Campbell – the whisky, the first of which was made in autumn 2022, is made using water from the on-site borehole and will, it is hoped, be influenced by the sea air while it matures in the on-site warehouse. Of course, this being whisky, there's nothing of the single-malt range to try as yet – it needs to be matured for at least three years to be classified as Scotch – but in the meantime you can sample whiskies from the Seven Sons range of blends and malts, made using whiskies from elsewhere.

You can do this on one of the tours or in the smart whisky lounge and bar, which has views over the **Pentland Firth**.

"John O'Groats is the literal end of the road north, so it's not hard to understand the appeal of making it out here."

The name '8 Doors' is a reference to the house believed to have been built by the town's namesake, Dutchman Jan de Groot, who ran a ferry between here and Orkney in the 15th century. De Groot had seven sons which, the story goes, caused arguments about who took precedence and could sit at the head of the table. To solve the problem, de Groot built an eight-sided house with eight doors and, within it, an eight-sided table. The house no longer exists, but it's thought to have stood to the east of the large building (now self-catering accommodation) that overlooks the harbour (the octagonal tower of which is little more than an homage to the original building, which would have been much smaller).

The island you can see across the water from here is South Ronaldsay, Orkney. Until September 2023, the *Pentland Venture* ran from John O'Groats harbour to Orkney – a very popular day trip and the cause of much coach unloading every day – but now the nearest crossing to Orkney from here is the car ferry run by Pentland Ferries (⊘ pentlandferries.co.uk) from **Gills Bay**, four miles west.

I suppose it makes sense that there should be a decent amount of booze at the end of the road, and the **John O'Groats Brewery** (⊘ 07842 401571 ⊘ johnogroatsbrewery.co.uk) is very handily located just east of the harbour and the famous signpost. As well as buying a bottle of two of its very good beer, which you can enjoy inside, outside with views of the harbour, or to take away, you can sample some of the beers on draught in the tasting room and learn more about the brewery on a tour.

Booze aside, one of my favourite reasons for a trip to Groats lies half a mile south of the main car park. **Puffin Croft** (KW1 4YS ⊘ 01955 611775 ⊘ puffincroft.com) is a wonderful little petting farm, run by 'Miss Puffin'. You can buy pots of carrots at the little shop to feed the animals as you go round – though if you're like us, you'll most likely need to go back for more at least once. There are donkeys, goats, sheep, rabbits, geese and pigs, among others, all of which will happily snuffle directly from your open palm. On one April visit, we turned up just in time to watch the lambs being bottle fed – and my kids were thrilled to be invited to help. The shop also sells a lovely range of local and handmade items, such as candles (made by Miss Puffin), key rings, tablet (like a hard, crumbly fudge), animal-shaped biscuits and goose eggs directly from the croft, which make for the most indulgent scrambled eggs.

"We turned up just in time to watch the lambs being bottle fed – and my kids were thrilled to be invited to help."

The hidden charm of John O'Groats lies in the coastline that stretches beyond it, particularly to the east. Just to the north of the brewery, you'll see the archway that marks the end (or start, if you're walking north to south) of the John O'Groats Trail (page 145), and just to the left of it, a huge red foghorn that was at Duncansby Head (page 153) until the lighthouse was automated. Beyond this is the coast path, which you can follow to beautiful Sannick Bay, a little over a mile away; if the tide is low enough, another – although rougher – option is to walk along the sand and rocks between the two. The strips of white sand en route are made up of discernible bits of shell, rather than the fine sand you would normally expect.

About three-quarters of a mile from John O'Groats is **Shell Beach** (♀ ND 39013 73780). As the name suggests, the beach here is made up of even more intact shells. Spend a while combing through them and you may well find a groatie buckie – the local name for cowrie shells – which is supposed to bring luck. Caithness artist Lisa Poulsen (page 118) says that searching for a groatie buckie 'enables you to tune into your surroundings' and I'd agree with her; one June morning, after I'd been woken early by the sun, I wandered out here and spent an hour combing the shore for them, losing myself in the activity rather than my thoughts. Needless to say, it was bliss.

The most traditionally beautiful beach on this stretch of the coast is **Sannick Bay**, with a sweep of white sand and clear waters – though, if you come at low tide you'll see that, much as is the case along this whole stretch east from Groats, rocky ledges preface the sand. The most intriguing thing about Sannick Bay is that some of the stones here have been carved with lines from poems by Chilean poet Pablo Neruda – rather than looking like graffiti, the neat script, which *"Some of the stones here have been carved with lines from poems by Chilean poet Pablo Neruda."* curves around the rocks, seems almost a natural part of the landscape. Though no-one knows who made the carvings, so far around 20 of them have been found here, some in quite inaccessible places; for the best chance of spotting them, come at low tide and scour both the shoreline and the rocks at the eastern end of the bay.

From Sannick Bay, you can continue east to Duncansby Head, a mile away along the coast, though the cliff edges can be treacherous, or a little less than that if you follow the road. If you want to visit the bay by road, your best option is to park at Duncansby Head and walk from there.

 SPECIAL STAYS

John O'Groats Luxury Holiday Lodges & Apartments by Together Travel ✆ 01625 416430 ⬠ togethertravel.co.uk/destinations/scotland/john-ogroats. An extensive range of self-catering options, some in the renovated and extended old hotel overlooking the harbour, and others in smart lodges. The one-bed Jan De Groot Penthouse, set over two floors in the octagonal tower, is particularly special, with amazing views over the water towards Orkney and a gorgeous copper bath for soaking in at the end of the day.

15 DUNCANSBY HEAD & THE STACKS OF DUNCANSBY

Two miles east of John O'Groats, **Duncansby Head** is mainland Britain's most northeasterly point. At its furthest corner sits its square lighthouse, built in 1924 by David Alan Stevenson and automated in 1997. Compared to others in the region, it's relatively small and compact, possibly in part because the original cottages here were replaced by smaller structures in the early 2000s. The waters the lighthouse looks out over may well seem placid when you visit, but don't be fooled – the Pentland Firth (page 154) between Orkney (visible from here) and the mainland is a particularly dangerous stretch of water, and many shipwrecks have occurred here.

The caves, natural arches and sea stacks south of the lighthouse make this a coastline as dramatic as the water that crashes against it. In the spring and summer months, the nooks and crannies of the cliffs become home to countless nesting seabirds, from fulmars and kittiwakes to guillemots and puffins. The best place to see them is at the Geo (a geo is a coastal inlet of water) of Sclaites (♥ ND 40494 72984) – a real gash in the cliffs. To get here from the parking area, turn left at the lighthouse to follow the fence, keeping with the coast as it curves, with nothing except waves and birds to your left. In spring and summer, you'll soon hear the sound of kittiwakes as you near the geo, which is about a quarter of a mile from the lighthouse, and as you get closer the eerie cries of countless birds echoing in the caves and crevasses will surround you. As with all birdwatching, patience is rewarded – particularly with puffins, which are much smaller than you might expect and don't always appear here in the same numbers as elsewhere. The ledges where the birds gather can be seen most clearly from the geo's southern side, from where you'll also be able to see a huge natural arch in the northern rock face.

From here, it's another half a mile to the star of the show: the **Stacks of Duncansby**. It's easy enough to pick out a path along the coast, passing a scattering of other stacks and coves as you do so, but if you don't have

---

◀ **1** The Stacks of Duncansby. **2 & 3** Look for guillemots and fulmars among other species at Duncansby and Dunnet heads during the spring and summer months. **4** Drop by the John O'Groats Brewery to sample its beers. **5** Freswick Bay curves round towards imposing Freswick Castle.

HELL'S MOUTH

The **Pentland Firth** between Caithness and Orkney is known as one of the most treacherous channels in the UK. The strait, which runs between Duncansby and Dunnet heads to South Ronaldsay and Hoy in the Orkneys, marks the point at which the Atlantic Ocean and North Sea meet; the tidal flow that travels through it creates one of the world's most powerful tidal currents. This, combined with the often volatile weather, makes sea conditions here frequently violent. Over the centuries the Pentland Firth has claimed countless lives – earning it the nickname 'Hell's Mouth'.

much of a head for heights you can follow an inland path instead. The famous view of these rather pyramidal giant stacks, with Thirle Door sea arch in front, can be had from about 100yds southwest of the geo; there's no doubt that it's a staggering sight, even when you've seen it a hundred times on tourist literature, but I'd recommend that you don't stop here – continuing along the coast allows you a close-up view that many others don't press on to, and you'll see that next to the most northerly stack sits a much shorter, stumpier one. Move further south still and the shape and thus your perception of the stacks seems to change – the northernmost in particular looks a lot more two-dimensional, while the southerly one is a lot chunkier than it appears from the north. Amazingly, when I walked out here one long, sunny June evening, I was the only person doing so – it was just me, the sea and the birds, with a lone seal watching from among the waves.

THE NORTH COAST

For much of its length, the coast between John O'Groats and the Sutherland border is comparatively flat and low-lying, offering up wide views across the Pentland Firth. As you travel along the A836 west from John O'Groats, you'll notice an island not far offshore – this is **Stroma**, uninhabited since 1997, though its buildings can still be seen standing sentry on the low hillsides. Just over six miles west of Groats is the **Castle of Mey** (⌂ castleofmey.org.uk), the Queen Mother's much-beloved Scottish holiday home. The castle is used annually in summer by King Charles III (now and when he was the mere Prince of Wales), usually coinciding with the Mey Highland Games (⌂ meyhighlandgames.com ☉ first Sat in Aug).

The highest point along this part of the north coast is **Dunnet Head**, the actual northernmost point of mainland Britain, and a fabulous birdwatching spot in spring and summer. Nearby is **Dunnet Bay**, one of the North Highlands' most spectacular stretches of sand. The biggest settlement in these parts, and Caithness as a whole, is **Thurso** – worth a stop for its excellent museum.

16 DUNNET HEAD
KW14 8XS

The most northerly point of mainland Britain is reached by winding through wild and barren moorland, with the sea hidden from view for much of the way. The area immediately around the lighthouse – which dates back to 1831 – is an RSPB nature reserve, reflective of its importance as a 'seabird city' in the spring and summer months, when puffins, razorbills, guillemots, kittiwakes and fulmars nest here.

From the northern end of the car park, a path heads northwest along the lighthouse's southern boundary wall before veering off to the cliffs to the bottom left of it. In late spring and summer, you should be able to see birds swooping in and out of the cliffs from here, but you might struggle to see any more than that. You used to be able to cross the fence to the left to get out on to the cliffs, but on my most recent visit this had been fully closed off with plenty of signs discouraging visitors from walking on the grass, due to ground-nesting birds – please do pay attention to this. The views stretch north across the Pentland Firth (see opposite) to the Orcadian island of Hoy, and the sight from the viewing area at sunset on a clear day is phenomenal, with shades of blue, purple, pink and orange washing the sky.

"The most northerly point of mainland Britain is reached by winding through wild and barren moorland."

If you want to get a closer look at the seabirds, head south down the road from the car park, cross the cattle grid and then turn right along the clear path towards the sea. Paths run in both directions along the clifftops but do make sure you stay on them because of the aforementioned ground-nesting birds. I've had the most success seeing **puffins** from a little rocky ledge (♀ ND 20193 76694) that juts out on the northern side of a cleft in the cliffs; to find it, follow the path northeast towards the lighthouse – it's only about 150yds or so northeast from the end of the brick wall. I sat here for close to an hour late one

June evening, watching a dozen or so puffins popping in and out of their burrows, flying in from the sea and cleaning themselves.

While most seabird species leave Dunnet Head come winter, you might still spot shags and, in the water, great northern divers. Even regardless of birdlife, Dunnet Head is worth the journey at any time of year, feeling every inch like a place that is at the far edge of the country.

The coastline to the southeast of the lighthouse is also worth exploring, and is even craggier; I've had luck spotting puffins at Bank Head (♀ ND 20559 76651), immediately east of the coastguard cottages. To get there, head east from the main car park, following the road for about 300yds till you see a path veering off to the right; when you reach the cliffs, Bank Head is to your left.

A path just before this one, opposite the disabled parking area, leads uphill to a viewpoint, from which there are fabulous – if inevitably rather windswept – 360° views across and beyond the headland. To the east, you'll see the low coastline towards John O'Groats and then two nearby lochs – Loch of Easter Head and Long Loch – while immediately around you you'll notice a number of small ex-military buildings. These date back to World War II, when they were used as RADAR stations.

17 DUNNET BAY & SURROUNDS

A glorious swoop of golden sand backed for much of its two-mile length by huge, bulbous, grass-covered sand dunes, Dunnet Bay is pure magic, whatever the weather. Sheltered between the bulk of Dunnet Head and the low-lying coastline that curves between here and Thurso, it's perfect for paddling, swimming – and even surfing. You can do the last here with **North Coast Watersports** (✆ 07982 649635 ⊘ northcoastwatersports.com), which also offers stand-up paddleboarding and private RIB tours.

The sand here is incredibly soft, and much of the northeastern end is shell-, pebble- and seaweed free. In the early evening on a bright day, the dunes and sand seem to glow, and whenever you come its size means that the beach inevitably feels empty and yours to enjoy, even when there are other people on it. There are a handful of access points along the length of the beach, with the most convenient being at the northern end, where there's parking by the campsite (♀ ND 21961 70526). My preferred entry point, not least because it tends to be less busy, is just over a mile further south, where there's a car park on the western side

A TASTE OF CAITHNESS

I'm a sucker for nice packaging, so it's hardly surprising that it was the distinctive ceramic bottles of **Rock Rose Gin** that lured me in. Fortunately, what's inside the bottle – an incredibly smooth gin with citrusy but understated undertones – makes for a superlative gin and tonic, and the company's credentials are just as impressive. In my mind, it's a perfect Slow tipple.

The gin is produced by **Dunnet Bay Distillers** (KW14 8WD ⊘ dunnetbaydistillers. co.uk ⊙ Apr–Oct 10.00–17.00 Mon–Sat; Nov–Mar 10.00–16.00 Mon–Sat), a small operation in the village of Dunnet, just northeast of Dunnet Bay, run by husband and wife Martin and Claire Murray. Martin, the master distiller, wanted to create a taste of Caithness in his gin making, and so, in the process of developing Rock Rose, walked a five-mile radius of the distillery to see what grew locally. The result – across their range, which includes vodka and rum, too – was the use of local botanicals like sea buckthorn, *Rhodiola rosea*, lemon balm, holy grass and rowan berries. Today, most of these botanicals are grown in the distillery's small garden, overseen by their gardener Hanna, who is passionate about encouraging biodiversity. 'It gives a flavour of the area,' my tour guide Andy said, 'but it may well taste different if it was grown down the road instead.'

There are two tours – a half-hour 'Express' and a 90-minute 'Premium' – and a weekly cocktail workshop is also available. The tours offer a great insight into the business, which feels very much like a family rather than an impersonal company, and a chance to see the stills, named Elizabeth and Margaret after the Queen Mother and Claire's mother respectively. You also get to visit the bottling and development area – it's a small enough operation that it all takes place in one relatively small space.

Perhaps most impressive of all is the company's commitment to sustainability, acknowledging that this also means being a fair employer that supports its local community. Drivers can take their tour tasting samples home but should bring their own bottles in order to do so. They also encourage people to buy a refill pouch to top up their empty gin bottles – alternatively you can buy a soap pump to give them a new life. (Having done both, I can attest that, while one is tastier than the other, the latter does look very stylish in my bathroom.)

At the time of writing, Claire and Martin are busy setting up the next part of their business: **Stannergill Whisky** (⊘ stannergillwhisky. co.uk). This will be made at Castletown Mill (page 160), which until the Murrays bought it had sat empty for 32 years, despite being a prominent and important feature on the local landscape. The mill won't just be a craft whisky distillery, rooted, as the gin and vodka is, in the local landscape, but also somewhere for traditional and contemporary arts and crafts, a centre for horticulture research, and a showcase for North Highland – and particularly Caithness – food and drink. At the time of writing, the visitor centre here was due to open in summer 2025, and I can't wait to see how it turns out. Visit the Stannergill website for up-to-date information.

of the road (♥ ND 21614 68893); from here a path leads alongside the appropriately named Burn of Midsand on to the beach.

While you're in the area, don't miss a chance to visit **Dunnet Bay Distillery** (page 157), which makes one of my very favourite gins (don't worry, I've sampled a few to come to this conclusion), just northeast of the bay in the village of Dunnet. From here, it's less than a mile northwest to **Mary-Ann's Cottage** (✐ 07771 756434 ◌ maryannscottage.org ☉ May–early Oct 14.00–16.30 Tue–Sat), an old crofting cottage that has been preserved to look much as it was when the eponymous Mary-Ann lived here. The cottage was built in 1850, when it was known as Westside Croft; its original occupant was John Young – Mary-Ann was his grandaughter, who lived here until 1990, when she moved into a nursing home. The cottage offers a fascinating snapshot of the years in which the family lived here – complete with peat fire and box bed – and is brought to life by the volunteers who take you around.

Arguably the area's best kept secret – such a well-kept secret that I'm half loath to include it here – is **Peedie Sands**, a staggering little beach of soft white sand and ridiculously clear, Mediterranean-coloured water. The catch is that you have to walk to reach it – but the payoff is that when you catch your first sight of the beach, you'll likely let out a yelp of joy. The most straightforward route is to drive northeast up the road from Mary-Ann's Cottage, following it as it swings left; park in the wide turning area (♥ ND 21121 72015) just before the evocatively named House of the Northern Gate (a holiday home). From here, you follow the signposted track west through the gate, which leads half á mile over rather exposed ground to the beach; alternatively, you can park at Dwarwick Pier (♥ ND 20706 71312) and walk the slightly rougher (and steeper) coastal path northwest for half a mile.

18 CASTLETOWN

This small village at the southern end of Dunnet Bay was established in the early 20th century by landowner James Traill to support the quarries he had opened here. These quarries were extracting **flagstone** – a material that had been used locally for thousands of years, thanks

---

1 The River Thurso running through Caithness. 2 The windpump tower on Castletown's Flagstone Trail. 3 Dunnet Head Lighthouse. 4 Dunnet Bay Distillery uses botanicals from its own garden in its gins. ▶

VISITSCOTLAND/PAUL TOMKINS

EMMA GIBBS

EMMA GIBBS

DUNNET BAY DISTILLERS

to being hardwearing and easily split into thin slices, known as flags – which led to Castletown being known as the 'Flagstone Village'.

At the northeastern end of Harbour Road, off Main Street (the A836), is the site of the old cutting yard and quarry, which has been repurposed as the **Flagstone Trail** ($\heartsuit$ ND 19558 68557). This short footpath of about a quarter of a mile winds through the now grass-covered old quarry, starting directly opposite the village's small museum, the **Castlehill Heritage Centre** (∂ castletownheritage.co.uk $\odot$ 14.00–16.00 Wed, Sat & Sun), built around a pretty courtyard. Signboards along the trail add context on the industry, and you can peer into decaying old buildings that were built from flagstones. The first and most intact structure you meet is the windpump tower, used to pump water draining out of the quarry, which was then used to operate an overshot watermill to power the saws. You can walk inside and peer out through the small window towards the sea. A little further north is a viewing platform, from where you can look across the bay to Dunnet Head. From here, you can either stick to the more defined gravel path, or dip downhill to look at the ruined and now rather overgrown old cottages.

The main path leads north out of the quarry area to come out along the coast. Walking right from here will take you past flagstone-built buildings to the large, flagstone harbour. It's a scenic spot, with Dunnet Head and the golden sands of Dunnet beach both in view. The harbour was built in 1825 and at first just shipped the flagstones down Britain's east coast, but before too long the stones were taken far beyond, to Australia and South America, among other places. It's very likely that you will have encountered flagstone before – it was used in pavements on the Royal Mile in Edinburgh, Sauchiehall Street in Glasgow and The Strand in London.

"This footpath winds through the now grass-covered old quarry, starting directly opposite the village's small museum."

Continuing past the harbour for about 600yds brings you to **Castletown Beach**, sitting at the far, southern end of Dunnet Bay and separated from the main beach by a small burn that you can easily wade across. The sand is more pebbly here, but it's still a lovely spot, with wide views of the curve of the bay towards Dunnet Head – the house you see on top of the far hill is the House of the Northern Gate (page 158). Overlooking the beach is 19th-century **Castletown Mill**, which was, for a long time, derelict and roofless but is now being beautifully repurposed and redeveloped as the home of Stanergill Whisky ($\oslash$ stannergillwhisky. co.uk), by the owners of Dunnet Bay Distillery (page 157).

19 THURSO

Arriving in Thurso from any direction feels at first like arriving in a metropolis – such is the shock of being somewhere that spreads out as far as it does after hundreds of miles of small villages. In reality though, Britain's most northerly town isn't a particularly large place. Thurso's main shopping area, along High Street, has seen better days, but there are some appealing 19th-century buildings in the neat grid of streets to its southwest, a testament to the town's expansion during this time. This was largely down to town planner Sir John Sinclair, who is commemorated with pretty **Sir John's Square** just off the southwestern end of Traill St (the A9). Overlooked by the 19th-century St Peter & St Andrew's Church, its enclosed, grassy centre is made colourful by its large flowerbeds.

Northeast of here, the rather grand-looking town hall on High Street looks a little out of place among the predominantly pebble-dashed buildings that surround; today it houses the **North Coast Visitor Centre** (KW14 8AJ $\mathscr{D}$ 01847 80502 $\oslash$ highlifehighland.com/north-coast-visitor-centre $\odot$ Apr–Oct 10.00–17.00 Tue–Sat; Nov–Mar 11.00–15.00 Tue–Thu, 11.00–16.00 Fri & Sat), with an excellent **museum** across three floors. Downstairs is the 'Stones Room', containing some local Pictish artefacts, and upstairs are a number of displays charting the development of Caithness; while there's lots to read, there are also plenty of interesting things to look at, and somehow it never feels overwhelming. I enjoyed sitting and listening to the stories and poems by local people, which were recorded between the 1950s and '70s, while kids can dress up as animals from the Flow Country (page 113). In a room right at the top a short film is screened on rotation, showing Caithness through the seasons: it's quite a nice little glimpse of life here. Don't miss, too, the exhibition on local nuclear power station Dounreay (page 164), which includes the control-room desk and display panels.

From here, a walk north up High Street and then a right turn on to Wilson Lane will take you through quiet residential streets in the older, more higgledy-piggledy, part of town to the ruins of **Old St Peter's Kirk** (KW14 8AZ), where the arched windows – missing their glass – give an indication of what the church would once have looked like. It's thought

St Peter's was founded here around 1220 by the Bishop of Caithness; it closed in 1832, but many of the graves and memorial stones in the churchyard are younger than this.

At the eastern end of Wilson Lane is the **River Thurso**, which you can follow north for about 200yds to its mouth; the castle-like building on the opposite bank is **Thurso Castle**. A castle was originally built here in 1664 but later demolished so that another could be built around 1875 – it's now in ruins and has something of a functional air about it. Directly north, beyond the castle, you should be able to see Dunnet Head and, to the left of that, the island of Hoy on Orkney. From the harbour, you can curve around southwest to walk towards Thurso's **beach**, a pleasant if unremarkable strip of sand. The waters here are known for being excellent for **cold-water surfing** and the annual Scottish National Surfing Championships is held here every March.

FOOD & DRINK

Olive 1–3 Brabster St ⬛. Bright, airy café festooned with plants and fairy lights – grab one of the cosy booths if you can. The menu of breakfast (till 11.30) and brunch dishes features a great range of standard and more interesting options, from filled morning rolls and chicken burgers to ramen and Mexican-style eggs, with a lot of decent veggie options. Themed evenings are often held (BYOB) – check Facebook for details.

SHOPPING

Coo's Tail Gallery 33 Traill St ✆ 01847 893623 ⬛ ◔ 10.00–17.00 Tue–Sat. This is one of my favourite shops in the North Highlands, crammed full of beautiful local artwork (including prints by Lisa Poulsen; page 119), as well as home furnishings (the orca- and seal-print lampshades are my favourite) and gifts. Framing is also on offer at a very reasonable price, so if you find a print you like you've no excuse for leaving it sitting around at home unframed.

20 HOLBORN HEAD

From Thurso, the land curves north to Holborn Head, 2½ miles away and the site of a fine coastal walk. To get out here, you can park at the busy harbour of **Scrabster**, which is also the terminal for ferries to Stromness on Orkney; the easiest place is the car park (♀ ND 10064

◀ **1** Holborn Head's unusual lighthouse. **2** Lichen Caithness Reindeer Centre – home to the most northerly herd of reindeer in the UK.

70358) right by the port, opposite the Ferry Inn. From here, continue northeast on foot – do take care as it can be very busy with vehicles. The route to Holborn Head, just under a mile away, starts to the left of the ferry terminal, up a narrow private road. As you reach the gates to the pretty lighthouse, turn left up the steps to follow the footpath sign, and then head diagonally right at the corner of the lighthouse garden to walk uphill. From here, it's a straightforward walk, keeping north on the path and climbing over a handful of stiles.

The views from the head, and particularly from the small cairn on it, are superlative, towards Orkney and Dunnet Head, and it's often a great place to catch glimpses of passing orca. There are various paths that you can follow around and beyond the head, and the coastline here is really quite spectacular, with many of the rocks cut in incredibly straight lines.

NUCLEAR CLEANUP

Travelling along the coast to the west of Thurso, you'll likely notice what looks like a large white ball sitting close to the cliff edge, some nine miles west of the town. This is **NRS Dounreay**: between 1955 and 1994 it was the centre of the UK's nuclear fast reactor research and development. Since being decommissioned, it has become the biggest closure project of a nuclear site in Britain; the cleanup of the site was originally due to be completed in 2023, but in 2024 it was announced that it would continue until the 2070s, at an estimated cost of almost £8 billion.

In many ways, this is good news for Caithness, particularly as the site employs over 1,200 local people and also uses hundreds of contract workers and local businesses. Dounreay has had a huge impact on the region throughout its lifespan, bringing highly skilled workers into Caithness, as well as providing jobs for local people – particularly vital in the 1950s and '60s when traditional fishing and farming work was in decline. Thurso expanded significantly in the 1950s as a result, with its population swelling from just over 3,000 to more than 8,000 within the space of a decade; new housing for the 'Atomics', as the incoming workers were called, was built to meet this demand.

Thurso's North Coast Visitor Centre (page 161) has a great Dounreay exhibition, which includes the interior of a control room and a model of the site's Prototype Fast Reactor. Views of the site can also be had from **Sandside Beach**, to the west of Dounreay, just north of the village of Reay; it's a lovely stretch of pale sand, but it's worth being aware that its proximity to the nuclear site means that radioactive particles have been found here, so if you visit you shouldn't remove any objects or materials, including sand, stones or shells, from the beach.

Walking immediately west from the cairn will enable you to see a cave cut into the rocks, the water wild and unforgiving below. Needless to say, do take care as you walk out here.

The lighthouse at the start of the walk really is very pretty, and also quite unusual, with its light tower built into the eastern wall of the two-storey lighthouse keepers' houses. Established in 1862 by David and Thomas Stevenson, it was automated in 1988 but discontinued in 2003 and is now a private home.

¶¶ FOOD & DRINK

Captain's Galley The Harbour, Scrabster ✆ 01847 894999 ⬦ captainsgalley.co.uk. This celebrated seafood restaurant is much nicer than its rather bare-bones exterior suggests. The menu includes oysters, locally spear-caught sea bass, mussels and an astounding seafood platter.

SOUTH OF THURSO

🏠 Ulbster Arms

The landscape south of Thurso is classic inland Caithness: neat, low-lying fields and stretches of moorland, with far-reaching views in all directions and dotted with small farming settlements and – in many places – windfarms.

21 LICHEN CAITHNESS REINDEER CENTRE

Harpsdale KW12 6UL ✆ 07496 879734 ⬦ 3reindeer.com ☺ prebooked experiences only; book 24hr in advance

If you were to ask my kids what their favourite place in the whole of the North Highlands is, Lichen Caithness would be their answer. Home to the most northerly herd of reindeer in the UK, here you can enjoy a 'Reindeer Reception', where you get to meet and feed the reindeer. The experience begins in a cosy little hut, where you find out about the small herd of three – Levvi, Sven and Mr Antlers – and the history of the species, which was native to Scotland until it became extinct in the 12th century. After this, you head into the enclosure to meet the boys for yourself, armed with bowls of their favourite food – lichen. The reindeer are incredibly patient, which is a blessing given my youngest had a habit of shrieking and dropping the bowl every time one approached, and are as beautiful as you would imagine. After they're fed, you head out of the enclosure to toast marshmallows over the fire and drink what is possibly the best hot chocolate I've ever tasted.

What really makes Lichen Caithness special is its owners, Chris and Elizabeth, who had dreamed of owning reindeers for almost two decades before finally making it a reality. It feels like a privilege to learn about these creatures from people so passionate about them – 'this is the story of them and their silliness,' Chris said – and to see that being a visitor attraction is secondary to the reindeer being part of Chris and Elizabeth's family.

In addition to the standard Reindeer Reception, you can also book 'Your Evening as a Reindeer Herder', a private-group experience, and numerous themed events are held throughout the year – check the website for more information.

Lichen Caithness is just over two miles south of the village of **Halkirk**, another settlement laid out in a tidy grid. Its location, six miles south of Thurso, makes it a good base for exploring both the north coast and inland. There's a handful of grand buildings at the northern end of Bridge Street, just before it crosses the River Thurso, including the Ross Institute with its little turrets and central clocktower.

"In addition to the standard Reindeer Reception, you can also book 'Your Evening as a Reindeer Herder'."

A pleasant walk of just over the mile can be taken from the other side of the bridge, where a footpath heads west along the wide river; as the river meanders, the path continues to follow Calder Burn, with farmland on either side and Morven visible in the distance. Around 150yds later, pass through a gate into what looks like someone's garden and then take a right turn up the side of a house into a quiet, tree-lined lane; turn right again at the end of this and walk up to meet the road, where you turn right again. This will take you along a minor road lined with fields, meeting the B874 after just under half a mile, where you turn a final right to return to the village.

The large green space opposite the turning on to the B874 is the site of the **Halkirk Highland Games** (⊘ halkirkgames.co.uk), held on the last Saturday in July every year and widely recognised as one of the best in the North Highlands. As well as caber tossing and hammer throwing by kilted strongmen, there's also athletics, clay pigeon shooting, children's events, and dancing and piping, plus fairground attractions and plenty of food and drink stalls.

 **SPECIAL STAYS**

Ulbster Arms Bridge St, Halkirk ℘ 01847 831641 ♦ ulbsterarmshotel.co.uk. Built as a family home in 1878, the Ulbster Arms overlooks the River Thurso as it meanders its way through the northern side of the village. Despite its size, it only has 13 rooms, many of which benefit from lovely, large windows. There's a comfy guest lounge with a wood fire, plus a restaurant and a cosy lounge bar; both serve meals that make the most of the local produce, including seafood delivered regularly from Scrabster (page 163).

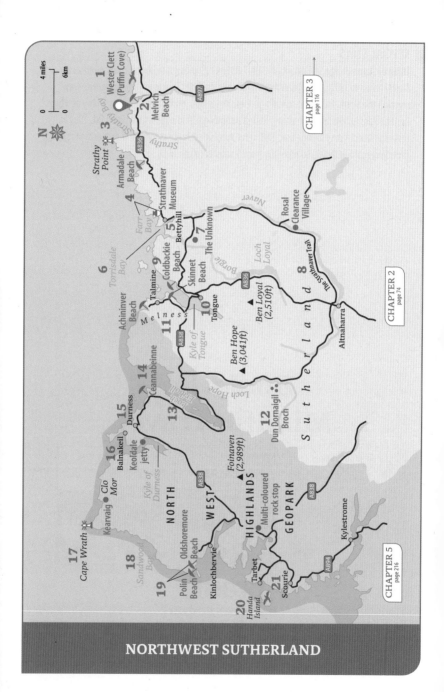

NORTHWEST SUTHERLAND

N

0 ___ 4 miles
0 ___ 6km

1 Wester Clett (Puffin Cove)

2 Melvich Beach

A897

3 Strathy Point

Strathy Bay

A836

Armadale Beach

Strathnaver Museum

Farr Bay

Strathnaver

4 Bettyhill

5

Naver

Rosal Clearance Village

6 Torrisdale Bay

Coldbackie Beach

9

Skinnet Beach

7 The Unknown

Loch Loyal

Borgie

The Strathnaver Trail

8

Talmine

Melness

Achininver Beach

10 Tongue

Ben Loyal (2,510ft)

A836

11 Kyle of Tongue

A838

Altnaharra

Ben Hope (3,041ft)

14 Ceannabeinne

Loch Hope

Loch Eriboll

12 Dun Dornaigil Broch

15 Durness

13

S u t h e r l a n d

CHAPTER 2
page 74

16 Balnakeil

Keoldale

Kyle of Durness jetty

NORTH

Foinaven (2,989ft)

Multi-coloured rock stop

A838

17 Cape Wrath

Kearvaig

Clo Mor

WEST

HIGHLANDS

GEOPARK

A838

Kylestrome

18 Sandwood Bay

Oldshoremore Beach

Polin Beach

19

Kinlochbervie

Tarbet

21 Scourie

20 Handa Island

A894

CHAPTER 5
page 216

CHAPTER 3
page 116

4

NORTHWEST SUTHERLAND

As you head west into Sutherland from Caithness, the scale and drama of the landscape begins to pick up pace: hills rise up to the south, the coast becomes ragged and, by the time you're approaching Bettyhill, mountains start lining up in the distance. Here, with settlements often few and far between, and even the main road frequently devoid of other cars, you really do feel conscious of being at the end of the mainland; take any road north off the main A836 and there's a real sense of driving to the end of the road, and half expecting the land to just suddenly drop away.

Along the north coast, taking these little roads north are usually necessary to reach the shore, with the sea often tantalisingly out of reach from the main road. Tucked into coves and crescents here you have some of the North Highlands' finest beaches, including – among others – **Melvich**, **Strathy**, **Farr**, **Torrisdale** and **Balnakeil**, many of which require a bit of a walk or a little effort to get to, and which reward you with swathes of golden, often empty sand. Round the almost impenetrable most northwestern corner are a handful of superlative white-sand beaches, including celebrated **Sandwood Bay**, only accessible on foot. In late spring and summer, the small harbour at Tarbet, just north of Scourie, provides access to the wildlife reserve of **Handa Island** – just a short distance offshore, though it feels a hundred miles away.

Along the way are small communities, many with little more than a shop and a café, many more with less than that, and long channels of water that create deep indentations in the coastline. As on the east coast, the ghosts of the Clearances still linger here, with a handful of sites – the Strathnaver museum and trail near **Bettyhill**, and **Ceannabeinne Clearance Village** near Durness – shedding light on this brutal period of history.

If you're approaching this region from the east and have never been before, then this will be your first taste of classic Highland drama. I will never forget what it was like to drive the roads of northwest Sutherland for the first time: open-mouthed with awe and caught between laughing and crying at the overwhelming preposterousness of the scenery, which every corner seemed to improve upon. Even after repeated visits, that feeling has never really gone for me. Take it slowly, stop often, and let the landscape of this area work its charms on you.

GETTING AROUND

Unsurprisingly, given both its mountainous terrain and distance from any major towns, northwest Sutherland is difficult to get to using public transport – and slow by car, too. For example, the journey between the eastern boundary (Wester Clett) and the southern boundary (Kylestrome) of this chapter is just 90 miles, but it'll take you about 2¾ hours to drive. Don't let this put you off – it isn't a drive you'd want to rush anyway.

BUSES

The good news is that though there are no trains in northwest Sutherland, there are buses – but if you're relying on them to get around then do make sure you check timings in advance as they can be rather irregular. Stagecoach (⬧ stagecoachbus.com ☺ Mon–Fri) service 274 runs twice daily between Bettyhill and Dounreay, calling at Melvich en route, though one of those departures is quite early. The Far North Bus (⬧ thedurnessbus.com) service 803 runs on Saturdays between Durness and Thurso (2hr 20min), calling at Tongue (50min), Bettyhill (1hr 25min), Strathy (1hr 40min) and Melvich (1hr 50min); on Tuesday and Thursday it starts/ends at Talmine (1hr 45min to Thurso). The Far North Bus also runs the term-time Monday to Friday 800 route from Bettyhill to Portskerra (35min), with two departures daily; the 805 runs Monday to Saturday throughout the year from Smoo Cave to Inverness (3hr 50min), via Kinlochbervie (55min) and Scourie (1hr 20min).

WALKING & CYCLING

Don't let the mountains put you off here – there are still fantastic **walking** possibilities even if you don't fancy scaling great heights. As always, the coast offers up fantastic options, the most famous of which is the four-mile walk across moorland to Sandwood Bay (page 206), often acknowledged as one of the most beautiful beaches in the world. Shorter and less famous is the walk out to Torrisdale Bay (page 181), with its huge, ever-changing expanse of sand. The wild headlands here provide some great coastal walking too, particularly at Faraid Head (page 204) and Scourie (page 213) – from the latter you can see beautiful Handa Island (page 211), which can only be explored on a four-mile footpath. At Melvich (page 176), there's a wonderful walk that combines beach and headland.

Walking in this area also gives you the opportunity to experience some of its Clearance history, particularly at Ceannabeinne (page 198) and Strathnaver (page 184). If you do fancy trying your hand at walking up a mountain, Ben Hope and Ben Stack are possibly the easiest – as always, use WalkHighlands ($\mathring{\partial}$ walkhighlands.co.uk) for detailed information, and ensure that you are properly prepared. This region also sees the last stages of the Cape Wrath Trail which, unsurprisingly, finishes at wild and remote Cape Wrath (page 205); it's a hard trail that's not suitable for inexperienced long-distance hikers, but the final section between Sandwood Bay and the cape is its shortest at just under eight miles.

Cycling is, generally, challenging, but there are a few options for off-road cycles, including part of the route to Sandwood Bay.

WESTER CLETT TO BETTYHILL

A scattering of beautiful, tucked-away beaches can be found between the eastern county boundary and the village of Bettyhill. The surrounding coast has a wild but not impenetrable feel – though you do have to be prepared to veer off the main road – and makes for some great walking experiences. In addition to the two beaches listed in the following section, another lovely one can be found at **Armadale**; there's parking space on the northern side of the main road (Q NC 79462 64015), from where you can follow the path down to the flat, wide sands.

1 WESTER CLETT (PUFFIN COVE)
Q NC 91933 65396

There's no signpost to tell you where to go or how to find Wester Clett – but don't let that put you off. It's a fabulous spot at any time of year, but in late spring and summer it's particularly worth coming out for puffin spotting. I'd go so far as to say that compared with Duncansby Head, Dunnet Head and Handa Island, this is the best place I've seen them, with the little birds flying right over my head.

The path ($\mathbb{Q}$ NC 91967 64488) down to the cove is situated about 40yds east of the Sutherland county sign and immediately to the west of the 'Welcome to Caithness' sign (assumedly the boundary line is on a diagonal between the two); look for it to the west of a now closed-off parking area on the northern side of the road. Parking is an issue when heading out here, so do make sure you do so responsibly – there are a couple of small parking areas a short walk west along the road, or you can pull in at the large layby one mile east ($\mathbb{Q}$ NC 93261 64538) and then walk back along the road.

The path is clear the whole way but can be boggy even in summer. When it splits, after about 260yds from the start, take the left-hand path to go down to the cove; from here, you walk straight on for a quarter of a mile before the path swings right to curve downhill into the rocky cove. Take it slowly when you walk here: the day before my visit, someone was airlifted to hospital after falling, and while I was there someone fell and twisted their ankle.

The cove itself is absolutely beautiful: clear turquoise waters and pale pebbles, with the almost triangular-shaped rock of Wester Clett blocking most of the entrance to it. The cliffs to the right of the cove and of Wester Clett itself are full of puffins from late spring until around late July, and from here you can sit and watch them swooping into their burrows and whizzing overhead, their little orange legs outstretched.

An even better view can be had from the headland to the right, which looks out directly on to Wester Clett. To get there, walk east from the cove to follow the path that winds up and around the cliffs. It can feel a little narrow and precarious at times, so don't rush. As you reach the top and begin to curve north, look down to your left and you should start to see puffins just below you. A little further on there's a good ledge to sit on, from where you can look directly onto the pyramidal hillside of Wester Clett, which is pockmarked by puffin burrows, and watch the little birds return from sea with their mouths full of fish or just shuffling

1 Strathy Bay. 2 Wester Clett is one of the best places in the region to look for puffins in season. 3 Melvich Beach. 4 At Strathy Point you can see the last traditionally manned lighthouse to be built in Scotland. ▶

GEORGE ROBERTSON/DT

HOLGERS/DT

13THREEPHOTOGRAPHY/DT

A loop around Melvich & Portskerra

❄ OS Explorer 449; start: Melvich Beach car park ⚲ NC 88695 64757; 4 miles; moderate

This delightful walk takes in the full scale of Melvich Beach, approaching via the Halladale River, before heading north along the coast to Portskerra. (You could easily reverse it if you want to save the beach for the end.) At high tide, there can be less shingle to walk along at the northern edge of the beach, so I'd recommend doing this walk at lower tides; whenever you walk it, the shingle and rocks at this end can make it rougher going for a short while.

1 Head through the gate at the eastern end of the car park; the path splits shortly after – take the right-hand route, which leads down to the shore of the wide and meandering Halladale River. Ignore the wooden bridge that crosses the water and instead stick to the shoreline, walking east. Depending on how far the tide is out, you'll probably be walking first on pebbles and then sand, with Bighouse Lodge to your right, and the green hills of the headland directly ahead. Follow the river as it curves around to the left, with the sand increasing as you do so.

2 As you round the dunes, you'll be able to take in the whole swathe of the beach. Walk west along the sand; as the beach curves north, a strip of shingle appears, with the sand eventually giving away entirely to shingle and bigger rocks. You'll see the concrete pier jutting out ahead; as you near it, you might find it easier to walk along the grassy bank, which runs past an old fishing building full of nets and ropes.

3 At the pier, continue north along the road; after about 90yds you'll reach the Portskerra Drownings Memorial on your left, dedicated to the local fishermen who lost their lives at sea during storms in 1848, 1890 and 1918, 'within sight of their homes', as the memorial says. It's worth stopping here too to take in the view back towards Melvich Bay, with the bay curving around to the headland of Rubha an Tuir. Continue up the road from here.

4 About 70yds after the memorial, a footpath sign to 'Portskerra Slipway' points to the right. Follow this, which is a largely grassy path, to curve along the coast. The sea below is easy to reach on the first stretch, and a nice area for rock pooling and swimming. Follow the path along the clifftops; just before Portskerra Slipway there's a steep climb uphill, but the views beyond the cliffs are wonderful and the water is so clear you can make out the rocks beneath.

5 At Portskerra Slipway there's a car park and scenically placed picnic benches; the pontoon here is almost entirely submerged at high tide. The shingle cove is a nice, sheltered spot for swimming. Continue up the road from the harbour; when you reach a T-junction, turn right and follow the road round, with houses ahead of you and the undulating coastline on your right; the sea dips in and out of view and the farmland is broken in places by craggy geos (inlets). After about 400yds, you'll see a small stone memorial, a little like a headstone, on your right, which is dedicated to

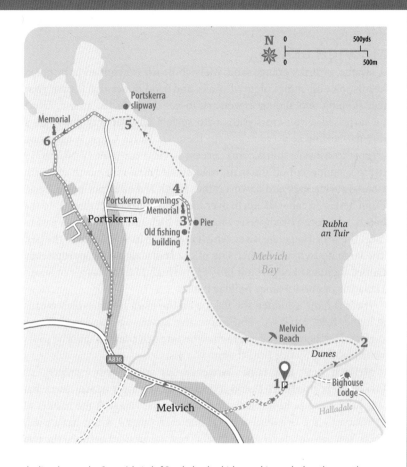

the lives lost on the *Snow Admiral* of Sunderland, which was shipwrecked on the coast here on 24 January 1842. In spring and summer, you'll be able to hear the seabird colony that lives on the big stack in the middle of the cove directly behind here.

6 Just after the memorial, the road curves left and gently climbs, and as it does so you get great views over croftland to Rubha an Tuir, Dounreay and even the island of Hoy on Orkney. Continue to follow the road, heading south back towards Melvich (ignoring the sharp left turn that takes you back north). At the T-junction with the main road (the A836), turn left – it's a half-mile walk back to the turning to the car park, on your left.

around. When I was there in mid June, the cliffs next to Wester Clett had ledges full of shags and their chicks, while kittiwakes swooped in and over the cove, their calls echoing around the walls.

2 MELVICH BEACH

A swathe of dusky orange sand, Melvich Beach is hemmed in by green headlands, soft-mint-coloured waves and sand dunes that'll have your feet slipping and sliding as you try to get down to the strand. Don't be surprised if you cross paths with surfers on your way down; it's a popular surfing spot (you can join them via North Coast Watersports ⊘ northcoastwatersports.com). Access is via a car park (♀ NC 88719 64758), signposted off the main road about half a mile north of North Coast Touring Park and down a rather rough and often pot-holed track. From here, you can walk north over the steep dunes to get directly to the beach, which can become very narrow at high tide, or continue east to meet the wide Halladale River, which meanders its way down to the bay. The large house on the other side of the Halladale is the appropriately named Bighouse Lodge, built in 1765 by Hugh Mackay, owner of Strath Halladale; it's now a fancy holiday house.

There is quite a sudden shelf/slope on the main beach, which means at higher tides you'll see some impressive waves – and understand why surfers flock here. Do be aware that the tide can come in quickly, so it's worth looking up tide times before you visit.

Melvich itself is a rather stretched-out village; unfortunately, its lovely hotel closed in 2023 and at the time of writing it was unclear what was happening to it. Immediately north of the village is the hamlet of Portskerra – the two kind of blend into each other – which has a small shop. You can do a lovely round walk (best at low tide) between the two (page 174).

3 STRATHY BAY

Blink and you'll miss the turning to Strathy Bay's lovely **beach** (signed 'Strathy east beach' on the A836) – a wide and wild stretch of sand that feels hidden away, even if you are likely to share it with surfers. Parking is next to Strathy Cemetery (♀ NC 83818 65677), where there's a toilet; from here, paths lead over the undulating, grass-covered dunes, brightened with wildflowers in spring, to the beach. The hue of the sand here seems to shift constantly with the sky – I've been here when it looked a light orange, while at other times it seemed more like the colour of Dijon mustard.

The eastern side of the beach is characterised by great, hulking rocks where the layers are so neat and visible that they give the impression of having been stacked, almost like pancakes. There are numerous outcrops, caves and stacks to explore here – including one that is so bulbous it looks rather precariously balanced – with the sound of water steadily dropping off the sides of the cliffs. Many of the rocks get quickly cut off as the tide comes in, so do keep an eye on the water level as you explore.

The peaty River Strathy empties on to the left-hand side of the beach, which is sheltered by the long, rocky coastline that leads up to Strathy Point. When I was last here, we found a huge piece of vertebrae that had assumedly come in on the tide – we could only guess that it belonged to a whale – which the kids were (understandably) both intrigued and appalled by. At this end of the wide bay you're also likely to find more shells and stones, making it great for beachcombing.

The tapered finger of **Strathy Point** juts out into the ocean 2½ miles (as the crow flies) north of Strathy beach, neatly marking the midpoint of the north coast. At its tip is its low and very functional-looking lighthouse, which was the last traditionally manned lighthouse to be built in Scotland, in 1958. It was automated less than 30 years later and then decommissioned in 2012 – a remarkably short lifespan. As you'd expect, it's a wild and rather lonely spot, but well worth the walk out here.

"The tapered finger of Strathy Point juts out into the ocean 2½ miles (as the crow flies) north of Strathy beach."

To reach the lighthouse, drive out to road's end at **Totegan** (♀ NC 82705 68593), where there's a parking area just to the left of the gates where it says you can go no further. (As always, park considerately and ensure you leave enough room for large vehicles to turn.) From here, walk through the gate and down the road, past a couple of low houses, and follow it around to the left, where you will see the lighthouse ahead of you. After about a quarter of a mile, the views to your right start to open up and you'll spot the bright white ball of Dounreay (page 164) along the coast. What I find remarkable about this view is that you can clearly see the difference between the Caithness and Sutherland coastline: the latter, which starts just before Melvich, is marked by higher, more rugged cliffs.

En route to the lighthouse you'll pass a couple of little lochans, the last of which has a small lighthouse on it that's arguably more picturesque than the real thing. The lighthouse proper is now private property so you can't climb the steps up to it. Instead, follow the path that heads to the left of the building, which opens up the view to the west along the coast, with an impressive dark-rock sea arch at the forefront. You can also walk to the right of the lighthouse, where the land splinters into the craggy rocks of the point. From here, you can either return to the road, or walk up the hill to the southeast of the lighthouse to an old concrete lookout post for more astounding views over the coast – as far as Dunnet Head if the weather allows – and then loop around the eastern side of the lochan to rejoin the road from there.

BETTYHILL & SURROUNDS

Don't get me wrong – I love the drive along the entirety of the north coast. But it's on the approach to Bettyhill from the east that the drama of the northwest really begins to reveal itself. This is particularly true three miles before the village, when you round a corner to be greeted by a distant line-up of mountains, the most prominent of which are Ben Hope and Ben Loyal, which will dip in and out of view for much of your journey west from here. It's practically obligatory to stop at the conveniently placed **Bettyhill Viewpoint** (♀ NC 74870 61962), where a helpful signboard names the various peaks you can see.

4 STRATHNAVER MUSEUM & FARR BAY

The road dips down just before Bettyhill, revealing the compact but appealing white building of Farr Old Church, built in 1774. Prior to the Highland Clearances (page 90), this was the main house of worship in the region, with a rather staggering 750 people in its congregation. The church closed in the 1940s and today houses the excellent **Strathnaver Museum** (✐ 01641 521418 ⬡ strathnavermuseum.org.uk ⊙ Mar 11.00–15.00 Wed–Fri; Apr–Oct 10.00–17.00 Mon–Sat; Nov–mid-Dec 11.00–15.00 Tue–Thu), which reopened in 2023 after a smart refurbishment and provides a fantastic, easy-to-digest (and enjoy) overview of the area's history. The section on the Clearances is especially moving – unsurprising given that they were particularly brutal in Strathnaver. You can sit in pews underneath the old pulpit and listen to accounts from the time – my seven-year-old was particularly taken with this, and spent days after retelling the story of how people had had to leave their houses naked, such was the brevity of the notice to vacate their property. There are a number of other nice touches that kids will enjoy, including a game in which you can find out what happens to various local residents after they were cleared off their land – kind of like a more depressing version of the Choose Your Own Adventure books I loved as a child.

Upstairs is the Mackay Centre, where you can find out more about this prominent local clan and – if you have Mackay roots – research your own history. A striking modern bridge takes you above the downstairs room with a tree overhead that was found in a peat bog and is thought to be a mind-scrambling 4,000 to 6,000 years old. There's also a bright, appealing annex across the graveyard that houses farming and fishing machinery – if that sounds dull then you'll be pleased to hear that it's anything but, with touchscreens providing more information on each implement. In the graveyard itself is the beautifully carved Pictish **Farr Stone**, which stands in the place it originated – showing that this was a site of worship long before the church was built.

"Even on a sunny day in high summer, you won't feel crowded, and the golden sands look idyllic under the Highland sun."

Behind the museum, beyond rolling dunes, is gorgeous **Farr Bay**. Overlooked by a scattering of houses on the low green hills on either side and enclosed by the headlands curving around it, this is a really lovely beach, and one on which my own family has spent many happy hours. Even on a sunny day in high summer, you won't feel crowded, and the golden sands look idyllic under the Highland sun. You can approach on its western side from Bettyhill (see below), but access is also available from behind the museum: a footpath sign (NC 71610 62306) points the way through the dunes from the road to the museum's overflow car park, behind the Farr Bay Inn.

5 BETTYHILL

Scenically wedged between the golden-sand bays of Farr and Torrisdale, Bettyhill was created as a resettlement village in the early 19th century by Elizabeth, Countess of Sutherland – thus the 'Betty' part of its name. Don't be fooled by the seemingly magnanimous nature of this gesture, however: the countess (later Duchess of Sutherland) was instrumental in clearing almost 15,000 people off her million-acre estate between 1809 and 1821 (page 90).

You'll see little evidence of the village's 19th-century origins on the rather sparse main road, with the exception of the hotel at its western end, built by the Sutherlands as a coaching inn in 1819. From the hotel's beer garden you can take in the sweeping panorama of Torrisdale Bay (see opposite), glorious even in the most dreich weather.

As elsewhere in the Highlands, the crofters that were relocated to Bettyhill – most of whom came from Farr, a mile downhill (page 178) – were encouraged to move into the fishing industry; the River Naver, which cuts between the village and Torrisdale Bay, is one of Scotland's best salmon rivers. Little remains of the village's once-thriving fishing port of Navermouth, but its now-forlorn-looking pier can still be seen; to get there, take the road that runs down the side of the village shop (on the A836) to its end, then turn left and follow this road as it curves west towards the bay to reach a car park. From here, you can scramble down the hillside to the pier, where Torrisdale's ever-shifting sands seem deceptively close. A short walk north along the path from the car park brings you to the remains of the salmon-netting station and ice house, in an evocative, wind-battered position by a series of jagged rocks. While it is possible to continue walking up and around the **Àrd Mòr** headland from here, the path soon peters out and there are numerous steep drops down to the sea so I'd only recommend it for more experienced hikers.

Much less perilous is the walk to Farr beach (page 179); head downhill alongside the A836 for about 500yds, until you reach a road on your left with parking spaces at its corner. Walk through the gate directly across from here, with the sea in the distance ahead of you, and follow the path gently downhill through fields towards the sand; I defy anyone not to pick up pace as the curve of the bay opens up. At high tide, you'll have to cross a little wooden bridge over the burn to get to the main part of the beach, but that only adds to the sense of adventure.

ᵘ FOOD & DRINK

In dry weather, there's no better spot for a drink than outside the **Bettyhill Hotel** (bettyhillhotel.com), overlooking Torrisdale Bay.

The Store Café KW14 7SS 07944 978332 storecafe.co.uk. A slice of homemade cake at this cosy, wood-clad café is the perfect incentive to get you back up the hill after a few hours on the beach. The menu includes breakfasts, burgers, hearty salads, curry and even a seafood platter, and there's a cosy nook of a bar for something a little stronger. The small terrace has a view of Farr Bay, and the café has the rather remarkable claim of being open every day – making it a complete rarity in these parts.

6 TORRISDALE BAY

A view over the wide expanse of Torrisdale Bay greets you at Bettyhill's western end: tantalising swirls of sea and sand that seem at once close and yet far away. It is, in my opinion, one of the very best of the region's beaches, not least because it always, no matter what the weather, feels elemental and wild.

There are two access points, alongside the rivers Naver and Borgie respectively. The first, on the bay's eastern side, is from the small huddle of houses at Invernaver. Parking is available just after the bridge over the River Naver (♀ NC 70951 60156), on the south side of the road; from here, walk 350yds west until you see a road on the right, signposted to Invernaver. Follow this to its northern end, where you'll see a footpath pointing across the grass, with the dunes in the distance – you can pick your way across to them, moving down to the sand within a few hundred yards if the tide is out, and it's about half an hour's walk to the main, most northerly stretch of beach. En route, you can detour uphill after about two-thirds of a mile to reach the remains of an Iron Age **broch** (♀ NC 69732 60976), which has arguably one of the finest views of any real estate in the region.

The second route to the bay is from Borgie, on its western side, about 6½ miles from Invernaver – the drive here seems to take so long that you might start to doubt you're still going to end up at the bay but have a little faith. Parking (♀ NC 68076 61121) is on the right about 500yds after the left turning to Torrisdale hamlet (keep straight on here); from here, a footpath leads down the hill through gorse and bracken towards the River Borgie, which you soon cross on a wooden bridge. The path winds alongside the river and for a short while feels as though it isn't going anywhere, but it doesn't take too long before the river widens out and the bay begins to appear – you can circle the dunes or climb over them to get to the main sand; at a steady pace, it takes about 20 minutes to reach the beach. En

"The path winds alongside the river... it doesn't take too long before the river widens out and the bay appears."

route to the beach, you will see a footpath to your right that leads up the craggy hill behind the bay; you can follow this for just under a mile to reach the broch on the western side of the bay (page 181), though note that it is quite steep and rough going in places.

The beach at Torrisdale Bay is undoubtedly one of the finest on the north coast; seaweed- and seashell-scattered at its western side before (at low tide at least) giving way to vast, almost buttery sands that constantly shift and change depending on the sky and tide. The water seems to swirl on its approach and retreat, creating shapes rather than straight lines. You could easily spend hours and hours here, walking and playing – take a picnic or, at the very least, some snacks. At low tide, part of the wrecked carcass of the SS *John Randolph* (♀ NC 68395 61857) is revealed at the beach's western end; the ship hit a minefield and sank in the Denmark Strait in 1942 – part of it was later recovered but ended up here after it broke from its tow in 1952. It's rather haunting to watch as its triangular fore section is slowly revealed by the sand.

7 THE UNKNOWN
Borgie Glen ♀ NC 68030 56780 ⊘ forestryandland.gov.scot/visit/borgie-glen

'I won't tell you what it's of, because I don't want to ruin the surprise of seeing it for yourself,' Marcel, the manager at the Tongue Hotel (page 190) said about *The Unknown*. So I hope you'll forgive me here for doing something that is the antithesis of guidebook writing – hinting at a place rather than telling you too much about it. In doing so, I hope it'll allow you a little child-like anticipation at discovering the sculpture for yourself. (Note though that you will see a photo of it if you visit the Forestry and Land website in advance.)

The area south of the A836 between Bettyhill and Tongue is a mix of Forestry Commission land and scraggy moorland. Standing on a hill in Borgie Glen, 2½ miles south of Borgie, *The Unknown* was made by Scottish sculptor Kenny Hunter in 2012. From the car park (ignore all the information boards if you want to keep the surprise), a circular gravel path weaves up the hill through the mixed woodland and then heather – I'd recommend choosing the left-hand path to walk up, which will keep the sculpture hidden from view until almost the last moment.

◀ 1 Torrisdale Bay. 2 Farr Bay. 3 Exhibits in the Strathnaver Museum. 4 The ruins of the settlement of Grumbeg on the Strathnaver Trail.

The sculpture at once feels both strikingly modern and ancient, which seems wholly appropriate as it faces out across the wide landscape that stretches across commercial forest and moorland to the brooding peaks of Ben Loyal, Ben Hope and Foinaven. Even if you know what the sculpture is of, however, it's still worth climbing up here to see it for yourself, and to enjoy the peaceful and pleasant (if sometimes steep) three-quarter of a mile walk up and down the hill.

8 THE STRATHNAVER TRAIL

The scars of the Clearances (page 90) are written especially vividly in **Strathnaver**, the valley that runs inland of Bettyhill along the River Naver and then Loch Naver. Beginning in 1814, within the space of 15 years some 40 townships in Strathnaver were entirely cleared of the people that lived in them – accounting for a not insignificant 388 families. The Strathnaver Trail was established as a way to link the history of these settlements with what (little) can be seen today, with 16 marked sites between Altnaharra and Bettyhill providing an insight into a valley population decimated by the Clearances.

You can follow as much or as little of the trail as you like, starting at either end. Here I've followed it in ascending numerical order, beginning east of the hamlet of **Altnaharra** to follow the B873 up to Syre (which then becomes the B871 as it continues north). The road takes you through a landscape that is largely scraggy moorland, punctuated here and there by clusters of deep-green forestry land. It feels so empty for much of the way that it's hard to reconcile what you see with the sobering thought that a couple of hundred years ago this area would have been full of thriving settlements.

"The road takes you through scraggy moorland, punctuated here and there by clusters of deep-green forestry land."

Each site is (theoretically at least) marked with a purple, numbered post, with information board(s) providing detail on what can be seen – however, the trail is rather old now, so it can be easy to miss the posts. I've highlighted those I think are most worth stopping at below; the numbers in parentheses correspond with the numbering used on the trail, which can be seen online at ⊘ theflowcountry.org.uk/assets/Uploads/StrathnaverTrailMap.pdf. Even if you don't stop, it's a beautiful driving route, with the loch or river always in view.

Travelling north, the first site you come to is **Grummore Settlement** (1; ♀ NC 61000 36669), from which its final 16 families were cleared in 1819. It's an extensive site, with the foundations of some 60 buildings – half were houses, half were used for farming – staggered up the hillside beside a winding burn, looking out over the loch, with Ben Klibreck in the distance beyond. Less than a hundred years before it was cleared, Grummore had only been home to five houses; it grew rapidly in the meantime, in part as people who had been cleared off land elsewhere were moved here – which of course makes it even more tragic that they were then cleared from here as well.

The parking area (♀ NC 60906 36578) for Grummore is 200yds southwest of the signposted starting point opposite the Altnaharra Campsite office, though you can also follow the paths up the hillside that start almost immediately across the burn. The first buildings can be found about 250yds up the rocky hill, and as you continue to climb higher you'll get a sense of just how big the village was – it's not hard to imagine this as a busy place when you see the outlines of dozens of buildings laid out below you.

Downhill from the village, immediately north of the campsite, is **Grummore Broch** (♀ NC 61083 36695). Though it's retained its circular shape, the broch is now little more than rubble, with trees growing out of its middle. Still, it's easy to see why this spot, right on the shores of the loch, would have been chosen.

Two miles northeast of Grummore is the smaller settlement of **Grumbeg** (2; ♀ NC 63499 38327); parking is across the road from the signpost. As at Grummore, clearance began in 1814, with the last villagers given notice in 1819 so that Patrick Sellar (page 90) could incorporate it as part of an extensive sheep farm. There are fewer ruins here, but they are closer to the road than at Grummore, and the hillside is less steep. The large walled area that you meet almost as soon as you climb up from the road is the old burial ground; to the west is the remains of a Neolithic chambered cairn, and the village buildings can be found further north and east.

Some six miles north, just where the B873 meets the B871, is **Syre Church** (4; ♀ NC 69358 43939), which, with its red roof and white corrugated-iron walls, stands out strikingly against the surrounding hills. It's a treat to be able to enter the small building, which is the picture of calm simplicity inside, comprised of little more than wooden pews and pulpit, a paisley runner and some of the unfussiest stained-glass I've seen. It was built in 1891 as a mission station to serve the Sutherland Estate's shepherds, gillies and gamekeepers, who at the time would have made up the strath's entire population, thanks to the Clearances.

To the south of here, on the opposite side of the river, is **Rosal Clearance Village** (5; ♀ NC 68567 41891 ♂ forestryandland.gov.scot/visit/rosal) reached by heading east on the B871 immediately after the church and taking the first (unsigned) right turning on to a forestry road. Running alongside the east bank of the River Naver, it's a bumpy, pot-hole scattered track, so do take it slowly. From the car park (♀ NC 68583 41925), about half a mile from the start of the road, tracks lead uphill to weave through trees to the enclosed site.

"It is quite something to sit and listen to MacLeod's words while gazing out at this now empty place."

What particularly marks Rosal out is its size – it was one of the largest pre-Clearance villages in Strathnaver and there are the remains of 70 buildings across the site, ranging from longhouses (where people would have lived) and barns to enclosures and corn-drying kilns. As you first emerge out of the trees, it's hard to see how big the site is; it's only as you wander around and every incline of the path reveals more building remains that you really begin to understand how large a settlement this would have been. You can follow posts to an audio bench, where you can listen to extracts from *Gloomy Memories* by Donald MacLeod, a first-hand account of the Clearances (there's a memorial to MacLeod himself at point 3 of the trail ♀ NC 68358 42146). It is quite something to sit and listen to MacLeod's words while gazing out at this now empty place, bringing home what was lost and giving extra meaning to the site when you continue to wander around it. How different this landscape would have seemed when the noises of children, farming and domestic work rang out across it.

THE KYLE OF TONGUE

Some 12½ miles west of Bettyhill is the shallow sea loch of the Kyle of Tongue, crossed by a causeway that at times – particularly when the tide is out and the loch seems to be predominantly swirling sand – appears to be a part of the natural landscape. The final, westernmost 200yds of the crossing is in fact a bridge; stopping at one of the two parking areas on the southern side of the road affords fabulous views across the water to the jagged ridges of Ben Loyal to the left and the bulk of Ben Hope to the right. The ruined castle in front of Ben Loyal is **Castle Varrich**, an easy walk from Tongue, the kyle's main settlement.

9 COLDBACKIE BEACH

As you head west out of the little crofting hamlet of **Coldbackie**, three miles northeast of Tongue on the A836, you'll catch a glimpse of its staggering beach: a curve of soft, cream-coloured sand and shimmering blue-green waters. There's no signpost down to the beach, which helps keep it secluded; park at the parking area (♀ NC 61040 60052) on the west side of the hamlet (immediately after the return to national speed limit, if coming from the east, and just before the village sign if coming from Tongue) and then head back towards the village sign – the path is just after this, on your left (there's another path about 100yds further on, if you miss this one), and leads quite steeply downhill and then over the dunes to the beach.

The cliffs along the back of the beach undulate in such a way that they look almost toe-like. The headlands at either end give it a sheltered feel, with lovely views across to Skinnet Beach (page 191) on the Melness peninsula, and the **Rabbit Islands** – here they are clearly two separate entities, but seen from Melness they often appear as one – and, to the far northeast, the more distant shape of **Eilean nan Ròn** (Island of the Seals), which was inhabited until 1938 but is now – surprise! – home to seals. The swell

"At low tide, you can spend ages exploring the nooks and crannies of the cliffs and the pools in the jagged rocks."

at the beach can be fierce, which has made it an increasingly popular spot with surfers. At low tide, you can spend ages exploring the nooks and crannies of the cliffs and the pools in the jagged rocks that pepper the sand.

The best view of the beach can be found along the clifftops to the east of it – you can either climb back up the dunes and look for a narrow path to the left that winds along the top (at the bottom of the fields), or park in the smaller space at the southeastern end of the hamlet (♀ NC 61532 59928) and follow the path down through fields though, as ever, do take care on the cliff tops. The hill behind the village is **Cnoc an**

Fhreiceadain, which Jeremy Clarkson infamously once drove a Land Rover up for *Top Gear*; you can head up the more respectful way – on foot – by following the footpath (♀ NC 61419 60007) that heads south off the main road, signposted just inland from the red phone box.

10 TONGUE
🏠 **Tongue Hotel**

It always strikes me how appropriate the name Tongue is for this small crofting village on the eastern shore of the kyle, given that the main road forms a V through the heart of the place, closely resembling the organ in question. The name actually comes from the Norse word *tonga*, which was used to describe a piece of land that juts out into a loch; referring here, one must assume, to the land that adjoins the causeway to the west.

The village's setting is its main selling point; to get a real sense of this, I'd recommend making a pleasant three-mile walk around its northern end. Starting at the curve in the A838, where the public toilets are, walk north along the western branch of the main road, so the Kyle is on your left and the loos and the back of the hotel on your right. Though you're walking along the main road here, it's generally not too busy, and you'll have increasingly good views across to the kyle, Castle Varrich (page 190) and – weather depending – Ben Hope. Shortly after you pass small **St Andrew's Church**, the pavement will run out – walk on the right-hand side of the road and move on to the verge when you meet traffic. As the road starts to curve left to go over the causeway, turn up the road on your right, walking uphill with your back to the water. You follow this road through woodland, full of birdsong, and past sweet little **Eddie's Garden**, which is open (free) to visitors, before curving right around old Tongue Mains. At the end of the road, with the kyle now in front of you, turn right to walk past the half-submerged old pier. You'll see the Rabbit Islands and Eilean nan Ròn in front of you, the kyle shimmering in a painter's palette of shades of blue. Follow this road up and round, climbing through woodland, and it'll eventually join the main road, where a right turn and careful walking will bring you back to the village after just over a mile, with increasingly good views of Ben Loyal's ridges ahead.

1 The ruins of Castle Varrich are a popular walk from Tongue. 2 Coldbackie Beach. 3 The jagged peaks of Ben Loyal from Tongue. ▶

KLODIEN/DT

EMMA GIBBS

EMMA GIBBS

The walk everyone does in Tongue, however, is the one to **Castle Varrich**, the neat little square ruin visible from the village. To get here, take the road that runs immediately south off the A838 and look for the footpath sign to 'Castle Bharrich' on your right soon after, about 100ft north of Ben Loyal Hotel. It's about a mile to the castle from the start of the footpath. The path is straightforward and well maintained, leading downhill and then curving left and then right to cross the wide and shallow Rhian Burn, before heading uphill through beautiful downy birch woodland. It's a fairly steep walk up, but a few benches here and there provide opportunities to rest.

"Cross the wide and shallow Rhian Burn, before heading uphill through beautiful downy birch woodland."

A fortification is thought to have stood on this prominent rocky hill since the 11th century, though what remains today most likely dates to the 16th century. Little is known about Castle Varrich, but it is assumed that, as its current size suggests, it would have been a relatively small structure, standing two storeys high. A public-viewing platform opened in the tower in 2018, which means you can climb up a metal staircase to the top and enjoy staggering views towards Ben Loyal, Ben Hope and down the kyle, as well as over the village itself, with its neat fields and hills.

SPECIAL STAYS

Tongue Hotel IV27 4XD ✆ 0808 506 5082 ⌂ tonguehotel.co.uk. Set in an old hunting lodge that was built by the Duke of Sutherland, this revamped hotel manages to perfectly combine cosy traditional style with unfussy contemporary sensibilities. Its position at the bend in the main road means some rooms have kyle views and others look over the wooded hillside or even towards Ben Loyal, and it's a great location from which to strike out on walks. Marcel and his friendly team are full of excellent suggestions for exploring Tongue and beyond, fresh milk is provided for in-room tea and coffee, and the bar is a great spot for a post-walk pint. The Varrich Restaurant is conveniently open all year and serves up particularly good seafood and fish, including Scrabster haddock. Don't miss the Cullen skink if it's on the menu.

FOOD & DRINK

Norse Bakehouse A836, IV27 4XW ✆ 01847 611332 ◼. With fabulous views over the sea and kyle, this great little place sells wonderful bread, focaccia and pastries, and really delicious pizzas. In sunny weather you can sit outside and soak up the views. It was for sale at the time of writing, so its future may be a little uncertain.

11 MELNESS

Heading north up the western side of the Kyle of Tongue there's no mistaking the townships that make up Melness as anything other than crofting ones: small rectangles of farmland line both sides of the road for much of the way, interrupted only by clusters of houses. It's worth coming this way for the views alone, across the ever-changing tidal waters of the kyle: north to the Rabbit Islands and Eilean nan Ròn; east to Coldbackie and the craggy hills of Cnoc an Fhreiceadain and Ben Tongue; and south across the causeway to glowering Ben Loyal and Ben Hope.

The main reason people head up here, however, is for the beaches. The first, and arguably the most spectacular, is **Skinnet Beach**; there's a parking area ($♀$ NC 58846 61819) in Midtown, across the road from which a footpath sign points to 'Skinnet Beach and the Ard'. Follow the path down between fields, with the rocky headland of the Ard directly ahead. At the gate at the end of the fields, turn right and you'll soon see the beach below you; keep the fence to your right and follow it around to the left to climb slightly before turning right towards the beach. There's a bit of clambering up and down the dunes to get to the sand.

"The main reason people head here is for the beaches. The first, and arguably the most spectacular, is Skinnet."

Marcel, the manager of the Tongue Hotel (see opposite) had told me to come here at low tide when the bay became 'desert-like'. I dutifully did, and now it's my turn to urge you to do the same; at low tide, the kyle seems to empty of water, and this description is perfectly apt for the vastness of sand that greets you, infinitely stretching out ahead – so much so that you feel you could walk the whole way to Ben Loyal, as the causeway in between is barely discernible. Low tide too means that there's more to explore – the rocky inlets and cliffs of the Ard, and the way the pale-blue water swirls through the sand. Do be sure to remember how quickly the tide starts coming in; it wouldn't take much to get stuck a bit too far out, lulled into a false sense of security by the lack of water.

On your way back to the car park, a right turn instead of a left when you meet the gate you came down to earlier will take you out on to the Ard itself, for more fabulous views over the kyle, the bay to the north and its islands.

SUTHERLAND SPACEPORT

The small hamlets on the northwest side of the Kyle of Tongue are part of **Melness Crofters' Estate** (MCE; 🖱 melness.scot), which covers 12,000 acres of land and has been community owned and managed since 1995. In many ways this landscape is typical of the North Highlands: small, green crofts dotted with sheep, wild swathes of moor, rocky coast and soft-sand beaches. The entire estate is common grazing, and most of the inhabitants are crofting tenants – many of whom were either born here or have lived here for a long time.

As with so many other places, MCE is faced with an ageing population and the need to encourage more families to move in – but people will only really come if there are jobs to be found. With many of the traditional industries, including oil and nuclear, in decline or disappearing, the estate has turned its sights on something rather bold and new: space.

In 2023, construction began on Sutherland Spaceport – the world's first carbon-neutral spaceport – on the estate. Dorothy Pritchard, MCE's chairperson, told me that the estate saw it 'as an opportunity to bring new industry to the Highlands, with new job opportunities attracting more people who want to live here.'

However, in December 2024, Orbex, the aerospace company behind the spaceport, suddenly announced that, despite a public investment package of £14.6 million, the project was being halted in favour of building a spaceport in Unst, Shetland. It remains to be seen whether an alternative might be found to take Orbex's place, or whether MCE will have to turn their sights elsewhere to attract new employment opportunities to the area.

Half a mile north is the pretty village of **Talmine**, stretched around and above an appealing bay. There's a useful **shop** here (Talmine Stores ⊙ Mon–Sat), and a very pleasant beach – or beaches, if you come at low tide when, as well as the main strip of sand, two smaller coves between the rocks are exposed.

Another mile and a half further on (keep straight on the road through East Strathan when the road forks towards Portvasgo and Midfield) – not quite at the end of the road but not far off – is beautiful **Achininver Beach**, which sits at the mouth of Strath Melness Burn. Access is from the parking space on its southern side (📍 NC 57433 64814), from where steps and a boardwalk lead down to the sand. This is another beach at its best at low tide, when the sands become huge and seem to stretch almost all the way to the two headlands that enclose it. It is possible to walk out here from Talmine, following the signed footpath to Portvasgo; detailed instructions can be found on WalkHighlands.

LOCH HOPE TO CAPE WRATH

Three further notable stretches of water lie between Melness and the very end of the north coast at isolated **Cape Wrath**: lochs Hope and Eriboll and the Kyle of Durness. The last acts of something of a boundary for the last swathe of land in the northwest, which is uninhabited and can only be reached on foot or via a ferry and minibus trip. By contrast, across the water is the busy little village of **Durness**, which swells in size during the warmer months and has more than enough to detain you for a few days.

12 DUN DORNAIGIL BROCH

It's easy to miss the narrow road that swings south off the A838 just before the road crossing Loch Hope, but it's another of those single-track roads that seems to go on indefinitely with very few other vehicles passing you en route. It traces the eastern side of Loch Hope for the whole of its six miles, with **Ben Hope** rising to the southeast; most of the tourists that you do meet along here will be travelling to or from the start point (♀ NC 46193 47680) to climb Scotland's most northerly Munro.

Just under two miles south of the starting point is Dun Dornaigil Broch (♀ NC 45707 45011), which still cuts an imposing figure when you spot it half a mile beforehand. Height-wise, this is the most intact broch (page 92) in the North Highlands, with its eastern wall still rising quite high, and thus giving at least a little sense of just how big these structures would have been. The small square-cut hole on the northern side was once its doorway, enabling you to think how much deeper it would have been, too; interestingly, it's never been excavated, so very little is known about it. Unlike brochs elsewhere, you can't actually go inside, but it's nonetheless interesting to get more of a sense of what others, such as those at Ousdale (page 120) and Nybster (page 147) would have looked like. You can walk around the outside of the walls, which now have moss and heather growing on top, and it's worth stopping for the views alone – the broch stands on the eastern side of Strath More, with the river winding directly below, Ben Hope rising to the north and undulating hills to the south.

"The broch stands on the eastern side of Strath More, Ben Hope rising to the north and undulating hills to the south."

SS

ALFIOFER/DT

SS

EMMA GIBBS

From the broch, the road makes its way through the sparse moorland of Flow Country (page 113) to the small crossroads settlement of **Altnaharra**, with mountain views increasingly opening up as you travel.

13 LOCH ERIBOLL

This sea loch's near ten-mile plunge inland forces the road to loop around it for most of its length, with its waters in view for most of the way. In addition to being long, it's also deep – about 195ft – which saw it used as an anchorage by the Royal Navy throughout the 20th century. The crews of some of the ships anchored here in the 1920s and '30s wrote out their ships' names in stone letters on the loch's western hillside (♥ NC 41400 60864), above the hamlet of Portnancon; they're hard to spot (I haven't yet managed it), but apparently you can see them with binoculars from road end in Portnancon (♥ NC 42708 60299). The stones are often called the **Hood Stones**, in reference to the most prominent of them, which was left

"What's particularly arresting about the sight of Ard Neakie are the old lime kilns set into the rough hills."

by the crew of HMS *Hood*, which was anchored here around 1935; the battlecruiser was sunk in May 1941 by the German warship *Bismarck* – all but three of the 1,418 crew died.

As the road curves round to meet Loch Eriboll from the east, one of the first things you'll see is the peninsula of **Ard Neakie**, joined to the shore by a thin isthmus. What's particularly arresting about the sight of Ard Neakie are the old lime kilns set into the rough hills on its southeastern side. Built in the 19th century, they heated the local limestone – quarried just behind the kilns – to produce lime that could be used to make mortar and render for buildings, and to improve soil quality so that crops could grow better.

It's worth getting out to explore the peninsula, particularly as most people just stop at the viewpoint to take a photo and then continue on; you can either follow the steep path down the hillside from the viewpoint parking area (♥ NC 45203 59929), or park in the small parking area (♥ NC 45069 59436) at the bottom of the hill – look for the road on the western side of the A838, which leads up to a closed gate.

◀ 1 View towards Ben Hope. 2 Loch Eriboll and the Ard Neakie peninsula. 3 The remains of the Clearance village of Ceannabeinne. 4 The Sculpture Croft at Loch Eriboll.

THE SCULPTURE CROFT

07761 220953 ⬧ lotteglob.co.uk ⬧ by appointment only

On the western side of Loch Eriboll, facing the island of Eilean Choraidh, is somewhere I'd honestly say is one of the most extraordinary places I've been to in the North Highlands – and I never expected this accolade to go to a place rather than a landscape. In many ways though, ceramicist **Lotte Glob**'s Sculpture Croft *is* a landscape – or, rather, it's very much part of it. First things first: this is not somewhere you can turn up to without an appointment, but – and I say this as someone who hates the idea of having to make appointments to visit things – doing so is more than worth it.

Lotte is a celebrated Danish ceramicist, but she's lived here in the North Highlands for the last 50 years – first at Balnakeil (page 201), and now on her 14-acre croft overlooking Loch Eriboll. Paths weave through the croft – first through trees (Lotte has planted a staggering 5,000 in the 20 years she's lived here) and then through heather – down towards the shore and then back up again. 'You can go anywhere,' Lotte told me.

There is so much to see; some of it is tucked into little dells, like the little village of tiny houses, while others spring up from the ground and from the trees. The ceramics seem at once alien and yet natural, and much of the work has been taken over by the world that surrounds it, with moss creeping on to things, and trees growing out of ceramic

At the end of the path across the isthmus is the old ferryman's house, built in 1831 – though, interestingly, 57 years later it was marked on the first edition of the OS map as the Heilam Inn, and assumedly used largely by ferry passengers who travelled between here and Portnancon

"You can continue up to the top of the hill for far-reaching views; listen out for the sound of oystercatchers."

on the opposite shore before the road was opened at the end of the 19th century. The kilns, further south along the shore, are a little less imposing close up than they are from afar, but still fascinating to peer inside. A steep path runs up the right-hand side of the kilns; at the top to the right is what looks like a little lochan, surrounded by steep rocky sides – this is actually the old limestone quarry. You can continue up to the top of the hill for far-reaching views in all directions; listen out for the sound of oystercatchers both here and along the shore.

On the western side of the loch is one of my favourite places in the whole of the North Highlands, the Sculpture Croft (see above), though note that a visit requires advance planning.

bases. This is not a place to rush through, but a place to really live Slow travel.

As I walked around, I found myself constantly astounded, and while at first my mind tried to make sense of what I was seeing – *is this a bird or am I misinterpreting it?* – the more I walked the more I realised that all that mattered was how it felt and appeared to me. Some of my favourites included the little elephant-like beasts rising out of boggy ground, and the three faceless winged creatures perched on rocks near them. I also loved the simplicity of other work, like the bright blue boulders that stretched in a line downhill.

What comes out the most from the Sculpture Croft is the importance of this landscape, and the deep love that Lotte has for it. So much of what she does is intrinsically linked with the place in which she lives, from the croft to the 'merstones' she made and cast off Faraid Head (page 204) three times a month for a year – some of which returned quickly to the beach, and others that have washed up on shores in Caithness and even west Shetland. 'You can't improve on nature,' Lottie said to me – a sentiment with which I'd completely agree, and so it seems only right that her work has become a part of it.

While here, you can also visit Lotte's small gallery and see and purchase some of her other work. Check her website, too, for her frequent exhibitions elsewhere in the region.

14 CEANNABEINNE

Almost as soon as the road turns west after circumnavigating Loch Eriboll, you catch a glimpse of the Caribbean-like colours of **Ceannabeinne Beach** to your right down below. Even dull weather seems to do little to dampen the colours here, and though it's far from the little-visited strands found elsewhere on this coast, it's unlikely to feel crowded once you're away from the car park. Steps directly across from the car park (♥ NC 44343 65307) lead on to a clear, well-maintained path down the grassy hill. Offshore are the islands of Eilean Hoan (the largest) and An Dubh-sgier (really a skerry or rocky island) to the northwest. The beach's Gaelic name, by which it is marked on OS maps, is *Tràigh Allt Chàilgeag*, which translates to 'beach of the burn of bereavement and death' – apparently because an old woman was swept to her death down the burn and into the sea. When the tide is at its lowest, you can walk northwest along the beach to find a natural arch and a cave. Many would disagree, but I can't help but think that the position of the **Golden Eagle Zipline** (⬙ durnesszipline.com ☽ weather permitting: Easter–Aug 10.15–16.00 daily; Sep & Oct 10.30–15.30 daily)

THE DURNESS RIOTS

The clearing of **Ceannabeinne** comes relatively late in the timeline of the Highland Clearances (page 90), despite the fact that areas east of here, including Eriboll, had been cleared a couple of decades previously. This is in part because the land here, unlike most other parts of Sutherland, was under the control of James Anderson – though, by all accounts, he wasn't the most pleasant of men.

On the day Anderson served notice of eviction to the tenants of Ceannabeinne, only the women were in the village – no doubt a careful calculation on Anderson's part. With the men unable to return quickly enough, the women took matters into their own hands, forcing the officer serving the writ to burn it. A few days later, police superintendent Philip Mackay from Dornoch brought a new writ, but he was chased away and also unable to serve it.

By this point, the Scottish press had heard about the events, though they were largely unsympathetic. Mackay later returned, hoping to raise a party of men en route to help him but unable to find more than three willing – and then only for those three to turn back when they heard that the residents, of both the village and the wider Durness area, were lying in wait for them.

rather ruins the more leisurely nature of the beach, but nonetheless it offers up a short alternate perspective of the sands.

Just west of the beach is the **Ceannabeinne Township Trail** (♀ NC 43664 65755), which takes you up on to the craggy hillsides where, until 1842, the township of Ceannabeinne was located. Prior to that year, there had been 14 houses and 50 people living here; as at similar places in the North Highlands, it's quite moving to stand on this now-deserted hillside and contemplate how this once would have been a busy settlement. In theory, a waymarked trail (just over half a mile) takes you around the township from information board to information board, but when I last visited many of the trail signs were broken and the bridge over the burn was severely damaged (though it was possible to cross via stepping stones); if this is still the case when you visit, take a photo of the route from the board in the car park to aid you as you walk around

15 DURNESS

⅄ Sango Sands

Stretching for a couple of miles along the northwesterly corner of the A838, with more than its fair share of gorgeous beaches, this scattered

When Mackay next returned it was with the sheriff and 14 special constables, arriving in the parish on the evening of Saturday 17 September 1841. This time a group of around 50 men met the officials, asking for the eviction not to be carried out on the Sabbath day, but this was declined. Shortly after, a crowd of locals amassed – by some reports, 300 in total – who charged at the inn and rounded up the constables, removing them from the parish.

When the sheriff of Sutherland returned a few days later, he threatened to carry out the eviction by force, making use of the 53rd Regiment from Edinburgh. A compromise was agreed – aided by the fact that the press was becoming sympathetic to the rioters – which allowed the tenants to stay until the May of the following year so that they would have time to find new places to live.

What perhaps makes the riots most significant is that after the event an enquiry was held, led by Francis Napier, in which no prosecutions were brought against those locals that were involved. Napier himself went on to lead the **Napier Commission**, which, in 1886, established the Crofting Act that finally gave crofters security of tenure.

crofting village has a definite holiday feel during the summer, but even out of season you'll find the campsite in use and at least a couple of other people on the sand. To many Beatles' fans, Durness is a familiar name as it was here that a young John Lennon spent his holidays; the small **John Lennon Memorial Garden** (♀ NC 41428 67241) on the main road is dedicated to him.

A deep chasm scours the coastline to the southeast of Durness, creating one of the north coast's most famous sites. The fact that you can't even catch a glimpse of **Smoo Cave** (♀ NC 41814 67143) without descending the hillside makes its appearance all the more impressive; there are two paths down to it and I'd recommend taking the right-hand one that winds more gently down the eastern hillside – when you turn sharply to walk towards the cave you get a great view of the wide, gaping mouth of its main chamber, cut deep into the limestone rock that characterises much of the Durness landscape.

Interestingly, this first cave you encounter has been formed and shaped by the sea, while its second chamber is a karst cave that was carved out by the river. The result is two very different but atmospheric caves. As you enter the main cave, look at the floor to your left to see a shell midden: the food waste of Stone Age people, which extends some

STORIES OF SMOO CAVE

Smoo Cave has long been used by humans, evidenced by the Stone Age shell midden and remnants from Viking times, including ship nails and pins made from antlers. Over the centuries it has become a large part of local folklore, too, with many stories swirling around it.

One such story tells that the cave's blowhole was created by the Devil himself, who blasted his way out of the cave after being discovered by a dog, who had been sent in by his owner to see if the Devil was in there. In the 17th century, Domhnull MacMhurchaidh apparently killed 18 people and disposed of their bodies down the cave's waterfall, sure that his crimes would never be discovered, thanks to the local belief that the Devil lived there. (MacMhurchaidh's tomb can still be found in Balnakeil Church, page 204, today). Then, in the 18th century, two Excise Officers were rowed beneath the waterfall and killed – well, it was either that or let them discover the illegal still hidden in the second chamber.

39ft below the ground – you'll see give-away clusters of shells. Ferns and mosses clinging to the misshapen walls give it an almost tropical feel, and you'll likely get dripped on from the walls and ceiling above you.

A covered wooden walkway leads into the second cave where you can see the gushing waterfall from a viewing platform and get a sense of the wider cave system continuing beyond. If you can, I really recommend taking the time to join a **tour** (✆ 01971 511492 ☍ smoocavetours. com ☉ Apr–Oct; cash only). Despite its rather basic set-up in the main cave, comprising a couple of trestle tables covered with photos and information, and a whiteboard waiting list on which you write your name and the number of people in your party, tours are run by experienced cavers – in the months the tours don't run, Fraser and his team are slowly but surely digging their way further into the cave system. Taking the tour does require a little sense of adventure and agility: you ascend down to water level via a ladder, climb into the rubber raft and duck under a horizontal limestone pillar before reaching the waterfall, and then, once out of the boat, pick your way to the end of the cave. It's hugely atmospheric, however, and the guides are insightful – and humorous with it (though my son was convinced they were telling the truth when they said they used to send little children – who never came back – down to explore

"Once out of the boat, pick your way to the end of the cave. It's hugely atmospheric and the guides are insightful."

the caves). Wear sturdy footwear and waterproof coats; hard hats are provided. Note that weather conditions dictate whether tours can run; when we visited, it was the first time in weeks that water levels had been low enough for them to safely do so.

Before you leave, cross the road by the car park to see the blowhole, allegedly carved out by the Devil (see opposite).

Durness's pièce de résistance is **Sango Bay**, just under a mile northwest of the caves. Access is via the large car park (♀ NC 40745 67701) immediately east of Mathers (a little shop), or a couple of smaller car parks on the single-track road that runs directly east from the A838 when the bigger road hairpins to the south. At high tide, the bay's beaches are divided into a handful of smaller, sandy coves, separated by great rocky outcrops, but at low tide it becomes one long stretch of sand that can look a pale pink in some light, and a bright, glittering gold in others. This is one of my kids' very favourite beaches: the rocks are perfect for climbing on and playing games of hide-and-seek around. Stretching above the beach is Sango Sands campsite (see below); wooden steps at the northern end of the campsite, accessible from the clifftop path that runs along its sea-facing edge, lead out to **Sango Sands Viewpoint** (♀ NC 40712 68035), which provides fantastic 360° views over the bay and undulating hills to the south. I'd particularly recommend coming out here at sunset, when the sky seems to scroll through an entire pastel-hued rainbow of colours.

SPECIAL STAYS

Sango Sands Sango Bay IV27 4PZ ⌀ sangosands.com. Without a doubt one of the best-placed campsites in the whole of the UK, stretching out along the clifftop above beautiful Sango Bay. Facilities are rather basic but clean plus there's a bar (summer only) and you're a short walk from the well-stocked Spar shop. Only 50 electric hook-up bookings are taken per day, otherwise it's run on a first-come first-served basis; in summer you'll need to arrive as soon as possible after noon to be sure of a space. You can still camp here in the winter months but toilets are closed – thankfully there are some in the public car park down the road.

16 BALNAKEIL

There's a real sense of heading towards the end of the road as you go out to the small hamlet of Balnakeil, just over half a mile northwest of Durness. Once you leave behind the last of its larger neighbour's residential buildings, the views open up: mountains to your left, Cape Wrath ahead, and the sea, the shimmering beach and Faraid Head to your right.

In the mid 1950s, the Ministry of Defence built an early warning station for a nuclear attack at Balnakeil – it was never used, however, and in the 1960s its low buildings were offered up for rent to people with skills and a decent business plan as part of the Far North Project. Despite the fact that the buildings initially had no plumbing or electricity, the project attracted applicants from all over the UK, evolving into **Balnakeil Craft Village** (⊘ balnakeilcraftvillage.weebly.com ⊖ check website; free entry), a small and thriving community of artists. If the words 'craft village' have you anticipating an orderly, prettified place then you'll be in for a surprise; there's a rather dishevelled feel to it, which suits its edge-of-the-world/ex-military base setting. It's now home to about 14 different

"Here, the delineation between land, sky and sea seems to disappear, with them all blurring into one."

businesses, most of them art based, from ceramics at Mudness (⊘ mudnessceramics.com) and stained- and fused glass by Lesley Smith (⊘ balnakeilglass.weebly.com) to the evocative landscapes of Ishbel Macdonald (⊘ ishmacpaintings.co.uk). You can learn about the region's fascinating geology in the small exhibition at Durness Deep Time (⊘ durnessdeeptime.com; free entry). Most visitors, however, make a beeline for Cocoa Mountain (page 204).

North of the craft village is another of those spectacular north-coast beaches that will have you laughing out loud in astonishment. All you really need to know about vast **Balnakeil Beach** is that the first time I visited, it was absolutely hammering it down – and I still came away thinking it was one of the most beautiful beaches I'd ever seen. Returning on a dry, bright day, it of course more than lived up to the memory. Here, the delineation between land, sky and sea seems to disappear, with them all blurring into one; the pale sand left almost silvery by the retreating tide, the water changing shades of turquoise and the sky ever-shifting above it. At low tide, the cream-coloured sand stretches uninterrupted

1 Balnakeil Church and cemetery. 2 Approaching Kearvaig Bay on the Cape Wrath peninsula. 3 Sango Bay, Durness. 4 Touring Smoo Cave. 5 Faraid Head peninsula and Balnakeil Beach. ▶

MARKFERGUSON2/A

HELEN HOTSON/DT

FRASER EADIE

SS

for almost 1½ miles, but at higher tides you'll need to join the path that runs along the back of the beach (from ♀ NC 39303 69580) to climb over the rocky outcrop in the middle to reach the sands on the other side. The rocks here are huge and rather prehistoric looking, perfect for exploring at low tide.

The beach is backed by huge sand dunes covered in long marram grass, which extend across much of the peninsula on which the beach sits. Do bear in mind that the dunes are fragile and a valuable part of the environment here, and walk gently between them. In the middle, the dunes are so huge and vast that you could almost think you'd strayed into the desert.

At the far end of the beach is **Faraid Head**, which can be explored by following the path north (you'll have to pick your way carefully through the dunes for a while) or walking the entire length of the beach and then climbing east uphill on to the grassy farmland at the end, eventually joining the road, which is used only by the MOD, which still has a base here. You can follow this road all the way to the MOD gates; turn right here on to a footpath that skirts around the site's perimeter before heading along the cliffs for a bit, with fabulous views towards Durness and Sango Bay (and beyond). The contrast to the soft beach is stark up here, with barren moorland stretching around you, though you'll likely spot the bushy tails of rabbits hopping away as you walk.

"In the middle, the dunes are so huge and vast that you could almost think you'd strayed into the desert."

Back on the beach, the view as you head back towards the car park (♀ NC 39153 68649) is exceedingly pretty, with the imposingly large Balnakeil House (now a holiday home) on the left and the shell of old Balnakeil Church on the right. The church itself can be accessed from its beach-facing side – today it's roofless, with ivy creeping up its remaining walls, but you can still get a sense of what it was like inside, and see the tomb of murderous Domhnull MacMhurchaidh (page 200).

¶¶ FOOD & DRINK

Cocoa Mountain Balnakeil Craft Village, IV27 4PT ⊘ cocoamountain.co.uk. A visit to this chocolate café is something of a rite of passage for visitors to this far northwest corner, who come for the incredibly rich hot chocolate. As well as fantastic chocolates (made on-site), there's a handful of savoury items including ham and cheese croissants.

17 CAPE WRATH

Ferry: ✆ 07719 678729 🖥 capewrathferry.wordpress.com; ⊙ May–Sep daily; check timings in advance via text or at Keoldale jetty ⚲ NC 37791 66134; Minibus: ✆ 07534 591124 🖥 visitcapewrath.com ⊙ May–Sep daily

The wild and isolated northwesternmost corner of mainland Britain is appropriately hard to access – not only can you only reach it on foot or by a combination of ferry and (organised) minibus, but the cape is also used as a training area so visits are subject to restrictions when MOD operations are taking place. And of course, as with so much in this region, getting out here is also dependent on the weather and tides. It's well worth the effort, however, and just adds to the feeling of adventure.

On foot, Cape Wrath can be accessed by a pathless 7¾-mile walk from Sandwood Bay (page 206), itself only reachable via a four-mile walk; this forms the end stage of the Cape Wrath Trail (page 171). If you're walking in, make sure you check when the cape will be closed for use by the MOD (🖥 gov.uk/government/publications/scotland-firing-times) before you set out – this is also indicated by red flags and lights. Much easier is the ferry and minibus combination; the small **Cape Wrath Ferry** departs from the tiny jetty at **Keoldale**, two miles southwest of Durness, to make the short (ten-minute) journey across the Kyle of Durness.

The ferry is met on the western side of the kyle by a minibus to make the 11-mile journey to the cape. Don't be fooled by this short distance – it takes about an hour to get there on a rather rough road and across rickety bridges, but the rugged scenery and commentary from the driver about the cape and the places you pass en route more than helps the time to pass. Once at the cape, you have around an hour to explore – it is possible to stay for longer, subject to arrangement with the bus driver. If you've walked into Cape Wrath and want to return by bus, you should inform the minibus company the day before; another option is to take the ferry over and back but walk up to the lighthouse, which would enable you to stop off en route at Clo Mor and Kearvaig (page 206) but again you should talk to the ferry operator about the return journey, and bear in mind that mobile reception can be patchy out here.

While 'wrath' feels like the appropriate word for this elemental, weather- and wave-beaten corner, the word actually comes from the Norse *hvarf*, which means turning point – reflecting its use as a navigation point. The lighthouse here was built by Robert Stevenson in 1828 and has been automated since 1998; the building itself is not open to the public, but there's a handy café and bunkhouse ($\mathcal{O}$ 01971 511314 $\odot$ 24hr) in the former engine room.

It would be a shame to come out here and just sit in a café, however. The cliffs at Cape Wrath are a Site of Special Scientific Interest (SSSI), home in the summer months to 50,000 breeding seabirds, including puffins, fulmars and guillemots. Look out too for seals and passing dolphins and porpoises. Here you'll also find the highest cliffs on mainland Britain, **Clo Mor**, rising sheer from the sea to 921ft – they are, however, over four miles from the lighthouse, so difficult to get to within your allocated hour here. Just west is **Kearvaig**, an absolutely glorious beach, overlooked by Britain's most remote bothy ($\mathcal{O}$ mountainbothies.org.uk).

THE FAR NORTHWEST

The craggy coastline of far northwest Sutherland is filled with tucked-away white-sand beaches, narrow inlets and scattered islands. The big sight for many people is **Sandwood Bay**, famously reached by a four-mile moorland walk, but nearby are some equally beautiful coves of soft sand that I'd argue are even more of a treat to discover. Here too is the fabulous nature reserve of **Handa Island**, which can only be visited in spring and summer when the seabirds come in to nest. If you're approaching from the north then this is the part where it often feels like the scenery really ramps up, with the main road (the A838) curving through an almost lunar-like landscape and the mountains rearing up around you.

The slightly industrial feel to parts of the road that runs out towards the start of the Sandwood walk is due to the presence of one of Scotland's major fishing ports, at the otherwise small village of **Kinlochbervie**.

18 SANDWOOD BAY

$\mathcal{O}$ johnmuirtrust.org

Gone are the days when this one-mile beach was a secret; Sandwood Bay has definitely been 'discovered'. Don't let that put you off, however – for a start, the beach is big enough to lose the crowds, if there could ever be any, but the four-mile walk across moorland to get here, with barely even a glimmer of the sea until the last stretch, is enough to put off all but the most dedicated. The walk itself is moderately easy – a few climbs, a couple of points where you need to stretch over stepping stones – but the path is well maintained and clear, and you don't need to be able to read a map to make the journey.

The only way to reach Sandwood is on foot (although you can also cycle to the half-way point); parking is available in **Blairmore** (♀ NC 19415 60028), just over three miles northwest of Kinlochbervie, where you'll find toilets, water and a map of the route. The path starts just to the east of the car park, on the opposite side of the road. For the main part, it winds through moorland, spotted with lochans that glitter appealingly in the sun, and with mountains rising to your right. After about a mile, you should be able to make out the white mark of Cape Wrath lighthouse in the distance. When the path splits, after just over a mile, take the left-hand branch, which runs alongside the loch, for a slight short cut – unless you're on a bike, in which case it'll be too rough – which soon rejoins the main path.

Bikes need to be left at the two-mile point; there are handy racks where you can leave them, and after this the path narrows and becomes considerably rockier. The landscape throughout the walk is studded with heather, making it a riot of colour in late summer. As you pass the last small loch, Loch Clais nan Coinneal, the contours, ridges and rocks of hills that you've been looking at for most of the last hour are suddenly revealed in full, technicolour detail, as though you're looking at them through a microscope.

From here, you climb the final hill and the large expanse of Loch Sandwood is exposed ahead, with a derelict cottage sitting by it. Soon after you're likely to be stopped in your tracks by the appearance of the bay in all its beauty – backed by the loch and dunes and looking wide and wild, with cliffs rearing up on either side. From here, there's still about half a mile left, up and over the dunes – be prepared to slide/slip down them if they become a bit steep.

"It's the size of Sandwood Bay that gets you when you first stand on it, particularly when the tide is out."

It's the size of Sandwood Bay that gets you when you first stand on it, particularly when the tide is out: vast and (most often) empty. It's another place where the colours seem to constantly change – turquoise sea moving to a deep blue, the sand shifting from a bright gold to bronze as clouds skid above you. At the far southwestern end (though you'll have to walk a little north up the beach to see it), is the 213ft-high sea stack of **Am Buachaille** ('the Shepherd').

Composed of red Torridonian sandstone, it looks like some kind of mad game of Jenga.

For all its wide, smooth sand, there's nothing bland about Sandwood Bay – texture is added by a couple of rocky deposits around the middle of the bay (on or off the sand depending on the state of the tide) that, at lower tides, you can climb on and explore. The beach, despite its huge size, feels as though it is constantly altering while you are there – when I started walking back, channels had appeared where previously there were none, forcing me to jump across rather deep water and in most places my footprints had already entirely disappeared.

The way back involves a bit more of an uphill slog at times, particularly over the dunes from the beach, but the good thing is that you're now able to better appreciate the scenery you're walking through. And the view of Polin Bay when it appears towards the end, stretching beyond to little lumpen islands, including Handa, is just as welcome.

19 POLIN & OLDSHOREMORE BEACHES

These two lovely stretches of sand more than hold their own against the might of Sandwood Bay – I might even go so far as to say that I think they're even more beautiful. Getting to both requires a short walk down through croft land, and when they appear in front of you, with paler sand than at Sandwood, it's still a real thrill.

With its little cluster of white houses, the hamlet of **Polin** is so picture perfect it'd be overrun in any other part of the UK. From the car park (♀ NC 19518 59175), continue down to the end of the road; the path to the beach is on the right, just before the last house. The path runs down through croft land, revealing the glorious, pale biscuit-coloured swathe of sand. A sign on the final gate down to the beach from the car park reads 'Here be mermaids', and it's not a stretch to believe it. Smaller and more sheltered than its more southerly neighbour, Polin beach is lapped by soft-mint-green sea, with undulating rocky cliffs on one side, and huge, jagged rocks scored by time and weather on the other.

"The path runs down through croft land, revealing the glorious, pale biscuit-coloured swathe of sand."

By road, it's two miles to Oldshoremore, but it's just over half a mile if you walk over the headland. To get there, take the path that runs along the cliffs at the southeastern side of Polin Beach: follow it to the left of a

MAD ABOUT MACHAIR

Oldshoremore, Polin and Sheigra are part of an SAC (Special Area of Conservation) and SSSI for their sand dunes, which, together with those at Sandwood, are home to one of Britain's most species-rich and least-disturbed areas of machair.

Gaelic for a fertile, grassy plain, machair is only found on west-facing shores in north and west Scotland and western Ireland, making it an incredibly rare habitat. It's not an entirely wild landscape though, as its makeup has been shaped over centuries and centuries by low-intensity farming. The sand here is rich in calcium carbonate, due to a high shell content, which enables a great diversity of plants to grow in the soil. As well as eight different species of orchids, other flora to look out for are pink mountain everlasting, yellow globeflowers and white Scots lovage.

fence, the sea on your right, initially keeping close to the sea. A few paths crisscross the headland here and it's quite fun to explore, with views across to Handa and Scourie and the mountains of Foinaven, Arkle and Ben Stack on the horizon. To reach the beach, you'll need to swing inland (east) to walk uphill between craggy rocks – it can be a little boggy – and then more or less keeping east until you reach a stile in the fence. While you can scramble down the rocks just southwest of here, it can be a bit slippery and I'd recommend instead turning right after you cross the stile to follow a stone wall for just over 100yds along the top of the dunes, turning left on a faint path to walk downhill on to the beach, which is rather rocky at this point. From here, the main expanse of sand is straight on.

Much larger **Oldshoremore** is bookended by particularly bulbous cliffs of Lewisian gneiss that is so characteristic of northwest Scotland, and overlooked by a scattering of white houses. Like Polin, it's a staggering stretch of buttery sand and vividly turquoise water. At its northern end is the hilly island of Eilean nan h-Aiteig, which you can walk on to at low tide

The dunes behind both beaches, and at **Sheigra**, another lovely beach two miles northwest, are home to particularly species-rich machair habitats (see above), where over 200 different plant species can be found, of which eight are orchids, including the purple northern marsh orchid and the harder to spot frog orchid.

Parking for Oldshoremore is by the hamlet's cemetery (◊ NC 20335 58481), where there are also toilets; from here it's just a short walk down to the sands.

¶ FOOD & DRINK

Old School Restaurant & Rooms Inshegra IV27 4RH ✐ 01971 521383 ⟁ oldschoolhotel. co.uk. Set inside an old school building, this friendly restaurant has a small menu of dishes such as homemade venison casserole and great fish and chips. The daily specials usually include locally caught fish or shellfish, and the homemade ice cream is divine. Book in advance. Also has a handful of very pleasant B&B rooms.

20 HANDA ISLAND

⟁ scottishwildlifetrust.org.uk/reserve/handa-island ⊘ early Apr–late Aug/early Sep Mon–Sat; ferry: ✐ 07780 967800 ⟁ handa-ferry.com ⊘ outward journey 09.00–13.30 Mon–Sat, weather dependent

The trouble with visiting Handa Island is that you're at the mercy of the elements – which means you may well be like me and thwarted numerous times before you can make it out here. Still, it's worth persevering to do so: Handa is recognised as being internationally important for its seabird population, which at the height of breeding season swells to a staggering 200,000 birds.

"It's worth persevering to visit: Handa is recognised as being internationally important for its seabird population."

The ferry to Handa departs from Tarbet pier, 5½ miles northwest of Scourie (page 213), via a single-track road that winds past lochs and lochans. Do check timings and details before you travel out here, however, as the service can easily be disrupted by the weather and the tides, and the season can often start and end earlier or later than planned. The price of the ferry ticket (cash only) includes access to the island; you land at one of two white-sand beaches on the island's eastern side, from where the ranger and volunteers lead you to the small hut for an introductory talk. After that you're armed with a map and left to explore the island by yourself: the only two stipulations are that you must stick to the paths, to protect the ground-nesting birds, and that you need to be back in plenty of time for the last boat. If you don't have your own binoculars, they can be hired from the hut (cash only) – I'd really recommend doing so as having them will make a huge difference to what you can see.

◀ 1 Oldshoremore is bookended by particularly bulbous cliffs. 2 Farmland at the start of the path to Sandwood Bay. 3 Handa Island is the breeding ground of 200,000 seabirds at the height of the season, including razorbills. 4 Polin Beach. 5 The sea stack of Am Buachaille, as seen from Sandwood Bay.

The path around the island is four miles in total; it's not particularly challenging, though it does climb gently uphill for a bit, and I'd recommended that you allow at least a couple of hours for exploration (it took me about 3½ hours, with leisurely stops for birdwatching and a picnic lunch en route); this is not the place to come if you have to be somewhere that afternoon, particularly as you might have to wait for room in a return boat (or for the tide to be right). Handa is a place for patience and time: sit, wait and watch, and more and more will be revealed to you.

The route starts out across moorland where the remains of a village can be seen – the island was last properly inhabited in 1847, when its residents were sent to Nova Scotia following the potato famine – and it's likely your walk will be accompanied by the constant song of skylarks. Look to your left as you walk and you should be able to spot the Old Man of Stoer (page 229) in the distance. The map you're given on arrival rather dauntingly advises on what to do if you're dive bombed by a skua ('hold up your hand and move on quickly'); both Arctic and great skuas nest here and can be very actively defensive of their nests.

The puffins are usually the main attraction for many visitors: up to 500 nest here each summer. You can usually see them on the **Great Stack**, among similarly coloured guillemots and razorbills, and at the **Geogdh na Goibhere**, a little further along. Their bright orange legs are usually a good giveaway. Don't forget to look up, too – I spotted a golden eagle while I was on the island – or down, as dolphins and whales are commonly sighted as well, and seals can usually be seen playing in the shallows of **Boulder Bay**, to the southwest. The cliffs westwards from puffin-less **Puffin Bay** are full of squawking, chattering birds, who perch and crowd and nest on the natural ledges cut into the cliffs; the more you study the rocks, the more birds you'll see, with others constantly circling and zooming in and out to take up their own places.

Make sure you wear decent walking shoes and pack layers for a trip out here. On my visit, it started as a grey, heavy day but was clear enough that I could, from the north coast, make out Oldshoremore and Polin beaches in the distance. Within half an hour, however, both had disappeared under a thick curtain of cloud, and before long the rain and fog had rolled on to the island and I couldn't see more than a hundred yards in front of me. Nonetheless, it was hugely atmospheric (if damp), with the squawks of the unseen birds billowing out eerily from the fog.

THE ROCK ROUTE

Along the northwest coast, from Loch Eriboll to Ullapool, you'll often notice a small Celtic symbol and signboards for the Rock Route, part of the **North West Highlands Geopark** (page 219). In some places, such as at Stac Pollaidh (page 250) and Knockan Crag National Nature Reserve (page 248), they mark places where you can get out and explore; in others, they sit in parking areas where you can observe the region's striking geology.

Particularly noticeable in northwest Sutherland is the so-called **Multi-coloured**

rock stop (♀ NC 23248 48606) opposite Loch na Fiacail, eight miles northeast of Scourie. Across the road from the parking area is an incredible rock face, banded by three strikingly different coloured instances of Lewisian gneiss – in particular, look closely to see the crystals in the pink band.

Audio guides and further information can be accessed from the geopark website (⌀ nwhgeopark.com/the-rock-route), which help to provide further context on the region's geology.

⫟ FOOD & DRINK

Shorehouse Seafood Restaurant Tarbet IV27 4SS ⌀ 01971 502251 ⌀ shorehousetarbet.co.uk. Run by the same family since it opened in 1977, this place, perfectly positioned right by the pier for the Handa ferry, is a great spot for a meal or a drink and a slice of (very delicious) cake after a trip to the island – lovely big windows allow you to soak up the views. The menu specialises, as the name suggests, in seafood, with an emphasis on shellfish, much of which is caught from the family's own boats. Fresh Handa crab and prawns are particular stand outs.

21 SCOURIE

Five and a half miles south of Tarbet is the appealing little village of Scourie, surrounded by lumpen, rocky hills and green croft land. The main part of the village sits to the east of Scourie Bay, which, at low tide, has a deep stretch of white sand (at high tide, what little sand there is is scattered with dark stones and seaweed).

At the southeastern end of the beach is a **community bird hide**, which is a pleasant spot from which to watch waders and divers on the shore – look out for rare red-throated divers. From here, it's well worth making the two-mile round-trip walk to Scourie headland, from which there are great views back towards the village, north to Handa and south to the Stoer peninsula. To begin, head to the northern end of the beach, where there's a signpost to the headland; go through the gate on the right-hand side of the cemetery and follow the wall round to then turn right and walk uphill, with a pebbly cove below you. A number of grassy paths run out to and around the headland, so it's easy enough to pick your own way: I'd suggest keeping to the right-hand paths on your way out, which will lead you past rocky shores, with views of Handa opening up.

The island to the northwest of the headland, separated only by a narrow, rocky channel, is **Eilean a' Bhuic** – 'Island of the Buck Goat', though there's no sign of any goats on there now. From here, you can head left to loop around the headland before turning back – either the way you came or along other paths. On your way back, you'll catch a glimpse of some of Assynt's mightiest mountains to the south, including Quinag and Suilven.

The award-winning Slow Travel series from Bradt Guides

Over 20 regional guides across Britain.
See the full list at bradtguides.com/slowtravel.

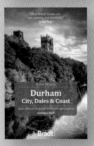

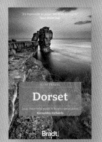

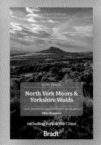

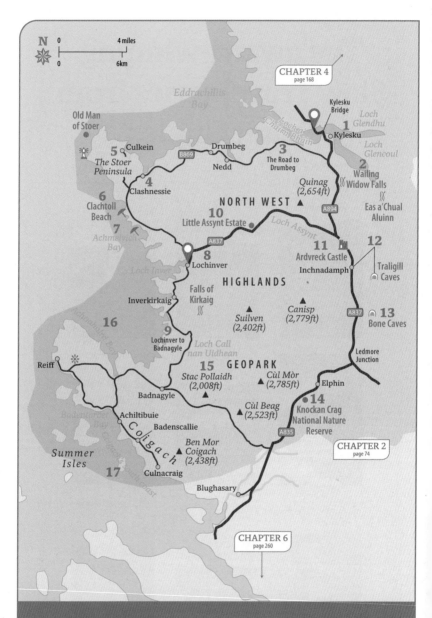

N
0   4 miles
0   6km

CHAPTER 4
page 168

Old Man
of Stoer

Kylesku
Bridge
Loch
Glendhu
1
Loch
Chàirn Bhàin
Kylesku

Loch
Gleneoul

5 Culkein
Drumbeg
3
B869
The Stoer
Peninsula
Nedd
The Road to
Drumbeg
4
Clashnessie

Quinag
(2,654ft)
2
Wailing
Widow Falls

A894

Eas a'Chual
Aluinn

6
Clachtoll
Beach

NORTH WEST

10
Little Assynt Estate

Loch Assynt

7
Achmelvich
Bay

A837

11
Ardvreck Castle
Inchnadamph

12
Traligill
Caves

8
Lochinver

HIGHLANDS

Loch Inver

Falls of
Kirkaig

Inverkirkaig

Suilven
(2,402ft)

Canisp
(2,779ft)

A837

13
Bone Caves

9
Lochinver to
Badnagyle

Loch Call
nan Uidhean

15
Stac Pollaidh
(2,008ft)

GEOPARK

Cùl Mòr
(2,785ft)

Ledmore
Junction

16

Reiff

Badnagyle

Cùl Beag
(2,523ft)

14
Knockan Crag
National Nature
Reserve

Elphin

Achiltibuie

Badenscallie

Coigach

A835

CHAPTER 2
page 74

Summer
Isles

Ben Mor
Coigach
(2,438ft)

17
Culnacraig

Blughasary

CHAPTER 6
page 260

ASSYNT & COIGACH

5
ASSYNT
& COIGACH

For many people, Assynt – and the neighbouring Coigach peninsula – is the epitome of the Highlands, a place of monumental landscapes gouged by glaciers, the elements and time. Here you will find some of the North Highlands' most recognisable mountains, not least Quinag, Suilven and Canisp, looming over lochan-scattered, boggy moorland. The coast, arguably the most rugged in the region, boasts coves of bright white sand and views over bays studded with islands.

Don't mistake this for an uninhabited landscape, however. While much of its interior – particularly that between Loch Assynt and Stac Pollaidh – is impenetrable except on foot, there are small settlements throughout, particularly along the curving B869 that loops north from the popular fishing village of **Lochinver**. Neither is it entirely barren – you'll find lush little pockets of woodland in places, particularly around Nedd, Lochinver and Inverkirkaig.

Though Assynt (essentially the area north of Elphin and south of Kylesku, and west of both) lies in Sutherland and Coigach in Wester Ross, I've included the latter here because it shares much in common with its better-known neighbour. This peninsula to the south of Assynt, with its long southern coastline overlooking the scattered Summer Isles, often feels all but forgotten about – most visitors travel just a short way inland to climb **Stac Pollaidh**. Water is never far away in Coigach, with views stretching across to the mountains of Wester Ross, and countless little coves to explore.

As well as mountain climbing, this is a fabulous region for water sports: the waters around Coigach are some of the best in the UK for sea kayaking, while the sheltered beaches of **Clachtoll** and **Achmelvich** are perfect for exploring on a paddleboard or kayak. In addition, both beaches, as well as **Achnahaird** in Coigach, are on bays that form part of the **North West Highlands Snorkel Trail** (page 234).

GETTING AROUND

This is one of the most difficult parts of the North Highlands to get around without your own transport – bus services are limited and infrequent, and there is no train line, so you'll need to plan carefully in advance if you want to rely on public transport. The major roads – the A894, A837 and A835 – run inland in this region; to explore the coast, you'll need to make use of the winding single-track roads that splinter off these. Most notable are the B869 'road to Drumbeg' and the so-called 'Wee Mad Road' south from Lochinver to the Coigach peninsula. With limited visibility in places, they're best avoided if you're in a motorhome or towing a caravan, or if you're an inexperienced driver. If you do take these roads, be prepared to pull over repeatedly, reverse into passing places, and take your time; in return, you'll be rewarded with phenomenal landscapes and breathtaking vistas.

BUSES

Rapsons Highland (⊘ rapsonshighland.com) offers a weekday service (route 809) from Drumbeg viewpoint to Ullapool (2hr) via Clashnessie (15min), Culkein (25min), Stoer (35min), Inchnadamph (1hr 20min) and Elphin (1hr 35min) once daily, with an additional service running from Lochinver just after noon (a request stop is available at Achmelvich, but you will need to book in advance by 17.00 the previous day). The T2 Assynt Dial A Bus service is available within the Assynt area, operated by Lochinver Taxi (⊘ highland.gov. uk/downloads/file/17767/t2_assynt_dial_a_bus ⊙ 09.30–17.30 Mon & Wed–Fri, 09.30–13.30 Tue); this is an on-demand service that needs to be booked by 18.00 the previous day.

WALKING & CYCLING

Assynt's landscape has given it a reputation as one of the best regions in Scotland for **walking**; indeed, if mountains are high on your list then you'll be spoilt for choice, with the mighty peaks of Canisp, Cùl Mòr and Quinag here, among others. As always, I've highlighted non-mountain paths within this chapter, and have also included the route up **Stac Pollaidh** (page 250), one of the most easily achievable Highland mountains. There are some great low-level walks too; one of the most accessible is the **Leitir Easaidh All Abilities Path** (page 242)

THE NORTH WEST HIGHLANDS GEOPARK

nwhgeopark.com

The complex geology of the northwest corner of mainland Britain has been key to scientific theories and research – including the discovery of Moine Thrust (page 248). This geology includes Lewisian gneiss, which at 3,000 million years old is some of the oldest rock in the whole of Europe. The North West Highlands Geopark, which has UNESCO accreditation, works to celebrate and conserve the geological heritage of this region, which stretches from Loch Eriboll to Ullapool, encompassing nearly 500,000 acres.

I'll be honest – geology is not my forte and I'm not going to try and fool you otherwise. Fortunately, that's where the folk at the geopark come in. In addition to handy, easy-to-digest signboards at important locations throughout the region (such as north of Scourie; page 213), they also arrange regular events and activities including walks, tours and talks.

The great thing about the geopark is that it brings geology to life at every turn – on the coast, in the mountains and the hills – and you can lay your hands on thousands- and millions-years-old rocks almost everywhere you go. Arguably the best place to do so, however, is **Knockan Crag** (page 248), which also makes a great first step when it comes to understanding (or trying to understand) the complex geological history and processes at work here. For more in-depth information and insight, visit **The Rock Stop** visitor centre (☉ summer 10.00–16.00 Sat–Wed) in Unapool, one mile south of Kylesku.

on the north side of Loch Assynt. Skirting lochans and with far-reaching mountain views, it's a joy for anyone to walk or wheel.

Some of the sights within this chapter can only be reached via a decent walk, most notably the **Bone** (page 247) and **Traligill** (page 244) caves; while they're relatively easy walks, they require a little fitness and an ability to cope with rough moorland paths.

If you are planning on **cycling**, you'll need to be prepared for a workout – the mountains can suddenly veer up and very little here is flat. The roads around Coigach, however, are particularly pleasant to explore by bike.

KYLESKU & SURROUNDS

The northern boundary of Assynt is marked by the sprawling lochs of **a' Chàirn Bhàin** and **Glendhu**, crossed by the strikingly modern Kylesku Bridge. The fishing hamlet of **Kylesku** itself is a fantastic base from which to explore the hinterland here, which is home to two staggering waterfalls – **Wailing Widow** and Britain's highest, **Eas a'Chual Aluinn**. The former can be accessed via a short walk, while the latter requires a rather tough-going six-mile round trip to see its 650ft drop; an easier option is to see it on a boat tour from Kylesku.

1 KYLESKU

🏠 **Kylesku Hotel**

This small hamlet has arguably one of the most spectacular locations of any in the North Highlands, sitting where lochs Glendhu and Glencoul meet and form the sea inlet of Loch a' Chàirn Bhàin, with views across the constantly changing water to a typically Assynt landscape of ridges and valleys. Despite this, however, its biggest draw remains the almost U-shaped **Kylesku Bridge** to its north, which has become something of a symbol of this part of the Highlands – and particularly the NC500 – in recent years; you'll often find the car park on the northern side of the bridge busier than anywhere else you've been on this road. That's not to pour scorn on either the parking area – from which there are phenomenal views of Quinag's peaks – or the bridge itself, the graceful modern simplicity of which somehow works against the rugged landscape that surrounds it. Prior to its opening in 1984, getting across the water to Kylestrome – just 350yds away – involved a small ferry or a road trip of around 100 miles.

"The bridge itself – a graceful, modern simplicity that somehow works against the rugged landscape that surrounds it."

One of the best ways to see Kylesku itself is on a circular walk; you can park either on the hill above it, just south of the bridge, or in the hamlet – I prefer the latter option as it means you can finish off with a drink at the lovely Kylesku Hotel (page 224). Walk to the northern point of the hamlet, where you'll see the old ferry slipway, now used by **Kylesku Boat Tours** (𝒫 07821 441090 𝄞 northwestseatours.co.uk ☉ Apr–Oct). These 75-minute boat trips take you out on to the sheltered waters of the surrounding lochs and offer the opportunity to see **Eas a'Chual Aluinn**, Britain's highest waterfall, as well as an array of wildlife – seals and various seabirds are

---

1 The much-photographed Kylesku Bridge. **2** & **3** The approach to Wailing Widow Falls and the beautiful waterfall itself. ▶

An alternate view of the Kylesku Bridge

❋ OS Explorer Map 445; start: Kylestrome car park ⚲ NC 21786 34562; 3.7 miles; moderate

This walk allows you to really enjoy Kylesku's setting – from the other side of the water. It follows the shore for its first half, with high chances of seeing the local seal colony and, if you're lucky, otters, and then climbs up through moorland on the return. For solitude and views of the bridge and Quinag, it's hard to beat.

1 Turn immediately right out of the car park and go through the wooden pedestrian gate to follow the road southeast. Keep straight as you pass the smart white estate buildings, with a stone wall on your right and a gentle slope to your left. As the wall ends, the view of Loch a' Chàirn Bhàin opens up, and you'll see a promontory ahead to your right.

2 After half a mile, just after the road curves right, a footpath sign points left to Loch Glendhu. Ignore this and continue on the road as it curves around the rocky promontory. If the tide is in, the bay to your left will be studded with little islands. Another third of a mile later, the hotel and bridge come into view across the water, with Quinag behind them. At the end of the road is the slipway; climb the grassy mound beside it for more good views, and to try your luck at spotting otters.

3 Retrace your steps back up towards the footpath sign. Just before you reach it, you'll see a small rocky ledge downhill to your left: this is a perfect spot for wildlife spotting – I spent a while watching seals playing in the shallows. At the footpath sign, turn right towards Loch Glendhu. Keep following the path straight on, ignoring the left turn after just over 100yds and instead following the curve of the bay to climb uphill. For a short while, you'll walk with vertical rock faces to your left before this gives way to a deer fence; the view over the loch and the often cloud-shrouded mountains feels increasingly elemental.

4 As you reach a cluster of downy birch, take the sharp left turn uphill, climbing on a clear gravel track, with a mix of gorse and heather on your right at first. Thankfully the path undulates rather than steadily climbing, and as you do so the views towards the bridge continue to get better and better. After about half a mile, the path levels out and curves right slowly – the views from here are wide ranging and quite amazing, over the estate boathouses, the lochs,

likely and if you're lucky you might spot golden or white-tailed eagles, puffins and even porpoises.

Head west from the slipway, along the side of the hotel, and you'll see steps heading uphill. Follow these to weave through scraggy, mossy ground, with birch trees clinging to the hillside. When you break through the trees, with the bridge almost directly ahead, the path weaves first

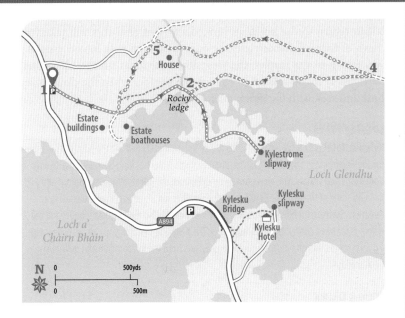

the bridge, the hotel and Quinag. After you pass through an open metal gate and cross over a burn on a bridge, keep straight, ignoring two left turns down to a house that surely must have one of the most enviable views in the region.

5 About 140yds after the second turning to the house, you'll come to a crossroads. Take the left-hand route, heading down towards the loch, with long moor-grass on either side. The path at first gradually descends before becoming steeper, and you'll soon see the estate houses below you. Keep straight on this track, ignoring the path to your right after around 400yds. After another 150yds, you'll reach the main estate road that you came in on; turn right to retrace your steps (about 400yds) back to the car park.

downhill and then up towards the car park; just before it goes uphill, you'll see a faint grassy path that leads down beneath the bridge. This is a great opportunity to get an alternate perspective of the crossing, and the view from here, with Quinag's ridges looming and the loch twisting out of view, is spectacular. You'll likely have the spot to yourself, with just the occasional rush of traffic and shriek of gulls overhead.

From here, walk back uphill and turn right to head up to the car park, which you should cross to its southern end. Follow the footpath sign that points downhill to Kylesku pier and, when you meet the road, turn left to return to the hotel; an immediate right after this will take you down to Kylesku Fishery Jetty, its sides piled high with lobster pots. As you return to the hamlet, the view down the loch is just tremendous, particularly if you catch it in changeable weather when the clouds play hide and seek with the mountains.

SPECIAL STAYS

Kylesku Hotel IV27 4HW ☏ 0333 2595989 ☖ kyleskuhotel.co.uk. At the hamlet's northern tip, looking out over Loch Glendhu, this unpretentious hotel has long been a favourite with both locals and visitors. The views can be enjoyed from the guest lounge, restaurant and bar, and some of the bedrooms; watching the weather roll in (or out) over breakfast is a real treat. Staff are friendly and helpful, there's an honesty bar in the guest lounge, and the whole place has a contemporary seaside feel. The restaurant (which you can use even if not a guest) serves up fantastic food, including mussels from the loch outside and deliciously fresh scallops.

FOOD & DRINK

Surf & Turf Kylesku Bridge 🅵. This summertime trailer is run by the same team as the excellent Dornoch take-away (page 83), from the big car park by Kylesku Bridge. Fresh seafood and Highland meat are the focus: it's hard to beat eating a lobster roll with a view of mighty Quinag.

2 WAILING WIDOW FALLS

Though just a fraction of the size of Britain's highest waterfall, nearby **Eas a'Chual Aluinn**, these beautiful falls are much easier to access, via a lovely walk in a steep-sided gorge. The starting point is a small parking area just off the A894 (♀ NC 24036 29574; marked as Loch na Gainmhich Waterfall Car Park on Google Maps) – note that if this is full (there's only room for a handful of cars), do not park on the grass verges but instead continue south up the hill to the next car park (♀ NC 23960 29212) and walk down from there.

It only takes about ten minutes to walk to the falls from the lower car park, though the gravel path alongside the burn soon becomes rocky – in places, it looks as though there is no path and you'll have to clamber along the rocks. Before long, the rocky, heather-clad valley walls are rising steeply above you; look for the pinnacle sticking out on your left, which adds to the rather fantastical feel. Keep low and close to the water, and take care as you walk.

The falls appear after only about 350yds of walking. It's a beautiful, rather skinny cascade, down dark rocks that are a little rounded at the top and then cut like steps at the bottom. It feels very glade-like here, with mosses clinging to the dark walls. On the way back, you can marvel at the way the rock has been eroded – curved in some places, straight cut in others – before Quinag looms into view.

ALONG & AROUND THE B869

Don't be put off by the rather uninspiring name for this section – the B869 is one of the most phenomenal roads in the North Highlands, winding through what is often a lunar-like landscape of moors and misshapen rocks, with views over craggy inlets. It starts two miles south of Kylesku and winds west to Drumbeg and Clashnessie before skirting the beautiful coastline – home to a scattering of northwest Scotland's most celebrated beaches – en route to the A837, just northeast of Lochinver (page 235). Note that the road east between Drumbeg and the A869 is not suitable for larger vehicles and should not be attempted in a motorhome.

3 THE ROAD TO DRUMBEG
🏠 West Coast Hideaways

Water is almost always in sight along the B869 west to Drumbeg, even if sometimes little more than a glimmer through the trees, with the route following Loch a' Chàirn Bhàin for most of the way. Just shy of two miles west of the A894, the views to your right open up and you'll spot the neat little island of **Eilean a' Ghamhna**, which rises to a hill on its eastern side. A further mile and a half on, the road climbs up through scraggy moorland as it weaves southwest, interrupted only by patches of downy birch. The road here feels so lonely for much of the way that it almost comes as a surprise to suddenly come across a few buildings as the road begins to descend towards **Loch Nedd**, with floodplains guarding the last stretch of the river.

The road climbs again to reach the old crofting village of **Nedd**, which, with its cluster of houses overlooking the water, has an enchanting

SS

WIRESTOCK/DT

EMMA GIBBS

JOHN ROBERTS IMAGES/S

position. This is the kind of place that outsiders would call 'remote' – whichever way you approach from, it's a slow, long journey – and yet, being here, in a place where people live and work, it feels like entirely the wrong word. The view from Nedd, of the undulating coastline opposite and Handa Island (page 211) in the distance, is sublime. I'd recommend parking up before you get to Nedd, at the head of the loch ($\mathbb{Q}$ NC 14715 31508), and walking up into the hamlet and beyond. As the road climbs, turn back for a phenomenal view of Quinag over the water; when I walked it once in the early evening, the mountain glowed purple while everything else was a deep amber.

Just over a mile northwest of Nedd is the small village of **Drumbeg**, prefaced by craggy, heather-clad hills. To its south lies Loch Drumbeg, overlooked by bulbous hills so characteristic of Assynt, while to the north is island-scattered **Eddrachillis Bay**. The focal point for most visitors to Drumbeg is the viewpoint, which offers a fantastic panorama of the bay.

A lovely short walk, and an even better view, can be had by heading right from the viewpoint and going downhill (east) between an abandoned house and a shed. Ahead you'll see an old, low wall: walk out towards it, following the faint, grassy path, and then keep it on your left-hand side, staying on the path to climb through the heather. Keep walking uphill – you'll see the remains of farm buildings on your right and the bay to your left; when you get to the top, you'll see another, lower hill ahead. Walk on to it, across the heather (you'll likely lose the path here) and when you get to the top of the knoll the bay entirely opens up below you. On a clear day, you can see as far as Handa, but it's beautiful even if the haar (sea mist) obscures the view. On one of my visits, the sky and sea were the same colour and it looked like the islands were floating in the air.

On your way back, once you're past the wall, you can turn right to follow a path downhill to the pebbly shore. While you're in Drumbeg, don't miss the opportunity to visit Assynt Aromas (page 228), a lovely little shop selling soap and candles with fragrances inspired by this corner of Scotland.

◀ 1 Drumbeg and island-scattered Eddrachillis Bay. 2 Clashnessie Bay. 3 While not particularly high, the falls at Clashnessie are still impressive. 4 Quinag looms over Loch Nedd.

SPECIAL STAYS

West Coast Hideaways Nedd IV27 4NN ✆ 01571 833219 ⊘ westcoasthideaways.co.uk.
Occupying a glorious hillside position in the old crofting township of Nedd, these three
shepherd's huts have been beautifully furnished and make the perfect hideaway for two.
With a bed by the window in each, you can spend hours – days – watching the weather roll
across sheltered Loch Nedd. Each hut has its own wood-fired hot tub outside, and sitting in it
under a blanket of stars is an unforgettable experience. Inside there's a wood-burning stove,
a compact but well-equipped kitchen, and a smart en suite. Owners Kari and Stefan, who
only took over in 2023, have big plans for their little croft, including growing vegetables and
yoga retreats.

FOOD & DRINK

If you're staying locally (even as far away as Lochinver), Drumbeg Stores (⊘ drumbegstores.
co.uk) can deliver groceries to your accommodation.

The Secret Tea Garden @ Assynt Aromas Drumbeg IV27 4NW ⊘ assyntaromas.co.uk. The
tea garden at the back of this tiny soap and candle shop really does feel secret, with benches
and wooden tables tucked under parasols and among flowers, and birdsong all around.
As well as delicious cakes, it also sells savoury 'light bite' boxes, from Highland cheeses to
smoked salmon, all with oatcakes and garnishes. Don't miss the opportunity to buy a candle
or two on your way out.

4 CLASHNESSIE

West of Drumbeg, the B869 always feels a bit easier – a little less winding,
and with (generally) better visibility of what (or who) is coming up
ahead. As you reach the southeastern end of **Clashnessie Bay**, the road
skirts narrowly between the rocks – high sided on the southern side –
before emerging with the bay running along your right-hand side. After
miles of rocky coastline dipping in and out of view, the first glimpse
of Clashnessie's pale sands can seem like a mirage. There's a parking
area (♀ NC 05742 30871) at the very southeastern tip of the beach; a
path leads down to the sand from directly opposite here. Lapped by
ridiculously clear water and with views of the rocky islets that scatter
the bay, it is a beautiful and peaceful spot.

While here, don't miss the short but lovely walk out to the wide
Clashnessie Falls. The walk begins 500yds southwest of the parking
area (leave your car there); look for the wooden signpost (♀ NC 05357
30753), marked 'Route to falls', on your left about 100yds after passing

a white house with a red postbox outside. The path soon meets a track; turn left on to it and follow it until the path splits, at which point you need to take the left branch. After around 200yds, shortly before a white house, turn left on to the path that takes you across the burn on stepping stones, and then turn right to follow the eastern bank of the burn. It can be quite boggy underfoot, but it's otherwise an easy walk of just under three-quarters of a mile.

The falls aren't especially high, but their width makes them impressive, with numerous streams cascading down, and the slight curve in the rocks gives the sense of the water tumbling into a hollow. You can, with care, walk close enough to the falls to feel the spray on your face.

5 THE STOER PENINSULA

Northwest of Clashnessie, the land juts out into an almost rectangular shape, peppered with jagged headlands and little coves. The B869 skirts the bottom of this peninsula, almost creating a boundary between the rocky hillscape that characterises so much of this area and here, where the land seems in the most part a little gentler.

"Just over three miles northwest of Clashnessie is the little hamlet of Culkein, with a scattering of white houses."

Just over three miles northwest of Clashnessie is the little hamlet of **Culkein**, with a scattering of white houses overlooking the bay at road end. As the road curves west towards the beach, you get an impressive view of distant Sutherland mountains to your right, often snow-capped into April. You can appreciate the view even more from the beach itself, particularly at low tide when the sands are dotted with small rocks, the water a shimmering turquoise.

On the opposite, southwestern end of the peninsula is the rather squat **Stoer Lighthouse**, built in 1870 by David and Thomas Stevenson. Parking is available just before the lighthouse, and the views from the cliffs on either side are quite something on a clear day: south as far as Skye, north to Cape Wrath and west to the Isle of Lewis. There's a well-placed bench just southwest of the lighthouse, looking over the rocky ledges and clear water below; one lunchtime, I ate my sandwiches while a seal watched from below, bobbing in the waves.

Just southeast of the lighthouse, by the car park (♀ NC 00464 32741), a sign points the way to the **Old Man of Stoer**, a rather phallic-looking

TO INFINITY – AND BEYOND

🖑 astronomy.scot

The skies of the northwest are among the darkest in the UK, largely because of the lack of light pollution here. 'It's what's known as a "Bortle 1" site – by contrast, Glasgow and London are Bortle 8/9,' Mark Washer tells me, 'so it's a special place for stargazing.'

The astronomy evenings offered by Mark and his partner Monica Shaw present the perfect way to become better acquainted with what's above our heads – whether you love staring up at the stars but need an app to help you identify them, or have a deep-rooted love of the cosmos.

With their own little observatory, complete with deep space and planetary cameras, the couple are able to really blow visitors' minds with what can be seen in this part of Scotland. 'You just don't know what you're going to see,' Mark tells me, 'which is part of the magic.'

Of course, here – as anywhere, really – the ability to see deep space, or indeed any stars, is dependent on a number of factors, not least the ever-changing weather. 'Being right by the coast means we have less heat haze and dust, and the air coming off the sea is much cleaner,' Mark says. 'The only problem is the wind and the aurora.' I laugh at this – to many people, seeing the northern lights feels like the pinnacle of night-sky attractions. 'It's a nice problem to have, but the aurora shuts down everything in the sky to the north.'

Based on the Stoer Peninsula, Mark and Monica run ad hoc **astronomy nights** and other events from their observatory, open to stargazers of all abilities, and are very happy to host visitors on these or on pre-booked evenings. They also have a fabulous little one-bed cottage on site (🖑 eatsleepwild. com/stay), for which they can provide evening meals ('We're massive foodies,' Monica says), and offer hiking, wild camping and other outdoor activities in the region. They're incomers – Mark is from Cornwall and Monica from the US – but it's hard to find two people more dedicated to this part of Scotland and to sharing the many joys of it, day or night, with both locals and visitors.

230ft sea stack just offshore. The path is fairly faint for much of the way, and you might have to pick your way somewhat in order to avoid boggier sections, but it's a great coastal walk – as always, do take care and avoid walking too close to the cliff edge. It's just over a mile and a half's walk to the Old Man, though you'll catch a glimpse of it before then, but the best view is right by it. The Old Man is a popular spot for rock climbing, and you might spot a hardy few attempting it. From here, you can continue to the **Point of Stoer** itself, another 600yds northeast, and then return inland for a different route – full details can be found on WalkHighlands (🖑 walkhighlands.co.uk).

6 CLACHTOLL BEACH

⚓ Clachtoll Beach Campsite

This superlative curve of white sand is, like nearby Achmelvich (page 234), a place that makes people exclaim 'I can't believe this is in the UK!'. Lapped by the kind of turquoise waters more commonly associated with exotic holiday brochures, and hemmed in by rocky headlands that are perfect for exploring, its sheltered nature makes it ideal for families, and you'll often see people exploring this stretch by paddleboard or kayak.

Access to the beach is via a large car park (♀ NC 03972 27305) immediately to its north; there are toilets and an informative little ranger's hut here where you can learn more about the wildlife of the area and find out about local events. The beach is reached by continuing down the road that the car park is on, from where a boardwalk leads across the dunes and on to the sands.

The distinctive tip of the headland to the south of Clachtoll is known as **Split Rock** – a triangular wedge of Torridonian sandstone separated from the land. You can walk out to the steep-sided cliff that would have once adjoined it by climbing up on to the croftland on this side of the beach. It's well worth walking up this way to seek out other, smaller coves, and for the fabulous views towards the mountains of Wester Ross and, beyond, Skye. Because it is west facing, sunsets can be sublime from both here and the beach.

On the headland to the north of the beach is the old salmon-netting station, a low white building that now houses some evocative old photos of fishing at Clachtoll. In its heyday, up to 100 salmon a day were caught here, but the netting station closed in 1995 – it was the last of the few west-coast salmon-netting stations to remain open – in order to allow the fish to replenish in the rivers.

"The old salmon-netting station is a low white building that houses some evocative old photos of fishing at Clachtoll."

Further around the headland are the evocative, partially restored ruins of **Clachtoll Broch** (⚲ clachtollbroch.com), which was home to an Iron Age family 2,000 years ago before being destroyed by a fire. To reach it, follow the road north from the salmon bothy – you'll pass a small cove on your left and then meet a metal gate with a sign saying 'Walkers welcome'. Go through this gate and then another two, keeping Clachtoll Cottage to your left, and after the

last gate climb uphill on to the grassy headland. Take the path heading left to walk out to the broch along the coast, or the right-hand path to head inland (which is a bit quicker); either way, don't forget to turn around to appreciate the views you're leaving behind. It's a great walk along the coast, where the elements have carved out huge slabs of rock. Along the way, there are little channels and stepping stones to cross over burns.

What can be seen of the broch today is the result of significant work by Historic Assynt; the exposed coastal position of the ruins, combined with the weight of the rubble that sat within the broch itself, meant that collapse was looking inevitable at the start of the millennium. The group worked to excavate, conserve and rebuild the broch – the result is, while not a complete structure, an evocative one that is a thrill to explore. Steps from the top lead down into the broch itself, and there are some fabulous views from here along the coast to nearby Stoer Beach (which it's possible to walk on to).

SPECIAL STAYS

Clachtoll Beach Campsite Clachtoll IV27 4JD ✆ 01571 855377 ⬧ clachtollbeachcampsite. com. Few campsites can beat this one, just a sprint away from the beach and with sea views from many of its pitches. It's exceptionally clean and friendly, with great facilities that include games and wellies to borrow, outdoor showers for a post-beach rinse, a nightly fire pit and – the icing on the cake – free use of kayaks, paddleboards, canoes and wetsuits. People come back year after year, and it's just as good for adults as it is for families. The night skies here, too, are amazing. Magic.

FOOD & DRINK

Flossie's Beach Store B869, Clachtoll IV27 4JD ✆ 01571 855222 ⬧. This little blue hut on the main road to the east of the beach is the perfect little daytime pit stop for coffee, filled rolls, soup, Scotch pies (a double-crust pie filled with minced meat) and toasties. There's also a decent selection of groceries and other self-catering supplies, and picnic benches on which to enjoy your food.

◀ **1** Achmelvich Beach is regularly voted one of the best in the world. **2** Hermit's Castle, Achmelvich. **3** Clachtoll's old salmon-netting station houses some evocative old photos of fishing in the area. **4** The 230ft Old Man of Stoer. **5** The distinctive tip of Clachtoll's headland is known as Split Rock. **6** The North West Highlands Snorkel Trail offers advice on the best places to get up close to underwater wildlife, like this dahlia anemone.

THE NORTH WEST HIGHLANDS SNORKEL TRAIL

Clachtoll, Achmelvich and Achnahaird bays are just three stops on the North West Highlands Snorkel Trail, which stretches down to the An Dun headland in Gairloch. The word 'trail' suggests you snorkel the entire length, but in reality it is made up of selected sites where you can snorkel to experience the diversity of the region's underwater life.

The best spots for beginners are Clachtoll, Ardmair (3½ miles north of Ullapool) and Big Sand (page 292), but each site has suggested areas for both beginners and more advanced snorkellers. The trail guide can be downloaded from ⊘ scottishwildlifetrust. org.uk/snorkeltrail; here you'll also find information about how to snorkel responsibly and particular species to look out for.

7 ACHMELVICH BAY

Just under 1½ miles south of Clachtoll as the crow files – or 5½ miles by road – white-sand Achmelvich Beach regularly makes it on to lists of the best beaches in the world. It's just under two miles west of the main road, which makes reaching it feel like more of an effort than Clachtoll; despite this, you'll often find it busy in the summer. I use that word lightly, of course – we're not talking Bournemouth Beach busy, just Highland busy.

I'll be honest, coming to Achmelvich after Clachtoll for the first time, I felt rather deflated – call me a snob, but with a caravan site immediately behind it (rather than tucked away from view like Clachtoll's), it felt a little less 'wild' than its northerly neighbour. Still, there's no denying the beauty of its gentle curve, or its ridiculously clear, Caribbean-like waters, and there's no better time to be here than at sunset, when the colours of the sand and the sea and sky seem to melt into each other.

I'll let you into a (rather well-known) secret though: the main beach at Achmelvich is not its best. To find the jewel in Achmelvich's crown, climb the northern headland and the next beach – known as **Vestey's Beach**, after the previous landowners – will soon be revealed. Getting to it requires a bit of a clamber down the rocks or a steepish descent through the croftland that backs it, but it's worth it. The first time I stumbled across it, it was like coming across the end of the rainbow – the main beach was 'crowded' but here was an untouched cove of the purest white sand, all to myself.

Immediately west of the main beach is **Sinky Sands** – it's actually part of the main strand at low tide but is cut off at high tide due to the rocks in between and so only accessible by water or another scramble down the rocks. Its name comes from the sand here, which in some places will see your foot entirely disappear.

You can follow a path up on to the western headland, which becomes increasingly rocky and is great fun to explore, peering down at little coves of clear water. Around 200yds southwest of Sinky Sands is the diminutive and rather Brutalist **Hermit's Castle** (♀ NC 05218 24771); if you don't know it's there, then stumbling over it comes as a bit of a surprise. It was built by an English architect, David Scott, in 1950. The story goes that he brought all the supplies over by boat over the course of six months, built the 'castle' and then left within days of its completion – apparently never to return again.

Calling it a castle feels like a bit of a stretch, particularly when you're up close and feel like you're dwarfing it. It is possible to go inside and, despite having to squeeze through the doorway, it is roomier than it appears from the outside, with an area to lie down in and shells pressed into the walls. It is still occasionally used by people as a bothy, but I don't imagine you'd get much privacy.

LOCHINVER & SURROUNDS

The B869 meets the A837 just northeast of Lochinver, the largest settlement on the west coast north of Ullapool. With easy access to mountains and beaches, this port village stretching around the head of Loch Inver is a great place from which to explore Assynt – and many people use it as such, meaning that in season it often has the feel of a small holiday resort. It's also a thriving little village in its own right, with a great community feel and some excellent places to eat. Lochinver is overlooked by two of Assynt's most iconic and recognisable mountains – Canisp and dome-shaped Suilven – but there are ample low-level walking opportunities too if you don't want to stretch your mountain legs.

8 LOCHINVER
🏠 The Albannach
If being the west coast's biggest settlement north of Ullapool gives you the impression that Lochinver will be a built-up place of traffic and noise, then that's pretty far from the truth. The main street – the very

end of the A837 runs into the village, following first the end of the River Inver's course and then curving around the loch – is lined by water-facing houses and a scattering of shops and restaurants. The far western end of the main road is home to the large harbour, used by the UK whitefish fleet as well as fishing boats from other European countries. **North Coast Sea Tours** (𝒸 northcoastseatours.co.uk ⊙ Apr–Oct) runs 90-minute wildlife trips from here on its catamaran, *Julie-Ann*, with seal sightings very likely – you might also get to see dolphins, basking sharks and white-tailed eagles.

Most of the area south of the harbour, between lochs Inver and Culag, is given over to beautiful **Culag Wood** (𝒸 culagwoods.org.uk), managed by a community trust. Paths wind through the woodland, including one up to a viewpoint that looks out on the lumpen hills and peaks that surround it – on a changeable day, the clouds seemed to constantly whizz about me, revealing and then hiding the mountains. The 'Are you brave enough?' path is a little more indistinct than the others, but nonetheless enjoyable and feels a bit more like an adventure (perfect if you don't like too much of a managed walk) – I met a couple of young red deer on one of my walks here. It eventually leads down to White Shore, the largest of the bays within the wood, with a sheltered pebble beach where each stone seems to be a different colour, all smoothed and rounded by the water. There are swings hanging from the trees, benches and a picnic table here, making it a great spot to linger and eat lunch, and it can also be reached on the easier Shore Path.

"Most of the area south of the harbour, between lochs Inver and Culag, is given over to beautiful Culag Wood."

There are other picnic tables dotted around the woods, as well as a play area, and part of the joy of wandering here is knowing that you can do so, following paths as they take your fancy, without getting lost. There are a couple of access points into the wood; the most central of which (and easiest on foot) can be found by taking the road that runs up the side of Culag Park (📍 NC 09269 22184), just east of the harbour. This leads straight up into the woods, though it's not a hugely scenic introduction. There are car parks (and alternate entrances) just off the road that runs south to Inverkirkaig: the first (📍 NC 09254 21975) is reached by taking the junction to the right just 350yds after turning on to the Inverkirkaig road and then following it for another 300yds; the second (📍 NC 09288 21479) is directly off the Inverkirkaig road, about 700yds further on.

🧳 SPECIAL STAYS

The Albannach IV27 4LP ✆ 01571 844537 🖥 thealbannach.co.uk. An incredibly special B&B, set on the northern side of Loch Inver, with spectacular views of Canisp and Suilven. There are two suites in the house and one – The Byre – in its own separate building, which has a hot tub outside and a private viewing area over the loch and mountains; there's also a small self-catering apartment. Owners Robin and Ballal have impeccable taste, and everything is beautifully designed and furnished, with the kind of attention to detail – like fresh milk and an espresso machine with compostable pods – that makes it feel more like a very lovely small hotel than a B&B. Breakfast is a treat, too – no heavy fry-up but instead dishes like shakshuka, mushrooms on homemade sourdough and overnight oats. Heavenly.

🍴 FOOD & DRINK

Delilah's Main St ✆ 01571 844333 🖥 delilahs.co.uk. Named after the owners' young daughter, this bright, modern restaurant has quickly become the heart of the community. Locally sourced ingredients, such as Lochinver lobster and hand-dived scallops, are at the forefront here, served with flair and imagination but no pretension; there are also good vegan options and a kids' menu on offer. Chef Sam is the son of James Hawkins, the artist behind Rhue Art (page 271).

Driftwood Café 12 Main St ✆ 01571 841233 🗜. 'The best coffee in town,' Ballal at The Albannach told me – so of course I had to try it and can happily confirm that it's excellent. Also on offer inside this small café are filled morning rolls (till noon), soup, scones, toasties and ridiculously good cakes.

Lochinver Larder Main St ✆ 01571 844356 🖥 lochinverlarder.com. The reputation of the pies here is such that chances are you'll have heard about them long before you arrive. Fillings range from classics like steak and ale and chicken and ham to venison and cranberry, and spiced butternut, sweet potato and goat's cheese. There are also sweet pies, and a non-pie menu of dishes such as Cullen skink and vegan bagels. Eat in or take away.

Peet's Culag Rd ✆ 01571 844085 🖥 peets.co.uk. Unsurprisingly, given its position right by the harbour, the menu at Peet's focuses predominantly on fish, including a fresh seafood platter and *moules frites*. Non-seafood options such as venison sausages and pizza are also on offer.

9 LOCHINVER TO BADNAGYLE

South of Lochinver, a single-track road winds its way down to the northeast of the Coigach peninsula (page 249). It's a staggering, if steering-wheel-clutching route that encompasses coastal, moorland, loch and, as you near Coigach, mountain views. At 12 miles long, it takes a typically Highland half an hour to drive; it's often referred to as 'The

River Inver loop

※ OS Explorer 442; start: car park on A837, immediately southwest of the Lochinver Larder
♥ NC 09483 22942; 4¾ miles; moderate

If you're after mountain views without the strain of climbing a mountain, this is an ideal walk, taking you alongside the beautiful River Inver, wooded for most of the way, before crossing moorland to reach Loch Druim Suardalain, with superlative views of Suilven and Canisp en route. I've started it from a convenient car park in Lochinver, but you could easily begin the walk from any point along the main road – it's easy enough to find your way. The convenient thing about this route is the proximity of the Lochinver Larder (page 237) to the starting point; stop to pick up a picnic lunch or reward yourself at the end.

1 From the car park, turn left to walk northeast up the A837, passing the Lochinver Larder on your left. Keep straight on, past the turning to Baddidarrach and Glendarrach, and just under 100yds further on, as the road crosses the river, you'll see a wooden fence on the right-hand side of the road, with a black sign welcoming visitors and hillwalkers. Cross the road and go through the small gate; the path runs alongside the peat-coloured river.

2 After about 600yds, the path splits – take the right-hand branch (the left-hand route is for anglers only). At this point, the route starts to climb, leaving the river below. You'll see a few paths heading off here and there, but keep straight on. As the path drops back down towards the river, you'll start seeing some fishing platforms jutting out into it. The path climbs again, and as it does it gains an enchanted forest feel, with tree roots snaking along it and birch trees springing from mossy mounds. Three-quarters of a mile after the first right-hand turning, you'll break out of the trees to walk on flat ground along the river; you might get a good view of Quinag ahead.

3 After about 400yds, you'll see another Inver and Kirkaig Fishings sign on your left, and a small post with a yellow footpath arrow pointing right, away from the river. Follow this path, which rises on to moorland, through bog myrtle, heather and bracken. It soon becomes a bit of a heart-pounding climb uphill, with a burn running beside you to your right, which you'll cross on a small wooden bridge after about 500yds. The moorland becomes increasingly barren as you walk, with Quinag to your left. About a quarter of a mile after the bridge is the ruin of a house, whose occupants were cleared during the early 19th century – you can walk around it and go inside. Back on the path, make sure you look ahead to your left for more great views of Quinag's long ridge.

4 A couple of hundred yards after the house ruins, you'll meet a gate; go through and almost immediately after you'll reach a T-junction, where you should turn right to head gently and then more steeply uphill. As you reach the top of the hill, you'll – weather allowing – get a wonderful view of Canisp and Suilven. Shortly after, go through a big metal gate, with Loch Druim Suardalain down below you. The pebbly path soon starts to descend steeply. As trees start to crowd in again, it becomes grassier and Victorian Glencanisp Lodge can be seen below. Go through another big metal gate, with a ruined building to your left.

5 At the bottom of the hill, you'll see a footpath sign to your right and a wooden building on your left. Go straight on, towards a green corrugated shed, and follow the road as it curves round after the shed to a T-junction. Turn right here (the left route is for the walk up Suilven) and, when you meet the lodge, keep to its right, passing between it and the estate office. As you leave the buildings behind, the loch is straight ahead of you. When you draw alongside the loch, look to your left for staggering views of Suilven and Canisp and, as you move further on, Quinag.

6 Follow the road alongside the loch, keeping straight on as you reach the walkers' car park on your right. The road moves away from the loch and about 600yds further on, you'll see a track to your right: ignore this and follow the road as it curves around to the left. Just over half a mile later, you'll reach a T-junction with the A837; turn right and follow the road all the way back to the car park.

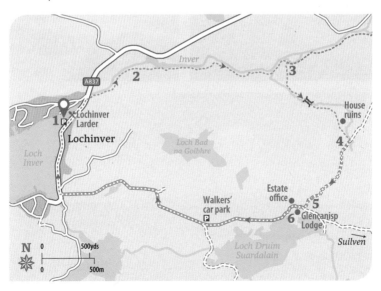

1

2

3

4

Wee Mad Road' – though that accolade also gets given to the Drumbeg road (page 225). Like that one, this road demands concentration, patience, a willingness to reverse and a stomach for twists and turns, but it's definitely worth it.

The stretch down to **Inverkirkaig**, the road's biggest settlement, is the easiest. Three miles south of Lochinver, this crofting hamlet curves around narrow Loch Kirkaig; it's a beautiful setting, with a pebbly beach on the loch and hills rising behind. The eastern side of the hamlet has some lovely woodland; a car park (♀ NC 08574 19345) next to the River Kirkaig, half a mile from the shore, is the starting point for a four-mile walk through the glen to the stunning **Falls of Kirkaig**. Do take care if you walk this path as it can be dangerously slippery close to the waterfalls.

"Loch Kirkaig is a beautiful setting for the crofting hamlet, with a pebbly beach and hills rising behind."

The road starts to climb steeply as soon as you're over the bridge southeast of the car park, winding first along the bay before heading inland to curve through birch and gorse, interspersed with barren moorland. As the road passes **Loch Call nan Uidhean** (♀ NC 09255 14930), you'll be treated to fabulous mountain views that will make you grateful for the parking areas where you can pull over. A mile and a half southwest, the road curves past a fish farm and shortly after you're treated to phenomenal views across exposed moorland to Stac Pollaidh (page 250); from here it's another two miles south to the junction with the road into Coigach.

LOCH ASSYNT TO KNOCKAN CRAG

East of Lochinver, the A837 curves its way through typical Assynt terrain of bulbous, heather-clad hills, glittery strips of water and looming mountains. Some 5½ miles beyond the village, the road follows the northern shore of lovely freshwater **Loch Assynt**, which stretches for just over six miles. From here, it's a wonderful drive south to Coigach, taking in some of the best of the region's geological sites en route.

◀ **1** The village of Lochinver. **2** Community-owned Culag Wood. **3** The Falls of Kirkaig are a four-mile walk from the village of Inverkirkaig. **4** The 2½-mile Loch an t-Sabhail circuit on the Little Assynt Estate.

10 LITTLE ASSYNT ESTATE

The western end of Loch Assynt is home to the Little Assynt Estate, managed by the Culag Community Woodland Trust, which also looks after Lochinver's Culag Wood (page 236). This is a beautiful area to explore on foot – and even, in the case of Leitir Easaidh, by wheelchair – offering expansive mountain views from a relatively low level.

The Little Assynt car park (♀ NC 15355 25137) next to Little Assynt Tree Nursery is the starting point for the wonderful 2½-mile **Loch an t-Sabhail** circular walk, with staggering views of Quinag and, at the end, Suilven. It's a well-marked and easy-to-follow path, though it climbs enough to be a little hard work at times; it's possible to extend the route by a quarter of a mile by branching off to the northwest on the equally well-marked 'Ken's Path'.

The Loch an t'Sabhail walk also connects to the **Leitir Easaidh** path, which is signed from the road as the **all-abilities path**. An easy and significantly flat route, suitable for wheelchairs, it trails around two lochs and provides some astounding mountain vistas. Parking is at ♀ NC 17227 26127, signposted off the A837; it's an out-and-back route of a mile and a half – the mountain views on the return are worth every second of retracing your steps.

11 ARDVRECK CASTLE

♀ NC 23917 23610

Standing on a craggy little promontory, connected to the northeastern shore of Loch Assynt at all but the highest of tides, the ruins of this late 15th-century castle command a great – if no longer imposing – position, with views up and down the loch, and the hulking Assynt mountains surrounding it. A decent gravel path leads from the car park (♀ NC 24283 23557) to the castle, with a few fainter grassy paths winding closer to the shore and over the hill.

"Today, the ruins are an evocative sight, and despite their small size make an atmospheric place to explore."

It's easy to assume that the diminutive ruins are just a fragment of a much larger structure, but Ardvreck was always fairly small as castles go. Built in the late 15th century by Angus Mor III, member of the Macleod clan, it was originally a three- or four-storey rectangular building, with the tower – the southern wall of which more or less remains today – added in the

THE MERMAID OF LOCH ASSYNT

No good castle is complete without a ghost story or two, and Ardvreck is no exception. The most compelling is that of the weeping mermaid who, some say, can still be heard when you walk around the site.

The story goes that when the Macleod chief was building Ardvreck he found himself in financial difficulty. Desperate to have his castle but with limited means to do so, he was approached by a stranger who offered to finance its construction. Of course, there's always a catch: and this stranger was in fact the Devil, so the price was Macleod's soul. That was, until the Devil caught sight of Macleod's daughter, Eihmir, and the price was changed to marrying his daughter.

Of course, greedy Macleod accepted and poor Eihmir was given no choice, though she had no idea to whom she was betrothed. The castle was built in just a few days, with the wedding planned to follow soon after. The night before the nuptials, however, Macleod, wracked with guilt, told his daughter who she was marrying.

Distraught, Eihmir threw herself off Ardvreck's tower, into the cold waters of the loch below. Though her body was never found, it was assumed that Eimhir had died. However, a weeping sound would often be heard by the loch, and people would sometimes catch sight of a flick of a tail: Macleod's daughter had become a mermaid, able to hide from the Devil in the caves beneath the water. They say that Loch Assynt's changing water level is due to her tears – when the water rises, the mermaid of the loch is weeping for the life she lost.

16th century. It was here, in 1672, that Macleod ownership of Assynt (which is thought to have been granted to them in the mid 14th century) ended following a 14-day siege by the Mackenzies of Wester Ross. The castle's ultimate destruction came a century later, however, when it was struck by lightning.

Today, the ruins are an evocative sight, and despite their small size make an atmospheric place to explore. In places, the walls are remarkably intact, and – particularly knowing that the original structure wasn't hugely bigger than what exists today – it's not a stretch to imagine what it would have been like in its prime. The rubble has created stone steps of sorts that lead up into the castle, from where you can peer out at the loch through the remains of the windows. Don't be tempted to climb up on top of the walls, however – danger aside, this is a scheduled monument that should be looked after. It's also worth exploring the rest of the promontory, for alternate views of the castle and up and down the loch; the castle only takes up a very small fraction of the land here.

From the sandy shoreline adjoining the castle, you can walk northeast to meet **Allt a' Chalda Beag**, a meandering burn that runs into the loch; on the other side of the A837, it rises to a lovely waterfall, scenically shaded by downy birch.

The ruined house south of the castle is **Calda House**, built for the wife of Kenneth Mackenzie in 1726 as she apparently did not like the austerity of the original building. The mansion would have been a fine sight at the time, notable for both its size and its – previously unheard of in these parts – symmetrical design, but it only lasted little over a decade. It was burnt by Mackenzie supporters after Assynt was purchased by the Earl of Sutherland, who were determined that it would never be inhabited by a Sutherland. Today, only its two ends and part of one wall remains.

12 INCHNADAMPH & THE TRALIGILL CAVES

🏠 **Inchnadamph Explorer's Lodge**

At the far southeastern edge of Loch Assynt, just 1½ miles from Ardvreck Castle, is the hamlet of **Inchnadamph**. Its name comes from the Gaelic *Innis nan Damh*, which means 'meadow of the stags' – which feels fairly accurate to me, given that I have often encountered deer here. The neat green fields of the hamlet are set against the moorland and hills that rise all around it, and the main reason to come here – as if the scenery itself isn't enough – is to walk.

Sitting at the northwestern end of Inchnadamph is the old **Assynt Parish Church**, a small, pretty church mere steps away from the water. The small cairn-like structure you can see on the hillside just north of here is a **memorial to Ben Peach and John Horne**, who developed the Moine Thrust theory at nearby Knockan Crag (page 248).

From the hamlet you can make the two-mile walk out to the **Traligill Caves** (📍 NC 27574 20603). The largest cave system in Scotland, these remind me of gaping mouths within the rocks they sit. Though only experienced cavers should venture inside, the path takes you up to three of them, and they are impressive to see from outside. The walk out here is straightforward, following a clear path through largely moorland landscape and – assuming the weather is on your side – with stupendous views of some of Assynt's mountains. Don't let dreich weather put you

1 Assynt Parish Church, Inchnadamph. 2 Ardvreck Castle. 3 The entrance to Uamh An Uisge – the 'Cave of the Water.' 4 Walking in Knockan Crag National Nature Reserve. ▶

off, however – the second time I walked this route, one damp day in October, it was particularly atmospheric, with low rain clouds dipping in and out of the valley, and the mountains only revealed as though part of a conjuring trick.

The caves are reached via a signposted two-mile walk off the A837; if you're travelling by car, use the parking area (♀ NC 25086 21610) just west of the Inchnadamph Hotel. From here, walk north up the road and follow the walking-path sign to go down the road towards Inchnadamph Explorer's Lodge. Continue on the track past the lodge and on to the road marked 'Private, no vehicle access', which soon leads past a couple of white houses to run next to the river, when it begins to climb uphill. Around 600yds after the turning to the lodge, you'll see a wood-and-metal bridge ahead – turn right when you meet a narrow path down to it and then cross over, turning left afterwards to walk up to meet the track. It can be rather boggy, so you may prefer to stay on the main track and cross at the less attractive concrete vehicle bridge.

"You'll see the craggy cliff and the cave – almost like a hideous toothy grin – the river winding around the rocks."

Once on the track on the other side of the river you pretty much keep straight on it, walking across scrubby moorland with hills looming around you. About 150yds after you pass an isolated holiday cottage, the path becomes grassier and the peak of Conival, with any luck, should be in view up ahead. A mile and a half of walking brings you to a sign pointing right to the caves; follow the path and keep straight on, soon crossing a small wooden footbridge over the river and then climbing uphill. The path will bring you to the first cave: Uamh an Tartair, or 'Cave of the Roaring'. The reason for the name is immediately apparent, with water rushing through the entrance, which is almost like a wide scar in the hillside.

From here, continuing left brings you to Uamh An Uisge, the 'Cave of the Water', where you can hear the water (but not see it from this level) – you can safely walk a short distance into this cave, soon meeting a dead end. Afterwards, head to the left of the cave to climb up its side and then on to the top of it, from where you can peer into the pothole, though do proceed with care and don't get too close.

The final cave is my favourite, reached by retracing your steps back over the footbridge and then turning immediately left to walk alongside the river. You'll soon see the craggy cliff and the cave – almost like a hideous toothy grin – ahead of you, the river winding around the rocks. Afterwards, head back up and then left when the path splits to join the path you came back in on. The views on the way back, across Loch Assynt, are fabulous.

SPECIAL STAYS

Inchnadamph Explorers Lodge IV27 4HL ✎ 01571 822218 ⬠ inchnadamph.com. This large old lodge is the perfect base for walking in Assynt, with a choice of private rooms and dorms in the main building and a handful of separate self-catering options, including a cottage, mini apartments and shepherd's huts. I loved the 'cosy cabin', which has a double bed, small kitchenette and toilet, decorated with fairy lights and kept warm with underfloor heating. The lodge itself has a good lounge, communal kitchen and dining area, a drying room (so warm on wet days you won't want to leave) and a shop. Staff are hugely knowledgeable and helpful, there's loads of information about walking in the area, and you can get straight out on to the track to the Traligill Caves.

13 BONE CAVES

♀ NC 26772 17036

Three miles south of Inchnadamph are the Bone Caves, so-called because it was here, in 1889, that geologists Ben Peach and John Horne discovered reindeer and bear bones, dating back around 14,000 years – from animals that local people would have tracked and hunted. More recent excavations have led to the discovery of bones from other animals now extinct in Scotland, including arctic fox, lynx and a fragment of a polar bear's skull that is more than 20,000 years old.

It's a walk of just over a mile from the car park (♀ NC 25321 17942) to the caves (though, as you ascend a few hundred feet, anticipate it taking at least 45 minutes), and of the two cave systems in the area this is my favourite walk. When I did it in autumn one year, I was completely alone, except for the rather eerie bellowing of stags on the hillsides above me.

The path initially takes you up the left-hand side of a scenic waterfall, before winding along the hillside, following the river for a while until the water disappears underground and you follow what is most often a dried-up riverbed. Just after you cross a shallow burn, a boulder with faint markings points right to the caves – follow this, which will lead you across the (dry) river to climb the path uphill, with a steep final slog up to the caves.

The caves are all hugely atmospheric, with water dripping down the dark rocks above. Unlike at Traligill (page 244), you can enter the mouths, but do take care – and, as at Traligill, only experienced cavers should press on beyond the entrance. To head back to the car park, rather than reverse the route entirely, you can continue walking beyond the caves, along the edge of the hill. Just when you feel like the path isn't going anywhere, it starts descending into the strath and then winds back towards the way you came, eventually joining the path you've already walked. When you're on the opposite side to the caves, do look to your left to see the caves from there – you'll likely be surprised (though your legs won't be) to see how far up you climbed.

14 KNOCKAN CRAG NATIONAL NATURE RESERVE

A835 ♀ NC 18784 09092 ∂ nature.scot

> **This landscape is**
> **masterless**
> **and intractable in any terms**
> **that are human.**
> Norman MacCaig, *A Man in Assynt*

I am, I must admit, rather obsessed with Knockan Crag – I can't drive past without stopping. In large part it's to do with the view from the car park, which I've seen in all seasons and all weather and which – rain, shine or snow – is never less than captivating, looking as it does across shimmering streaks of lochans and lochs to the mountains of Coigach.

It is also a hugely important place in terms of geology and our understanding of the world and our place in it. Knockan Crag is home to some of the oldest rocks on Earth, which in their layers show how the planet has changed – through collisions, pressure and upheavals – over billions of years. This is where in 1882 Ben Peach and John Horne (the geologists who uncovered the history of the Bone Caves; page 247) figured out that older rocks can be pushed up and on top of younger rocks through a process called thrust; the Moine Thrust Belt, which stretches for around 120 miles from Loch Eriboll (page 195) near Durness to the Isle of Skye and defines so much of this stretch of the North Highlands, was at the heart of this discovery.

Regardless of whether you have any interest in geology, Knockan Crag should be on your must-stop list. Three trails wind up the hillside from the 'Rock Room', which introduces visitors to the history and science here in a clear and accessible way. The real impact, however, comes from the paths themselves, where you can lay your hands on the very rocks you've been reading about – my kids were flabbergasted to learn they were touching rocks that were billions of years old (I mean, how can any of us really comprehend that amount of time?). Along the way, quotes (such as the one on the opposite page) and stone artwork complement the scenery and rocks that surround, with signs (carved on to rock, of course) detailing where the land we know as modern-day Scotland would have been located at various points in time. The result is a walk that feels as much an exploration and investigation as anything else; my kids loved seeking out the signs, finding the fossils of pipe worms in the rocks and, best of all, being able to touch the Moine Thrust itself.

"You can really appreciate the largeness of the landscape – on a clear day, the view stretches as far as Ullapool."

Exploring the reserve even on the lower trails involves a bit of hillside climbing, though for all three trails the paths are well marked and easy to follow. I'd recommend at the very least walking out on the Thurst Trail, which takes you past the beautiful *Globe* sculpture by Jo Smith and up to the Moine Thrust itself, before returning back on the Quarry Trail. It's a steep climb up to the top of the crag on the Crag Top Trail, but at only just over a mile long in total it's not particularly arduous for much of the rest of the way. From the top, you can really appreciate the largeness of the landscape – on a clear day, the view stretches as far as Ullapool.

FOOD & DRINK

Elphin Tearooms A835, Elphin IV27 4HH ⊘ elphintearooms.co.uk. A sweet little café selling local arts and crafts, and a small selection of local farm foods, plus puzzles and books to keep you occupied on a miserable day. Coffee is excellent, and the food on offer – toasties, soups, quiches and cakes – is simple but decent.

COIGACH

Travelling west from the A835 into Coigach, there's a real sense that you are heading somewhere tucked away; the road narrows, the mountains of Stac Pollaidh and Ben Mor Coigach tower on either side, and gorse presses in tightly around you, in striking contrast to the bare scrubbiness of the landscape you've just turned off. 'It feels like an island even though it's not,' said Ruth Bradley, manager of Acheninver Hostel (page 258), and there's no better way that I can think of to describe it.

One of the best views in Coigach is from the viewpoint on the road that runs west from Achnahaird (park at ♀ NB 98522 13274 and walk up the hill on the path from there), which looks across the Summer Isles and down the coast, the landscape undulating between sea and mountains.

15 STAC POLLAIDH

The distinctive ridge of Stac Pollaidh (pronounced 'Stac Polly') soon greets you as you drive northwest into Coigach – and you'll spot it looming in the distance from many places in the area. Its western ridge looks, I think, as though someone has pulled the land up by their fingertips. Despite being rather imposing, it's only a wee mountain – at just over 2,000ft, it's a Graham rather than a Munro – which makes it a popular option for people who want to tackle a mountain but aren't sure they have the legs or the stamina for anything too gruelling.

"The distinctive ridge of Stac Pollaidh (pronounced 'Stac Polly') soon greets you as you drive northwest into Coigach."

If you're planning to climb Stac Pollaidh, particularly between May and September, I'd recommend getting to the car park (♀ NC 10754 09545) prior to 10.00, or after 17.00 when the daylight hours are long; it can fill up quickly, and while there is limited parking space immediately to the west along the road, it doesn't take much before parked cars take over the road. The path up and around the mountain is clear and easy to follow the whole way, beginning directly across the road from the car park and immediately climbing uphill. When the path splits, take the right-hand branch towards the gate in the deer fence, with the mountain straight ahead of you. As you climb up, the views open up behind you and the craggy ridges of Stac Pollaidh will come into increasingly, and rather intimidatingly, clear view, before you curve around the side of the mountain to approach from the northeast.

After just under a mile, the path splits again; take the left to head up towards the ridge. The top here isn't actually the top of the ridge but rather its lowest part – nonetheless, it still feels like a good achievement and the views (assuming the weather plays ball) are phenomenal, stretching as far as the Point of Stoer and Suilven. You can head higher,

TAKE TO THE WATER

'Coigach is the best place in west Scotland for sea kayaking,' Ruth Bradley, the manager of Acheninver Hostel (page 258) told me, 'but nobody knows about it.'

It's certainly a winning combination: a wild, ragged coastline; wildlife-rich waters (seals are most commonly seen but dolphins are also frequent visitors); and uninhabited islands to explore. Whether you've been kayaking before or fancy giving it a try, there are two excellent and well-recommended outfits that can get you out paddling here:

Kayak Summer Isles
🖉 kayaksummerisles.com. Page 266.
Summer Isles Sea Kayaking 🖉 07900 641860 🖉 summerislesseakayaking.com. Half- and full-day tours, plus camping trips, family adventures and kayak and canoe hire.

up to the eastern end of the ridge, but this involves a short scramble. (The mountain's true summit is at its western end and should only be attempted by experienced climbers; despite its diminutive height, Stac Pollaidh is considered one of the most difficult summits in the UK.)

You can either rejoin the path by heading back the way you came and turning left to continue circling the mountain or, as you start to descend back down to the main path, look to your left for a path that clings to the hillside; after about 300yds it joins the main path, where you should turn left to continue. You can of course just retrace your steps downhill the way you came, but it's ultimately more fulfilling to circle the mountain; it's also a quieter return route and offers up sublime views over the Summer Isles and beyond. It feels wilder and lonelier on this part because less people walk it – it's also boggier so you may have to pick your way in places.

The ever-changing nature of Highland weather means that you can easily start the walk in blistering sun and end in pouring

"You can retrace your steps downhill the way you came, but it's ultimately more fulfilling to circle the mountain."

rain; pack layers, sunscreen and plenty of water and snacks. It took me about 2½ hours to walk, but it could easily take longer than that if you factor in more time to rest – or it could also take less time, as the people who run up and down it can attest! When I climbed Stac Pollaidh, I did it on a day where I could see the low clouds clinging to the top so I knew a lack of visibility would be a risk. I had amazing views on my way up and down, but of course the clouds completely descended as I climbed

to the top, and in the end I could see nothing but a wall of white. Did it matter? Not really. I had a great time, but I know lots of people climbing that same day were hugely disappointed, so do bear this in mind before you set off.

16 ACHNAHAIRD BAY

Parking at ♥ NC 01552 14018

Despite its island feel, Coigach doesn't have an abundance of sandy beaches – but the sands of Achnahaird Bay, which stretch south for a mile, more than make up for this. Approaching from the parking area on its northwestern side, you're greeted by a frankly stupendous line-up of mountains: Cùl Mòr, Stac Pollaidh, Cùl Beag and Ben Mor Coigach, and on to An Teallach and the mountains further south down the coast. Having first come here on a clear, bright day, I'd say that my favourite visit was in fact on a changeable day in mid Autumn, where the clouds hung low over the mountains when I arrived, completely hiding their peaks, before rising slowly to reveal them, like the curtain on a theatre set.

En route between the car park and the beach are an abundance of little pebbly coves, many of which have footpaths leading down to them, or which can be reached at low tide by clambering over rocks from the beach. Here are stones in blushing colours of pink and purple, rounded and smoothed by the tide, and in all sizes. On one visit, I found a plethora of tennis-ball shaped stones, which, rather appropriately, bounced off the other stones when I threw them against the rocks.

The sands here are a mellow golden-pink colour that seems to shift as the tide changes and the channels of water widen, streaking the sands in silver and blue. The further back you walk, the more the human footsteps in the sand fade away, replaced only by the tiny crisscrossing prints of birds' feet.

17 COIGACH'S SOUTH COAST

 Acheninver Hostel

Coigach's long southern coast is where most of the peninsula's settlements lie. Most northerly is the small community of **Reiff**, at road end to the north; the sea cliffs here have a reputation as some of the best

◄ **1** The distinctive ridge of Stac Pollaidh. **2** Sea kayaking through a natural arch in the Summer Isles. **3** Achnahaird Bay.

for climbing. The south coast is full of excellent, relatively easy coastal walking possibilities, with a few small hills to climb for great views; an easy option is to head up the hill immediately south of Port a Bhaigh campsite (page 259) in Altandhu – from the top you get fabulous views over the Summer Isles.

Just over three miles south of Altandhu is **Badentarbet Bay**, where the long pebble beach (with some sand at low tide) has an enviable position, with views of Ben Mor Coigach to the right and then the other mountains of Wester Ross, including the Dundonnell Range, further out. It's the kind of place you can lose a lot of time just contemplating your surroundings. Though this is a quiet spot today, the pier was once regularly served by steamers bringing supplies to the peninsula. Salmon, along with lobster and herring, were big business here, and salmon, farmed off the Summer Isles, and local langoustines are still exported today. Some detritus from the fishing industry lines the grass behind the bay, including huge metal buoys and rusting anchors.

"Just over three miles south of Altandhu is Badentarbet Bay, where the long pebble beach has an enviable position."

Summer Isles Sea Tours (✆ 07927 920592 🌐 summerisles-seatours. co.uk 🕑 May–Sep Mon–Sat) runs tours out to the Summer Isles from the pier, as well as sea-angling trips; you'll be able to see the local seal colony and, if you're lucky, could also spot basking sharks, dolphins and otters. At the end of Badentarbet pier are a few picnic benches, from which you can sit and soak up the wide views down the coast and across to Tanera Mòr and some of the other Summer Isles (page 258); the small building just before the pier is Am Bothan, which has self-service tea, coffee and cakes, as well as acting as an information point for Tanera Mòr and hosting a variety of community events.

Less than a mile southeast is Coigach's main settlement, **Achiltibuie**. The village stretches out along the road for some way, with most of its buildings facing the water on the northern side of the road, providing wonderful views of the Summer Isles and the Dundonnell Range. There's a well-stocked little petrol station and shop here (Achiltibuie Stores, IV26 2YG 🌐 achiltibuiestores.co.uk 🕑 Mon–Sat), and the Summer Isles Hotel – one of the loveliest places to stay, eat and drink in the region, it was sold at the end of 2024 and is unlikely to reopen before summer 2026. Check the website (🌐 summerisleshotel.com) for the latest information.

A lovely 2½-mile coastal **walk** out to the headland of **Rubha Dùnan**, south of the village, starts on the outskirts of Achiltibuie: park at the community hall (♀ NC 02886 07698) and then continue southeast along the main road until, just after a house called 'Lochanside' on your right, you see a wooden fingerpost pointing down steps, marked 'To the Broch and coast'. The path leads down towards the shore, where you might spot seals, particularly when the tide is out. About 600yds from the main road, on your right, are the ruins of a broch, wedged between two ruined houses. What's remarkable here is that the broch itself is largely hidden between the more modern buildings, so you can almost clamber unwittingly on to it. The houses were built using stones robbed from the broch.

From here, the path more or less follows the coastline, climbing up a rocky hill to head north, with the cliffs to your left becoming steeper. It can be very boggy and steep in places, but the views you gain – north towards Reiff and west towards Loch Broom – are more than worth the effort, with the calls of birds and the constantly shifting light (and often, weather) adding to the atmosphere. Just before the pebbly beach at Port Mhaire, the path heads east to meet a track that will take you back up to the community hall.

A further two miles down the road brings you to the scattered settlement of **Badenscallie**, boasting what I think are even better views of the Summer Isles. The colours of the sea and sky at Coigach, and particularly here, often remind me of watercolour paintings, with something almost dreamlike about the way the water and mountains look from a distance. The coast south of here is particularly worth an explore; a lovely walk starts half a mile down the road, at the parking area (♀ NC 04470 05990) by the signpost to Acheninver Hostel (page 258).

"The colours of the sea and sky at Coigach, and particularly here, often remind me of watercolour paintings."

From here, a path leads south, following the burn along its right-hand side; go past the bridge to the hostel and when you reach another little bridge across the water, cross it to walk down to a stretch of deep pinky-brown sand, backed by pink pebbles.

Afterwards, return to the other side of the bridge, turning left to go down to the rocky shoreline on this side. You can walk for a while on the rocks, which are cut like huge, flat steps, but you'll get to a point where you have to retrace your steps to get on to the grassy path that runs behind the shore. As you walk, look for shags and gulls drying themselves on the rocks, and seals bobbing in the water. The views are far-ranging, with the island directly west of you actually made up of two: larger Horse Island to the south and Meall nan Gabhar immediately north, both of which are uninhabited but where sheep were overwintered until as recently as the 1990s. It's less than half a mile to reach the beach at Badenscallie, which is backed by a cemetery. Follow the fence along and then down to reach a gate that opens just above the rocks – it's a bit of a steep clamber so take care and use your hands for leverage if need be. The beach is a pretty curve of pebbles (and sand at low tide), and the sand when you see it is a deep, almost red colour. When I was here, it was just me and a flock of ringed plovers wading in the shallows.

At the far end of the beach, across the burn, you'll see the remains of two houses. The one closest to the sea was, in the 19th century, home to Katy Campbell and her husband. They were forced to build the cottage after Katy had been identified as the ringleader of a rebellion against the clearance of tenants from Badenscaille, which in the 1850s was part of the Cromartie Estate. While the cottage's position may look scenic, it was built below the high-tide line and thus subject to regular flooding – a particularly cruel punishment. From the burn, you can follow the steep road back up to the main road, and then turn right to walk the half mile back to the car park – the views from the road across the water are astounding.

Coigach's most southerly settlement is **Culnacraig**, little more than a scattering of houses just after road end. There's a parking area a few hundred yards before the track down to the hamlet, at the foot of Ben Mor Coigach. It's worth driving out here for the views alone, with the mountain rearing up on your left, Isle Martin and Rhue to the south, and Scoraig, An Teallach and the peaks of Fisherfield beyond. If you want to explore further, you could follow the road (really just a track) down into Culnacraig on foot, turning right when it splits to reach the small coastal settlement of Achduart and then looping up and round to the main road and back to the car park.

---

1 Assynt's mountains line up on the approach to Achnahaird Bay. 2 Some 20 islands, skerries and rocks make up the Summer Isles, off the coast of Coigach. 3 The lovely 2½-mile coastal walk out to the headland of Rubha Dùnan. ▶

THE SUMMER ISLES

Tantalisingly lying just to Coigach's west, the Summer Isles (not to be confused with Summerisle, the island in *The Wicker Man*) are made up of around 20 islands, skerries and rocks, and seem almost constantly in view as you travel around the peninsula. The nearest is small **Isle Ristol**, immediately west of Old Dorney Harbour – at low tide, it's possible to walk out to the island, which has a blindingly beautiful beach on its northern coast. Furthest away is the RSPB reserve **Priest Island**, which is an important site for nesting seabirds, and, near Ullapool, **Isle Martin**, which can be reached by ferry (page 268).

The largest island, **Tanera Mòr** (⌂ tanera. org), was bought by a London-based financier in 2017; the island is now undergoing considerable regeneration, which is being delivered by a charitable trust in order to retain the ecology of the island and ensure that it 'retains community at its heart', as the website says. It'll be fascinating to see this unfold over the coming years – the project already employs 150 people, many of whom are local. While the rest of the Summer Isles are uninhabited, Tanera Mòr does have a small population now thanks to the people working here.

The best way visit the islands is by boat, either on a tour with Summer Isles Sea Tours (page 254) or one of the Ullapool operators (page 266), or by kayaking (page 251).

There is a seven-mile waymarked path from here to Blughasary, itself seven miles north of Ullapool. Known as the **Postie's Path**, because this was the route used by the postman in the 19th century, it is one for only very experienced hikers – for a start, it takes around 4½ hours to walk and though it doesn't go up Ben Mor Coigach, is very much a mountain route, with difficult terrain for much of the way and climbing a total of 656ft. If you do want to do it, make sure you read up about it first, organise transport for the other end, and pack lots of snacks and water.

SPECIAL STAYS

Acheninver Hostel IV26 2YL ✆ 07783 305776 ⌂ acheninverhostel.com. There's no car access to this hostel, so you have to park up and walk the 550yds down to it (wheelbarrows are provided for your bags) – but it's more than worth it. It has a phenomenal position on the hillside, next to a burn, with views that'll distract you for hours and hours, if not days. The main building has a dorm, fully equipped kitchen and dining area, and is popular with walkers. There are also three 'sleeping pods', each of which has a double and a single bed, plus a microwave, small fridge, sink and en suite – all linen is provided, and the views are superlative. They're cosy and comfortable, and in the mornings you can eat breakfast while you watch the Stornoway ferry come into Ullapool.

FOOD & DRINK

Am Fuaran Altandhu IV26 2YR 🖉 01854 622339 ⊙ amfuaran.co.uk. Though it doesn't look like much from outside, the bare brick walls and roaring fire inside create a cosy setting for a meal or a drink. It specialises in freshly caught seafood, such as local langoustines and hand-dived scallops, and salad leaves and herbs are grown on site. In summer, the terrace is the perfect place to soak up the views over a drink. The same people also run the fantastic **Port a Bhaigh** campsite (⊙ portabhaigh.co.uk), just a stumble away, and which has a handy little shop.

SHOPPING

FISK Gallery Polbain IV26 2YW 🖉 01854 622302 ⊙ fisk-gallery-achiltibuie.co.uk ⬛. This little gallery shop is a real treasure trove, stuffed full of beautiful locally made items, many of which are created in the artists' studios upstairs. I always love seeing the ceramics by Lesley Muir of Summer Isles Studio, painted with fish and oystercatchers, among other things, and can never resist the candles by Ali Mac, all created on a local theme (Haar is particularly divine). And there's plenty more besides — it's well worth a trip.

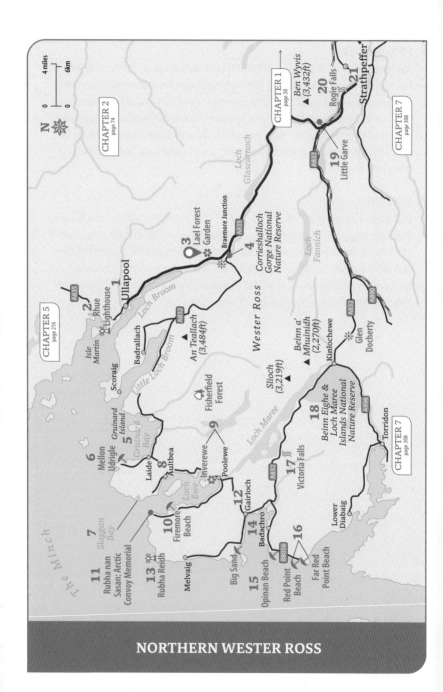

NORTHERN WESTER ROSS

N

0   4 miles
0   6km

CHAPTER 1
page 38

CHAPTER 2
page 74

CHAPTER 5
page 216

CHAPTER 7
page 308

CHAPTER 7
page 308

The Minch

Wester Ross

Isle Martin

Slaggan Bay

Loch Ewe

Gruinard Bay

Loch Broom

Little Loch Broom

Loch Maree

Loch Glascarnoch

Loch Fannich

1 Ullapool
2 Rhue Lighthouse
3 Lael Forest Garden
4 Corrieshalloch Gorge National Nature Reserve
5 Gruinard Island
6 Mellon Udrigle
7 Rubha nan Sasan: Arctic Convoy Memorial
8 Aultbea
9 Inverewe
10 Firemore Beach
11 Rubha nan Sasan
12 Gairloch
13 Rubha Reidh
14 Badachro
15 Opinan Beach
16 Red Point Beach
17 Victoria Falls
18 Beinn Eighe & Loch Maree Islands National Nature Reserve
19 Little Garve
20 Rogie Falls
21 Strathpeffer

Badrallach
Scoraig
Laide
Poolewe
Big Sand
Melvaig
Far Red Point Beach
Lower Diabaig
Torridon
Kinlochewe
Glen Docherty
Braemore Junction
Ben Wyvis (3,432ft)
An Teallach (3,484ft)
Slioch (3,219ft)
Beinn a' Mhuinidh (2,270ft)
Fisherfield Forest

A835
A835
A832
A832
A832
A832
A835
B8056
A896
A890

260

6
NORTHERN WESTER ROSS

Look at a map of northern Wester Ross and it appears to be largely comprised of fingers of land jutting out into the Minch (the strait between the mainland and the Hebridean islands of Lewis and Harris). With much of the accessible area of this region being coastal, these headlands and promontories will colour your experience of it: venture up them and you'll find small crofting communities above the shoreline; drive between them and you'll traverse hilly moorland, coloured yellow with gorse in spring and purple with heather in late summer, with mountains dipping in and out of view.

These mountains take up almost the entirety of the inland area of northern Wester Ross, creating a landscape of peak after peak, from **Beinn Dearg** and **An Teallach** in the north to **Slioch** and **Beinn Eighe** further south. The roads skirt round the outside, making the only way to explore these remote inland areas on foot – and then only really by the most experienced of walkers.

Unsurprising, then, that the coast is the focus for most visitors here. The major attraction is undoubtedly its beaches, which range from the white-sand, dreamlike **Mellon Udrigle** to vast, dusky-coloured **Red Point**. Superlative walking, too, brings people here; there is plenty to suit those who don't want to conquer mountains, from exploring the headlands to trekking inland.

Wester Ross's biggest settlement – in fact, the biggest settlement on the northwest coast – is the port village of **Ullapool**, which has a particularly lively feel in summer and on sunny days throughout the year. In the south of the area is **Gairloch**, another popular holiday village, set around an attractive, wide bay; here, as in many of the area's other settlements, you can learn about the region's important role during World War II. Two impressive natural sites can also be found in this northern part of Wester Ross: dramatic **Corrieshalloch Gorge** in the north, and **Beinn Eighe National Nature Reserve** in the south. The latter, situated on beautiful **Loch Maree**, boasts some of the best and most accessible mountain views in the whole region, and is home to Britain's only waymarked mountain trail: the perfect place to start if you do want to scale some heights.

Also included in this section are a handful of places on the far eastern side of Wester Ross: the old spa town of **Strathpeffer**, the salmon-leaping **Rogie Falls**, and **Little Garve**, where a delightful riverside walk provides a perfect journey breaker before you head further west or east.

GETTING AROUND

There are two major roads here: the A835, which runs up to Ullapool, and the A832 from Braemore Junction, 12 miles south of Ullapool, which curves around the coast to serve Aultbea, Poolewe and Gairloch. On the latter, look out for wild goats on the roadside around Dundonnell – they love eating the gorse and are always a source of great amusement. Trains here only run as far as **Garve** and **Achnasheen**, so buses are your best bet if you want to explore by public transport.

BUSES

Most useful for exploring the area are two MacKenzie & MacLennan services (⊘ mackenziemaclennan.co.uk/westerbus): the 700 (⊙ Mon & Fri am) runs from Gairloch to Inverness (2hr 40min) via Poolewe (25min), Aultbea (40min), Laide (45min), Dundonnell (1hr 10min) and Braemore Junction (1hr 25min); and the 700A (⊙ Tue & Sat) connects Laide with Inverness (2hr 30min) via Aultbea (5min), Poolewe (20min), Gairloch (35min) and Kinlochewe (1hr 10min). Both services, plus the Wednesday-only 711 from Poolewe to Dingwall (1hr 50min), also call at Garve (1hr 25min–1hr 40min) and Strathpeffer (1hr 45min–2hr). Also useful is the Thursday 707 from Gairloch to Ullapool (1hr 50min), via Poolewe (25min), Aultbea (40min), Dundonnell (1hr 15min) and Braemore Junction (1hr 30min). MacKenzie & MacLennan also runs a few school-days-only services, between Gairloch and South Erradale (30min), Melvaig (45min), Mellon Charles (40min) and Shieldaig near Torridon (1hr 5min) via the various settlements in between. As they are effectively school buses, the services generally run to Gairloch in the morning, and in the opposite direction in the afternoon; check the website for details.

A Citylink service (⊘ citylink.co.uk) runs twice daily between Inverness and Ullapool Pier (1hr 20min), calling at Braemore Junction (1hr) en route and timed to link up with ferry departures to Stornoway on the Isle of Lewis. D&E Coaches' (⊘ decoaches.co.uk) service 61 runs from Inverness to Ullapool (2 daily: Mon–Fri in term time, Mon–Thu in school holidays), calling at Strathpeffer (30min), Garve (45min), Braemore Junction (1hr 10min) and Leckmelm (1hr 25min) en route. Travelling further north from here, the weekday service offered by Rapsons Highland (⊘ rapsonshighland.com; route 809) runs from Ullapool to Drumbeg viewpoint (1hr 55min, request stop only) via Elphin (35min), Inchnadamph (50min), Lochinver (1hr 10min), Stoer (1hr 30min), Culkein (1hr 35min) and Clashnessie (1hr 30min; request stop only).

WALKING

Vast swathes of northern Wester Ross are mountainous and uninhabited – not least **Fisherfield Forest**, which lies between Little Loch Broom in the north and Loch Maree in the south, and is often referred to as 'the Great Wilderness', due to its complete lack of settlements and being home to Scotland's most remote mountains. It goes without saying that accessing Fisherfield should only be attempted by experienced and well-equipped hikers; as always, WalkHighlands (⊘ walkhighlands.co.uk) is the place to visit for more information.

For those of us less inclined to hike up a hard-to-access mountain, northern Wester Ross has plenty of lower-level options; I've included a few of my favourites here but there are plenty more to be discovered, and every road seems to have dozens of fingerposts to be found and followed. For a relatively easy climb with good views, head into the Ullapool hills (page 266), while nearby Inverbroom (page 272) is home to a great low-level riverside walk with fabulous mountain panoramas. There's also a wonderful walk inland behind Gruinard Bay (page 276), and, on the eastern side of the region, some beautiful options around Garve (page 302) and Strathpeffer (page 304), including the salmon jumping Rogie Falls (page 302).

This region is also home to beautiful Beinn Eighe & Loch Maree National Nature Reserve (page 300); don't miss a chance to explore the regenerated woodland on the Woodland Trail or, if you fancy more of a challenge, to climb up on the UK's only waymarked mountain walk.

CYCLING

As usual, hills will likely be your biggest challenge when it comes to cycling in this region. That said, there are a handful of flatter routes, including the track out to Slaggan Bay (page 278) and the winding, narrow road to Rubha Reidh lighthouse (page 293). Visit Wester Ross (visitwester-ross.com/see-and-do/cycling) has a handy page about cycling, detailing a number of routes.

BIKE HIRE

Badachro Inn IV21 2AA 01445 741255 badachroinn.com
Ullapool Bike Hire Shore St 07724 640446 ullapoolbikehire.co.uk

ULLAPOOL & SURROUNDS

Regardless of which direction you approach **Ullapool** from, it'll be the biggest settlement you'll have seen for a while. Still, don't expect a 'bright lights, big city' vibe – this is the Highlands, after all. With a lovely setting looking down and across skinny **Loch Broom**, it makes a great base from which to explore the wider region, particularly on foot: there are fabulous walks up into the hills, out to **Rhue Lighthouse** to the north, and in and around lovely **Lael Forest Garden** to the south.

1 ULLAPOOL

 Ecotone Cabins

The neat fishing village of Ullapool sits on the shores of Loch Broom, surrounded by hills – stand on Argyle Street and you'll particularly feel this, with the land rising up all around you. People have lived here and in the surrounding region for thousands of years, and the deep, natural harbour has long been important; it was from here, in 1773, that the *Hector* set sail, carrying close to 200 men, women and children who had been cleared off local lands to a new life in Nova Scotia, Canada. Thomas Telford was commissioned by the British Fisheries Society to design a village and port for the herring industry here in 1788; the tidy grid pattern of this 'modern' village and some of its original buildings still survive today. One such is the three-storey 18th-century warehouse on the corner of Shore and Quay streets, which now houses a hardware shop on the ground floor and a gift shop above.

Ullapool's position, with water on two sides, is particularly bonny and I never fail to be entranced by the view down Loch Broom from Shore Street, with the loch narrowing in the distance as layers and layers of hills and – eventually – mountains build up. On sunny summer days, the promenade (which was unveiled in 2023) fills up with holidaymakers watching the water, eating ice creams and relaxing, and you'll often find people stone skimming, paddling or taking to SUPs from the pebble beach on the western side of the harbour (look out for seals here, too). For a slightly quieter water view, head round to Western Terrace on the west side of town, where there's a picnic table and a scenically set bench.

Juxtaposed against the village's pretty white buildings and lovely views is the large, modern ferry port; the arrival (and departure) of the Stornoway ferry sees Ullapool swell twice a day – the only time you're likely to encounter any heavy traffic. Still, it's fun to watch the cars and lorries trundle off, particularly the latter which often seem too huge to fit on the ship.

"Ullapool's position, with water on two sides, is particularly bonny and I never fail to be entranced by the view."

Telford also left his mark in the village in the form of the Parliamentary church on West Argyle Street, a street back from the pier. This is one of just 32 Presbyterian churches (often referred to as 'Telford kirks') that were built in Scotland under Telford's management between 1823 and 1830, in order to serve the Highland parishes where villagers lived a considerable distance from their parish church. This one was built in 1829 to a simple T-shape design, as many of them were. It now houses the small **Ullapool Museum** (✆ 01854 612987 ⌂ ullapoolmuseum.co.uk ◷ Apr–Oct daily), where you can climb up into the original pulpit and, upstairs, sit in the old pews to watch a video about the village and region. 'We only charge an entrance fee so that we can maintain this historic church,' the volunteer on the front desk told me, somewhat apologetically.

Quite apart from offering the opportunity to look at the interior of the church, the museum is worth a wander; it's the best kind of local-history museum, with enough information to provide context on the village, but not too much that you end up overwhelmed and skimming everything. I particularly enjoyed finding out about the 'Coigach

ACTIVITIES IN & AROUND ULLAPOOL

Ullapool is a great base for an active holiday, with fantastic walking on the doorstep including up Ullapool Hill (see below) and out to Rhue Lighthouse (page 269), and plenty of opportunities on the water. In addition to the companies below, bike hire is available on Shore Street (page 264).

BOAT TRIPS

Seascape Expeditions sea-scape.co.uk. Choose from a one-hour loop around Loch Broom, a two-hour tour of the Summer Isles, or a three-hour whale and dolphin option that sails out into the Minch. Private hire also available.

Shearwater Cruises 07713 257219 summerqueen.co.uk. These popular cruises out to the Summer Isles (page 258) have been running since the 1970s, often encountering seals, porpoises and dolphins. Private hire also available.

WALKING & CLIMBING

Hamlet Mountaineering 01854 622754 hamletmountaineering.com. Hill walking, mountain and rock climbing and scrambling, and canyoneering.

Mckenzie Mountaineering 07580 171325 mckenziemountaineering.com. Day walks and longer adventures, from hillwalking just outside the village to long-distance trails. Bike and hike options, too.

WATERSPORTS

Kayak Summer Isles
kayaksummerisles.com. Trips by kayak or canoe, ranging from half days to overnight tours with camping.

WhatSUP Ullapool Small Pier, Shore St 07731796206 whatsupullapool. co.uk. SUP hire from central Ullapool, plus introductory lessons in small groups or privately. Book at least 24hr in advance.

Cowboys' – men from Coigach and Lochbroom (as the area around Ullapool is known), who emigrated to Montana to work as shepherds. There's also lots to keep kids entertained, including dressing up, colouring and Lego activities.

"It's hard to beat a walk up Ullapool Hill on the eastern side of town. Views stretch up and down Loch Broom."

On a fine day, it's hard to beat a walk up **Ullapool Hill**, on the eastern side of town. From here, views stretch up and down Loch Broom and while it's a bit of a steep walk, it's not as bad as it looks when you're staring up at the hill from the village centre (it's only just over half a mile to the top – about 30 minutes' walking). There are a couple of access points for the hill, but I like to start from the northern part of town; a footpath sign points the way off Broom Park (confusingly labelled Broom Court on the street sign closest to the road, which is also the name of the street immediately to the south), with the path (♀ NH 13066 94594) beginning at a wooden gate that you can see from the start of the road. The path runs uphill behind houses at first, winding up and around the hill; there are some handily placed benches along the way where you can catch a breather. From the top, where you can look up and down the loch, you can make a longer loop by heading down to the Braes of Ullapool (details on WalkHighlands ∂ walkhighlands.co.uk), or head back the way you came, changing the route slightly by heading over the little bridge you'll see on your left (♀ NH 13360 94430) just after you begin the final descent. The path here is a little rougher and can be a bit slippery, but it brings you out around the back of the Royal Hotel, with the seafront almost directly in front of you.

"The village is home to Lugger Fest, a maritime festival that sees lots of traditional boats take to the water."

Every May, the village is home to the two-day **Lugger Fest** (∂ luggerfest.wordpress.com), a maritime festival that sees lots of beautiful traditional boats take to the water, along with talks, ceilidhs and chances to take to the water yourself.

 ## SPECIAL STAYS

Ecotone Cabins Leckmelm Wood, IV23 2RH ∂ 07483 102111 ∂ ecotonecabins.com. An incredibly special place in the hills above Loch Broom, 2½ miles southeast of Ullapool. Owner Sam and his family have lived here since his parents bought the site from the Forestry Commission 30 years ago, and since then they've worked hard to restore biodiversity and create environmentally sustainable businesses. There are just two modern wooden cabins here – one sleeping two and the other sleeping four – built on-site by the family's construction company, and which have wide views over the loch to the hills opposite. The interiors are modern but cosy, with everything you could need and a balcony from which to soak up the location. Sam is a passionate advocate for sustainable, environmentally friendly living, and has created the perfect Slow accommodation. You can easily get here by bus, which stops right outside, or on foot from Ullapool along the hillside.

 ## FOOD & DRINK

Ceilidh Place 14 West Argyle St ∂ 01854 612103 ∂ theceilidhplace.com. Relaxed bar-restaurant that's also a celebrated music venue. As well as staples like fish and chips and burgers, the menu features some more interesting dishes, from roasted veg with za'atar

ISLE MARTIN

islemartin.org; ferry: Ardmair jetty ● NH 11053 98423 ✆ 07522 929145 ⊙ Mid-May–mid-Oct 11.00–16.30 (last boat from island) Fri–Sun

Three miles northwest of Ullapool is the southernmost of the Summer Isles (page 258), community-owned Isle Martin – which is also the only one you can get to by ferry. It takes just ten minutes to get to the uninhabited 400-acre island, which rises to a hill on its bulky northern side. It was donated to the RSPB in 1980 to be managed for conservation: the previous owner had cleared it of both sheep and cattle for this purpose, and under the RSPB woodland regeneration and surveying of breeding birds was carried out. However, managing the island proved to be difficult for the charity, and in 1999 the island was given to the Isle Martin Trust, established by the local communities of Loch Broom and Coigach.

Most visitors come for just the day (you are also welcome to come out here with your own boat), but it's possible to wild camp on the island or stay in either the bunk house or the small self-catering Croft House (sleeps five). You can explore on a number of way-marked trails, heading up the hill for fabulous views; in the small New School building is a tiny museum where you can learn about the island's history. There's also a so-called 'Library of Stuff', with useful things to borrow like wetsuits and wellies, as well as an honesty shop offering drinks and snacks, and events are often held here (see website for details). It's worth coming out early so you have the whole day to explore.

chickpeas to flatbread with fried chicken and pickles. It's a great place to stop for a coffee and a piece of cake, or for a pint of local beer outside on a sunny day. There's also an excellent little bookshop, plus accommodation upstairs. Check website for gig details.

Cult Café West Argyle St ▪️. This little Antipodean-inspired café serves up fabulous all-day breakfasts like rhubarb French toast and salmon hash cakes, as well as a couple of bigger lunch dishes including a vegan buddha bowl and beef stew; the menu changes seasonally. Coffee is excellent, and kids will love the milkshakes.

Deli-Ca-Sea West Shore St ✆ 01854 612141 delicasea.co.uk. Every seaside town needs a good fish and chip shop and this is Ullapool's. Much of the fish comes from straight across the road, so it's super fresh, and the batter is light and crispy. Perfect for eating on the beach or the promenade wall.

Seafood Shack West Argyle St seafoodshack.co.uk. A visit to the Seafood Shack is something of a rite of passage on a trip to Ullapool, and the food more than lives up to the hype. Delicious fresh, local seafood on a menu that changes daily but which often includes haddock wraps, scallops and langoustines. No reservations: just turn up, order, and hopefully grab one of the wooden tables. There's also a gin bar for drinks.

West Coast Delicatessen 5 Argyle St ✆ 01854 613450 🖥 westcoastdeli.co.uk. This great little deli is packed with foodie delights, with an emphasis on Scottish produce, which makes it perfect if you're self-catering or in need of a picnic. Also great coffee, filled rolls, soups, salads and amazing toasties.

SHOPPING

Ceàrd 21 West Argyle St 🖥 ceard.co.uk. This fabulous little shop is crammed full of art and gifts from Scottish artists and makers, including my favourite Ali Mac candles from Coigach and gorgeous ceramic items by Fergus Stewart. Everything feels carefully curated, and it makes a great change from the more twee items you often see in gift shops.

Ullapool Bookshop Quay St ✆ 01854 612918 🖥 ullapoolbookshop.co.uk. It's always remarkable these days when any place in the UK has more than one independent bookshop, but even more so in a village as small as Ullapool (the second is in the Ceilidh Place, page 267). This is a really fantastic store, selling a great range of fiction and non-fiction, and with a lot of local interest on offer too – many of which aren't easy to find elsewhere. There's a fab kids' corner, and a selection of stationery, cards and small gifts.

2 RHUE LIGHTHOUSE

Loch Broom's northeastern headland is marked by this unusual small lighthouse. Little more than a tower with a light, it's quite a contrast to the other lighthouses in the region, standing alone as a beacon on the rocks above the entrance to the loch. It's a spectacular location, with views down the water towards Ullapool, across to Scoraig (page 275) and Dundonnell, and over to Isle Martin (see opposite) and Coigach.

There's a small parking area (♀ NH 09664 97250) at the end of the public road in the small hamlet of Rhue, about 3½ miles northwest of Ullapool. From here, you'll see the lighthouse ahead; take the road to the left-hand side of the car park, past a house and then on to a grassy track that curves left to a kissing gate. Once through the gate, with the lighthouse ahead, the path curves to *"My kids loved the rock pools, but my favourite thing was watching the weather roll in over Ullapool."* your right, running above a pebbly cove, with bracken on either side. It can get a little muddy in places, particularly as the path crosses a small burn, but it's a straightforward ten-minute walk (around 550yds) to reach the lighthouse from the car park. The rocky ledge is filled with little rock pools, which my kids loved exploring, but my favourite thing was watching the weather roll in over Ullapool and Ben Mor Coigach.

On your return, you can scramble down the hillside to the pebble cove you saw on the way out, which is perfect for stone skimming. A faint path on the far side leads up steeply to the gate you entered through.

While in Rhue, it's well worth popping into **Rhue Art** (IV26 2TJ ✆ 01854 612460 🖱 rhueart.co.uk ⊙ Apr–Oct 11.00–17.00 Mon–Wed, Fri & Sat; Nov–Mar call in advance), a striking art gallery overlooking the water, owned by Flick and James Hawkins and showcasing a varied and interesting array of contemporary art.

3 LAEL FOREST GARDEN

A835, IV23 2RS 🖱 forestryandland.gov.scot

This lovely mixed woodland is Forestry and Land Scotland's most northerly arboretum, featuring around 200 species from around the world, including giant sequoia and Serbian spruce. There are two car parks, one at its northern end (♀ NH 19557 81056) and the other at its southern end (♀ NH 19567 80604). Entering from the southern car park, I'll admit that at first I found the woodland fairly pedestrian, but it quickly becomes more interesting, particularly as you climb away from the road and head deeper into the trees. A number of trails wind between the two car parks, making it fun to wander somewhat aimlessly – labels handily point out the more interesting and unusual trees. On the bottom path, you'll see dozens of fallen trees, which have been overtaken by moss and lichen in such a way that they have become indistinguishable from the ground, creating a rather magical, dell-like feel.

"This lovely mixed woodland is Forestry and Land Scotland's most northerly arboretum, featuring around 200 species."

At the northern end of the garden, you can follow the burn up past the car park to a pretty waterfall. If you're able to manage a steeper walk, you can follow the red waymarkers up and over the top of the garden, into the forest that surrounds, to see Allt na h-Ighine gorge. The walk is only about a mile in length but does involve a fair amount of climbing. The southern car park is also the starting point for a lovely walk (page 272).

◀ 1 The fishing village of Ullapool on the shores of Loch Broom. 2 Exhibits in Isle Martin's tiny museum. 3 Lugger Fest in Ullapool is a two-day maritime festival held every May. 4 Rhue Lighthouse is situated on the northeastern headland of Loch Broom. 5 James Hawkins at work at Rhue Art.

Inverbroom riverside walk

❄ OS Explorer 436; start: Lael Forest Garden south car park, off A835 ♀ NH 19567 80604;
2.9 miles; moderate

This delightful walk follows the path of the River Broom to a waterfall before returning along the hillside, with beautiful views of fields, water, mountains and hills along the way. Though it's a straightforward route, it's not without a bit of a climb, and the path can be a little hard work at times.

1 From the car park, cross the A835 (taking care as traffic goes quickly) and go over the bridge directly in front of you. The view is very scenic with the hills rising ahead and fields edged by old dry-stone walls. Turn left as soon as you're over the bridge, through a metal gate with a signpost saying 'Auchindrean Path', and up on to a raised grassy path that runs alongside the river. You'll soon see the peak of Sgurr Morr ahead, and the gorse will begin to crowd in on either side – in spring, it smells like someone has spilled a vat of coconut oil. The path veers to the right briefly before heading south again, soon moving a little away from the river.

2 After about half a mile you'll cross a little wooden bridge as you walk through the trees, with the path becoming rockier as the river reappears ahead of you. It can be narrow and muddy in places as you weave through the trees, the river now below you. A quarter of a mile further on, the river goes around a green island; just after the end of the island, cross another wooden slatted bridge over a burn and continue on the rather faint path.

3 After another quarter of a mile, a couple of hundred yards before you reach a line of Scots pines, a path leads to the left between trees; take this, walking around to meet and then follow the water. This, as the sign says, is Junction Pool, where the Broom and Cuileig rivers meet. There's some flat grass and a bench seat made out of stones here, providing a good spot for a picnic. Follow the path round to the right to go gently uphill, coming out on the path you turned off, with the line of Scots pines now ahead on the left. Take the left-hand path, walking up to meet the pines, and continue on the path, soon winding through downy birch and then crossing a burn on stepping stones. Soon after there's a sign marking Linn Pool and, across the river, you'll see a measurement post in the concrete structure opposite. The water here is brown from the peaty soil but extremely clear.

4 At the top of a slight incline, where you meet a track at a T-junction, you'll have a great view of the waterfall ahead to your left; turn left here, to go down steps and then over a couple of rocky burns to reach Falls Pool, with a lovely view of the waterfall crashing down the rocks, cut like steps here. You can go up the (actual) steps to the right of the Falls Pool sign to walk along the muddy path at the top for an alternate view – be careful on the steps as they can be slippery, and note that the bridge you can see ahead is broken and not in use. When you reach the fence, retrace your steps back to the pool, turning left to return to the T-junction. At the top of the steps, take the grassy path to the left to go uphill, with your back to the falls, and weave through the bracken.

5 At a T-junction, go left over a burn to meet a wooden gate; go through and turn right on to the gravel track, in the opposite direction to the Culaig Path sign. This climbs uphill through young woodland, and as you walk the views of the hills approaching and beyond Ullapool open up. It's exceedingly pretty, particularly in spring when the bright yellow gorse contrasts against the green fields. You'll go through three gates, to keep out deer; after the final one the path descends to run alongside a dry-stone wall. When you meet the farmhouses, turn right to walk past the old farm buildings before curving slightly right between pretty cottages. As the road curves left slightly, you'll see the bridge and the car park ahead.

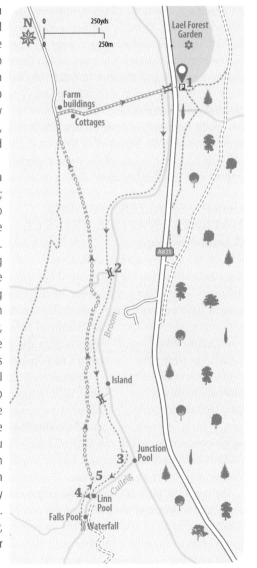

BRAEMORE JUNCTION TO RUBHA MÒR

At Braemore Junction, 12 miles southeast of Ullapool, the A832 heads inland to traipse through a rather wild-looking landscape of moorland backed by an almost endless supply of rugged mountains and hills, before heading through the trees as the Dundonnell River appears on the eastern side and then on to trace the coast. Before you get too far, however, be sure to stop at the **viewpoint** (♀ NH 19567 78419) one mile northwest of Corrieshalloch Gorge – from here, you look down over the flat green farmland of Inverbroom (including the area covered by the walk on page 272), hemmed in by steep hills and the distant glimmer of Loch Broom. It is one of the most superlative views to be had in the region, and you don't need to climb a mountain for the privilege.

4 CORRIESHALLOCH GORGE NATIONAL NATURE RESERVE
🏠 Sound of Durnamuck
IV23 2AB; NTS; free admission but parking charge

'Ugly hollow' is what the Gaelic word *Corrishalloch* translates to – which definitely seems like a misnomer when you're staring down into this narrow gash between steep, tree-clad sides. The focal point here is the 147ft Falls of Measach, one of a number of waterfalls in the gorge, which can be seen from a suspension bridge high above it.

"It's somewhat surprising that this dramatic and wild gorge should sit sandwiched between two major roads."

It's somewhat surprising that this dramatic and wild gorge should sit sandwiched between two major roads (though, I use 'major' within the context of the Highlands, so it's not like it's next to the M25 and the M4), but this does of course make it both easy to access and hugely popular – don't be surprised if you struggle to find a parking space in the summer months.

The main car park is home to the smart, modern visitor centre, with a café and toilets, and the wheelchair-accessible Woodland Walk, which takes in a couple of other waterfalls en route to the star of the show. If you're able to manage a rougher path then I'd recommend beginning at the old (but still in use) car park (♀ NH 20231 77918), half a mile northwest from there and labelled as 'The Falls of Measach Car Park' on

Google Maps. From here, take the left-hand gate ('Lady Fowler's Fern Walk'), which initially winds alongside the road past downy birch; despite the proximity of the road, you're more likely to be aware of birdsong, and soon a view of Loch Broom opens up. Shortly after this, as the path starts going downhill, it begins to feel a bit more interesting and wilder, with a viewpoint over the northern part of the gorge and its moss- and fern-covered sides. The path meets the Woodland Walk just before the metal suspension bridge, and it's this that you follow over the gorge.

The bridge, which was built in 1874 by Sir John Fowler – one of the designers of the iconic Forth Rail Bridge near Edinburgh – can only hold six people at a time, so you might have to wait to cross. It's also a little bouncy, which means more nervous visitors may not enjoy it too much. The River Droma, which flows through the mile-long gorge, drops a staggering almost 330ft over the course of it. From here though,

THE ISLAND PENINSULA

The mountainous peninsula of land jutting between Loch Broom and Little Loch Broom is home, at its skinny northern tip, to the community of **Scoraig**, which today can still only be reached by boat or on foot. Though it sits on a landmass that is part of the mainland, Scoraig is in many ways an island, not least because it feels almost entirely separate.

For a long time, Scoraig had existed as a fishing and crofting settlement before being abandoned in the 1950s. However, new people moved in in the 1960s, creating an alternative, off-grid community that still exists to this day – around 70 people currently live here. Homes – and the school – are powered by wind and solar energy and the distance from the mainland has led residents to be creative when it comes to building, by reusing and repurposing things as much as possible. There's a small primary school in Scoraig; older children go to Ullapool, boarding in a hostel during the week. Some of the residents were born and raised here, while others have made the decision to make it their home.

The walk out to Scoraig begins at the small community of Badrallach, on the southern side of the peninsula, where the road ends; from here, it's about a five-mile walk along a clear, exposed coast path. Full details can be found on WalkHighlands (⊘ walkhighlands.co.uk). Alternatively, you can get out here by boat from Baluarach Jetty (⚲ NG 99642 94803); a small on-demand ferry is run by Jonah (✆ 07730 422718), or you might be able to get a lift with someone else heading over. Alternatively, you can head out with Mckenzie Mountaineering (⊘ mckenziemountaineering.com), which offers a one-day walk and boat trip to the peninsula.

assuming you have a head for heights, you can look down to see the full depth of the gorge and length of the waterfall – even if you do have a head for heights it is a somewhat head-swimming view. On the eastern side, a path runs northwest to another viewpoint (also with a six-person weight limit), which juts out over the gorge and allows you to see the waterfall in its rushing, gushing entirety.

SPECIAL STAYS

Sound of Durnamuck 1 Durnamuck, IV23 2QZ ✆ 07939 391617 ✆ soundofdurnamuck. com. The location alone is reason to come here – looking across Little Loch Broom to Scoraig (page 275) and backed by An Teallach. There are three accommodation options, all a little quirky in the best possible way: the Rustic Barn (sleeps two), with its own sauna; Tiny House Elegance Grand (sleeps four), a skinny little house with two bedrooms; and the Western Wagon (sleeps four), with a bunk-bed room and a fold-out double bed, which is incredibly fun and cosy. Each has its own outdoor area with a barbecue (the barn also has a pizza oven), and you can buy fresh eggs from owners Linda and Mike. An excellent spot from which to explore the region, with plenty of information provided and walks from the doorstep.

5 GRUINARD BAY

Coming from the east, Gruinard Bay first appears as a shimmer of water on the horizon, broken by the long stretch of Gruinard Island (see opposite); from the west, you'll see it first just after Laide, backed by bulbous, rocky hills that look like something out of a sci-fi film and, beyond them, a ragged assortment of mountains. The eastern coast of the bay is home to a number of lovely patches of golden sand, the largest of which is just east of **Little Gruinard**. Parking (♀ NG 95182 89860) is available directly across the road from the boardwalk and steps that lead down to the beach. At low tide, the dusky pink sands stretch for almost three-quarters of a mile, but high tide creates little coves among the rocks. This is the kind of beach that my kids can always spend hours enjoying: exploring, digging holes and clambering on rocks.

While you're here, don't miss the chance to walk to the **waterfall** (just over 1½ miles away) up the Inverianvie River – my seven-year-old declared it 'the best walk ever!' when we did it as a family, which is high praise indeed. To get there, walk to the western side of the beach to meet the Inverianvie River and then climb up to the road. Cross over and go through the gate: the path straight on leads through bracken to a lovely

ANTHRAX ISLAND

Less than a mile offshore in Gruinard Bay is low-lying **Gruinard Island**. It may look innocent enough, but mere decades ago it was known as the 'Island of death', thanks to its role during World War II. Purchased by the Ministry of Defence in 1942, it was used by scientists from Porton Down in Wiltshire to test the use of anthrax as a biological weapon.

Sixty sheep were tethered to the island and 30lb of explosives containing anthrax were detonated; within days, most of the sheep had died. The experiment was seen as a success, but anthrax bombs were never used by the MoD – and the anthrax detonated on the island remained there, keeping it off limits for decades, though none of the signs warning people to keep away mentioned anything about it until the 1960s. The experiment had been carried out in secret, though rumours began to swirl when animals on the mainland started dying with no explanation.

Thanks to the work of militant group Dark Harvest Commando bringing the island to the public's attention, decontamination finally took place in 1986: heather was burnt, the most contaminated topsoil was removed, and the ground was drenched in diluted formaldehyde, though the island wasn't declared entirely free of anthrax until 1990. Today, the only way to see the island is with your own boat or kayak.

view of the rocky river running through gorse-clad slopes. When the path runs out, head left to curve uphill and then right to join the main path to the waterfall. Gravelly at this point, it curves uphill and becomes grassy as it heads through bracken and gorse, the river below you. It's a simple route and the path is easy to follow, if a bit rocky under foot at times (and muddy, too). The steep waterfall is tucked among craggy rocks, with downy birch clinging precariously to the sides, and plunges into a deep, dark pool that looks deliciously inviting on a hot day.

There's a smaller but equally lovely beach 2½ miles north at **Mungasdale** (φ NG 96483 93166); parking can be tricky, but you might find a little space available on the verge (φ NG 96525 93119).

6 MELLON UDRIGLE

From Little Gruinard, the road curves northwest around the coast, past the appropriately named Second Coast, First Coast and Sand, before reaching the small village of **Laide**. A single-track road heads north from here up the east coast of the **Rubha Mòr** peninsula to the pale pink and gold sands of Mellon Udrigle. It's an absolutely beautiful beach, set against a staggering backdrop of mountains that look as though they've been lined up solely for your viewing pleasure, and is at its most magical at low tide, when the retreating bottle-green water leaves the sand shining and catching the reflection of the clouds.

On the beach's eastern side, paths lead over the dunes to jagged rocks, where low tide leaves behind some fabulous rock pools – some so large and rectangular they look like mini swimming pools. You can also head up on to the moorland to the north of the beach for a walk up to and around the headland of Rubha Beag; the views towards Coigach and the Summer Isles are superlative.

7 SLAGGAN BAY

The most northerly beach on Rubha Mòr's western coast is a beautiful, sheltered stretch of golden sand, facing the distant islands of Lewis and Harris. The catch? You have to walk (or bike) just over three miles to get there, but it's a straightforward route, following a path the entire way, and the scenery is more than enough to distract you. Do bear in mind that you're walking over a large expanse of exposed ground, however, so if it's sunny you'll definitely need sunscreen and a hat.

"The most northerly beach on Rubha Mòr's western coast is a beautiful, sheltered stretch of golden sand."

Parking is available on the eastern side of the road (NG 88743 94139), just over a mile south of Mellon Udrigle; from here, walk about 100yds south to find a footpath sign on the right-hand side of the road pointing the way to the bay down a track, through a metal gate. Keep on the track throughout – you'll pass two lochs on your left-hand side and at times the gorse will crowd in, but by and large you'll be travelling through undulating moorland, dotted with occasional copses.

After about 2½ miles, you'll crest a hill and the water of the bay will appear in the distance, a streak of deep turquoise, and, closer by, you'll see the ruins of a house – pretty much just two gable ends. This is the most intact part of the ruins of the old crofting township of Slaggan, which was once big enough to have had a school but by the start of World War II was home to just six people. The house burned down

---

1 Gruinard Bay. 2 Corrieshalloch Gorge National Nature Reserve and the 147ft Falls of Measach. 3 A gun placement on the Loch Ewe Wartime Trail. 4 Look out for yellow globeflowers among the machair. ▶

ATMOSPHERE!/DT

BOBBROOKY/DT

DMITRY BABURIN 2/S

in the early 1940s and the village's remaining family, the Mackenzies, moved to Achgarve, the village immediately to the south of the walk's starting point. You can wander around the ruins, though be aware that the ground here can be quite boggy.

From the house, a grassy path heads down to the right of old farm walls; when it splits, take the left-hand route down towards the sand. Though the beach isn't particularly wide, at low tide it stretches quite a way; pale, golden sand, streaked with pink from the Lewisian gneiss rocks, and water – as clear as glass – that shifts from turquoise to cobalt blue. It's a great spot for a picnic and a paddle (or a swim, if you can brave the chill).

LOCH EWE

This beautiful sea loch stretching between the Rubha Mòr headland in the east and Cove in the west may look serene today, but during World War II it was the base for the Arctic Convoys (see opposite) making their way to Russia. At the time this meant that general access to Gairloch parish, in which Loch Ewe sits, was restricted and locals were required to carry passes. A number of fortifications and other structures were built around the loch, many of which can still be seen today – the **Loch Ewe Wartime Trail** (⊘ racmp.co.uk/history-learning/loch-ewe-wartime-trail) highlights many of the sites used; check the website and look out for the silhouetted figures as you travel around. Beyond its wartime history, the area around the loch is also home to some beautiful beaches and the abundant Inverewe Gardens.

8 AULTBEA & SURROUNDS

The appealing village of Aultbea curves around a bay on the northeastern shore of Loch Ewe, with a long, pebbly shore and lovely views of the Isle of Ewe, less than half a mile offshore at its closest point. The island is still crofted and inhabited by the same family – the Grants – who have lived here since the 19th century. Today, as well as crofting, Alasdair Grant builds traditional-style boats by hand (⊘ isleeweboats.co.uk) – if you're lucky, you might catch a glimpse of some of them on the water.

During World War II, Aultbea was a hub of activity: the loch was filled with ships, and the village was home to a mess camp on Aird Point, the little headland where the jetty is, as well as a cinema in what is now

THE WORST JOURNEY IN THE WORLD

Loch Ewe's deep waters made it an important and secretive site for the Royal Navy from the end of the 19th century, but it was during World War II that it became particularly vital. After Hitler's invasion of the Soviet Union in June 1941, the Allies transported vital supplies – not just food and fuel but ammunition, tanks and aircraft as well – to the Russians. The aid was taken from Loch Ewe to the Soviet Union by Merchant Navy ships that were protected by warships; a dangerous route that involved travelling close to Norway's occupied northern coast and between Arctic pack ice.

In addition to the dangers that war brought, travelling through the Arctic brought its own challenges: ferocious gales and huge waves, which, combined with the extreme cold, would freeze to the ships as soon as they crashed on board. It's hardly surprising that Winston Churchill referred to this as 'the worst journey in the world'. Over the course of the four years that the convoys operated, more than 3,000 Allied servicemen died, and over 100 Merchant Navy ships were lost. Despite its dangers, four million tons of supplies were successfully delivered, playing an important role in the battles on the Eastern Front.

Aultbea Hall and officers' quarters in the now-closed Aultbea Hotel. You can find out more about wartime activity in the village at the **Arctic Convoy Museum** (Birchburn ✆ 01445 731137 ⌂ racmp.co.uk ⊙ Apr–Oct 10.00–16.00 Mon–Sat), set back from the A832 on the eastern outskirts of the village, which has a huge amount of information and artefacts, including model ships and aircraft.

One of the most fascinating sights around Aultbea has to be **Boom Beach** in the little village of **Mellon Charles**, three miles northwest of the museum. The parking area for the beach – beyond a sign telling you that it's still part of MoD land and the Aultbea Training Area – feels like an inauspicious start, being a huge expanse of concrete, but don't let that put you off. The beach itself is soft golden sand, with views across to the Isle of Ewe, Firemore (page 285), Cove and, to the southeast, the mighty Torridon range.

But what makes the beach particularly interesting is that it is littered with huge concrete blocks with metal loops on their tops and sides. The first time we visited we were yet to read anything about what they were, and the kids especially had a great time hypothesising: anchors for a huge boat, or a giant's building blocks were two suggestions. They are in fact concrete weights, which were used to anchor (so the kids weren't too wrong) an anti-submarine net – known as a 'boom net' – to the seabed; this net was stretched across the loch to guard it from enemy ships and submarines, with a gate in it that allowed friendly ships to enter the loch. More information can be found at the signboard (♀ NG 84499 91168) on the northeastern side of the parking expanse – look for the silhouetted figures.

The signboard also has a picture of what the beach and surrounding area looked like as a naval base in 1946, including the large pier that jutted out from the shore. Today, only a small amount of the pier remains, with its columns looking rather eerie silhouetted against the sea and distant hills.

If you want to get out on the water in the area, contact Conor at **Ewe Canoe** (✆ 07980 588467 ⏿ ewecanoe.co.uk; minimum age 8 years), who offers three-hour private canoe and kayak sessions.

9 INVEREWE & POOLEWE

Whichever way you approach **Inverewe** (IV22 2LG ⏲ garden: end Mar–mid-Nov 10.00–17.00 daily; house: Jun–Sep 10.00–16.30 daily; estate: year-round; NTS), it'll seem like a lush enclave within the typically rugged Wester Ross landscape. Sitting on the southeastern shore of Loch Ewe, overlooking the small village of Poolewe, which sits at the head of the loch, it feels – particularly when the sun shines – like a little corner of paradise.

"Sitting on the shore of Loch Ewe, it feels – particularly when the sun shines – like a little corner of paradise."

In the mid 19th century, the estate owner, Osgood Mackenzie, decided to establish a garden on what he called his 'barren peninsula'. He imported so-called good soil in order to grow flowers, fruit and vegetables, and within a decade had planted thousands of trees to create a windbreak. The introduction of exotic trees and plants soon followed, including palms, Himalayan blue poppies and rhododendrons – so many of the last that there is always one in flower here every day of the year – which were able to benefit from Inverewe's unique microclimate. Osgood's daughter, Mairi, who continued her father's work, gave the garden to the National Trust for Scotland in 1952, shortly before her death.

Even today – and even expecting the garden to look like it does – it's an astonishing place to explore in this corner of Scotland. When I visited one October, I was fully prepared to find the garden wilting and fading, but it was still abundantly green and colourful: the walled garden brimmed with magnolias and roses, kale, chard and cabbages, while on the Jubilee track I was surrounded by towering pines and, at ground level, the tiny purple lantern-like flowers of St Dabeoc's heath.

The best way to explore Inverewe is to wander and follow the paths as they appear and take your fancy, stumbling across hidden groves and places to sit and contemplate. While it's a popular place, it doesn't take much to get beyond the crowds and find solitude. At times, you might have to push past plants crowding the paths, such as a very large, spreading rhododendron, which gives the place a wild feel. Don't miss Camas Glas, the bay at the far end of the garden, from where there are staggering views across and along the water; there are more beautiful views to the west of here, at Cuddy Rock. **Wildlife boat cruises** run by a local fisherman from the jetty near Cuddy Rock (book in advance online via NTS website; additional fee) give you the opportunity to spot seals and white-tailed eagles, among other animals.

"If you are able, it is worth walking these harder paths for the views they afford over the water and hillsides."

The vast majority of the garden's paths are easy to walk (and a decent amount can be explored by wheelchair, too), and those that aren't – including the dauntingly named Devil's Elbow Path – are labelled as such. If you are able, it is worth walking these harder paths for the views they afford over the water and hillsides. That said, the walk up to High Viewpoint is largely an 'easy' path; from here, on a clear day, you can really make out the contours and crags of the landscape on the far side of the loch.

I really liked the so-called Wet Valley, just before the Pond Garden, where the huge leaves of the giant rhubarb (*Gunnera manicata*) have taken over – perhaps unsurprising given that their leaves can grow to be up to 8ft wide. Right on the shore, just beyond the Walled Garden, the peaceful Rock Garden, with its view of Poolewe and the mountains behind, has an impressive tree that looks a bit like it's been dressed in camouflage.

The village of **Poolewe** itself, just 350yds south of the gardens, also boasts an incredibly scenic position on Loch Ewe. On its shores, next to where the River Ewe turns its final corner to empty into the loch, is **Pool House** (☏ 01445 781272 ⬦ pool-house.co.uk ☺ Apr–Oct: house tour

16.30 Mon & Sat, spooky tour 16.30 Thu; Nov–Mar by arrangement), which bills itself as 'part museum, part comfy home'. The house was used as the Royal Navy Command Headquarters for the Arctic Convoys (page 281), from which the convoys entering and leaving the loch were controlled. It remains a family home today, which means that while crammed full of toys, World War II memorabilia and period furnishings – including an amazingly ornate and beautiful Chinese marriage bed – it doesn't have that detached feel that some stately homes do. The house can only be visited on a tour, but the café (see below) provides an opportunity to have a glimpse of the interior when the rest of the place is off limits.

¶¶ FOOD & DRINK

Pool House Poolewe IV22 2LD ⊘ pool-house.co.uk/cafe. Set in the Pool House's Rowallan Room – with its central billiard table, piano and ship's figurehead – this café feels much fancier than its prices suggest. The wooden bar is always set out with a decadent array of cakes and traybakes (if the lemon Victoria sponge is on the menu, snap it up), and there's a great range of hot and cold drinks, including excellent local Ewe Brew beer. If the weather is nice, forgo the fancy surroundings for a seat in the garden, overlooking the loch.

10 FIREMORE BEACH

Parking at ♥ NG 81317 88441

The single-track road that runs along the west side of Loch Ewe (the B8057) is a wonderful one, with views right across the loch and the Isle of Ewe, and passing through small crofting communities of predominantly white houses. There are little coves of pebbles and sand along the way, but the best and biggest stretch is six miles north of Poolewe at the evocatively named Firemore Beach. This is a long, glorious strand of pale terracotta-coloured sand lapped by spearmint-green water, looking towards distant mountains. A rocky outcrop makes the beach feel as though it's split in two; the southern half is bisected by a burn that flows down from nearby Loch Sguod, to the southwest, while the northern half feels more like a classic curve of sand. It's my favourite kind of

◀ **1** The River Ewe at Poolewe. **2** Boom Beach is littered with concrete weights that were used to anchor an anti-submarine net. **3** The beautiful gardens at Inverewe. **4** Pool House was used as the Royal Navy Command Headquarters for the Arctic Convoys.

beach: you feel like you could happily walk and walk and walk, or spend hours climbing up on the rocky headlands. The gulf stream here means the water can be a little warmer than elsewhere, and its sheltered nature makes it a good spot for watersports in summer.

11 RUBHA NAN SASAN: ARCTIC CONVOY MEMORIAL

♀ NG 81492 92104

I'll be honest: this was one of those places I traipsed out to half-heartedly, muttering 'for the sake of the book', rather than because I was really interested. Thankfully, as so often, I was proved wrong – and even if you too have no real interest in military history, I'd urge you to make the effort for the views alone: towards the Isle of Ewe, Boom Beach and the mountains further inland.

"Even if you too have no real interest in military history, I'd urge you to make the effort for the views alone."

From Firemore, the road continues three miles further north, past the hamlet of **Cove** to the stark promontory at Rubha nan Sasan; to get out here, you have to pass a sign that says 'End of public road', but be reassured that there is a public car park (♀ NG 81417 92057) just before the memorial. Once you've parked, return to the main road and turn left to walk up the road towards the headland; it curves towards the memorial after about 70yds. The simple stone, in memory of those who lost their lives at sea 'in the bitter Arctic sea battles', commands a formidable position on the headland, looking out across the very loch that the convoys would have sailed out of, unsure of whether they would return.

Beyond the memorial, and all around the headland, are small concrete buildings; operating as Cove Battery during World War II, the site was used to watch for enemy attack, and two large naval guns were mounted in the bunkers here. As with so many military sites, there's a desolation to this headland, with the functional buildings and empty moorland in stark contrast against the sea and the hills and mountains across the loch. Do be cautious if you decide to explore – the buildings are close to the cliff edges and although there are visible paths, it has been fenced off to deter people from risking their lives. Instead, I'd recommend you head back down the hill and, when the road turns to the right, continue straight on to follow a path up to a bench (climbing over a low fence to do so), which offers up stupendous mountain views – with any luck, you might be able to spot Beinn Eighe and Liathach.

A right turn just before you reach the bench takes you uphill to a triangulation station (♀ NG 81492 91916), dated to 1951, and even better views, including south along the coastline. Immediately to the south, you'll see an impressive natural sea arch in the rocks.

GAIRLOCH TO RUBHA REIDH

The undulating moorland between Poolewe and Gairloch is such that for a while it feels as though there will be nothing but this vast moonscape of heather, rocks and lochs. You know you're getting closer to Gairloch when skinny pines start to dot the southern side of the road, and soon after the waters of wide Loch Gairloch streak the horizon. There's plenty to keep you occupied exploring the village and its surrounds for days, including to its north where the isolated lighthouse of Rubha Reidh looks out over the islands of Skye, Lewis and Harris.

THE SPIRIT OF THE PLACE

'For me, it's about the spirit of the place, that's what I strive for,' Gairloch-based artist Fiona Mackenzie (⬦ fionamackenzieart.co.uk) tells me. This is strikingly clear in Fiona's landscape work, which captures the wild, elemental nature of the Wester Ross coast. Clouds, sea, shore and mountains are distinct and yet blend into each other, creating a constant sense of movement. In her painting *Incoming – bad weather* you can almost feel the thick, rolling cloud pulling in across the landscape, while in *Sea Haar* the mist dances above silver-flecked water.

Fiona works in a variety of different mediums, from pencil and inks to watercolours, oils and acrylics. 'My mood can move from expressive large works, with big strokes capturing light and air, to more introspective, detailed capture in my wood engraving,' she says. These smaller pieces often focus on wildlife, particularly birds, and the level of detail is quite astounding: on her Instagram account (📷 fionamackenzie3), she shares fascinating snippets of the process, from initial pencil studies to note-scribbled test prints. Despite only studying the art form since 2019, in 2024 Fiona deservedly won the First Time Exhibitor Award at the Society of Wood Engraver's annual exhibition for her beautiful engraving of a peewit.

You can find cards of some of Fiona's work in the Gairloch Museum (page 289); check her website for full-size artworks (available to buy) and details of her forthcoming exhibitions, many of which are held in the North Highlands.

12 GAIRLOCH

Come to Gairloch on a warm, sunny day and it feels every inch the holiday village: people queuing for fish and chips, kids paddling in the sea, couples wandering hand-in-hand along the sand and boats bobbing in the water. Of course, this is a holiday village in the Wester Ross fashion, which is to say relaxed and understated, with pockets of complete solitude not hard to find.

Gairloch's position – strung out around the head of Loch Gairloch and encompassing a handful of small settlements – makes it feel mightier in size than it actually is. Along the B8021, which runs west from the A832, you'll find the community hall and a scattering of hotels, cafés and gift shops facing towards the shore, which is pebbly at high tide with some nice stretches of sand appearing at low tide, and a view towards the mountains of Torridon and Skye.

Back on the A832, 200yds south of the junction with the B8021 is the **GALE Centre** (IV21 2BH ✆ 01445 712071 ✆ galeactionforum.co.uk/the-gale-centre), which serves as the village's tourist information centre,

ACTIVITIES IN & AROUND GAIRLOCH

Given the huge number of activities on offer both on and off the water in Gairloch, it's no surprise that this is a popular spot for family holidays, with many people returning year after year. In addition to the activity providers listed below, there are lots of opportunities for excellent walking, particularly around Flowerdale Glen (page 292).

BOAT TRIPS

Gairloch Marine Wildlife Centre and Cruises Charleston Harbour, Pier Rd ✆ 07751 992666 (text for booking enquiries) ✆ porpoise-gairloch.co.uk. Choose between a two-hour 'wildlife survey' cruise on Loch Gairloch and into the Little Minch, or a four-hour 'cetacean and seabird city cruise' that takes you straight into the Minch and around the fascinating seabird-rich Shiant Isles, both run by marine biologist Ian.

Glass Bottomed Boat Pier Rd ✆ 01445 712647 ✆ glassbottomedboat.co.uk. Carrying just 11 people, this small glass-bottomed boat is a particular hit with kids who love being able to see what's going on under the water. It sails around the little islands in Loch Gairloch, and you can expect to see the local seal colony.

Glendale Boat Hire Gairloch Harbour ✆ 01445 712228 ✆ glendaleboathire.com. A choice of three small boats for self-drive hire of up to eight hours, with a maximum capacity of four people.

Hebridean Whale Cruises Pier Rd ✆ 01445 712 458 ✆ hebridean-whale-cruises.co.uk. Offering RIB trips out into the open waters of as well as a community café (page 292) and gift shop selling books, maps and local gifts and crafts.

Another 150yds further on, set back from the road in an old nuclear bunker (yes, really), is the splendid **Gairloch Museum** (IV21 2BH ✎ 01445 712287 ⌂ gairlochmuseum.org ☉ late Mar–Oct 10.00–17.00 Mon–Sat). This is a fantastic example of how you can cram in a lot of exhibits and interesting detail into one space in a lively and captivating way – if you want to visit just one museum in the North Highlands, it should be this one.

The building, which was one of four anti-aircraft operations rooms built in Scotland to withstand a nuclear attack, was decommissioned in 1956 – before it was finished – but parts of it were used for civil defence during the 1960s and '80s when Cold War tensions flared up. Pictures and a scale model in the museum show what it originally looked like – they've done a fantastic job of making a very utilitarian building look more appealing (painting it white and adding a couple of windows has definitely helped).

the North Minch for the best chance to see whales and dolphins; choose between the 2½-hour Whales and Wildlife cruise, the four-hour Ultimate Orca 1, and, at the start of the season, a three-hour trip to the Shiant Islands. Autumn trips vary depending on conditions.

HORSERIDING
Gairloch Trekking Centre Red Point ✎ 01445 741743 ⌂ gairlochtrekkingcentre. co.uk. Pony trekking on the beach for both novice and experienced riders (and everyone in between), with half- and full-day kids' experiences also available.

WALKING & CLIMBING
Climb Ride Explore See right
Gairloch Kayak Centre See right

go further Scotland Melvaig ✎ 01445 771260 ⌂ gofurtherscotland.co.uk. Guided mountain walking and scrambling, and rock climbing – from the crags around Gairloch to sea stacks.

WATERSPORTS
Climb Ride Explore ✎ 07737 413268 ⌂ climbrideexplore.co.uk. Stand-up paddleboard hire and guided SUP exploration (age 8+), plus coasteering, canyoning, mountain biking, and mountain and rock climbing.
Ewe Canoe Page 282.
Gairloch Kayak Centre Shieldaig Lodge, IV21 2AN ⌂ gairlochkayakcentre.com. Half- and full-day kayaking trips, in Shieldaig Bay or Loch Maree, suitable for beginners. Bike hire and mountain climbing also available.

The exhibits, which cover between them the whole gamut of the parish's history, from Bronze Age items to the original lens from Rubha Reidh lighthouse (page 293), are a good mix of things to read and look at, and things to do. I particularly enjoyed sitting in a booth and listening to Gaelic stories, and seeing the huge wooden pulpit that was used for outdoor services in Shieldaig in Torridon until 1920 and which could be easily dismantled for transporting. The upstairs galleries include a great crash course in geology where you can see and touch examples of the many kinds of rocks found in the region – perfect for contextualising what you might see on your explorations. The excellent café (page 292) is also upstairs, while downstairs, next to the well-stocked little shop, is a gallery space that hosts some interesting exhibitions.

When you leave the museum, don't miss the opportunity to head across the road to the 'Outdoor Museum'. Here you'll find information about the local fishing industry and geology, with fishing implements and rock examples in situ. You can also head behind the museum to walk the Achtercairn Archaeology Trail around the remains of 12 Iron Age roundhouses; the first is a short distance from the museum, but you'll need a couple of hours for the whole trail, and decent footwear.

"Despite its proximity to the village, there's a real sense of wildness to this beach, with mountains behind."

The view from the museum cannot help but steal the show, looking down on the wide sweep of beautiful **Gairloch Beach** and the scenically placed Gairloch Free Church (♀ NG 80504 76016) that sits above the middle of it. You can access the beach from the parking area to the south of the church, though it's much easier from the large car park (♀ NG 80701 75634) next to the golf course, just 500yds further down the road; from here, it's just a short walk along a boardwalk on to the golden sands. Despite its proximity to the village, there's a real sense of wildness to this beach, with mountains behind and islands dotting the water in front, yet it's sheltered enough to make it popular with families. On hot days it can get busy, but it's quieter and more sheltered at the far southern end.

Immediately south of the beach, on the other side of the headland of An Ard, is **Charlestown**, the most southerly of the settlements that

1 The picturesque lighthouse at Rubha Reidh. 2 Looking towards Flowerdale Glen and the Old Inn, Gairloch. 3 Exploring Gairloch Museum. ▶

EMMA GIBBS

EMMA GIBBS

MARK APPLETON

make up Gairloch. This is where you'll find the harbour, home not only to Gairloch's fishing fleet but also to a number of activity operators (page 288). The harbourfront walkway has been prettied up with a community garden, which has plenty of places to sit and soak up the lovely views across the bay.

On the other side of the A832, scenically positioned next to the old bridge across the burn, is the Old Inn (see below), an enviable spot for a drink on a warm, sunny day. From the other side of the burn, paths lead into beautiful **Flowerdale Glen** – the best of which heads a mile and a half upriver to a lovely waterfall. It's a wonderful walk, particularly on a sunny day in spring when the trees are back in full leaf and the gorse is singing with colour. The path is well signposted, and takes you past attractive old Flowerdale House, which has been home to the Mackenzie family since 1738.

¶¶ FOOD & DRINK

Am Bàrd Gairloch Museum ⊘ gairlochmuseum.org/café. Bright, big-windowed café on the first floor of the museum (page 289), with a loch-view terrace for fine weather. Soups, sandwiches and quiches are available for lunch, plus lots of delicious sweet treats.
Black Pearl Creole Kitchen IV21 2BP ✆ 07300 337201 ⊘ blackpearlcreolekitchen.com. Hands-down the best and most exciting place to eat in Gairloch, the Black Pearl started life in a converted horsebox and now has a casual but stylish restaurant just off the A832. My personal favourite is the chickpea curry served with a Trinidadian bara flatbread, but there's enough to keep you coming back again and again, including jerk chicken and barbecue pork ribs. Come early to grab a table, or order take-away. Out of season, check its Facebook page for pop-up events around the region.
GALE Centre (page 288). Lovely cakes made by local bakers, plus more substantial lunch items, which can be eaten inside the modern building or on the loch-facing terrace outside.
The Old Inn IV21 2BD ⊘ theoldinn.net. Beautifully positioned at the start of the walks into Flowerdale, the Old Inn makes the perfect spot to enjoy a pre- or post-walk (or hey, both) pint of local beer, with tables outside by the river perfect for soaking up the surroundings on a sunny day. It's cosy inside too, and the menu features locally caught fish and seafood.

13 NORTH TO RUBHA REIDH

Three miles northwest of Gairloch, reached by following the B8021 west, is the glorious swathe of **Big Sand beach**, which more than lives up to its name. The campsite here, which somewhat claims the beach as its own, provides the only real parking and easiest access to the sands, though you'll have to pay a few pounds for the privilege. Otherwise, you can walk up from the village and use the pedestrian access on the southeastern side of the beach (φ NG 76047 77905); you might be able to find roadside parking a mile or so down the road, but as always do be mindful of not blocking houses or traffic, or ruining verges. The island just offshore here is uninhabited Longa Island.

From here it's a further ten miles north to the end of the road, and the attractive lighthouse at **Rubha Reidh** (also spelled Rubh Re, as you'll see in Gairloch Museum where its original lens is on display). Beyond the hamlet of **Melvaig**, the road becomes one of the narrowest I've encountered in the Highlands – the fact that it has a 20mph speed limit is a testament to just how tight it is, often with very limited visibility. If you're of a nervous disposition or not a confident single-track driver then I'd recommend that you use the parking area (φ NG 74034 87096) at the northern end of Melvaig and walk the three miles from there.

"From here it's ten miles north to the end of the road, and the attractive lighthouse at Rubha Reidh."

There are a number of small, designated parking spaces along the way, but the last one is at just under half a mile from the lighthouse; park here (φ NG 74066 91461) and then continue up to the lighthouse on foot. Surrounded by sheer, rocky edges, the lighthouse was built in 1912 and engineered by David Stevenson – though he had in fact recommended it be built six years earlier. Automated in 1986, it's now a holiday let.

The views from the headland here – and en route, though if you're driving you're more likely to be able to enjoy them on your return journey – are phenomenal. On a clear day, you can see Skye and even Lewis and Harris astonishingly clearly, and, if you walk around to the eastern side of the headland or to the top, as far as Coigach. You can walk down to the jetty, just a little further along the track from the lighthouse, or higher up on to the headland – heading east (with care though, as the cliffs are perilous) will take you to beautiful **Camas Mòr** beach, which can only be reached via a tricky scramble.

THE OVERSIDE

The southern side of Loch Gairloch is known locally as the Overside – a great name, I always think, even if it gives little away about the charms of this coastal area. The B8056 winds west and then south through it, with the coast largely in sight for most of the way, past appealing crofting and coastal communities and with enviable views across the Minch as far as Skye.

14 BADACHRO
🏠 **Arrowdale**

Eleven miles from Gairloch, set around an incredibly picturesque natural harbour that looks directly on to **Isle Horrisdale**, is the attractive village of Badachro. The water here always seems to be peppered with colourful boats, though these are just a fraction of those that would have been seen in the mid 19th century when the cod-fishing industry was flourishing – a number of curing stations were built here at this time, including on tidal **Dry Island** (⊘ dryisland.co.uk), which offers self-catering accommodation. The island, which is attached to the mainland by a floating footbridge, is owned by Ian McWhinney, whose family have fished here for generations and who still fishes himself. A fabulous way to experience this is on one of Ian's **Shellfish Safaris** (✆ 01445 741263 ⊘ shellfishsafari.co.uk), which take you out on a working fishing boat – you'll watch creels and lobster pots get hauled up and have the chance to hold and feel small sea creatures like starfish and crabs. It's a fun and totally unique experience that really helps you engage with the landscape and its history – and the people who live and work here.

"Set around a picturesque natural harbour that looks directly on to Isle Horrisdale, is attractive Badachro."

Just southwest of Dry Island is the small-scale family-owned **Badachro Distillery** (Aird Hill ✆ 01445 741282 ⊘ badachrodistillery.com ⊙ 10.00–16.00 Mon–Fri), whose gin uses local botanicals such as gorse blossom and elderflower. As well as Badachro Gin, the team makes and sells Dancing Puffin Vodka and Bad na h-Achlaise whisky. You can try some of these on a distillery tour (minimum age 14), which begins with a G&T and ends with a tasting of five spirits in the beautiful sunroom.

Keeping with the alcohol theme, the main reason many people visit Badachro is the lovely **Badachro Inn** (see opposite), in a prime position overlooking the water as you enter the village. It was originally built in the early to mid 19th century, most likely in association with the nearby curing stations. Inside, it's everything you want a waterside pub to be:

cosy, relaxed and with lots of wooden furniture, and you can soak up the views from the lovely terrace in fine weather. Just up the road from the pub is **Latitude 57** (✆ 07818 616488 ⬧ latitude57.net), a dinky but well-stocked gift shop specialising in appropriately nautically themed items.

SPECIAL STAYS

Arrowdale Leacnasaide, IV21 2AP ✆ 07762 793644 ⬧ arrowdaleholiday.com. Quite possibly the Platonic ideal of a self-catering property and one of nicest I've ever stayed in. Clare has thought of everything, from cosy spots to sit – the window seat overlooking the bay is the winner – to everything you could possibly need in the kitchen, along with insulated picnic bags, blankets, kayaks and a drying cupboard for wet gear. Her fresh baking greets you upon arrival, and she can make you dinners and various treats in advance and during your stay. Clare lives just up the hill and welcomes the chance for a good chat, but overall the place feels blissfully, utterly private.

FOOD & DRINK

Badachro Inn IV21 2AA ✆ 01445 741255 ⬧ badachroinn.com. If you can grab a window seat at this fine little pub, you will most likely feel like you've won the lottery. Food is excellent but unpretentious, there's local beer and gin on the drinks menu, and wood-fired pizza on offer through its sister business, Stag and Dough (⬧ staganddough.com). For a special experience, book ahead for the table in the little Boat House cabin outside. E-bikes are also available to hire from here.

15 OPINAN BEACH

Parking at 📍 NG 74493 72347 and NG 74585 72643

> **The sun began to sink, and gradually the sands turned from ash blonde to ochre and dun, the colours of a lioness.**
> Annie Worsley, *Windswept*

Dusky Opinan Beach, just under three miles southwest of Badachro, seems like it's hidden in plain sight – if you're not looking for it, you'll most likely drive past as only the briefest flash of the sands is seen from the road. Backed by grass-covered dunes, surrounded by crofting land and a scattering of houses, and with rocks at either end, it feels secluded and private. Views stretch across to Skye and, on the clearest of days, to Lewis and Harris.

On one visit in October, the tide was out and a milky sun was making the sea gleam a startling white, giving the whole beach an unreal feel. Kids will love finding the stepping stones across the river channel at

the northern end, and if you've read Annie Worsley's book, *Windswept*, you'll easily locate the sea log seat she speaks so fondly of.

16 RED POINT BEACHES
Parking at ♀ NG 73185 68737

The road through the Overside ends at the tiny settlement of Red Point, which is also the name of the bulbous peninsula to its southwest. There's a viewpoint (♀ NG 73186 69247) on the right about 500yds before the road descends to the parking place at the end of it (♀ NG 73174 68707), which gives you a sense of **Red Point Beach** before you reach it – a fabulous stretch of sand wedged between two rocky headlands. When people talk of Red Point beach, they're generally talking about this one, but there are in fact two, both of which can be reached from the parking area at the end of the road.

> "When people talk of Red Point beach, they're generally talking about this one, but there are in fact two."

At the southern end of the car park are two farm gates; the right-hand one leads to the north beach, with a grassy path leading through ferns and heather, the sea and Skye in the distance. It doesn't take long before the high terracotta dunes that back the beach are revealed, and the path becomes sandy. This is a glorious stretch of beach, with the colour of the sands shifting from a honey to terracotta as often as the clouds move, and a burn snaking its way around its southern end. If you're willing to ford the burn, which is easiest at low tide (or with bare feet/wellies), you can climb up to the headland of Red Point itself, and pick out a faint path around the peninsula to the southern beach (1¾ miles) – be warned that it can get very boggy, however, so much so that I aborted my attempt when I tried it one autumn.

Alternatively, for a quicker – and easier – route (about 20 minutes), you can retrace your steps back to the car park, and once you're through the gate turn right to go through the kissing gate to the right of the metal farm gate, on to the farm track, which is signposted to Diabaig. Keep straight, following the path to the right when it turns, and then continue straight on to pass right through the farm, with the farmhouse to your

---

◀ **1** Badachro is set in an incredibly picturesque natural harbour. **2** Victoria Falls at Loch Maree. **3** Stills at the family-owned Badachro Distillery. **4** Loch Maree, with Slioch in the distance.

left and outbuildings to your right, to reach another kissing gate to the right of a farm gate, accompanied by a footpath symbol. You'll pass through two more kissing gates on this track; at the third, you'll see a big cluster of gorse on your right and machair ahead. When the track veers left, after crossing a peaty burn, turn right and you'll see the sea ahead of you. Walk towards it and the beach will soon appear.

"A flock of ringed plover took to the sky in a great mass of wings before settling back down on the shore again."

The sands of **Far Red Point** are shallower than at its northerly sister, but longer and more graceful, and slightly paler, particularly on its far southern side. At low tide, you can walk out to the grass-topped rocky island of **Eilean Tioram**, which creates a kind of T-shape with the beach. At the southern end of the beach, you'll see a few derelict buildings: the most intact, though entirely roofless, was once the fishing station.

Personally, Far Red Point has the edge for me, in part because of its expansive views. To the south are the Torridon Mountains and the Applecross Peninsula, layer upon layer of hills and mountains, while to the west are Rona and Skye, and to the northwest you might just catch a glimpse of Lewis and Harris. I was here once on my favourite kind of Highland day: with intermittent rainbows and the light and clouds constantly playing a game of hide and seek, making the sea change from silver to aquamarine and back again quicker than I could keep track, while a flock of ringed plover took to the sky in a great mass of wings before settling back down on the shore again. Bring a picnic and stay all day.

Red Point is the furthest you can go by road on the Overside, but further down the peninsula is the picturesque hamlet of **Lower Diabaig** (page 317), which can be reached by road from Torridon, or on foot from here. It's a seven-mile walk, so you'll need to arrange a pick-up from the other end – or be prepared for a long round-trip, which you may consider worth it given the prospect of Gille Brighde (page 319) at the other end.

LOCH MAREE

Stretching for 12 miles from just south of Poolewe to just north of the village of **Kinlochewe**, Loch Maree is undoubtedly one of the most scenic lochs in the North Highlands. Its northern shore, towered over by Slioch in the southeast, backs on to Fisherfield – or the 'Great Wilderness' as it is known, on account of it being untouched by roads or settlements, and accessible only on foot.

Eight miles southeast of Gairloch, the A832 follows the southern shore of Loch Maree almost the entire rest of the way to Kinlochewe, with the water dipping in and out of view between trees. Even if you don't plan to properly stop along here, I'd recommend at the very least parking up for a few minutes at **Coille na Glas-Leitir** (page 300), from where you get staggering views over the loch, with Slioch glowering from across the water. Whatever the weather, it never fails to catch my breath.

17 VICTORIA FALLS

IV22 2HW; parking at 📍 NG 89315 71204

Though not a patch on the more famous African waterfalls that share their name, these skinny little falls are beautiful nonetheless. They are named after Queen Victoria, who visited the area in 1877, staying at the nearby Loch Maree Hotel – which at that point was only five years old. From the car park, you get lovely views over the loch, and it's just 300yds from here to the lower viewing area along a wide, smooth path.

LOCH MAREE ISLANDS

Clustered at the loch's widest point are the Loch Maree Islands, which, thanks to their isolated position, are home to patches of ancient woodland that are considered to be among the least disturbed by humans in the UK. As a result, the islands are home to rare plants, insects and birds, including black-throated divers, which breed here. The largest island, **Eilean Sùbhainn**, even has a loch of its own, which in turn has an island on it – something you won't find anywhere else in Britain. On small **Isle Maree** is a burial ground containing 19th-century gravestones; this is also supposed to be where, in the 7th or 8th century, St Maelrubha founded a chapel – the loch's name apparently derives from his.

It's possible to explore the islands by kayak – if you don't have your own gear, or would like a guided exploration, contact Gairloch Kayak Centre (page 289). NatureScot issues excellent guidance (⊘ nature.scot/lochmareeaccess) on exploring the loch and its islands, both in terms of minimising your impact and protecting the wildlife, particularly in relation to nesting birds from April to August. Camping on the islands is only permitted from September to March, and outside of this time you shouldn't stay on any one island for more than half an hour.

Depending on recent rainfall, the falls can be either a thin stream or a wide, gushing cascade, which twists itself down numerous drops through the trees. You can also continue up along the burn to the top of the falls – this trail is a little more strenuous but worth it for the view of both the falls and the loch.

18 BEINN EIGHE & LOCH MAREE ISLANDS NATIONAL NATURE RESERVE

⌖ nature.scot ☉ visitor centre: Apr–Oct 10.00–17.00 daily

The UK's oldest National Nature Reserve stretches from Loch Maree to the top of Beinn Eighe mountain, covering an astounding 18 sq miles of shimmering beauty. There are numerous places to stop and explore the reserve; the most accessible are at the **visitor centre** (♀ NH 01990 62993), a mile northwest of Kinlochewe, where you can find out more about exploring the reserve. The short, flat **Pinecone Trail** weaves through the towering pines behind the centre, while the mile-long **Buzzard Trail** climbs uphill for a short distance to afford fabulous views of Beinn Eighe's peaks. There's a bird hide by the visitor centre, and pine martens are known to rummage in the bins here in the evenings.

"The UK's oldest NNR stretches from Loch Maree to the top of Beinn Eighe mountain, covering an astounding 18 sq miles."

More exciting are the trails that start two miles north at **Coille na Glas-Leitir** car park (♀ NH 00201 64997), which provide fabulous views over the island-studded loch. In fact, you don't even have to head off on one of the trails; you can walk down to the shore for one of my favourite views in the whole of the North Highlands: across to the ridges of mighty Slioch and Beinn a' Mhuinidh. It would be a shame to miss out on walking one of these trails, however. The one-mile **Woodland Trail** is the most easily achievable, climbing a short way up the mountainside through birch, young pines and weather-beaten

GLEN DOCHERTY VIEWPOINT

If you're driving the A832 south of Kinlochewe, look out for this viewpoint on the eastern side of the road, three miles south of the village. From here, you have a fantastic view down the glen, with the road curving scenically towards the spread of Loch Maree, with mountains crowding in on either side and some of the loch's islands visible.

'granny pines' – the last, remnants of the old Atlantic rainforest – for more staggering views across the water. The four-mile **Mountain Trail** is a little more intense, climbing higher and billing itself as the country's only waymarked mountain walk – if you have a few hours to spare, and the fitness for it (it climbs pretty steeply uphill), then you'll be rewarded with astounding vistas.

In the 70 years since Beinn Eighe became an NNR, some 800,000 trees have been planted here, linking up strands of ancient forest: the result is a wide forest that colours the lower slopes of the mountain, made up of Scots pine, juniper, birch and aspen. They've planted the last of the 'links' that help to extend the forest, so are now, amazingly, in a position to just let natural regeneration take place. Of course, this has been achieved and will continue to be achieved by careful deer management through culling – the reserve office has a deer larder where the dead animals are prepared to be used as meat by local businesses such as The Torridon (page 316) and private buyers.

SOUTH OF BEN WYVIS

This is a slightly awkward corner of Wester Ross, in that it sits closer to Easter Ross than it does to the places in the rest of this chapter. With so much of inland Wester Ross virtually inaccessible except to the hardiest of walkers, the handful of places I've included on the southern side of isolated **Ben Wyvis** feel like the exception – though, despite the dominating mountain to their north, they have a rather different feel to much of the rest of Wester Ross.

"Ben Wyvis is generally accepted as one of the easiest Munros to climb with a four-mile route to the summit."

Ben Wyvis is generally accepted as one of the easiest Munros to climb; the four-mile route to the summit starts from a car park (♀ NH 41025 67131) four miles north of **Garve** village. The roads across Wester Ross to Garve from Kinlochewe (the A832) and Ullapool (the A835) are beautiful: the former follows the route of the Kyle Line (page 24) as far as **Achnasheen**, with fabulous views along the strath; while the latter takes you alongside **Loch Glascarnoch,** with its dam that always makes me think of James Bond movies. There are ample opportunities along both to stop and take in the views, and to hike up into the hills and mountains – as always, don't head out without a map and adequate kit.

19 LITTLE GARVE

Parking at ♀ NH 39581 62941 ⟣ forestryandland.gov.scot/visit/little-garve

This is a glorious forest walk of just over two miles along the evocatively named **Black Water River**, which rushes and tumbles over rocks below you for most of the way. The path from the car park, which is just over a mile north of Garve, is easy to follow, heading south to cross over pretty Little Garve Bridge, built in 1767 and from which there are gorgeous views both up- and downstream – the peat-coloured river wild and rocky among trees on your left and wider and flatter to the right, with fields and tree-clad hills in the distance.

Once over the bridge, follow the signposted trail towards **Silverbridge** (if you've got kids in tow you might want to detour straight ahead to the natural playpark). This is a clear gravel path that meanders alongside the river through a woodland of predominantly Scots pine.

"On both paths there are places where you can get down to the river – perfect for a paddle on a warm day." After about three-quarters of a mile, you'll see a picnic table on the left with a good view of a shallow waterfall, which makes a lovely lunch spot. There's another waterfall almost immediately after you continue walking from here, which the path crosses on a wooden bridge. Shortly after, continue left when the path splits and you'll soon see two larger bridges: the modern road bridge and Silverbridge itself, once used as part of an old drovers' route.

From the bridge, you'll be able to see the impressive but also fairly shallow falls – once you've crossed over, you can walk through the car park to a viewing spot on the right, more or less opposite the toilets. The path back on the western side of the river is a little rougher, dipping down closer to the water in a few places. On both paths there are clear places where you can get down to the river – perfect for a paddle on a warm day.

20 ROGIE FALLS

A8345, IV14 9EQ ⟣ forestryandland.gov.scot/visit/rogie-falls

The Black Water River waterfalls at Little Garve seem rather sedate compared to those at Rogie Falls, six miles to the south. Here, the

---

1 At Little Garve you can take a forested walk of around 2 miles along the Black Water River. **2** The spa town of Strathpeffer. **3** Watch salmon jumping from the bridge at Rogie Falls. **4** Look for red deer on the slopes of Beinn Eighe. ▶

RPHSTOCK/DT

DAVID MASSIE/DT

P BANNON/DT

EMMA GIBBS

dark river is squeezed down steep rocky walls, foaming and gushing as it descends. It's a glorious spot, tightly hemmed in by jagged rocks and trees, even in winter when the trees have been stripped of their plumage.

What brings most people here though is the annual **salmon-jumping** spectacle; as at the Falls of Shin (page 98), salmon make their way upstream in summer in order to lay their eggs in the place they were born. The falls here are arguably more spectacular than those at Shin, with an option of two trails to reach them: the there-and-back half-mile **Salmon Trail**, or the slightly longer **Riverside Trail**, which is a little rougher underfoot. Both head through the Scots pines of surrounding Torrachilty Forest, with the latter following the river for a while – wide and flat before it reaches the falls.

"The falls here are arguably more spectacular than those at Shin, with an option of two trails to reach them."

By the falls is a suspension bridge, providing great views up and down the water – you can also cross here to head further into the forest on the other side. Spotting the salmon sometimes requires a bit of patience, but you should be able to see them from both sides of the river and the bridge. It feels a little cruel to say, but there is something quite comical about these large fish launching themselves out of the water in order to make their way up the falls – often they don't quite make it, and even once they make it up the first part of the falls there's still more to make their way up before they're in the clear.

21 STRATHPEFFER

Genteel Strathpeffer feels every inch the old Victorian spa town it is, with 19th-century buildings – some graceful, some typically grandiose – strung out along the main road. Sulphurous springs were discovered here in the 18th century, with a pump room built in 1819; Strathpeffer's heyday as a spa town came after the (now defunct) railway line was opened in 1885, which – amazingly – linked it directly to London. Unfortunately, few spa buildings remain in the town today. One exception is the **Spa Pavilion** (The Square ⊘ highlifehighland.com/strathpefferpavilion) – if it looks rather European that's because it was modelled on Baden-Baden's casino. Today, it's community owned and used for concerts, exhibitions and other events. The little brick building tucked away in the car park immediately south of the pavilion is the old **pump room.**

Two hundred yards north, a sign points west up a residential street to the **Eagle Stone** (♀ NH 48509 58512), in a small enclosure among fields and trees. It's just a fragment of the original Pictish (page 67) stone, but its carvings – a horseshoe above an eagle – remain clear. It was originally placed lower in the valley, where it was apparently used to mark the graves of local clansmen who had been killed in a battle. In the 16th century, the Brahan Seer – often referred to as 'Scotland's Nostradamus' – prophesied that if the stone fell three times the valley here would flood and ships would sail up the valley, using the stone as an anchor. Having fallen twice already, the stone now sits in a concrete base.

From the stone, you can head back downhill to meet the main road; turning right on to it and then taking the next left turn soon after will bring you to the old red wooden train station. The grounds here, including what was once the line, have been turned into lovely gardens that include monkey puzzle and sequoia trees introduced by the Victorians. The spa town's popularity waned considerably after the world wars, and the train station closed entirely in 1951. The building was renovated in the 1980s and now houses a gift shop, beauty salon, the small **Highland Museum of Childhood** (⬙ highlandmuseumofchildhood.org.uk ☉ Apr–Oct 10.00–15.00 Tue–Fri, 11.30–15.00 Sat), with displays of toys and games from different periods, and a pleasant café.

"The grounds here have been turned into lovely gardens that include monkey puzzle and sequoia trees."

As you continue back towards the village centre, the next left turn leads up to the **Touchstone Maze** (♀ NH 49086 57684) on the edge of **Blackmuir Wood.** It's a steep walk from the car park at the bottom of the road (don't try and park further up the road), but worth it for the views across the town and hills that surround it. The stone labyrinth, which kids will particularly enjoy, is made up of 80 rocks from around northern Scotland, including ancient Lewisian gneiss (page 219). From here, you can continue south or west on the Touchstone Maze Trail (2¼ miles) to loop through the woods. Alternatively, you can park at the eastern end of the woods (♀ NH 47885 57313) in the forestry car park, which gives you the opportunity to follow the shorter (1¼ miles) Red

Kite Trail, which also enjoys lovely views, particularly of Ben Wyvis. Both are well-established gravel trails, but they do require a fair amount of walking uphill.

¶¶ FOOD & DRINK

Deli in the Square 1 The Sq ✐ 01997 421259 ⬛. This small, friendly deli-café is a great spot for lunch, offering dishes ranging from toasties to a substantial Cullen skink.

Adventures in Britain

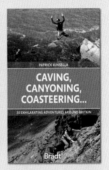

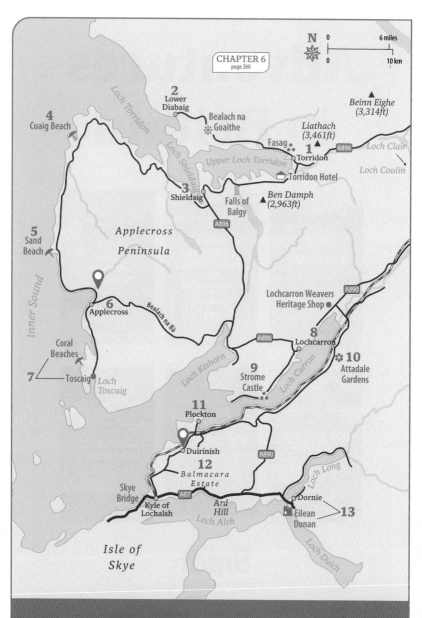

N

0   6 miles

0   10 km

CHAPTER 6
page 260

Loch Torridon

2
Lower
Diabaig

Bealach na
❋ Goaithe

*Beinn Eighe
(3,314ft)*

*Liathach
(3,461ft)*

4
Cuaig Beach

Fasag

A896

Loch Clair

Torridon

Upper Loch Torridon

Loch Shieldaig

Loch Coulin

Torridon Hotel

3
Shieldaig

Falls of
Balgy

*Ben Damph
(2,963ft)*

Applecross

Peninsula

A896

5
Sand
Beach

Lochcarron Weavers
Heritage Shop ●

A890

Inner Sound

6
Applecross

Bealach na Bá

A896

8
Lochcarron

10 ❋
Attadale
Gardens

Coral
Beaches

Loch Kishorn

9
Strome
Castle

Loch Carron

7   Toscaig

*Loch
Toscaig*

11
Plockton

Duirinish

A890

Loch Long

Skye
Bridge

A87

12
*Balmacara
Estate*

Dornie

13

Kyle of
Lochalsh

*Ard
Hill*

Eilean
Donan

Loch Alsh

Loch Duich

*Isle of
Skye*

SOUTHERN WESTER ROSS

7
SOUTHERN WESTER ROSS

Four sea lochs influence the geography of the southern part of Wester Ross: Torridon, Kishorn, Carron and Alsh. Combined with the Inner Sound, which runs between the mainland and the isles of Rona, Raasay, Scalpay and Skye, and the mountains that dominate both the interior and distant Skye, it often feels like an area caught between the mountains and the sea, with the colours (and weather) constantly changing.

Unsurprisingly, given the topography of the region, the few settlements that are here cling to the coast and lochs. The very south of the area, between **Lochcarron** – the region's biggest settlement, though still far from a town – and **Dornie**, is the most populous and, due to being on the main routes towards Skye, the roads here can often feel surprisingly busy compared to those further north. Don't let that put you off – aside from tour-bus crowds at instantly recognisable **Eilean Donan** castle, it's just as easy to find pockets of solitude here as anywhere else in the North Highlands.

To the north is the triangular Applecross Peninsula, famous as the end point of the **Bealach na Bà**, a twisting mountain pass that often turns up on lists of 'the world's scariest drives'. The peninsula itself, hemmed in by mountains and sea, is more than worth the effort, with lush pockets of forest and plenty of tucked-away beaches to reward Slow travellers. To the east is the pretty village of **Shieldaig**, stretched around the loch of the same name and a lovely spot for pottering around on the water. The mountains increasingly crowd in as you head further east, with the small village of **Torridon** one of the North Highlands' best and most popular walking destinations, both up into the mountains and skirting the bottom of them. Wherever you end up in this region, though, and however you explore it – from the water, on foot or behind a wheel – the views are superlative.

GETTING AROUND

Travelling by public transport is easiest in the south of the region, where the magnificent Kyle of Lochalsh train line runs to the village of the same name, just before the Skye Bridge, and you can make use of buses running between Inverness and Skye. Here, too, is one of the region's major roads: the A87, which follows the northern shore of Loch Alsh. The A890 runs inland from here to head east towards Inverness via Strathcarron (for Lochcarron) and Achnasheen, while the other major artery, the A896, often feels anything but, particularly in the section between Kinlochewe and Torridon, with mountains looming on every side.

The **Bealach na Bà** (page 330) is for many people the main route on to the Applecross Peninsula – the eleven miles of hairpins and steep gradients aren't to everyone's liking, but there's no doubt that the views from the top, towards Skye, are more than worth it. Alternatively, you can take the coastal road on to the peninsula, though be warned that the first few miles west of the A896 can be just as difficult to drive, if not more so, thanks to limited visibility in parts.

TRAINS

Regularly referred to as one of the most scenic train journeys in the UK, the **Kyle Line** (⌀ scotrail.com) runs from Inverness to the Kyle of Lochalsh (2hr 40min), just before the Skye Bridge, providing staggering views of lochs and mountain peaks along the way. Useful stations for this chapter include Strathcarron (for Lochcarron), Attadale Gardens and Plockton. There are usually four services a day in each direction, but the wait between trains can range from two to four hours.

BUSES

The most regular bus service in the region is the City Link bus (⌀ citylink. co.uk ⊙ four daily) that runs from Inverness to Skye, stopping at Dornie Bridge (handy for Eilean Donan; 1hr 55min), Reraig (for Balmacara; 2hr) and Kyle of Lochalsh (2hr 10min). Lochcarron Garage (⌀ 01520 722997 ⌀ lochcarrongarage.co.uk/bus) runs a bus on Mondays and Saturdays between Inverness and Lochcarron (1hr 45min), with stops at Kishorn (2hr), Shieldaig (2hr 15min) and Applecross (3hr 15min) available on request. Seat bookings should be made before 18.00 the day before travel. MacKenzie & MacLennan (♂ mackenziemaclennan. co.uk/westerbus) offers a school-days-only service from Shieldaig via Torridon (15min) to Gairloch (1hr 5min), running in that direction in the morning and back to Shieldaig in the afternoon.

WALKING & CYCLING

On a dry weekend, you'll often see clusters of cars beside seemingly random parking places along the roads here, most often marking the start of a walk up a Munro. But don't get put off by the proliferation of peaks in this region – there's also a fantastic range of lower-level walks, both inland and by the coast, offering far-reaching views of mountains and water. There are several waymarked trails in Balmacara (page 342) and around the northern shore of Lochalsh (page 345), while the area around Plockton (page 335) is a great place for relatively easy coastal walking.

Torridon has a well-deserved reputation for walking, particularly in the mountains, but there are also some good paths in and around the village that don't require too much hard work, as well as some fabulous low-level walks further out. For a more challenging option, you can walk from Lower Diabaig (page 317) to Red Point (page 297).

There aren't really any set mountain-bike routes in this area, but plenty of opportunities for on- or off-road **cycling**. The Balmacara Estate has some cyclist-friendly paths, particularly north of **Coille Mhòr** and south of **Balmacara Square**, as well as near Plockton. Some of the paths by The Torridon (page 316) are suitable for mountain biking, and the hotel also offers guided mountain biking.

 BIKE HIRE

Skye Mountain Bike Adventures Church Rd, Kyle of Lochalsh ♂ 01599 534731 ♂ skyemtbadventures.co.uk.

TORRIDON & SURROUNDS

The name Torridon is used for both the village of Torridon, which sits at the head of Upper Loch Torridon, and the hills and mountains that surround it – much of this area falls under the National Trust for Scotland's Torridon Estate. The approach to Torridon village from Kinlochewe, along the A896, is in my opinion one of the best roads in the entire North Highlands. It's single track for most of the way (but with plenty of passing places and good visibility for much of it), and as you drive west along the valley the mountains increasingly crowd in around you. Head west on the A896 just before sunset and you'll catch the mountains glowing shades of pink, purple and orange, and feel as though you're chasing the sun. There are a couple of walkers' car parks along the way, the most famous of which is **Coire Dubh Car Park** (for Beinn Eighe and Liathach; ♥ NG 95738 56828), from where you'll get fabulous views up and down the strath.

1 TORRIDON VILLAGE
🏠 Ben Damph Estate 🏠 The Torridon

Approaching from the east, there's no real sign of Torridon village until you reach it; from the west, you'll catch glimpses at a few points as you round the road, its houses often little more than white dots at the bottom of the towering mountains behind. On our first visit, we stumbled upon Torridon by accident rather than by design – the name felt evocative and we wanted to see where the road went beyond Applecross – and were surprised to have the shore of the loch entirely to ourselves, despite it being the tail end of a beautifully bright day in high summer. With the tide out, the rocky beach felt like an adventure playground, dotted with huge chunks of rock and enclosed by mountains.

"With the tide out, the rocky beach felt like an adventure playground, dotted with huge chunks of rock."

That's not to say that Torridon is always quiet or unvisited, far from it. Sit by the main road through the village for any amount of time and you're bound to see a fairly steady stream of walkers pass by, but many of them are doing just that – passing through en route elsewhere, and you're unlikely to find it crowded. Torridon's name comes from the Gaelic *Toirbheartan*, meaning 'place of transference', a reference, it is thought, to taking boats and goods from Loch Torridon to Loch Maree.

The road through the village veers off northwest from the A896, just as it turns south to skirt around the head of the loch. After about 700yds, on the right-hand side of the road, is **Loch Torridon Community Centre** (✆ 01445 791361 ⊘ lochtorridoncentre.co.uk), which is home to small gallery and exhibition space that showcases the work of local artists, a café (page 317) and a **craft market** on alternate Thursdays

(☉ Apr–Oct 10.00–15.00); there's usually an interesting range of sellers here, including Ewebrew (⌂ ewebrew.beer), which makes an excellent range of beers from its base on the shores of Loch Ewe.

A path on the eastern side of the centre's car park leads up on to the low hillside immediately behind to follow a circular trail of only about half a mile in length. This takes you around the ruins of the old crofting township of **Doire na Fuaran**, which was cleared around 1845. The Torridon glens were subject to particularly harsh Clearances (page 90) in the mid 19th century, overseen by the then estate owner, Colonel McBarnet; those people that were not moved were only given a very small amount of land and allowed to keep just one cow. By 1859, all inhabitants had been shifted to Annat, on the other side of the loch.

Torridon's fortunes changed when the estate was sold in 1872 to Duncan Darroch, a wealthy man from near Glasgow, who cleared the sheep off his land, gave crofts back to the evicted tenants and established a deer park that still exists in Torridon today. One of the nicest ways to see the deer park, and to explore the village, is on a circular two-mile route; you can start at any point along the way, though I'd recommend starting at the parking area (♀ NG 89663 56511) by the loch, diagonally across the road from Torridon Stores (page 317). From here, a sign points the way to the shore path; keep on the track rather than veering on to the footpath and you'll see the little peninsula of **Am Ploc** ahead, curving to the right. When you reach a left turn signposted to Am Ploc, follow it (the gate straight ahead is marked private) and within 100yds or so you'll reach the remains of an **open-air church**, with its neat stone pews.

Though the pews may look as though they are arranged to face towards the water, it's thought that the pulpit would have been just

ACTIVITIES IN & AROUND TORRIDON

As well as the self-guided walks listed on page 314 and, of course, mountain climbing, there are a number of activity options in and around the village, with the outdoor centre at The Torridon being a particular focus.

Ranger-led walks The National Trust for Scotland offers weekly guided walks (90mins; donations suggested) with a ranger. Email ✉ rshannon@nts.org.uk for information and bookings.

Torridon Outdoors The Torridon (page 316) ⌂ thetorridon.com/torridon-outdoors. A huge range of activities for both guests and non-guests, including sea kayaking, guided mountain biking, gorge scrambling, snorkelling and archery.

uphill of the seating (look for the narrow gap between two rocks), so the congregation would have sat with their backs to the water – I suppose they would have been less distracted that way, given the views.

From here, retrace your steps and take the first right to follow the shore path; the water here is very shallow and perfect for paddling, and there are benches along the way to soak up the view. As you head north, you'll see The Torridon hotel (page 316) ahead – up close it's rather grand, but from far away it's dwarfed by Ben Damph.

The path veers away from the shore to go through a gate, turning left to head east at a white building. After just under 100yds, look for the signposted right turn along the bottom of the deer enclosure, which takes you to a wildlife hide, with views over the loch. Back on the main path, you'll have the deer enclosure to your right and soon the white buildings of Torridon Mains on your left. On the eastern side of the second building is the entrance to the National Trust for Scotland's **Deer Museum** (⊙ open access) – a small room stuffed full of antlers, deer skulls and other bones, as well as photos of deer stalking. Particularly

WALKS IN & AROUND TORRIDON

One of the many wonderful things about Torridon is that you don't have to climb up high or be a particularly hardy or seasoned walker to get fabulous views – even a short stroll around the village will offer those up. As always, arming yourself with the OS app or maps (❋ OS Explorer 433 and OS Explorer 428) will be invaluable and help you find other footpaths to explore. Wherever you walk, whether high or low, do pack layers, water and snacks – the weather can change in an instant.

Am Ploc and the deer enclosure Page 313. An easy walk along the shore to an open-air church and then on to the NTS deer enclosure.

Ben Damph Viewpoint Start: public car park at The Torridon ♀ NG 88938 54149; 2

miles; difficult. A real heart-pounder of a walk; follow the signpost for the Viewpoint Trail from The Torridon to climb steeply up to the main road and then continue uphill on the other side. The path proceeds to climb through skinny-legged pine trees, and after crossing two small burns begins to rise above the treeline. Don't keep climbing indefinitely (there's no real sign for the viewpoint) as you'll end up climbing Ben Damph itself, but walk for a mile and then turn around and soak up the view – over the loch and the village and beyond.

Fasag See opposite. Lovely views over Loch Torridon from this path that leads through the ruins of an old crofting village.

Falls of Balgy Start: parking area on north side of A896, three miles west of The fascinating is the stack of antlers that belonged to the same deer, Crafty, showing how they changed over the course of eight years.

The **deer enclosure** is also part of the National Trust for Scotland's estate and provides an easy way to see beautiful red deer who might otherwise prove elusive in the wild. That said, the enclosure is a decent size, so you may still have to peer into the distance to see them – they are particularly well camouflaged in the autumn.

From here, continue northeast along the road; shortly before the NTS Countryside Centre (closed until further notice at the time of writing), a path leads into the woodland on the left, taking you over a wooden bridge and coming out on the road into the village. Turn left here and you can walk back to your starting point.

Fasag

Torridon village is also known as Fasag (though you might be more likely to come across this on a map than on the ground), which was also the name of a village here that was emptied by the Highland Clearances.

Torridon ♀ NG 84759 54316; just under 1 mile; easy. This is a short but often boggy walk up to wide and powerful waterfalls on the River Balgy. From the parking area, walk west for 100yds and look for the wooden gate on the southern side of the road, which leads on to a path alongside the river. It's less than half a mile to the falls, from where you can turn back and retrace your steps; alternatively, you can walk another half mile along the river (look out, en route, for a signposted viewpoint over the hills), taking a left turning shortly after you meet Loch Damph to walk three-quarters of a mile back to the main road, from where you turn left to walk another half a mile to the parking area.
Lochs Clair and Coulin Start: car park on northern side of A896, seven miles east of

Torridon village ♀ NH 00239 58161; Loch Clair: 2 miles; Loch Coulin: 5½ miles; moderate. Staggering mountain views without the climb – if you don't fancy the full length then you can still enjoy beautiful scenery by walking to the southern end of lovely Loch Clair and back. To start the walk, cross the road opposite the parking area and follow the path along the eastern shore of Loch Clair; when it splits take the left-hand path to circle Loch Coulin.
Torridon Trail Start: public car park at The Torridon ♀ NG 88938 54149; 1 mile; easy. This lovely walk winds through the beautiful grounds of The Torridon (page 316), with views across the loch to the village. It can be easily combined with other walks from the hotel (⏃ thetorridon.com/things-to-do/torridon-trails).

A pleasant (if often muddy) walk of just over 1¾ miles takes you through the remains of the village, with wonderful views over the loch and Ben Damph beyond. From Torridon Stores, walk northwest along the main road for 250yds; when the jetty appears on your left, take the path that leads uphill on your right, winding through bog myrtle and heather, with the loch below you.

After you cross a wooden bridge over a tumbling, tree-lined burn, look up to your right to see a series of waterfalls rushing over rocks. You'll cross a few other burns along the way, usually hidden by foliage but nonetheless loud as they rush down the hillside. The hillside is bare for a lot of the way – look out for the patches of bracken, which indicate where animals were grazed – and you might struggle to see the ruins, which are obscured among the plants, though you can still make out an old broken wall here and there. Shortly after picking your way on stones across a burn, the path begins to descend towards the road. Here, turn left to head back to the village. As you do so, do make sure you look up at the hillside above you, as the remains of the village are a bit clearer from lower down.

After about 650yds, you'll pass a small **memorial stone** (♀ NG 88973 56661), dedicated to the 100 men from the estate who carried the body of Duncan Darroch (page 313) to his family resting place in his home town of Gourock. As Gourock was some 250 miles away, and with numerous mountains en route, this would have been no small task. On the hillside above here is a well-placed bench where you can soak up the views before walking the final half a mile back into the village.

 SPECIAL STAYS

Ben Damph Estate IV22 2EZ ✆ 07725 764842 ⬠ bendamph.com. Three self-catering options on this beautiful 14,500-acre estate on the southern side of Loch Torridon, all with amazing views of water and mountains: the striking modern Ben Damph Lodge (sleeps eight), complete with a wood-fired hot tub; Thrall House (sleeps eight); and the Bothy (sleeps four). The Bothy is back-to-basics, with gas rings for simple cooking (and kettle boiling), woodburning stoves in the bedrooms, and only candles to light your way at night – it's a hugely atmospheric place to stay, and unlike anywhere I've ever been. Listening to the stags bellow from outside during the autumn was memorable to say the least. There is a decent shower and a long-drop 'loo with a view'.

The Torridon IV22 2EY ✆ 01445 791242 ⬠ thetorridon.com. You can't miss The Torridon, in all its turreted, red sandstone glory, standing on the opposite side of the loch to Torridon village. This is exactly what you want from a luxury Highland hotel: roaring fires, comfy lounge, whisky bar (with enough different drams to try a new one every day of the year), and beautiful grounds that run down to the loch. Elegant food with a local focus is served in the main restaurant, while the relaxed pub-style option Bo & Muc offers heartier (and cheaper) dishes. Rooms in the main building are incredibly luxurious, the best of which have loch and mountain views; the Stable block offers cheaper options. On site is an outdoor activity specialist (page 313).

¶¶ FOOD & DRINK

As well as the places listed below, there are two restaurants at The Torridon (see opposite).

Torridon Stores & Café IV22 2EZ ⊘ torridonstoresandcafe.co.uk. The village shop also doubles as a cosy café, with views over the loch and to Am Ploc. The menu is simple, with soup, filled rolls, toasties and cakes on offer. The shop has a decent array of food, booze and other supplies like hiking socks and torches.

Wee Whistle Stop Café Loch Torridon Community Centre, IV22 2EZ ⊘ 07570 540212 ⊘ lochtorridoncentre.co.uk. Bright, big-windowed café in the community centre, whose slightly elevated position affords amazing views over the loch, even on dreich days. Food is fantastic and fresh, with offerings like sautéed mushrooms and wilted spinach on toast for breakfast and roasted salmon for lunch, and it's also a great place to pop into for a piece of cake and a coffee. On Friday evenings, it runs 'Fish Fridays', for which bookings are essential.

2 LOWER DIABAIG

The journey between Torridon village and Lower Diabaig, on the northeast shore of the loch, exemplifies the kind of distance versus time equation you're confronted with in the North Highlands: despite being only nine miles from each other, on largely 60-miles-an-hour roads, the journey takes at least 20 minutes. Nonetheless, it's a superlative, if winding, road that swings inland to gain elevation before dropping down into the scenic little hamlet of Lower Diabaig, literally at the end of the road. En route, though easier on the way back to Torridon, it's worth stopping at the **Bealach na Goaithe view point** (♀ NG 82716 58732) to look over the loch and mountains beyond; a handy diagram points out which peak is which.

Lower Diabaig is in a beautiful, sheltered spot, with trees behind and north along the bay (tellingly, Diabaig means 'deep bay') and a great, craggy headland jutting out to its south, peppered with little white houses. The views across the water, which is often dotted with colourful

boats, stretch to the north of the Applecross Peninsula. Just seven miles separate Lower Diabaig from Far Red Point beach (page 298) to its north, but it's a distance only possible on foot – by road, it's 45 miles away.

FOOD & DRINK

Gille Brighde IV22 2HE ✆ 01445 790245 ⊘ gille-brighde.com. This petite restaurant is why most people make it out this far, and with good reason: the emphasis is on local and sustainable food, so you'll see the likes of local hand-dived scallops with wild-garlic butter, home-cured wild sea trout and wild-venison steak. There are a few outside tables for good weather, too, from where you can soak up the views across the bay. Booking is essential all year round – it's a long way to travel if you can't get a table!

3 SHIELDAIG

On the loch of the same name, Shieldaig, with its neat row of shore-facing cottages, boasts an exceptionally lovely position. Across the water is lush, wooded Shieldaig Island, beyond which is the Applecross Peninsula; to the north is the rocky peninsula that lies to the south of Lower Diabaig. Behind the village rise the formidable Torridon peaks; from afar, Shieldaig is little more than a white streak on the landscape.

"Shieldaig Island is a bird reserve owned by the National Trust for Scotland – herons nest in the trees here."

The village's name comes from the area's Viking past and means 'Herring Bay' – despite this, the modern settlement was originally built in 1810, with the aim of training sailors to fight Napoleon. However, with the Frenchman's defeat at Waterloo just five years later, none of the village men were ultimately called upon to fight, and the population turned instead to crofting and fishing.

Shieldaig Island is a bird reserve owned by the National Trust for Scotland – herons nest in the trees here, and there's a resident pair of white-tailed eagles. The only way to get to the island is by boat: **Shieldaig Outdoor Adventures** (✆ 01520 755369 ⊘ shieldaigadventures.com) offers tours of the loch by canoe and kayak, which might give you a chance to see some of the local wildlife, including otters and seals.

◀ 1 Torridon village. 2 Looking out towards the snow-capped Torridon Mountains from near the Ben Damph viewpoint. 3 Lobster pots line a wall in Shieldaig village. 4 Lower Diabaig is in a beautiful, sheltered spot.

For more beautiful views, walk out to the **An Aird peninsula**, to the north of the village. To get there, follow the main shoreline road north and, when you reach a crossroads, go straight on up the side of the primary school, before bearing left at the next corner. Once the road becomes a path, it remains easy to follow, and you get some tremendous views of Loch Shieldaig towards Loch Torridon, and then of Upper Loch Torridon and Torridon village. It's just a three-mile round trip in total, with plenty of places to stop and soak up the views as you walk it.

FOOD & DRINK

Loch Torridon Smokehouse Main St ⊘ lochtorridonsmokehouse.co.uk. Just up the side of Rosebank house on the main street (look for its painted red windowsills), this little wooden smokehouse sells cold- and hot-smoked salmon – smoked on site. Buy a pot of the hot-smoked salmon pâté if they have it – it's perfect with oatcakes.

Nanny's Main St ⊘ nannysshieldaig.co.uk. Named after Nanny Grant, who was the last in her family to run the original shop (in a tin shed) on this site, this friendly little café at the southern end of the village is a popular spot with both locals and tourists. At breakfast time there's filled rolls and porridge, and at lunch the likes of hot-smoked salmon chowder, sandwiches and toasties. The bright room is decorated with work by local artist Lisa Fenton (⊘ lisafenton.co.uk) who also has a gallery studio on the outskirts of the village.

THE APPLECROSS PENINSULA

There is no easy way to explore the Applecross Peninsula – either you enter via the infamous Bealach na Bà (page 330) to the south, or from the north via the coast road, which may be less famous but I'd argue at times could do even more damage to frayed nerves thanks to poorer visibility. Despite both being best for confident drivers, there's no doubt that they are amazing roads to travel, with equally amazing views. For most people, Applecross village is the main focus – and it is a special place – but the good news is that that leaves the rest of the peninsula comparatively quiet and underexplored, making it perfect for those of us that want to take our time. Much of the interior of the peninsula is hilly moorland, dropping away to croftland and the coast, with views across the Inner Sound to the isles of Rona, Raasay and Skye. There are pockets of forest

"The rest of the peninsula is comparatively quiet, making it perfect for those of us that want to take our time."

scattered here and there, which are infrequent enough to feel like little oases, particularly around the village of Applecross.

Although the route into the peninsula via the Bealach has been there since the 1820s, it wasn't tarred until the 1950s – and the coastal road from Shieldaig wasn't opened until as recently as 1976, so before that to get from the north to the south of the peninsula was only possible on foot, horseback or a bike, or by boat. Today, about 200 permanent residents live on the peninsula, which stretches northwest from the turn-off from the A896, just over a mile south of Shieldaig, before heading south to road end at Toscaig. Beyond here, the land continues a further two miles south and then seven miles east along Loch Kishorn: miles of rather impenetrable land.

4 CUAIG BEACH
⌂ Spindrift

Few people take the time to explore Applecross's northern coast, which means that this beautiful beach, tucked away north of the crofting hamlet of **Cuiag**, is all but overlooked by the vast majority of visitors. Reaching it feels like a bit of an adventure in itself, which adds to the fun, particularly when the blushing pink sands are finally revealed. Do check tide times before you visit – at high tide, the beach entirely disappears. Also, note that this walk (just over half a mile in length) involves some stepping stones, which may be a bit of a stretch for very little legs. Pack your swimming costume and a picnic, and make a day of it.

You can park by the side of the road where the Cuaig road sign is (♀ NG 70514 57835) though, as always, use your discretion and if it's too busy you'd be better off pressing on to the viewpoint (♀ NG 69854 56822), a mile further southwest down the road. From here, walk east and then north to reach the starting point, either along the main road or following a faint path that runs close to it, which is far from unpleasant if a little rough at times. From the Cuaig parking area, walk west up the road, and look for the gate on the right shortly after crossing the bridge, with a hand-written 'No parking' sign on it. Go through the gate and follow the grassy path uphill slightly, with the sound of the river gushing to your right. The path soon gets rockier and may be quite wet underfoot depending on how recently it has rained; when you see two fence posts ahead, pass between them – if you're very tall you may have to duck under the wire. Follow the path downhill, with the hills now hemming you in and the river ever closer. As the path curves very slightly, you'll see the bay ahead.

Go through the gate you meet and follow the path to the river, where you'll see some distinct stepping stones. Cross here – depending on how high the river is, some of the stones may be partially or fully submerged. The other side of the river is quite rocky, and at lower tides you can pick your way along here, but there's also a clear grassy path above the rocks that twists its way among boulders. Depending on the state of the tide, you may want to clamber down to the sand – a gentle mix of gold and red – or continue along the rocks. The little island you can see in the distance is Sgeir an Oba, which means, appropriately if unimaginatively, 'Rock of the Bay'.

Cuaig Beach is a peaceful spot, and when you're down on the sands the road feels miles away, though it's only actually half a mile distant. You could easily spend ages exploring the rocks and the little rock pools left behind by the tide. I stayed here for a while when the tide was on its way out, watching the water ebb and flow, leaving behind channels and wave lines as it receded.

🧳 SPECIAL STAYS

Spindrift Kalnakill IV54 8XL ✆ 01520 744407 ⊘ spindrift-applecross.co.uk. There's just one bedroom at this gorgeous B&B – though it's more of a suite than a room, with a little kitchenette, dining table, and a sofa perfectly positioned to soak up the astounding views across to Rona and Skye. Sue and Andy live next door but you have your own private entrance, and both have a huge amount of local knowledge and are incredibly friendly and approachable. Sue provides freshly baked bread, plus eggs, salmon, cheese, ham and milk so you can make your own breakfast. It's hard to beat watching the sea and sky change from your bed.

5 SAND BEACH

Despite its does-what-it-says-on-the-tin name, Sand is a glorious (and, compared to Cuaig, easily accessible) stretch of beach. Five miles north of Applecross, there's parking (📍 NG 68392 49318) on the (unsigned) road that leads down to it, on the western side of the road; you'll see the

---

1 A road with a reputation: Bealach na Bà. **2** The path to Cuaig Beach on the Applecross Peninsula. **3** The Applecross Walled Garden. **4** Fish and chips with a view at the Applecross Inn. ▶

EMMA GIBBS

CHRIS 148/DT

EMMA GIBBS

beach briefly as you descend from the north before it ducks out of view again – if it makes a reappearance then you've gone too far. From the parking area, continue on foot down the road, which is marked post car park with a sign that says it's a private MoD road. After about 120yds, you'll see a path to your left, across a shallow burn. It's a clear path, through bracken at first, but can be quite muddy underfoot.

"You may have to wade through channels – wellies can be a good idea unless you're happy getting your feet wet."

You can't tell from afar but there's a reddish hue to the sands here, which at low tide form a deep if not hugely wide beach. Hemmed in by low, green headlands and with hills and (if the weather is playing ball) mountains on the horizon, there's a wonderful wildness to it. Depending on the tide, you may have to wade through channels – wellies can be a good idea unless you're happy getting your feet wet.

The Ministry of Defence site here, which sits to the south of the beach, is BUTEC (British Underwater Test and Evaluation Centre), used for testing underwater weapons and equipment like torpedoes and sonar between the peninsula and the Isle of Rona.

6 APPLECROSS VILLAGE

For many visitors, the entire focus of their time on the peninsula is Applecross Village. It's not hard to understand why, particularly if you descend from the hairpin bends and heights of the Bealach na Bà (page 330) – surrounded by trees and edged by water, with little more than a scattering of low-level white buildings, Applecross is exceedingly pretty.

The trouble with such prettiness – particularly in the Highlands, on the North Coast 500, and in the village at the end (or start) of a notoriously hard road that everyone wants to try – is that it comes at a price. Of course, it shouldn't: Applecross should be able to be pretty, and loved, and respected. But the village and its surrounds has seen many of the worst parts of tourist behaviour: huge motorhomes struggling (and sometimes failing) to make it over the Bealach; people camping where they shouldn't; excrement dumped into burns. One visitor, former Prime Minister Boris Johnson, allegedly pitched a tent in a field without permission from the farmer. Such behaviour has led to the community putting things in place, such as protection around the head of the bay to prevent people from camping, and asking for the village to be removed from NC500-branded tourist literature, but considerate visitors will never feel anything less than welcome here.

The main part of the village sits on the eastern side of wide **Applecross Bay**, immediately west of the junction with the road that leads to the Bealach na Bà. At the corner of the junction you'll find a little but well-stocked gift shop, **The Coalshed** ($\mathcal{O}$ 01520 744206 ![f]), and just under 200yds further on, past the small petrol station and car park, is the Applecross Inn (page 328) – the perfect place to head after negotiating the road into the village – and a neat line of cottages that open right on to the narrow road. The shore here is predominantly pebbly, stretching into sand at low tide when the full size of the beach is exposed.

The best views from the village can be had from the main part of the beach itself, the head of which can be accessed about a mile north of the Bealach junction, at the eastern end of the bay. Here, sheltered by the hills, you see the mountains upon mountains on the distant islands: Raasay, Scalpay and Skye, all in one shot. The beach itself, with its strands of pebbles and seaweed-clad rocks interspersed with dusky orange sand, isn't perhaps as classically beautiful as Sand (page 322), but at low tide it can be as much as half a mile deep, making it the biggest beach on the peninsula. It is at low tide that the sands, some of which still shimmer with water, are at their best, and you feel as though you could walk the whole way to Raasay.

The bay is bisected by the River Applecross, which, just east of the beach, is a popular swimming spot. Around 300yds northwest of the road bridge across the river is the **Applecross Heritage Centre** (parking at Q NG 71157 45743 $\mathcal{O}$ 01520 74447 $\mathcal{O}$ applecrossheritage.org.uk $\odot$ Apr–Oct noon–16.00 Mon–Sat), which crams a lot of information about the peninsula into a small space – it's a good spot to gain a bit of background detail, if not the most engaging of local-history museums.

On the eastern side of the river is Applecross House, now holiday accommodation ($\mathcal{O}$ applecross.org.uk); the grounds here, neat and green fields to start and then giving way to woodland before the hills rise up, are crisscrossed with a number of paths. Set just back from the house is **Applecross Walled Garden** (page 328); though the focus is the café-restaurant, you don't have to be dining to enjoy the walled garden that surrounds it ($\odot$ always open). Neat paths wander through the abundant garden, which is thoughtfully planted but still has a wonderful

Applecross River & Roe walk

✳ OS Explorer 428; start: Applecross Walled Garden car park ♀ NG 71994 45590; 2½ miles; moderate

There are a number of paths that wind across Applecross Estate, and this combines two of them: the River and Roe paths near the Walled Garden (page 328). It's a relatively gentle walk, with a bit of a climb uphill in the middle, though the result is that you get to enjoy wonderful views over the village and the bay.

1 From the car park, head east up the path signposted 'Keppoch', climbing gently. After around 100yds, cross the road and keep straight on the Keppoch track, crossing a burn via a simple bridge shortly after and then immediately following the path right to snake through the trees, climbing uphill. The path crosses the property boundary through an open fence, after which you'll be walking with ferns on either side, fenced in by trees to your left. As you continue to climb, views of the hills open up to your left.

2 At the top of the hill, you meet a rough road; pause to look back at the view and around you, and then turn left, following the sign to the River Route. Continue straight to cross over a noisy burn on a stone bridge, ignoring the path to your right. At this point, with trees ahead and to your left, you can really appreciate the mixed woodland, with spindly granny pines, monkey puzzle and silver birch trees. As you descend, the track starts to feel more like a road.

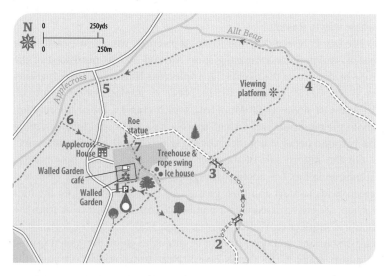

3 At a crossroads of signposted paths, go straight on, crossing a small burn shortly after. About 100yds after the bridge, turn right at the signpost labelled 'Roes' Walk', going through the smaller gate to follow the path through more mixed woodland. The path can be a bit stony and muddy in places, with the hills almost always in view. About 500yds after the gate, look for an uphill path on the left; this leads a short but steep distance up to a wooden viewing platform, from where you can enjoy panoramic views of the surrounding mountains, Applecross Bay and the islands across the sound. Afterwards, head back down and pick up the route. Shortly afterwards you'll meet a tall wooden gate in the deer fence; go through and you'll soon see the river rushing below, after which you'll begin to descend in parallel to the river.

4 At a T-junction, with the Allt Beag river ahead, follow the stone steps to turn left and then continue along the water, keeping it on your right-hand side. It's incredibly scenic here, with two forks in the river joining and then the watercourse widening out. Follow the path as it curves. As the river goes through a sluice gate, go through another wooden gate yourself and follow the path round towards a metal gate, the river now out of sight. Soon after the gate, the river – now the River Applecross – will be by your side again, and the mountains will feel closer. For a while you play hide and seek with the water, until it finally drops away and as its sound begins to fade again into the background you'll go through another metal gate.

A couple of hundred yards later, the path leads through mature woodland, where old tree stumps have been transformed by moss. You'll eventually see the river and a bridge ahead; when the path splits left towards a wooden outbuilding, continue to follow the river on the narrow path through the trees, and over a narrow wooden bridge (good for Pooh sticks) across a burn.

5 When you meet the bridge across the river, ignore it to continue straight across the road and through a wooden kissing gate. Follow the river, still on your right, as it calms a little. The path moves you away from the water for a little bit – look to the left for a glimpse of the white buildings of Applecross House – before becoming stony and delivering you back alongside the river. It's particularly beautiful along here, with flat grassy ledges overlooking the water that are perfect for picnicking.

6 When you see a wooden gate in the fence to your left, take a sharp left (ignoring the gate!) to walk away from the river, between two white fences. Applecross House shortly appears ahead; continue towards it as the path heads along an avenue of old trees. When you meet a crossroads, keep straight on, past the back of the house, to head back into the trees. ▶

Applecross River & Roe walk (continued)

7 ◄ At a T-junction, shortly after crossing a burn, look to your left to see a statue of a roe, before turning right to go through a wooden gate. You're now back in the grounds of the Walled Garden. You'll see a couple of gates in the fence on your left as you walk – the first leads off for more exploration of the grounds, while the second provides access to a treehouse and rope swing. When you meet a T-junction, head left through a gate and cross a lovely babbling burn to climb gently. On the left, a sign points to the old ice house, a subterranean cavern that you can (if the light is working) peer inside. Back on the path, follow it as it curves round to cross another burn – this one has a beech tree by it that in September was resplendent in its autumnal finery. The path then climbs up and around, with the mountains appearing again; at the crossroads, turn right to return to the car park.

wildness about it, with archways to duck under and places to sit and contemplate. As well as flowers, fruit and veg are grown for use in the café. The parking area here makes a good starting place for walks around the wider estate, one of which I've included on page 326.

¶¶ FOOD & DRINK

Applecross Inn IV54 8LR ✆ 01520 744262 ♂ applecrossinn.co.uk. It may sound like hyperbole but I will always remember the pint of Applecross beer I had here after driving the Bealach for the first time as the best pint I've ever had – though for the sake of research I've sampled it a few times since and it more than lives up to the memory. Unsurprisingly, it can be hard to get a table inside the wood-clad room of this lovely old inn without a booking, but in milder weather you can grab a table outside, overlooking the bay and Inner Sound. The food menu has an emphasis on local produce, including haggis, oysters and crab, with a good range of pub standards and more interesting dishes. The airstream trailer outside, **Inn-Side Out**, also serves the inn's fantastic fish and chips (choose between haddock or monkfish), as well as prawn and crab salads, sausage rolls, coffee and ice cream, so even if you can't get a table you can still eat outside – and of course get a beer from inside. Rooms are available too.

Applecross Walled Garden IV54 8ND ✆ 01520 744440 ♂ applecrossgarden.co.uk. Intimate café-restaurant in the lovely Walled Garden, with lots of windows making the most of its position and a ceiling strung with fairy lights. You can come for just cake and hot drinks, or a more substantial meal. Food is hearty and unpretentious, with a mix of tapas-style small plates, such as Strathdon blue cheese arancini balls, and larger options like seafood linguine.

7 SOUTH TO TOSCAIG & THE CORAL BEACHES

For many visitors, Applecross village acts as road end – though in fact this is 4½ miles further south at **Toscaig Pier**, at the head of little Loch Toscaig. The hills on the opposite side are only accessible on foot – it's rather rough going though so recommended only for experienced hikers (see ⌀ walkhighlands.co.uk for routes). Today, the pier is more car park than working port, but in the mid 20th century it was from here that the ferry service ran to Kyle of Lochalsh – seven miles away by water but 45 miles by road. It's nonetheless a scenic spot, with the rough hills on the other side of the loch, a scattering of white houses that make up the hamlet, and views towards the very eastern end of Skye.

On the coast northwest of Toscaig are two lovely **coral beaches**, also only accessible on foot, though the walk to each is relatively easy, if a bit steep in places (it's a trip of just under four miles return to visit both). To reach them, park just before the signpost to Ard Dhubh on the main road (♀ NG 71394 39837), 1½ miles north of Toscaig Pier and 500yds south of the small hamlet of **Culduie**. From here, head south over the small bridge over the burn and then immediately turn right down the single-track road to Ard Dhubh, following the left-hand side of the bay for around 400yds until, at the top of a bit of an incline, you meet a path going left, signposted to Coille Ghille and Ardbain. Take this, following the path inland across moorland studded with rocks and heather. As you start climbing gently, the view on the right opens up, across to the Inner Sound and Raasay. The path undulates up and down for a while, and after around three-quarters of a mile descends down big rock steps to another junction.

"It's rather fascinating to pick up a handful and look at it in more detail – it's almost like little bits of bone."

Take the right-hand path, signposted to **Ardbain**, skirting another bay before climbing up on to what can be rather boggy moorland; the beach is about 650yds from the junction. From the shore, you can see across to Raasay (straight ahead), and Scalpay and Skye (to your left). The pale sand here is not actually made up of coral, as the name of these beaches suggest, but calcified seaweed, known as maerl. It's rather fascinating to pick up a handful and look at it in more detail – it's almost like little bits of bone. At low tide, the rocks here are particularly fun for rock pooling and to climb on.

THE BEALACH NA BÀ

I'd read so much about the Bealach in preparation for my first trip along it that when the time came I was – I'm not afraid to say – a bag of nerves. Articles with headlines like 'Is this the scariest road in Britain?' certainly did not help. In reality, it was nowhere near as bad as I'd feared – in fact, I'd go as far as to say that the coastal road to Applecross is more of a challenge. That's not to say that the road should be taken lightly: if you're an inexperienced driver, unhappy negotiating hairpin bends or reversing, or travelling in a large motorhome or with a trailer or caravan, you should avoid it. There are, sure, plenty of people who ignore this, but that's also why there are not infrequent occurrences of ambulances being unable to get through or large vehicles getting stuck.

The road – which translates to 'the pass of the cattle' – was built in 1822, although the route had long been used by cattle drovers prior to this. Single track for its whole way, it climbs to 2,053ft and incorporates, on its southern side in particular, a number of very tight hairpin bends. Despite this, however, visibility along the route – unless you're driving in heavy cloud, in which case I'd urge you to avoid it if you haven't driven it before – is good and you can often see the next passing place ahead of you and the oncoming traffic before it reaches you. Though you may see people tearing up it, the way to drive the Bealach is slowly and steadily; make use of passing places to pull over for oncoming traffic, and don't stop to take in the views. And do bear in mind that it's not just a tourist route – locals use this road and will be grateful if you pull over to let them and other faster traffic pass.

Arguably the best direction to drive the Bealach in order to see the full twists and turns is east; just before you descend from the top you'll see the classic view of it laid out below you, though it might make your stomach flip over. At the very top of the pass is a viewpoint with a large parking area (though it easily fills up): from here, the view – on a clear day at least – is stupendous, looking across to Raasay and Skye. I've been up here on a bright, sunny day when the view was amazing, but I'd argue the best time was on a changeable, overcast day when Skye and Raasay were bathed in shades of blue and grey, with the Inner Sound like liquid metal in between. Even better views can be had by climbing the hill to the southeast of the viewpoint; to get here, walk 150yds south down the road and look for the path on the left-hand side of the road that leads up to a transmitter mast. At 2,536ft, it's not actually the highest point of the mountain, but it affords great views.

To reach **Coille Ghille**, which is the bigger of the beaches, retrace your steps back to the last junction and turn right to head through woodland. When you emerge from the trees, you'll see Skye and a ruined house ahead; just before the house, a sign points to your right down to the beach. The path can be quite boggy on the descent here, but its a lovely pale stretch of maerl, meeting rocks on three sides, and with yet more views across to Raasay.

LOCH CARRON

Winding from the Inner Sound and the southernmost shores of the Applecross Peninsula to just south of the hamlet of Strathcarron is lovely Loch Carron. With trees covering much of the slopes that rise around it, the area feels particularly lush – this is especially noticeable if you've arrived from the north where trees are often few and far between.

8 LOCHCARRON

This appealing village stretches for over two miles along the northeastern shore of Loch Carron, earning it – so the local tourist literature claims, anyway – the title of the longest village in Scotland. Originally known as Janetown and then Jeantown, it became Lochcarron around the time the Parliamentary roads in the region were introduced: first from Kyle of Lochalsh to Strome Ferry (on the southern side of the loch) and then from Strome (on the northern side) to Lochcarron in 1817. Amazingly, there was no road between Strome and Strome Ferry until 1970 – travelling between the two meant using the ferry (or driving via Inverness – some 143 miles in total). The building of the A4890 along Loch Carron's southern shore led to the closure of the ferry – so Strome Ferry is now very much Strome Ferry (no ferry), as all the signposts say.

With two grocery shops and two petrol stations, a handful of B&Bs and restaurants, plus a campsite up the hill, Lochcarron is what passes for a busy place round here. Its long, linear nature along the loch – with buildings only lining the inland side of the road – means there are fabulous views as you stroll along the main road, with layers of hills on all sides. Come at dusk at the end of a clear day, when most of the tourists have passed through, and the hills and loch seem to glow in a multitude of pastel shades. The

"Come at dusk at the end of a clear day and the hills and loch seem to glow in a multitude of pastel shades."

shore here is pebbly but pleasant to wander along, and you might be lucky enough to catch a glimpse of an otter or two. Even better views can be had from Croft Road, which runs along the hill above the village; access it by turning left (west) at Lochcarron Garage in the northern part of the village. From here, among houses and croft land, you really get a sense of the village's position, with the loch below and hills on all sides.

Arguably the biggest tourist draw in the village actually lies on its outskirts: **Lochcarron Weavers Heritage Shop** (IV54 8YS ✐ 01520 722212 ◌ lochcarron.co.uk), which claims to be the 'world's leading manufacturer of tartan'. Today, the company's tartan is made in Selkirk, in the Borders, but it was here in Lochcarron (though not on this spot) that the company's first tartan was woven, after they'd taught local women the art of weaving. There's quite an astonishing range of tartan colours and items here, as well as lots of other gifts – you can buy kilts, scarves, blankets and even scrunchies, among other things. Also on site are a couple of other small, craft-based businesses, including **Freedom Framery** (✐ 07375 593123 ◌ freedomframery.co.uk ◷ 11.00–15.00 Wed–Sat), which specialises in creating beautiful frames but also sells gorgeous local artwork and little handmade gifts.

⊺⦙ FOOD & DRINK

The Bistro Main St ✐ 07449 575509 🆕. Celebrated local restaurant serving a short but interesting menu specialising in local seafood such as mussels and scallops, as well as a couple of meat and veggie dishes.

Kishorn Seafood Bar Kishorn IV54 8XA ✐ 01520 733240 ◌ kishornseafoodbar.co.uk. This little blue seafood restaurant, four miles west of Lochcarron, looks like it's been transported here from New England. The menu ranges from an abundant seafood platter to dressed crab, local oysters and hot-smoked salmon, with a couple of burger options to suit non fish eaters. Its location makes it a good stop pre or post Bealach.

The Old Butchers Main St 🆕. Great little coffee shop on Lochcarron's main drag, serving up decent breakfasts (not in winter), lunches and absolutely delicious cakes. Also doubles as a photography gallery.

9 STROME CASTLE

📍 NG 86247 35470

On a little rocky outcrop, just over three miles southwest of Lochcarron, are the ruins of Strome Castle – though to be honest, the word 'ruins' might suggest that there's more here than there is. Little remains of the original structure, except for part of its western and northern walls, but if, like me, you find more atmosphere in ruins than complete castles, it's well worth a little detour to see it. The castle has a wonderful position, overlooking Loch Carron: on a clear day, the view stretches across the clear blue waters to Plockton (page 335) and the mountains of Skye. The castle is thought to date back to the late 15th century, when it was used as a stronghold by the Lord of the Isles. It didn't last long though – it was blown up by the 1st Lord Kintail, Kenneth Mackenzie, in 1602, following a siege.

Parking (♀ NG 86283 35625) is possible at the northern end of the road to the ruins, just after the farm gate on the left-hand side, from where it's a 200yd walk to the short path to the castle. You can walk up the hill into the ruins to explore them close up, and the window on the western side provides the perfect frame for the view – climb through it in order to appreciate the full scale of the setting. On either side of the ruin are rocky shores that you can walk down to.

10 ATTADALE GARDENS

IV54 8YX ✆ 07860 403605 ⚲ attadalegardens.com ☺ Easter–Oct 10.00–17.00 daily

You could easily spend hours exploring these enchanting gardens on the southern shore of Loch Carron. Laid out around 18th-century Attadale House – which, with its white walls and turret looks rather French – they contain so many different sections that it's a delight to try and discover every nook and cranny.

'It sits within a wild area, so it can't be totally tame,' Attadale's owner, Joanna Macpherson, told me as she showed me around the 20 acres of gardens. And that definitely feels true: while the gardens have been planted, curated and cared for, they don't seem entirely managed, but instead allowed to develop in such a way that they have become part of the natural landscape.

"The gardens contain so many different sections that it's a delight to try and discover every nook and cranny."

There have been gardens at Attadale since the house was built; these included, it is thought, the still in-place sunken garden to the south of the house. In the early decades of the 20th century, paths and steps were laid around the garden, and rhododendrons and redwoods introduced. But a lot of what you see today is thanks to Joanna's parents: her father bought the estate in 1952 and her mother, a painter, planted over a thousand trees. During a couple of big storms in the 1980s, a number of large trees fell down, leaving behind big holes filled with water – this gave Joanna's mother the idea of introducing some ponds

and bridges, in homage to Claude Monet. (Look for the very Monet-inspired bridge over the pond by the main entrance.)

There's much to marvel at while you wander the pathways, including the many sculptures dotted around, from bronze animals and birds to a slate obelisk and letters cut into a cliff face that read 'Life is not a rehearsal'. In many instances, they are part of the landscape rather than separate from it, and spotting them is part of the fun. Perhaps my favourite of all the things here isn't really a thing as such: it's the 'borrowed landscape' in the Japanese Garden, where a gap in trees provides a perfectly framed view of the Applecross hills across the loch.

There's a small, self-service café on site, serving cakes and other goodies, and you can stay here in one of the estate's holiday cottages. Attadale also has its own train station on the Kyle Line (page 310), which is just across the road.

11 PLOCKTON & SURROUNDS

I'm naturally sceptical of anything that sounds like marketing talk, but I do admit that billing Plockton as the 'jewel of the Highlands' never feels inaccurate. Situated on an east-facing bay on the southern shore of Loch Carron, it feels almost entirely enclosed by hills, with the nearest, tree-covered slopes giving it a lush, tucked-away feel.

No matter how many times I see it, the view from Harbour Street – particularly where it meets Innes Street, with the pier more or less in front of you – is never less than sublime. In sunny weather, the water glitters and the white boats give it a feel of somewhere more exotic, while in rain the low clouds cling to the surrounding mountains in wispy strands of cotton wool. If the village seems a little familiar then it may be from its appearance in the late 1990s television series *Hamish Macbeth* and classic 1973 folk horror film *The Wicker Man*. Thankfully, though, these are both low-key enough to avoid bringing the crowds here.

"No matter how many times I see it, the view from Harbour Street is never less than sublime."

The island directly in front of the central pier is **Eilean nan Gamhainn**, which translates to 'Cattle Island', though it's also commonly known as

---

◀ 1 Picture-perfect Plockton on Loch Carron. 2 Attadale Gardens is set out around the 18th-century Attadale House.

Tidal Island – appropriate given that it gets cut off by the tide. If it's low tide, it's a pleasant walk out to and around the island (though you'll benefit from wearing boots or wellies), with paths that'll have you ducking under trees here and there.

It would be a shame to be in such a wonderful setting and not get out on the water. The affable Calum runs **Calum's Seal Trip**s (✆ 01599 544306 ⌖ calums-sealtrips.com ⊘ Apr–Oct up to four daily) on the *Sula Bheag*, which sails around the loch to spot seals – with a money-back guarantee if you don't see them – and other wildlife. It's a lovely, fun trip, which offers a chance to view the village and its surroundings from another perspective – as well as watching seals slip off small islands into the clear water, my kids were thrilled when Calum offered them the chance to steer the boat themselves. Two-hour sunset cruises on the smaller *Spindrift IV* and private hire are also available. If you fancy paddling yourself, contact **Sea Kayak Plockton** (⌖ seakayakplockton.co.uk), which offers coastal explorations for beginners, families and more experienced kayakers.

"It's a lovely, fun trip, which offers a chance to view the village and its surroundings from another perspective."

On Innes Street, about 500yds southwest of its junction with Harbour Street, tucked up on the northern side of the road, is the old **open-air church**. A signpost points the way up steps and under an old stone bridge to a clearing, crowded in by rocks on its northern side and gorse and bracken on the other two sides. It's a little less obviously evocative than the open-air church at Torridon (page 313), but nonetheless an interesting place to wander into.

Harbour Street heads north from its junction with Innes Street, with the shoreline on your right, sometimes distanced by small gardens that belong to the cottages on the opposite side of the road. Plockton was established at the end of the 18th century by the Earl of Seaforth, though it was bought four years later by Hugh Innes of Lochalsh, by which point it was already growing; most of the houses along Harbour Street date back to the early 19th century. What you might mistake for

1 Exploring Loch Carron by sea kayak. 2 Cleaning lobster pots in Plockton. 3 The remains of 15th-century Strome Castle. 4 Take a boat trip from Plockton to be in with a chance of spotting seals. ▶

A coastal walk from Duirinish

✳ OS Explorer 428; start: Duirinish train station 📍 NG 77915 31535; 2 miles; easy

This is a really lovely, non-strenuous coastal walk that allows you to take in some of the fine coastal scenery south of Plockton. As it starts and ends at Duirinish station (parking is available just south of the level crossing), you could easily get here from Kyle of Lochalsh, Plockton or further afield.

1 Begin on the southern side of the level crossing, crossing over to follow the road, with the river below to your right. After about a quarter of a mile, you'll pass the little cove of Port Bàn – you can walk down here for great views across to the Applecross Mountains – and then the road starts to climb up on to more exposed moorland ground, with the views across the loch opening up as you go. As the road dips down, with a house and burn on your left, go through the metal gate and continue into the hamlet of Port an Eòrna.

2 As you cross a metal bridge, look first to your right for more views of the Applecross Peninsula and beyond, before taking the left turn immediately after the bridge, signposted 'Coastal Path to Drumbuie', walking uphill. The path passes a house and splits soon after; take the right-hand path, following the little wooden arrow sign, and then as you near another fence, look for the narrow footpath to your right with an NTS waymarker. The path winds up and around and can be quite boggy in places, passing a couple of crofts at first and then through bracken over open ground, with the coast never too far away.

3 After about 300yds from the road junction, look to your right for a narrow path that leads to an exposed, rocky outcrop overlooking the water – from here there's yet more fabulous views across the water and inland. Back on the main path, it soon becomes stonier with a view of the Skye Cuillins up ahead, and the path starts to swing south. You'll cross a burn via boulders and then climb over a stile. The Applecross Peninsula is now behind you and Skye to your right, with dark-rock, pebbly shored beaches ahead.

4 The path curves around the back of the first bay you meet, before climbing quite steeply up a small hill. As you come down to meet a second rocky bay, the path disappears – look ahead and you should be able to see a marker on the small hill directly ahead, so you can pick your way across the stones or walk along the back of the bay to reach it (though if doing the former, take care as the rocks can be slippery). On the far side, look for the steep, narrow path that leads up to the post; from here, you'll see another bay, this one less craggy. The grassy path skirts the back of the beach here, but it's worth going down to the shore if you can. You'll see that those rocks that look quite uniformly grey from a distance are in fact made up of many different colours, worn smooth by the sea.

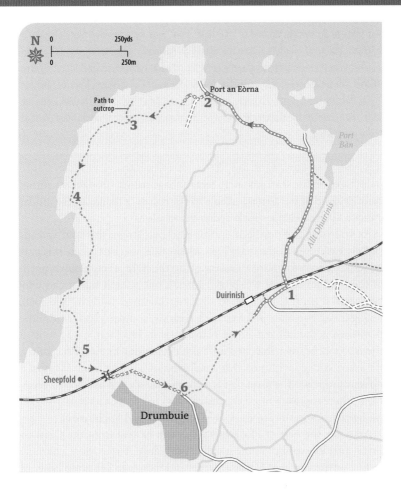

5 At the edge of the bay, veer left with the path and follow it as it turns right to lead uphill, before turning left as a sheepfold appears in front, and you'll see the railway bridge ahead. Follow the path up to meet the track over the railway bridge, following it over – the views here, with the railway line cutting through gorse, moorland and patchwork fields, and the bulbous hills and the white houses of Duirinish in the background – are really lovely. Keep on the track, and you'll pass a green shed on your right and then a metal farm gate. ▶

A coastal walk from Duirinish (continued)

6 ◄ On the other side of the farm gate, in the hamlet of Drumbuie, the track becomes a road that splits to go straight on and to your right. Here, look for a wooden footpath sign to Duirinish station on your left. Follow the sign to go downhill; the path is grassy at first but soon becomes more distinct and gravelly. Cross the stile on to a low wooden bridge, and then another stile on the other side, walking across fields towards a low ridge. You cross another stile as the path turns right and climbs uphill slightly and then cross another to walk along the ridge. You'll soon see the station ahead of you, with the path dropping down to meet the road where you started.

palm trees on the seafront are in fact cabbage palms, brought over from New Zealand in the 1960s and able to flourish here thanks to the milder climate that the village's sheltered position affords.

As you near the northern end of Harbour Street, the land spreads slightly east towards the main pier. At low tide, you can access this part by walking across a narrow causeway (on the right, about 300yds north of the road junction ♀ NG 80497 33668), but at high tide it can only be accessed from Cooper Street, another hundred yards up the road, giving this area a bit of an island feel. Near the southern end of this little peninsula is the last remaining blackhouse in Plockton, easily spotted thanks to its heather-thatched roof. Built sometime in the 19th century, it's a low cottage with just two small windows on its front; it's now a holiday property. The main pier is at the far eastern end of Cooper Street, from where there are more expansive views of the loch as it narrows on its approach towards Strome Castle (page 332) and Lochcarron.

Arguably the best of Plockton's views can be had from the **Càrn an Frith-aird Viewpoint**, to the north of the village. To get there, continue to the northern end of Harbour Street and then turn left on to Frithard Road, following it for about 300yds until, just before the road curves round to the left, you see a small metal gate on the right-hand side of the road, with a signpost for the viewpoint. From here, it's about a 500yd climb up to the viewpoint, where there are benches from which to soak up the vista: across the loch to Applecross to the north and southeast towards Skye.

On the western side of Plockton's train station (which is itself just over a mile southwest of the village centre), beyond the small airstrip, is the village's **coral beach**. It's just over a mile and a half to the beach from the village centre, an easy if rather unexciting walk, or you can park immediately northeast of the path (NG 78861 32867) that leads 500yds down to the sands. Follow the path through the gate, with thick gorse on either side. Shortly after you see water ahead of you, the path descends down rocky steps through silver birch. A final clamber over rocks takes you on to the beach, which is surprisingly large at low tide. This is a great beach for exploring, particularly if you're with kids, with big rocks to climb on, huge mounds of seaweed and shells aplenty. Like on the Applecross coral beaches (page 329), the sand is not made up of actual coral but rather calcified seaweed. Backed by a grassy area that is populated by dog roses, ash and birch trees and ragged rocks, it has a rough, wild beauty.

The coast southwest of Plockton is also well worth a visit, and easy to explore on foot (page 338); conveniently, you can take the train to Duirinish from Plockton.

¶¶ FOOD & DRINK

Harbour Fish Bar 1 Innes St ☏ 01599 544479 ◼. Regularly appearing on lists of the best fish and chips in the UK, this little chippy is the kind of place that people will urge you to visit Plockton for. It's take-away only, but there are a couple of benches outside and the harbour wall is mere steps away.

Plockton Hotel 41 Harbour St ☏ 01599 544274 ⊘ plocktonhotel.co.uk. You can't miss this pub-hotel – not just because it's the only building on the waterfront with a dark façade, but because it's the only hotel in the village that faces the water. It's a great place for a drink, whether inside the cosy bar or, in fine weather, outside on its wooden terrace overlooking the bay and surrounding hills.

THE NORTHERN SHORE OF LOCH ALSH

The northern shore of wide Loch Alsh runs east from Kyle of Lochalsh and the Skye Bridge towards the instantly recognisable castle of **Eilean Donan**. The castle itself sits where Loch Alsh meets two others – Loch Long, to its north, and Loch Duich to its south – an undeniably stunning setting for one of Scotland's most tourist-friendly images. Wedged between two tourist honeypots (the other being the Isle of Skye) means that this southern boundary of Wester Ross tends to get

THE SKYE BRIDGE

Even if you're not planning on heading to Skye (but if you are, Bradt's fabulous *Inner Hebrides* guide is what you need), you won't be able to miss the graceful curve of the road bridge on the horizon as you explore this area. The bridge took three years to build, opening in 1995, and construction cost a staggering £39 million. Prior to this, from around 1600, a ferry service had run between Kyle of Lochalsh and Kyleakin on Skye. While the opening of the bridge obviously brought benefits to the local residents, it has also brought a whole load of tourists, many of whom zoom up the A87 from Fort William.

zoomed through as people head to or from the island on the A87, which is one of the busiest roads you'll encounter in the North Highlands, particularly in the summer season. In between however, are plenty of reasons to stop, not least for walking.

This area's main settlement, **Kyle of Lochalsh**, marks the end of the rail route from Inverness and feels a lot more functional than the villages in the rest of this region; while it's not somewhere to necessarily go out of your way to visit, if you're self-catering it's a handy stop, with a decent-sized Co-op, a butcher's and an excellent seafood shop and take-away, **Fisherman's Kitchen** (Old Ferry Slip, IV40 8AF ✆ 01599 534002 🖰 fishermans-kitchen.co.uk).

12 BALMACARA ESTATE

🏠 **Avernish Lodge**

Information: The Square, Balmacara; NTS

This 6,000-acre National Trust for Scotland estate covers a large part of Loch Alsh's northern shore, encompassing within it ancient woodland, croftland, shoreline and over 14 miles of paths. In practice, it includes much of the western stretch of the land between lochs Carron and Alsh, including Plockton, Duirinish and Drumbuie, but for the sake of this book I've used it to refer to the section immediately in and around Balmacara Square.

Though it sounds like a street, **Balmacara Square** is in fact a hamlet, with low, predominantly white cottages set around its northern and eastern side, and an old mill pond in its middle. On the western side of the hamlet, which is, appropriately enough, set around a square, is a café, gift shop and gallery, in renovated 18th-century farm buildings, run by the NTS. The **Steadings Gallery** holds frequent, changing exhibitions by local and national artists in its small space, and makes an interesting place to begin your explorations. The landscape around the hamlet is exceedingly pretty, with horses grazing in the green fields; crofting – there are around 80 crofts on the estate – remains central here, and many of the people living and working on this land have been doing so for generations.

Balmacara Square is the starting point for a number of excellent walks on the estate; while some of them are waymarked, I'd recommend having the OS app or map to hand as it can be easy to lose them. In addition, a useful route card can be downloaded from Forestry and Land Scotland (⊘ forestryandland.gov.scot/visit/balmacara-woods).

For fabulous views, I'd recommend the two-mile **Skye View Trail**, which you can start from the visitor centre. From here, head south along the main road for 100yds to pick up the signposted 'Forest Walks' path on the left-hand side of the road; just inside the gate is a blue waymarker. The path follows a burn to begin with and can be quite muddy before it gets rocky and starts to climb uphill; don't forget to look back as you do so, to take in the views. You can follow the blue waymarkers throughout, which makes it fairly easy; one thing to note is that when the path meets a track, after about half a mile of walking, you need to ignore the first right turning and continue straight until you meet a crossroads, at which point you take the right-hand track, and then veer right again after just under 300yds when the track splits. At times, you'll pass conifer plantations, some of which may have patches of felled trees that look rather desolate, but it matters less when you see the views towards Skye, over the shimmering waters of Loch Alsh and Kyle Rhea.

It's worth noting that the viewpoint (♀ NG 81089 27662) isn't actually marked with a post – I walked right past it without realising and had to backtrack – so look out for a grassy track to your right that meets the path you're on just as the path turns left, about 1½ miles from the start of the walk. To be honest though, the views are more open as you're coming down the hill before this, with the bonus of tree stumps to perch on.

Ard Hill
IV40 8DH ♀ NG 81897 27061 ⊘ forestryandland.gov.scot/visit/ard-hill

More panoramic views can be had from this hill, 1½ miles southeast of Balmacara Square. Strictly speaking, it's not part of the NTS estate,

but the shoreline below it is, and it's so close that it doesn't really feel separate – particularly as you can use the footpath trails to link between Balmacara Square and here.

From the car park, a clear path loops around the hill for about 1¼ miles, at first through gorse with larch trees behind, and then less scrubby as the air becomes fragrant with the pine trees towering above you, their bark coloured with strands of bearded lichen. As you walk east, there are lovely views towards the flat marsh- and grassland south of Kirkton, the hills rising up all around, framed by the trees; to the west you'll see the smooth curve of the Skye Bridge, and to the northwest the neat village of Balmacara itself (different and separate to Balmacara Square), with its white buildings facing the shore. When I walked here in early October, it was a feast of colour, with the deep shades of the evergreen trees set against the rust-coloured bracken and the last of the purple heather. Look out for otters, seals and porpoises in the water below.

"There are lovely views towards the flat marsh- and grassland south of Kirkton, the hills rising up all around."

Lochalsh Woodland Walks

NG 80059 27799

Paths run through the Balmacara Estate's skinny shoreside stretch of woodland just over two miles west of Ard Hill, signposted south off the main road. While the trails are clear and easy to follow, they've been laid out in such a way that they feel natural and retain the wildness of the place – and, despite running alongside the A87, it's most often the sea below that you'll hear roaring.

The paths head west from the car park – the shortest is the Caorann (Rowan) Trail at just under half a mile. Just over a mile in length, the Giluthas (Pine) Trail takes in the whole length of this woodland, circling from the northern edge to the southern, with a couple of link paths joining the two so there are options to shorten the route.

The mixed woodland is hugely pleasurable to explore and among the familiar pines and oaks you'll spot more exotic species like bamboo and rhododendron, which were bought here in the 1950s. I'd recommend

◀ **1** The instantly recognisable Eilean Donan Castle. **2** The view from Ard Hill near the Balmacara Estate. **3** The village of Dornie.

following the top path first, which takes you over burns that tumble over the dark rocks of the hillside. At the western end of the upper path, looking through the trees, the water at high tide appeared almost like a wall – the position of the straight-limbed trees against the sea and land played tricks on my mind.

"The position of the straight-limbed trees against the sea and land played tricks on my mind."

On the lower path, just before the coach house, look out for steps down. These lead to a bench and a view of the rocks below and across to Skye on the other side of the loch. From here, the path takes you round the back of the Balmacara estate office – it looks like you're going into private property but keep walking through (ignoring the footpath up to the left unless you want to climb back up to the upper path) and you'll soon join the estate road, which follows the shore for a little while. Once the buildings drop away, the coast is rocky and wild, looking across to Ard Hill (page 343). Keep an eye out for seals while you're here.

SPECIAL STAYS

Avernish Lodge Avernish IV40 8EQ ✆ 07748 911155 ⬦ avernishlodge.com. Five miles east of Balmacara Estate is this incredibly smart modern lodge, built on the hillside overlooking Loch Alsh and the mountains. The plush sofas are perfect for sinking into and watching the changing colours of the sky and loch, and at night you can see Eilean Donan twinkling in the distance. There's underfloor heating, a woodburner, a fantastic shower and extremely comfortable beds. Though it sleeps – and is more than big enough for – four, it would also make a cosy, very private escape for two.

13 DORNIE & EILEAN DONAN

The little village of **Dornie**, on the southeastern shore of Loch Long, boasts a particularly pretty outlook, with views south to Eilean Donan and the Glenelg peninsula, and west to the mountains of eastern Skye. With an iconic castle literally just down the road, Dornie is often overlooked, but it always feels like a lovely bit of breathing space before (or after) contending with the sheer number of visitors at the castle. I always enjoy walking northeast up Caroline Street, which runs parallel to the shore; the views along Loch Long just get better and better, and often the water is as still as a mirror.

The current bridge across Loch Long only dates back to 1991; the previous one, opened in 1940, was smaller, and operated as a toll bridge for its first six years. Old Dornie bridge itself replaced a ferry that crossed the river between the village and Ardelve; the building of the bridge meant locals could travel all the way to Kyle of Lochalsh by road.

On the high road that leads south out of Dornie, which runs parallel to the A87, just under half a mile from the village centre, is a viewpoint that offers up arguably one of the best views of Eilean Donan, looking down across the trees to the island and the castle that stands on it, and beyond to Glenelg and distant Skye.

It's a short walk from the village to the castle; to get there, follow the road south from the Clachan (page 348), unmissable with its blue walls, and loop round the right-hand side of the pretty community garden. You'll see a path to the right at the northern end of the garden, which leads to an underpass that goes directly to the castle car park – from here you need to head left to get to the main entrance.

I'll be absolutely honest: the best thing about **Eilean Donan Castle** (✆ 01599 555202 ⌖ eileandonancastle.com ⊙ Feb–mid-Dec daily, check online for hours) is the exterior. It is, of course, a hugely recognisable building – it stands for the Highlands in countless bits of tourist literature, has appeared in films like *The World is Not Enough* and *Highlander*, and has been photographed so frequently that it's highly unlikely that you won't feel even a glimmer of recognition. And there's no doubting its beauty from outside, particularly with its setting on an island between three lochs, the mountains of Skye rising behind and an attractive arched bridge linking it to the mainland. Come on a day when the loch is glittering and the mountains are hazy in the background and you'll see why everyone flocks here.

"This is one of the best views of Eilean Donan, looking down across the trees to the island and the castle."

The trouble with the castle is that inside it is devoid of atmosphere. In some places, like the Banqueting Hall, it looks like it's been done up as a cheap Hollywood approximation of a laird's castle. In others, like the bedrooms, the furnishings are rather dull – and this is all added to by a lack of contextual information to tell you why any of these things are here.

Part of the problem with Eilean Donan is that what you see now is the result of substantial renovations. The first fortified castle here was built sometime in the mid 13th century, but it was left in ruins following a Jacobite uprising in 1719. In 1911, it was bought by Lieutenant Colonel

John MacRae-Gilstrap, who spent 20 years restoring the castle – much (or even most) of what you see inside today is reflective of its reopening in the 1930s. Even the kitchen is set up as it would have been for a celebration at the end of the summer of 1932.

Far better, in my opinion, to stick to the outside of the castle (during opening hours you can buy a grounds-only ticket, and out of hours you're free to explore), from where you can wander around the island and its craggy coastline, take in the architecture, and enjoy the superlative views up and along the three lochs.

ᵼ❘ FOOD & DRINK

All the Goodness Aird Point, Ardelve IV40 8DY ⊘ allthegoodness.co.uk. It's worth going out of your way to time a visit to this little weekend-only café: the coffee is excellent and the cakes are sublime. Don't miss the malt whisky brownie, made with Talisker (from Skye), or the sticky buns. There are places to perch by the window inside and picnic tables outside, from where you can see across to Eilean Donan. It also sells beautiful art by one of the owners, Lorraine Tolmie, which, whether painted or etched, manages to perfectly capture the colour and contours of the Highlands and Islands.

The Clachan 13 Francis St, Dornie ⊘ 01599 555366 ▪️. You can't miss this bright blue pub in Dornie village, emblazoned with the word 'PUB' on its roof. It's a great spot to head for a pre- or post-castle pint and is particularly well known for its regular traditional live-music evenings – and it serves decent pub meals, too. Food is only served from March to October.

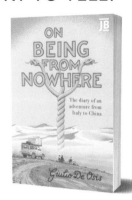

INDEX

Entries in **bold** refer to major entries; those in *italics*
indicate maps.

INDEX OF ADVERTISERS

THE BRADT STORY

In the beginning
It all began in 1974 on an Amazon river barge. During an 18-month trip through South America, two adventurous young backpackers – Hilary Bradt and her then husband, George – decided to write about the hiking trails they had discovered through the Andes. *Backpacking Along Ancient Ways in Peru and Bolivia* included the very first descriptions of the Inca Trail. It was the start of a colourful journey to becoming one of the best-loved travel publishers in the world; you can read the full story on our website (**bradtguides. com/ourstory**).

Getting there first
Hilary quickly gained a reputation for being a true travel pioneer, and in the 1980s she started to focus on guides to places overlooked by other publishers. The Bradt Guides list became a roll call of guidebook 'firsts'. We published the first guide to Madagascar, followed by Mauritius, Czechoslovakia and Vietnam. The 1990s saw the beginning of our extensive coverage of Africa: Tanzania, Uganda, South Africa, and Eritrea. Later, post-conflict guides became a feature: Rwanda, Mozambique, Angola, and Sierra Leone, as well as the first standalone guides to the Baltic States following the fall of the Iron Curtain, and the first post-war guides to Bosnia, Kosovo and Albania.

Comprehensive – and with a conscience
Today, we are the world's largest independently owned travel publisher, with more than 200 titles. However, our ethos remains unchanged. Hilary is still keenly involved, and **we still get there first**: two-thirds of Bradt guides have no direct competition.

But we don't just get there first. Our guides are also known for being **more comprehensive** than any other series. We avoid templates and tick-lists. Each guide is a one-of-a-kind expression of an expert author's interests, knowledge and enthusiasm for telling it how it really is.

And a commitment to wildlife, conservation and respect for local communities has always been at the heart of our books. Bradt Guides was **championing sustainable travel** before any other guidebook publisher. We even have a series dedicated to Slow Travel in the UK, award-winning books that explore the country with a passion and depth you'll find nowhere else.

Thank you!
We can only do what we do because of the support of readers like you – people who value less-obvious experiences, less-visited places and a more thoughtful approach to travel. Those who, like us, take travel seriously.

Bradt GUIDES
TRAVEL TAKEN SERIOUSLY